# BASEBALL DIAMONDS

This book is for our first colleagues in baseball:

Paul Grossinger
Johnathan Towers
Bob Towers
Phil Wohlstetter
Jay Zises
Patrick J. Kerrane
Barry Kerrane
Cary Nelson Davis, Sr.
Artie Wrobel
Terry Dougherty

# BASEBALL DIAMONDS

*Tales, Traces, Visions, and Voodoo from a Native American Rite*

Edited by Kevin Kerrane
and Richard Grossinger

Anchor Books
ANCHOR PRESS/DOUBLEDAY, GARDEN CITY, NEW YORK
1980

*Baseball Diamonds* was formerly published as *Baseball I Gave You All the Best Years of My Life* by North Atlantic Books (three editions, 1976, 1978, 1979).

Anchor Books edition: 1980

Library of Congress Cataloging in Publication Data

Baseball diamonds.

  Originally published under title: Baseball, I gave you all the best years of my life.
  1. Baseball—Addresses, essays, lectures.  I. Kerrane, Kevin.  II. Grossinger, Richard, 1944–    III. Title: Baseball, I gave you all the best years of my life.
GV867.B35  1980    796.357

Library of Congress Catalog Card Number 79–7601

Authors wish to acknowledge and thank the following for permission to reprint material owned by them:

JOHN ALLMAN
  "The Knuckler." By permission of the author.

ROGER ANGELL
  "Box Scores" and "The Interior Stadium" from *The New Yorker;* reprinted in *The Summer Game* (Viking Press, 1972). By permission of the author.

MAX APPLE
  "Understanding Alvarado," from *The Oranging of America* (Viking Press, 1976). By permission of the publisher.

CHARLES BARASCH
  "Curve Ball," "World Series." By permission of the author.

PAUL BLACKBURN
  "7th Game: 1960 Series." By permission of the author.

ROY BLOUNT, JR.
  "Soil Is the Soul of Baseball." Copyright © 1978 by Roy Blount, Jr. By permission of the author.

JAMES BOGAN
  "You're Too Far in the Future." By permission of the author.

ROB BREZSNY
  "Qabalistic Sex°Magick for Shortstops and Second Basemen." By permission of the author.

BOB CALLAHAN
  "The Athlete," from *Algonquin Woods* (Turtle Island Foundation, 1978). By permission of the author.

DONALD CHALLENGER
  "White River Spools," from *Delaware Literary Review* (Fall 1976). By permission of the author.

FRED CHAPPELL
  "Third Base Coach," "Fast Ball," "Spitballer," "Junk Ball," and "Strike Zone" from *The World Between the Eyes* (Louisiana State University Press, 1971). By permission of the author.

TOM CLARK
  "Oakland Coliseum," "1971," "What Happened During Outfield Practice," "Septem-

ber in the Bleachers," "Great Catch," and "Clemente (1934–72)" from *Blue* (Black Sparrow Press, 1974). "Interesting Losers," "Son of Interesting Losers," and "And You Are There" from *At Malibu* (The Kulchur Foundation, 1975). "To Nelson Fox," "To Al Dark," "To Bill Lee," "To Vida Blue" from *Fan Poems* (North Atlantic Books, 1977). "Baseball & Classicism" and "A Difference." All by permission of the author.

STEPHEN CORMANY

"Jerome Herman's Higher Education," "Big Six and Alexander The Great," "The Boudreau Shift," "Culture vs. Nature," "The Frenchman," and "Gumbo" from *Catch*, edited by Virgil Smith (Shelly's Press, Kent, Ohio, 1977). By permission of the author.

RICHARD COUTANT

"Layers of Sound: Fisch Farm." By permission of the author.

DANIEL CURLEY

"After the Game Is Over" from *The Massachusetts Review* (1972). By permission of the author.

FIELDING DAWSON

"Leo 1675" from *Two Penny Lane* (Black Sparrow Press, 1977), the second novel in a series of five. By permission of the author.

FRANZ DOUSKEY

"Babe & Lou." By permission of the author.

WILLIAM EMPSON

"Another Version of Pastoral," excerpt from 1976 interview with Kevin Kerrane. Photo of Mr. Empson courtesy of George Lanning.

DAVID ALLEN EVANS

"Will You Sign My Brand-New Baseball, Louie?" from *Train Windows* (Ohio University Press, 1976). By permission of the publisher.

GENE FEHLER

"Mel Stottlemyre." By permission of the author.

ROBERT FRANCIS

"The Base Stealer," "Catch," and "Pitcher" from *The Orb Weaver* (Wesleyan University Press, 1953). By permission of the author.

A. BARTLETT GIAMATTI

"The Green Fields of the Mind," from *Yale Alumni Magazine* (November 1977). By permission of the author.

BARRY GIFFORD

"Willie Miranda." By permission of the author.

PAUL GORRIN

"For Mickey Mantle's 500th H.R. Hit Off Stu Miller . . ." By permission of the author.

RICHARD GROSSINGER

"Baseball Psalm," "Baseball Variants," and "Three Repeating Baseball Dreams" from *The Slag of Creation* (North Atlantic Books, 1975). "Baseball Voodoo" from *The Unfinished Business of Doctor Hermes* (North Atlantic Books, 1976). By permission of the author.

DONALD HALL

"Fathers Playing Catch with Sons" from *Playing Around* (Little, Brown and Company, 1973). "The Country of Baseball" from *Dock Ellis in the Country of Baseball* by Donald Hall with Dock Ellis (Coward, McCann & Geoghegan, Inc., 1976). By permission of the author.

SANDRA SOTO HATFIELD

"Riverfront." By permission of the author.

JONATHAN HOLDEN

"Hitting Against Mike Cutler" and "How to Play Night Baseball" from *Design for a House: Poems* (University of Missouri Press, 1972). By permission of the author.

# Contents

# Preface

## KEVIN KERRANE

Start at Key West. Draw a line west-northwest to intersect the boundary of the United States and Baja California at the edge of the Pacific, and let the line proceed as far into the ocean as you wish the left field wall to be. From Key West again, project the right field line through Cape Hatteras, Cape Cod, and into Canada by way of the Bay of Fundy. Within these United States of Baseball lie the flowing base paths of the Ohio and Mississippi, and beyond them the lonely center field of the great Northwest.

This daydream, like dozens of others connected with baseball, has haunted me for a generation of seasons. When Richard Grossinger and I began co-editing an anthology of contemporary baseball writing, I tried to make sense of the map by translating it into rational terms: the image of the continental diamond led me to look for literary work exemplifying peculiarly American qualities of the game. For, even as we enter the 1980s, baseball still expresses profoundly who we are, and were, and might be. In the unit entitled "North America," and all through this book, imaginative writers offer testimony on such persistent cultural values as open space, open-endedness, individualism, statistical accountability, and the glorification of competition.

At an early point in our editorial work I began to suspect that my map of baseball was too parochial—for example, in ignoring incarnations of the game in Latin America, the Orient, and even the Old World. But, thanks to Richard Grossinger, our anthology was never in any danger of becoming chauvinistic or narrowly sociological. Richard's own insights, basically anthropological, led toward a second main theme in the book: baseball's dimensions of ritual, myth, and magic. These archetypal aspects of the game have in fact permeated the history of baseball storytelling. From the dime-novel fantasies of the last century, to light Hollywood entertainments, to sophisticated modern fiction by Bernard Malamud, Robert Coover, Philip Roth, or Jerome Charyn, baseball has been rendered less often through the conventions of realism than through symbolic fables with magical events. Similarly, much of the written and graphic work assembled here is preoccupied with dreams, telepathy, voodoo, American Indian rites, Celtic witchcraft, oriental enlightenment, solar myth, arcane symbolism, and sheer imaginative possibility. The material suggests, in short, that the United States of Baseball are also states of consciousness.

Pastoralism, also pervasive in the history of baseball literature, is well represented as a third theme by our contemporary writers. The source of this aesthetic value lies in the aesthetic of baseball itself, especially its freedom of time, or rather its power to *stretch* time—across a long afternoon in which the rituals of resin bags and infield chatter assume a meaning of their own, or across a long season in which one game seems only a tiny part of some great scheme of things, or across a whole life in which the textures of baseball continue to evoke the green openness of a simpler personal or national past. As a result, many of our selections celebrate pure moments of baseball, images whose vividness remains undimmed by time. Others describe seasonal rhythms or the pleasures of landscape, baseball's promise of oneness with the elements. And still others explore the games of childhood or express nostalgia for seasons past, bearing out Thomas Wolfe's observation that baseball is "really a part of the whole weather of our lives."

Balancing the pastoral ideal of baseball as play, this anthology also documents the reality of baseball as contest, and even blood sport. Diamonds can serve as mirrors of psychological and social conflict, and many of the works included here point once again to fundamentals of American life by isolating precisely those aspects of baseball that are *not* cricket: its tolerance of argument, brawling, and clever cheating, its encouragement of plebeian rather than patrician style, and especially its historical development from amateur pastime to professional sport and commercialized spectacle.

One of the most persistent themes in this book is that the major leagues, despite their mythic stature and images of pure excellence, cannot begin to encompass the full imaginative power of baseball. The term "major" has never referred simply to the achievement of the best professional players of an era; if it had, then—contrary to the official histories—the old National Association of 1871–75 (controlled by labor rather than capital) and the segregated Negro leagues of the 1920s, '30s, and '40s would assuredly be recognized as major. Instead, the word has usually connoted stable corporate control and statistical completeness. And today, even as the major leagues set yearly attendance records, thoughtful fans must contend with new dimensions of commercial adulteration: strikes, lockouts, a megabuck mentality, show-biz distractions, and sports palaces with the dreary sameness of airport architecture.

By contrast, many of our selections show how baseball retains its vitality within the aleatory spaces of backyards, schoolyards, sandlots, and city streets. "The October Series broken down into a hundred thousand atomistic possibilities"—this is how Richard Grossinger describes the continuing energy of amateur ball, recreation as re-creation. And in his writing Richard has given the Codornices softball field in Berkeley its own mythic stature.

Moreover, baseball never reduces itself to one kind of experience. Let me illustrate with a personal chronology.

For five summers I had tried to continue ballplaying by hanging in on a tavern softball team in a slow-pitch league. But one day, a mere half block from my own house, I chanced on a sandlot hardball game being performed by seventeen men. Most wore uniforms, but no uniform matched any other; salvaged from softball, rescued from closets, or bought for fifty cents at Goodwill, they created a riot of color expressing the spirit of that game. The loudest player, a rock-and-blues musician named George Thorogood, invited me onto the field, and I entered a kaleidoscopic contest in which lineups shifted every inning, pitchers threw as hard as they wished but without benefit of called strikes, and the action swung from heroic to sloppy to miraculous—sometimes on the same play. I mentioned how different it felt to be hitting a baseball again: there was no sense of the *splat* a softball makes, and sometimes there was no feeling at all, other than of a current of energy as ball and bat met. "This is baseball," George barked. "Softball, that's like methadone. Time enough for that stuff when we get older . . . if we do."

He was home for the summer, after instructing his agent not to schedule any more out-of-town work that might interfere with playing ball for free. And through that summer he brought to the games exactly the same energy and awareness he brings to the music of Chuck Berry, Bo Diddley, and Robert Johnson. When someone kidded him about trying to be an "athlete," he snorted: "This isn't athletics. It's religion." By the end of the summer the players had coalesced into a team called the Destroyers— named after George's band, but perhaps also invoking the god Shiva, many-armed master of defense—and we arranged to join a local Roberto Clemente League the following year as one of the few non-Latin entries.

At that point I had to bid, and I bid now, an affectionate farewell to one dimension of baseball. As the season began, I was trying to lead a double diamond life, on the tavern team and in the Clemente League, until I shattered a leg in a collision on a softball field, an injury that promises to curtail most future versions of playing the game instead of watching it. George stopped by my house, trying to inspire me by talking about his favorite major leaguer, Bobby Valentine, who came back from a similar injury: "And look at him now—a crooked-legged utility player on a marginal team in the twilight of a mediocre career." But for a long time baseball simply meant lying around watching games on TV, and studying newspaper box scores so carefully that you might have thought I was searching for my own name. Still, one day I managed to hobble around the backyard on crutches, flipping batting-practice pitches to my kids. And that evening I called Richard Grossinger.

"It may be," he said from California, "that the major leagues will make more sense to you now. And so might good games with your kids instead of people your own age. The states of baseball *are* united." He paused. "You know, I've always had the feeling of being invulnerable on a diamond—that nothing really bad could happen to me within those lines." "I still have it," I said, taking a tighter grip on the receiver that linked us at two ends of the continent—Richard in deep left, me in shallow right—knowing that what binds us together also unifies this book.

Some of the 1978 Delaware Destroyers: George Thorogood (first row, Mets' cap) and Kevin Kerrane (back row, center).

# Preface

## RICHARD GROSSINGER

This book is the most recent in a series of baseball anthologies, the first of which appeared in 1971 in Cape Elizabeth, Maine. That volume, entitled simply *Baseball Issue*, was number 10 in the *Io* series. *Io* itself was begun in 1964, when I was an undergraduate at Amherst College, named then after a moon of Jupiter and edited by a group of students as an alternative to the school literary magazine. The group dissolved after two issues, and the journal continued to be edited, after I went to graduate school in Ann Arbor, by me and my wife, the poet Lindy Hough. Number 4 began a series of issues on subject matters, with the sequence, through eight, being: Alchemy, Doctrine of Signatures, Ethnoastronomy, Oecology, and Dreams. Although the topics varied, the basic import of the series was to get at the mythological and deep historical meanings of contemporary art and science. It was, and, in fact, still is, a journal of origins.

Baseball began to occur as an image almost from the beginning, but the first substantial statement was in the Ethnoastronomy issue where I wrote a piece blending my memories of baseball games with American tribal histories and statements of the formation of matter. At various places in the issue were collages including box scores, lists of leading hitters and pitchers from Sunday papers, charts of the Solar System, diagrams of the structure of the cube, Hebrew letters, and various shapes from the animal kingdom. In the following issue (Oecology), I went at the idea more fully with a sweeping piece called "The Southern Cult of the New York Yankees." In essence, I set the formation of the Yankees during the 1950's and 1960's parallel to the archaeology and ethnohistory of North America. I opened: "There is a movement of men, ships, seeds, languages; the New York Yankees come to the Mississippi, batting .309 as a team, and found the Southern Temple Cult." The first paragraph ends: "There is never a clear beginning; the Mars of the 1940's is the first Yankee pennant of the twenties is the Creek and Chickasaw nations that Ponce de Leon comes upon, Dale Long in search of the fountain of youth." At the crescendo, I wrote:

"And for archaeologists I will teach a course on the mad streak of the New York Yankees, its possible origins in the twenties, sites in the thirties, and fluorescence in the fifties, right through 1964, when they return to the archaic leaving nary a trace. And for Yankee fans to know, they must review the Hopewellian culture, the burial mounds of the heroes, the pots and polychrome designs, the incised animals; they must learn of the coming of the Mississippi era, with its vast farmlands and temples and cultigens; the yearbooks of all these seasons are critical, the origin of Mickey Mantle and the players in the southern cult, before the historical period, before the coming of the European."

There is no clear thesis here, but there is the intimation of something. In the Dreams issue, I suggested that some future volume contain a small "local" section on baseball. After a science fiction issue on the planet Mars (number 9), there was enough work to put together a full-fledged volume on baseball. Furthermore, the Mars number had opened the gates to pop culture.

Issue number 10 was 232 pages, and used the 6-by-9-inch format of the other *Io*'s. It was mainly but not purely baseball; it also included volleyball, horse racing, pinball machines, football, basketball, and other non-sports work that was on hand at the time. The contents included a number of interesting baseball derivations, similar to and yet different than my own. Other writers had their own mythologies of baseball. The core of the Baseball issue was a long section compiled out of old history books and ethnographic journals, deriving baseball first from ancient England, and next from American Indian games. This particular fantasy is discussed in my piece "Baseball Variants" in this book.

Almost nothing made it from this volume to the following ones. The tribal mythology bias was later dropped, and, in any case, most of the works were fairly esoteric, or fragments from journals, or dealing with baseball only partially.

Between *Io*/number 10 and this book lie three editions of an enormous anthology entitled *Baseball I Gave You All the Best Years of My Life*, 400, 416, and 432 pages, respectively, done in an oversize 8½-by-11-inch format. Virtually all the contents of this book appeared in these anthologies, along with many other pieces that could not be carried over into the smaller format.

*Io*/number 10 I had edited by myself, with a bit of help from some of my students then at the University of Maine at Portland. *Baseball I Gave You All the Best Years of My Life* was co-edited by Kevin Kerrane and me, with help from five major and numerous minor regional contributing editors. At the time this collaboration began (1975), I was living in Vermont, teaching at Goddard College, and Kevin was living in Newark, Delaware, teaching at the University of Delaware. One of his courses was in baseball literature, a serious American Studies survey of the important writings in this area. *Io*/number 10 was used as a course book, so Kevin invited me to Delaware to talk to his class. This was our first meeting.

During my visit, Kevin and I discussed what a model baseball anthology would include. He showed me material he had been assembling for his course over a number of years. He also had the idea of turning it into an anthology but had never acted on it. It was an enormous, time-consuming and probably impractical project. In the course of our discussion, we simultaneously realized that we could do it together from our separate collections.

Looking back over the process of preparing this book, I realize how ideal a pair of co-editors we were. Kevin knew the standard literature of baseball thoroughly, and he brought almost a thousand pages in resources to the collaboration, 90 per cent of them already published as poems, essays, or chapters in novels. I knew very little of this material, but, as an anthropologist and a writer with roots and connections in various radical and underground American literary traditions, I was able to find a body of baseball writing totally outside the mainstream. Much of it came from unpublished writers, writers associated primarily with small presses, and writers who had only a single baseball piece in their work. We also had the help of contributing editors David Wilk, Jack Shoemaker, Lewis Warsh, and Geoff Young, plus innumerable other people who passed the word for two years. In 1977, the first edition of *Baseball I Gave You All the Best Years of My Life* appeared in Oakland, California (where I had moved). It was edited out of several thousands of pages of work and issued as *Io*/number 24 under my own press's imprint, North Atlantic Books. This title went through three printings, the second one being a major re-editing with about eighty new pages and the third one a minor re-editing with twenty new pages.

The editing of these anthologies has been a continuing process. The first edition of *Baseball I Gave You All the Best Years of My Life* reached large numbers of people who had not known about the project and who submitted work to North Atlantic Books or who told us about pieces we did not know. In order to fit the best of the new work into the second edition, we took out 15 per cent of the book including some very interesting individual documents, such as George Altman's diary of playing ball in Japan, a complete series on the Red Sox by George Kimball, and a series of short stories on childhood baseball by a variety of authors. The third edition then added more new work.

*Baseball Diamonds* also had the benefit of an extended time frame, so it has work we were not aware of at the time we did the other books. However, the intention was to do a smaller anthology, more economical, and with a wider audience. It is a new book, graphically and in its reconception of the entire project, but it is not as encyclopedic as the earlier volumes.

Work was omitted from it for reasons of economics of individual pieces or sheer space.

All three earlier editions, as well as *Io*/number 10 and Tom Clark's complete *Fan Poems,* are available by writing North Atlantic Books at 635 Amador Street, Richmond, California 94805. These titles are no longer generally in stores. Kevin and I have also begun assembling work for a follow-up baseball anthology and would be pleased to hear from readers who have contributions for a book of this genre. There is no reason the anthologizing need stop now any more than with the earlier books. Daniel Rudman is also editing a companion basketball anthology for North Atlantic Books.

If there is a Major League Baseball strike, we hope that our anthology will help make a season for people. We have certainly participated in the Major League myth in this book, with its players, cards, statistics, and so on, but baseball exists first in the imagination, and there are many other seasons and games without the Majors. Both owners and players have taken advantage of the myth, and fans can tolerate their greed for a while because fans enjoy the enacting of the baseball ritual as a national vision. If, however, the players and owners persist, the connection to the great baseball myth will snap, and they will find themselves without a following. The baseball myth is quite capable of generating other versions, both regional and national. The game will be played, and it will continue to live as wild as the Celtic and Creek Indian games that lie behind it.

Kevin and I would also like to thank the many contributors for their generosity in allowing their works to appear here. Without this generosity, a major anthology of this scope would not have been possible.

# Prologue ⸻

ROBERT KELLY

## A Pastoral Dialogue on the Game of the Quadrature

*Strephon*
*Prynikos*

*Str:*  I've long wondered why when we come this way you often walk apart from the other shepherds & climb that greasy little hill alone. Commonly you walk in our midst, & talk correctly of our proper businesses, love affairs, prosody, new songs & the price of wool.

*Pryn:*  Come with me, Strephon, and I'll show you. The hill is easier than it looks. Leave your sheep with mine. Pedantic Corydon surely has another hour of talk in him, & will watch a little against the wolf while Alcman & Philaster drowse beneath his argument.

*Str:*  I'll fill my pockets with dried figs, & pelt you with them if this climb isn't worth it.

*Pryn:*  It will be worth your while if you keep your eyes open. We'll suck those figs together—you may want to linger up there with me.

*Str:*  That seems unlikely. This hill I notice doesn't even have a sacred grove—grass is all I see, & the top is just like the bottom. Hardly worth the climb. Especially for you, my fleshy friend.

*Pryn:*  It isn't where we are but what we see. Look down there on the meadow. What do you see?

*Str:*  I see little boys playing ball in the field. Is that your pleasure, voyeur, to look on graceful young men? I thought your pleasure lay with girls—you've never sung us of Himeros & the love of like —maybe there's hope for you yet.

*Pryn:* Not in the sense you mean. Not who or what the boys are, but what they do—that's why I'm here.

*Str:* Looks like baseball to me.

*Pryn:* That's what it is.

*Str:* A stupid game. They're not even naked as they play; it's slow, unathletic. It's so boring.

*Pryn:* Have you ever watched it at length?

*Str:* Among the merchants in Alexandria I have often stayed; those weary empty men turn on their television boxes & look at this, or seem to, while they repose from parched acts of commerce in the market, & count their assets. Really, what they watch is as boring as they are themselves—a perfect wedding, I think—a game that does not move watched by men who do not live. I mean, how can you find this interesting? How can you?

*Pryn:* There's something in the use of the game that's bad. And that's in our air, isn't it, the box your merchants watch, the air of their markets. They can turn all things rotten—if you feel you need to make such judgments. I'm content to watch. Watching is instructive, especially when I'm strong enough not to react; just watch.

*Str:* It still is nonsense. It might be fun to play that game. It might even be fun to play the game down there, your baseball, but there's nothing to watch. The pitcher fusses & preens, the batter dusts & fidgets. A ball is thrown. The batter watches it go by. Sometimes he swings at it; sometimes, though more rarely, his bat hits the ball. If it goes beside him, or behind, they forget all about it, except that some little kid chases the ball & brings it back long after it's forgotten. Sometimes the batter hits the ball ahead of him. Then all the hitherto motionless people begin to scurry around, the batter runs, they all run. But soon it all runs down like a cheap clock, & everything stops again. More fussing, preening, dusting, fidgeting, tapping the bat on the ground, hitching the pants, nervous gestures, suspicious peering in all directions. Nothing happens. A ball is thrown, the catcher catches it, the crowd roars, the batter goes away, a new one comes up. Nothing *happens.* Tell me, Prynikos, is that your idea of holy play, a game? It should be a beautiful wedding of sense & intellect in muscled play. I have seen the oiled bodies of the wrestlers throwing & holding & being held—it flashes, Prynikos, flesh coming to flesh, giving the slip, the twist of it, the torque—my breath catches in my throat when I watch that, I feel each hold, I fall & am delivered, I writhe & triumph, & it all is beautiful.

*Pryn:* You're right, wrestling is beautiful, I say it gladly, but it teaches us nothing, or nothing that Love doesn't teach better.

*Str:* But that play is a form of Love, & what is *this?*

*Pryn:* This is the other side of love, the stages by which we go beyond the traps of love into Love for Love's sake, for Love's sake wielding our minds, Strephon, our minds in Love's service.

Str: What are you talking about? You mean fantasy?

*Pryn:* I mean perception. Love is to perceive & be perceived.

Str: So they say.

*Pryn:* I mean the this & the that, the proportions by which all experiences are united in the experiencer. That was Egypt before there ever was an Alexandria. This game teaches us to see.

Str: I think a Persian juggler, a Magian with sleight of hand could teach that better—the eye is quicker than the hand, after all, when it's trained & ready. That idiom I hear so often: Keep your eye on the Ball: if your baseball teaches that, & I suppose it does since there's nothing else to watch, then it's of some service, I guess. But that's just a metaphor, Prynikos; if you see it once, you've seen it all.

*Pryn:* Truth in what you say. If you do truly see something once, whole and entire, then that *is* once for all. How often do we see that way, though? Even the best of us shepherds loses count—especially when we start looking *for* something; then all we naturally see we don't see at all. We're just looking for, not seeing. The anxious eye cancels out the world.

Str: See, don't see, what has all that to do with baseball?

*Pryn:* I'm not sure, but we were talking about baseball, so it led us here.

Str: It led you there. I'm still wondering why it's worth your while to watch this game, and worth mine to climb up here with you. Want a fig?

*Pryn:* You see where the batter stands—that's home plate, or *home*. If he gets a hit he runs to first, or second if he sometimes can, or sometimes third . . .

Str: I'm familiar with the game, for my sins. I played it as a child—never very good at it, kept losing interest.

*Pryn:* Where did you play?

Str: In Boeotia, where I was born.

*Pryn:* I mean, what position did you play?

Str: Right field mostly.

*Pryn:* It's far away.

Str: Nobody ever came out to visit me, at any rate.

*Pryn:* The bases are ninety feet apart.

Str: What?

*Pryn:* I said, the bases are ninety feet from one another, along the course the runner must cover.

Str: So?

*Pryn:* The circuit around the square, the so-called rhomb or *diamond,* is three hundred sixty feet.

Str: Evidently.

*Pryn:* The number of degrees in a circle. When a runner passes through all three hundred sixty, he comes home. A run is scored—a unit added to the sum of all experience.

*Str:* You are representing the runner as a kind of solar myth? Very interesting, in a fin-de-siècle way.

*Pryn:* Each base is an obstacle in his path, yet a qualifying of his course: a definition of it, in fact. Home is the vernal equinox, perhaps, and First the Summer solstice. Second base, the keystone, is the autumn equinox, where we of the City start the year. Third base, most difficult of all, eccentric, chthonic, is the Winter solstice, where the sun turns round and the runner has his last chance at terra firma before he makes his dash for the goal.

*Str:* *Sharmant*, as I heard a Goth say the other day. But your analysis will work as well for any four-part thing.

*Pryn:* But it is not a solar myth, or sun god, you see. It is a man. That's the point: a man, and a ball comes at him.

*Str:* From another man. No God, no Hero.

*Pryn:* Yes, from the pitcher. *Inside* the diamond—sixty feet six inches away—again the theme of sixes. What is important is that it comes from inside the system.

*Str:* Why should that be important?

*Pryn:* Because the system is so designed, the world is so designed, that each gesture of matter, each new atomy of hydrogen, enters from inside, or appears to. *Nothing* is outside. Yet that *Nothing* must be a positive, or where would the gesture come from?

*Str:* At the risk of scoffing at your fugue, let me remind you that the outfielders are outside. I should know, I was one.

*Pryn:* Consider the foul lines—they extend the diamond until the lines reach an impenetrable barrier, the outfield *wall*. The outfield, as an extension of the diamond, is thus the scope or scatter of the diamond's focus. It is the diamond's field of action, its implicit result. Note that wherever baseball is played, the exact measurements of the diamond are preserved, carefully and identically. But each stadium has its own outfield wall—no two are the same—they can vary considerably in size, height, texture, and (above all) distance from the plate. In other words, the precise rules of the game specify the diamond's measure, but only hint at the shape of the wall—specifying in fact only a minimum distance the foul lines must extend before they reach the outfield wall. This combination of rule and approximation means to preserve and signify that randomness we detect at every point of observation in the world. Our perceptual system cannot process every item into percept, nor can our brains process every percept into meaningful array with all other percepts. What falls outside the grid of our perceptual-interpretational system we call random.

*Str:* A flimsy use of the word, it seems to me. But don't talk to me about random—I've heard the sophists chew that one down to irreducible gristle. It means everything and nothing. In all rigor, there is no such thing as random.

*Pryn:* Or random is a *range* of possible events—like the outfield walls.

*Str:* This seems fetched far and sold dear, Prynikos. These thoughts surely do not vex the heads of those blundering boys down there on the field.

*Pryn:* Why should they? They are the dancers of a most ancient ritual . . .

*Str:* How boring, when everything is suddenly intuited as ritual!

*Pryn:* . . . most ancient ritual, I say: the Squaring of the Circle. Which was always a dance. And never an equation. They are the dancers, each responsible only for his own conformity to what he guesses of the pattern. Years later, when he can use the insight, he will stand and watch, as we are doing, and then he will see. Boys don't need to know the things we're talking about, Strephon; it would do them harm and not good. Now they are perfect dancers, and as such they carry forward through time into the visible world these old mysteries.

*Str:* That is pretty; I'll allow that. But what mysteries?

*Pryn:* I'll take a fig now, a sweet one. You've been playing with them in your pocket, and have softened the dry fruit with your kneading, worked it tender again. Thank you for that.

*Str:* Is that ritual too?

*Pryn:* Now reflect: there are nine players on each team. The cycle of three-six-nine goes on. These numbers are no accident; perhaps you're right to scoff at the solar journey, but the numbers are there, and by their remorseless internal consistency remind the watcher that some meaning lies in or near the game. The number set may be no more, after all, than a trick to catch the attention, or a bona fides of the conscious, deliberate origin of the game.

*Str:* Conscious? I thought it started among rustics in old America, puritans like as not, from the rough sport of rounders.

*Pryn:* Freemasons. The earliest American leaders were initiates of the various lodges and temples that claim some filiation from the Egyptian workshops. Early American history was a dance again, a set of instructions on the art of transcendence. Thirteen nomes, thirteen stars, stripes, arrows, olive leaves, stone courses in pyramids—the early national cult celebrated the Sun in the Thirteenth Degree of the Crab as its chief holy day.

*Str:* This tedious occultry soils the golden afternoon. How can you finger such mechanical superstitions and still talk of transcendence?

*Pryn:* Because they found their way. Instead of being trapped by all their good ideas, they founded a game for their children. The game, once started, will always somehow stay in the world. And it teaches their transcendence without gimcrack symbols. They set only one problem: how to get out of the circle.

Str: *O pour briser un seul cercle!* one of our shepherds sang.

Pryn: Exactly: to be able to break even one circle, just one—& get out. And be gone!

Str: Spirit anxious to escape from matter?

Pryn: What you call the golden afternoon is too lovely to escape from. Instead, we learn to escape *through*.

Str: It is comfortable here, after all.

Pryn: Baseball enacts the parable. *Nine* means where the cycle begins again, and thus where a man can gear his being in with a higher cycle . . .

Str: Such language!

Pryn: Or better, slip past and have done with cycles. Nine men on each team. Each team has nine innings. See why I call numbers remorseless?

Str: Lots of multiples of three. I grant that. Your insistence on these numbers, as if on some arcana, seems peculiar, unsound, unstandard. Aren't these numbers, all numbers, the children of chance?

Pryn: I'll give you more. Three, the number of the individual beginning his work, must become six, which is the base for the measure of circles. If a man does not exceed, get beyond, his three, he cannot then engage his own life and energy in the world of spirit *or* matter. He has three chances—three strikes and he's out. If the pitcher throws four balls, that is, exceeds the three that *he's* permitted, then the batter is liberated to begin his cycle on the squared circle. You see, if the batter does not get beyond his three, he can no more make his perfect circuit than a circle itself can be generated without $\pi$—that sacred number which is *more than three*—the enigmatic never-resolving cipher of transcendence and completion.

Str: These funny numbers weary men, Prynikos. It seems to me I've heard this sort of thing before.

Pryn: See it through a little longer with me. To the basic three of any batter, what any one of us starts with in the world, the batter must add the next three bases (First, Second and Third) to win his Six. Then, in the arcane and terrible passageway between Third and Home, he can at last exceed his Six. That passageway, much spoken of, in more or less veiled terms, by the South Thebans in their Book of Coming Forth by Day, ah Strephon, I want you to know, and not just from memory, what a bitter passageway that is. Especially when the squeeze is on, and the individual is forced into the Gate again, again, past the Guardian of the Threshold into the world again. It is a numinous alley, Strephon, a birth canal, a highway of theophany!

*Str:*   Control yourself. I think you're dithering. Rhetoric is no better than numerology.

*Pryn:*   But think of it! The batter has come home. He has fulfilled his destiny, and by fulfilling it, transcended both the game and the idea of destiny itself. He has squared the circle. His karma (I use Philostratus's word, that enthusiast) is improved; a run or unit has been added to the tally.

*Str:*   Strange that with all your threes and nines, the score increases only by ones.

*Pryn:*   Only one man at a time reaches enlightenment. But don't think about the goal, for a moment. In all baseball, there's hardly a moment more exciting than when the runner leaps from Third, hurtling into the irretrievably dangerous. Many a swift young man has been trapped there between those archons, the squat Catcher in his devil-mask, and the swifter Third Baseman like lithe graceful Death running him down! It all holds together, Strephon—the game enacts. As in any wrought Egyptian symbol, every fact and gesture of it holds and limns and beckons. It is played to remind us.

*Str:*   But does anybody know this? Isn't this all your dreamy interpretation of a common thing? It sounds good, a little, but can it really be the instructive symbol you make it out to be, if nobody in fact is instructed by it? Of all the people who watch or play this game, who cares about all this?

*Pryn:*   They *feel* it, Strephon, and their feelings make their minds. Their feelings are being worked on in the game, in their thousands in the stadium, millions maybe watching the Visual Box, all being worked on, taught to exult in certain special things and certain special contours of action that achieve them, taught to esteem transcendence above all else. They don't know all this as abstract proposition—they are instructed deeper in themselves than they know.

*Str:*   Unprovable. And I fret this "working on the feelings." The barbarous Romans roar in their circuses at the deaths of men and animals, the sprout of blood. Their feelings are being worked on too.

*Pryn:*   Your own objection answers itself: it is death and brutality that the Romans teach, and the weird pleasures to be found therein. Consider however what it is that makes the thousands roar at a baseball game. They do not roar at a kill or even an injury; even the suspicion that a pitcher is trying to hurt the batter provokes the low murmur of censure before which lancers quail. The crowd does not roar (the way they do in football, say, or the Dance of the Basket) at a simple enactment on an easy symbolic plane of the biological commonplace, the old putting-it-in-the-hole, the net, the goal. Those games of simple-minded phallic naiveté may be innocent enough, but with their *insertion of ball in slot* they always celebrate, alas, the enslavement of spirit to matter. But in baseball, sweet baseball, they roar their exultation at the Home Run, the white ball sailing, infinitely unreachable, over the outfield wall.

*Str:* The ball then is the soul?

*Pryn:* I see you are convincing yourself. Soul or self, how shall a man know what to call it? It isn't the sperm entering the egg. No. It is the Other Way. Getting out. Baseball's paragon moment, then, is when one breaks out of the whole system. Its truth is the leap across the Abyss. Supreme. Swan time. To go. Supreme, that is, for living men.

*Str:* I feel some of your excitement, but you're not being too clear.

*Pryn:* And the hunger of the mob for Home Runs—how wise that noisy furor is!

*Str:* They tell me that Home Runs are far more common these days than in the past years of baseball.

*Pryn:* So I've heard too. If that is true, and the chronicles hint that it is, it must mean a growing hunger throughout our populations, a weariness with progress and lotos-eating; it must be the start of an immense striving. The ball players feel it, the obscure men who make the baseballs feel it, and wind into the mysterious lively planetary interior of the ball some of their own sensed urgency for liberation. The ball is *alive*, we say. The ball gets lively, the batter practices not placing the ball but instead that flex of wrist that can give the long loft. Maybe even the pitcher, in a mystery, himself yearns too for all men to enter the road of transcendence, and, like a dreaming bodhisattva, spares his own glory to serve up, maybe hardly even knowing he wants to, that fine fastball, a little high, a little outside. That's the kind I used to like.

*Str:* Prynikos?

*Pryn:* Yes?

*Str:* Do you know that the boys are gone? They finished their game and went home.

*Pryn:* So they did. We are alone.

*Str:* We're up here on a hill, with nothing but words and figs between us and the night wind. Let's go down.

*Pryn:* Was it worth the climb?

*Str:* If what you've been saying has any sense, it must be a sense that will develop as I watch the game. All I ever really care for is the body, its absolute beauty, grace of its turn. I'll let you know if all this hermeneutic of yours gets me anywhere. Strange that we missed the end of the game. We don't even know who won.

*Pryn:* We don't even know who was playing.

# 1

# Archetypal Baseball

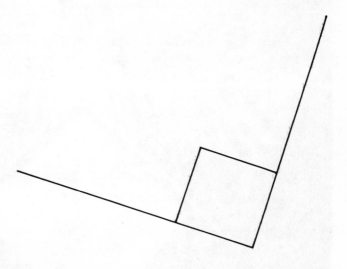

**KEVIN KERRANE**

## Season Openers

At one end of a three-acre field, tucked away in a university town along the BosWash Corridor, is a garden, fifty feet by sixty, where on this April Saturday we are enacting a ceremony. Michael, barefoot and shirtless even in the cool of mid-morning, hums along with the roto-tiller, plowing under winter rye grass. Pam, his beloved, plants dill and basil, marigold and nasturtium; she bends beautifully to her work from a yogic stance, forming a pyramid as she nudges each seedling into the earth with the gift of her total concentration. But my thoughts aren't really so elevated: as I watch Pam's jeans stretch, I'm shoveling compost, last year's death, atop a freshly plowed patch where the kohl crops will go. The rot of leaves, manure, stalks of old garden refuse, slimy kitchen garbage—some of it is still undissolved, and the stench is occasionally so dizzying that I scoop on extra puffs of lime.

On one side of the field are railroad tracks, where two people have committed suicide this year; as we work the trains hurtle by every ten minutes or so, drowning out all other sound for a long moment. On the other side are the chartered back yards of middle-class homes. And at the far end of the field, up near a municipal tennis court where my wife has just punched a nice forehand shot from the baseline (why isn't she out here helping?), a half dozen boys are shagging flies. Oddly, the fielders aren't spread out; instead they stand in a tight knot as the oldest, about twelve, tries without much success to direct fungoes to them. A ball rises slowly against the sky as Michael shuts off the tiller, and now the "plink" of the metal bat carries down to us. The ball drops toward the knot of boys, and every one of them raises his glove and seems (head back, mouth open) to call for it. It falls to the ground in their very midst just as we begin to hear their confident sopranos.

"Baby birds," Michael says next to me. "Like a nest of little guys all calling for the worm." I'm not amused, not by their awkwardness or his wit. I feel refracted, unthawed, out of phase with the season—maybe sluggish from too much compost, or jarred by too many Metroliners barreling past, or just jealous. Of Sheila and her uncomplicated tennis freedom. Or of Michael: in my pocket, in my wallet, is the poem I wrote for Pam six weeks ago, the day we planted tomato seeds in peat pots. I haven't had courage or foolishness enough to give it to her.

## To a Tomato

*Juicy, taut, you'd tempt a carnivore*
*To practice vegetarian good taste*
*By teaching him your silent metaphor:*
*Organically, nothing goes to waste.*
*Out of a quiet place, a leafy bed*
*Of darkest green along the nightshade vine,*
*You pulse with pure life-energy, blood-red:*
*Uncanny beauty! Saucy valentine!*

I need a break. Pam gives me a soft yes when I ask if she wants a beer. "Ditto pour moi," Michael says. "Hey, bring the radio back out. Later on we can catch the Phils. At Chicago—so we'll pick up ivy vibes while we plant." He mimes a windup. "And Carlton's gonna chuck."

"No thanks, I'm tryin' to quit." I can't resist nettling him. Pam shoots me a grateful look. Last week she and Michael had a fight over a game on tv: when she switched channels in the ninth inning, he accused her of disrupting an "energy field" protecting the Phils, later pretending (he must have been) to think that she bore some of the blame for their dramatic loss two minutes later. Pam's interest in baseball has reached a new low. But next week, after Easter, she and Michael are leaving for ten days in Canada, and he's been threatening to stop at Cooperstown on the way up.

Michael sees us sharing a glance. "Are you serious?" he asks me, now serious himself. He walks to the house with me to puzzle out my tone and mood—or maybe just to make sure that the radio is brought back out to the garden.

"Look, I'm not even gonna be here. I've got softball this afternoon, a practice game."

His brow furrows. "Yeah, well, I wanted to talk to you about that."

I know where he's headed, and I don't feel like dealing with it, so I just rush on, going with the role: "Anyway, the Phils're bloated. They've got the bloat. Sluggish sluggers. Schmidt's workin' on his season quota of 180 strikeouts,"—

"He'll get hot."

"He better. They've dropped him to the gristle of the batting order. You should have seen him on opening day."

"You told me, you told me."

I keep remembering that game, like fast food that you can still taste hours later. After what seemed like three hours of pre-game fanfare and Bicentennial tableaux, the Phils played like fat statues, finally blowing it in extra innings on outfield errors. Schmidt struck out twice and popped up; he looked distracted and swollen. I was bloated too, loaded up on tough hot dogs and lukewarm beer, trying to will the season into being after all the labor-management banality of March. The giant scoreboard, an afternoon of cartoons, gave me a strobe headache. And I was even alienated from the crowd: I watched Johnny Oates, the Phils' catcher, writhing on the ground with a broken collarbone after Dave Parker ran right over him at the plate, and I heard fans around me boo Oates for dropping the ball. "The Philly fans are still thinking hockey here in goddamn April."

"Not me!" Michael says, putting a sincere hand on his chest as we enter the kitchen. "And no goddamns about it either. Tomorrow's Easter. It's a beautiful day, a beautiful spring, and we got the big red machine out there in the garden, a Troy-Bilt roto-tiller beautifully engineered in Troy, New York, home of the Troy Haymakers, baseball terrors of the nineteenth century. What more do ya want? Come on—you get the beer. I'll get this honkey working." The radio is already cradled under his arm.

"Hold on." I wash my filthy hands in the kitchen sink (after first making sure that my kids aren't around to see me do the very thing I've nagged them about—just like drinking milk right out of the carton), and then head for the living room bookcase. Moments later I hand Michael a dog-eared copy of Updike's *Rabbit Redux,* pointing dramatically to an underlined passage. He reads it aloud in a bemused tone:

> But something has gone wrong. The ball game is boring. The spaced dance of the men in white fails to enchant, the code beneath the staccato bursts of distant motion refuses to yield its meaning . . . Rabbit yearns to protect the game from the crowd; the poetry of space and inaction is too fine, too slowly spun for them. And for the players themselves, they seem expert listlessly, each intent on a private dream of making it; they seem specialists like any other, not men playing a game because all men are boys time is trying to outsmart.

"This is all in your head," Michael announces as soon as he finishes. "What's it got to do with the Phils?"

"It's the majors, the whole big-league game. Bloated. Like *you* always say this whole country is—top-heavy, too high on the energy chain." He doesn't answer; he just continues reading silently while I lapse into a monologue: "It's all down to dollars . . . one more thing to consume . . . Finley calls it an 'entertainment product' . . . it's to baseball what McDonald's is to food." No wonder he doesn't respond; God, I'm even boring myself. And the unspoken truth is that I've lost my faith—or my naiveté. At 34 I can't give myself to a team, rise and sink with its fortunes, the way I used to, even in my twenties. It's only a game. "Neanderthal owners . . . greedy players . . . a plague on both their houses." My one-time love for the majors has diffused into a neutral aesthetic appreciation of well-played games; into a sporadic interest in individual players, most of them flaky pitchers (Tiant, Hrabosky, Ellis, Lolich, and especially

McDowell—now retired, or fired); and into an odd conservatism, a resistance to almost any change in the game, that seems to have little connection to the rest of my life. (I'm not nostalgic for two-lane highways or medicine before penicillin.) "Distances in meters . . . freeze-dried fields . . . man-eating scoreboards . . . the designated hitter"—

"That's in the other league," Michael says without looking up. "Hey!" He suddenly holds the book up and stares at me accusingly: "This is about a *minor*-league game! And you're givin' me a grouch sermon about the *majors*."

"So what?" I try to sound indignant. "The majors have even less soul. More dollars, more specialization. And they're expanding again . . . while the minors contract. An inverted pyramid—what's that if not the bloat?"

He waves my words aside. "Just quit analyzing and get into it. The Phils are gonna make it this year, take it all . . . and go right into the Series against Boston." He reads my look and laughs: "The Bicentennial. Dig it!" Halfway out the door, he pops back in. "And it's the centennial of baseball."

"Not baseball—just the National League." I'm straining to catch up. "Also the centennial of Budweiser. Another great entertainment product."

He takes a swig. "The Bud stops here."

Pam's not in the garden; obviously tired of waiting for her beer, she's strolled up to the tennis court to talk to Sheila. Michael plays with the radio dial, but the batteries are weak and there's only static. Some of it sounds like crowd noise, but it's much too early for any game to be on. He yanks the useless aerial, turning it and the dial and himself around in different directions. Impotence. He walks around the kohl patch drinking his beer and radiating energy. "Well how about some wiffle ball?" he demands. He unbands his Jesus hair. "Come on."

I stand confused in compost, but he's already pushing the mower to a spot just outside the garden fence, a few feet from a cornerpost. The motor starts on the first pull, and he revs it up good and high, unchokes the sound to a steady hum, and begins cutting. After forty feet a left turn, another forty and left again—and now the swath is clearly a basepath. He rounds third, completes the diamond, pauses, and then mows another swath from home to a putative pitcher's mound. (They used to have this alleyway on old baseball fields. Why? And where did it go?)

Michael's so intense that this energy should be infectious, but I'm still trying to will it. I become preoccupied with mere number, measuring the distance from home, next to the garden, down the left-field line to the backyard fence. I pace it off as 72 feet, and 81 to the power alley in left-center. There's no fence at all in right field, where baseball space stretches outward to infinity. Michael has laid out lengths of garden hose as foul lines, but the green is hard to see in the grass, so he brings the bag of lime out of the garden.

This is all as goofy as that Kentucky farmer's reconstruction of Crosley Field on his south forty. But it's not all Michael's fault; the game, the game itself, encourages this sort of pastoral foolishness. Baseball's not only a country pastime that was brought into the city, but also the opposite—the imposition of sophisticated forms on an artificial natural setting. Just like our garden: an "imitation" of a farm, and no real exercise in self-sufficiency. The game was nostalgic even at the beginning. One day in 1846 Alexander Joy Cartwright and the boys from the Knickerbocker Club took the Barclay Street Ferry over to Hoboken, to a lovely five-acre tract actually named the Elysian Fields. And in that first formal game, even before all the rules had found their natural form, the players were already using the old farm metaphors of "outfield" (grazing land) and "infield" (where the crops are, closer to home).

Michael's own pastoral rituals have caught the fancy of my daughters, eight and ten. Taking their cue from me, they lean idly against the backyard fence as he peels off bases from an old chunk of spoiled hay. But then he smiles out at them—"Wanna play? Get some kids."—and they're off, yelling through the yard and down the street. I fetch the wiffle ball and plastic bat, ready now to humor Michael and maybe to teach the kids a thing or two about ball. By the time I return we're faced with six girls, all gangly and pre-pubescent, waiting for us to pattern their play. We divide them into teams: Michael calls them the Farm Team and the Kernels, but they pay no attention to his pastoral allusions or to the country nicknames (Rube, Bobo, Bubba, Cy, Ty, Pie) he keeps tossing around. I am the permanent pitcher, trying with a soft underhand arc (and too much advice) to help the kids hit. Michael's at shortstop, where his main job seems to be allowing grounders to roll dead for hits, so that the kids have enough offense to keep them interested.

The rules evolve as we go. No called balls or strikes. No leadoffs for baserunners. And we restore an ancient tradition, "soaking" the runner, from proto-baseball: the ball can be thrown at a runner who's between bases, and if it hits her she's out. The kids profess fear, until they learn that it doesn't hurt and that a missed soak is usually good for at least one extra base. One rule that baffles them is the need to tag up on fly balls, and I keep re-explaining this, finally enforcing it magisterially, until they grasp it. On the other hand, they have no trouble with the idea of an imaginary runner: when the Kernels load the bases and my daughter Kate saunters in from third to bat, she tells us that she's been replaced by "a ghost runner." "That's an astral projection," Michael replies.

At first it's more of a ceremony than a game, for Michael and I have an unspoken agreement to work for a tie between the teams. But we can't control everything, and we haven't reckoned on the ineptness of the kids' fielding; the Farm Team girls, especially, seem to find the skills of catching and throwing a wiffle ball every bit as arcane as dancing with boys. When Janice laces a fly to right that's misplayed (twice) for a homer, the Kernels lead 10–3. After the third out Michael announces that he's just been signed as a free agent by the Farm Team.

Without Michael on defense three quick hits bloop in. Then he waits on one of my high arcs, and lofts a monster fly that sails like the tail of a kite over the fence (and a young white birch) in left-center. By the time we get three outs the Farm Team leads 14–10, and I acquiesce modestly when the Kernels demand that I come in to hit with them.

Michael lobs the ball to me as I did to him, but the big arc has me vapor-locked. It's like slow-pitch softball, where the batter is really contending with himself, trying to wait for the muscular initiative to flow outward from the breath. I'm jerky. I'd prefer wicked fastballs, wifflescrewballs, or anything that might force me to respond with direct reflex rather than allowing time for thought to get in the way. Waiting for that ephus ball to get to the plate, I press to remain alert, but forget to be loose, and now the girls are giving *me* advice. "It's healthy for kids to see grown-ups fail," I tell them after two weak fouls. Then I hit a lame pop-up that Michael backs up to take at shortstop, calling for it and then brushing two of his own uncomprehending fielders out of the way.

The kids' lack of interest is becoming palpable. When I come to bat again, the Kernels sense that even if I smash one (I don't), the game now has perverse possibilities of shaping up as a bloated Home Run Derby between these two bizarre men. And when Michael digs in on me in the next inning, his Farm Teammates, winning and bored, decide they want to quit. I'm tempted to issue a sermon on the elementary Kid Code that prohibits leaving just after getting your "ups." But, of course, that's not a code you learn from an adult. Why should I care more than the kids do? Kate, thin and intense, fidgets at shortstop and talks about tomorrow's Easter egg hunt. Her more placid sister, Quinn, pets a cat in center field. Let 'em go.

When the game dissolves, I see my four-year-old son playing in the garden, digging with a trowel at an empty bed. I consider but reject the idea of having him take some hitting; the fact is, I'm shy about coaching him. The last time I talked with Sean about baseball, he told me that he now understood the game—that it was like the story of the Three Little Pigs! "First you have to run to the first house, and then you get chased to the second house, and around." Good enough. I want him to learn the values of slow games, strategies for living in a culture addicted to speed, but precisely because baseball has been so central in my life I don't want to force it on him. Nobody forced it on me: my own immigrant father had little interest in the game, beyond a vague identification with the eccentric Dodgers and his own baseball-crazy sons. Wait until Sean suggests it himself—let baseball be a rite of passage into boyhood, just as football might later be a rite of passage into adolescence.

"Kemosabe," Sean says to me in the garden, pointing to a flat of kohlrabi seedlings. He stares in wonder, his face a distillation of my own. The plants look strange, thick little leaves resonating in the breeze as if they were receiving signals from some UFO; and soon enough these stems will be tendrils, like a catfish's, snaking up from the outside of each chartreuse ball. Sean watches us plant: Michael and I are cruder than Pam—

we lack her ability to focus attention—but we make sure that the soil around each seedling is well aerated. Michael finds the larva of a Japanese beetle, holds it between his fingers and studies it, then squashes it with a trowel: "Come back higher."

"I hope he gets reincarnated as a gardener."

"Or that you don't get reincarnated as a beetle."

"I probably will. I hate those sonsabitches for what they did to the corn last year. When I kill one, I can't be serene. I wish they were bigger, the size of mice or something, so I could garotte them with piano wire."

Across the patch Sean seems startled by my shrill tone, and tosses me a quizzical look. Michael's amused: "Hey, take it easy. We'll get 'em. You gotta go *with* this thing, not against it. Jack told me a new way to beat bugs. When do the beetles come out? End of June? OK, so we catch a couple dozen, put 'em in your kitchen blender—let me finish—in your blended with water, zap 'em, strain the mess, and then dilute it and just spray it on corn and stuff. Simple."

"You mean we don't smoke it first? Listen, let's just rise above our principles and get some Sevin. We won't spray much. It'll only be a venial sin."

"You're still too Catholic. And don't sneak any poison in here while I'm in Canada. Anyway, that'd be like doing cortisone for your arm."

"I wouldn't rule cortisone out. Maybe once or twice over the season. If I really needed it."

"You *never* need that stuff. Whoo, I can tell you guys are really serious. Why don't you just get the hell out of that league? We could play in the Church League—no pressure, no uniforms, no power trips from managers. Hank says the Unitarians need players."

Michael's made this pitch before. Last year it was for the Friends, whose lineup included a retarded kid—"a beautiful guy," Michael said, who hit with power and grace and who was made to feel a part of things, even if he did need to be told when and where to run and throw.

"What happened to the Friends? I don't figure you for a Unitarian. How'll you get along with all those rationalists?"

"The Unitarians are nice. Nice people. I could definitely see Baba Ram Dass in center field for them. The Catholics are the only ones in that league who get weird. They're into winning. They all wear spikes."

"If I played for you guys, would you let me wear my spikes? I mean, I just wanna be able to tell the difference between your games and wiffle ball."

"Hey, forget it. Go ahead and play in the City League, and make everything serious. All it is, is Little League for big people."

"Are you kidding? We're not serious *enough*. We've got our first practice game today, and we still haven't had a real practice of our own yet. Know what we do when we get together? We divide into teams and play rounders and drink beer. Except for George, who doesn't need the beer; he showed up last time on some high-octane stuff of his own—God knows what, probably beetle juice. He claims he tracks the fly balls by following their vapor trails." Michael doesn't look up from his silent planting. "Would you feel better if we had a retarded guy on our team? Maybe then we'd be silly enough to suit you."

"That's just shitty."

I know it. I know it is. But it's also me, wedded to categories, half afraid that heaven wouldn't be heaven if everyone could get in, and looking for a rational middle ground between the extremes of Michael's paradoxical enthusiasms. "I gotta play in the best league I can cut it in." He still won't look up. How do you talk to a knee-jerk head? He's closer to me than my brother, but sometimes his consciousness is so high I can't get over it. Once before when he pulled a stunt like this, retreating from a political debate into a set of yoga postures, I wrote a West Virginia haiku:

> Just 'cause it ain't
> Fulla shit don't mean clear water
> Can't drown ya damn dead.

When I showed it to him a week later, I told him it was about someone else. He said he liked it: "It fits lotsa trips."

Maybe I could salvage a poem out of this day. Or maybe I could at least figure out how to give that tomato poem to Pam. But I can't wait any longer for her to come back from the tennis courts. All I can summon up is one more baseball meditation, another piece of fruit for this still life. I stand up. "Look, Michael, I have to go. If I don't see you guys again before you leave . . . have a good trip. And if you do stop off in Cooperstown, why not take in something worthwhile? Go visit the Farmer's Museum." He looks up. "No, I'm serious. It's a good place. Pam'd like it. Nobody'll try to tell you that agriculture got invented by Abner Doublehay. You can just catch the exhibits, some beautiful old-time tools, the Cardiff Giant"—

"The what?"

"The Cardiff Giant. It's a ten-foot statue, carved from gypsum about a hundred years ago. The guy who did it tried to pass it off as a petrified man. He charged admission to see it, and made a bundle. And then he made even more when he admitted it was a hoax. He just billed it as 'The Famous Hoax,' and the crowds flocked in. That's what the Hall of Fame oughta do with Doubleday. He's like the Cardiff Giant."

"I don't get it. What about Doubleday?"

"He didn't invent baseball. Nobody did. It just evolved."

"Shit"—Michael laughs at my pedantry—"it didn't evolve. It was discovered!" He stands up to say good-bye, a quick soul handshake.

On my way in to change clothes for the game, son Sean on my shoulders, I laugh too, full and free. I like the idea: baseball was there all the time, waiting to be found. Like a set of pure relations, a Pythagorean theorem. Or like the American earth.

* * * * * * *

I return to the garden five hours later, in the cool dusk. Still wearing my uniform and spikes, I step lightly into the kohl patch to retrieve tools that Michael and Pam have left. The radio lies to one side, next to a wheelbarrow full of compost. I try the batteries again, hoping for some kind of communication through skip distance, and in between bursts of static I catch the faint strains of Taj Mahal's mellow guitar ("Satisfied 'n' tickled too . . .")—which vanishes just as I begin to move to the rhythm. I switch off the radio and begin shoveling, allowing my beery head to buzz with words. Through some skip distance of its own, my brain is picking up antiheroic couplets. Shaggy doggerel—

> Spirit's re-creation: game today
> Against the Body (visitor, in gray).

I take a practice swing with the shovel. Earlier, in the softball game, I'd tried to brown-nose the life-force by using a real wood bat instead of inorganic aluminum. But I was still stymied by the impossible arc. Standing in the batter's box, waiting, waiting for each pitch to drop, I thought about my income tax. I thought about the Franco-Prussian War. I thought about Jane Fonda. And I still swung too soon, every time, suffering from what felt like a permanent case of premature bat.

Still, I'd felt at home in the outfield distances. There were no fences, and in the early innings before the softball softened I played a deep right, afraid of giving up a cheap homer. I ignored the busy-ness of infield noise ("Hum bay, hum that pea," I used to prattle from third base) to talk mostly to myself. After a lead-off double in the third inning: "OK, man on second: the throw's to third on a fly, second on a grounder. But take it home if you can charge one on the hop." Even as I was envying the hitter's level swing, I'd begun moving in and toward the line; the ball sliced in and bounced once, right into my glove, and I planted my spikes and fired home without aiming. The throw sailed into Vern's glove two feet off the ground and just to the third-base side of the plate. When he made the tag he hardly had to move. I laughed out loud—not only because I felt like Martin Dihigo, that great *jardinero* ("You no run on me, boy, you no run on me!"), but also because of a fleeting sensation that I'd been just an agent, that in the absence of time for thought *It* had thrown.

> Can't play this game against a clock. To go
> Outside yourself, just let the season flow.

We lost 7–3, but not before a final comic rally. With Nick on first, Stormy poled a fly to center; Nick trotted back to the bag to tag up, but the ball kept carrying and jumped past the fielder's outstretched glove. By the time Nick got in gear, Stormy was right behind him and the two of them rounded the bases stride-for-stride, turning third like twin gyros and converging with the relay at the plate. Nick slid straight in, got tagged, but took the catcher with him, and Stormy scored standing up. A home run on fielder's choice? The play defied charting—or would have if any of us had been bothering to score the game in a book.

If baseball is a democratized version of cricket, then this game was a democratized version of baseball: the essential populism of slow-pitch, with an extra man per side, every hitter making contact and every fielder getting more action. But beyond that there were the rowdy and plebeian textures, beer and dust and bench-jockeying, far from the civility of Sheila's tennis. Here the action was spread out, not just in space and time but socially—the relationships shallow but expansive, treasuring the eccentric, without middle-class sport's obsession with form. And through the flow of the season this team of bureaucrats and bartenders, carpenters and college teachers, salesmen and musicians and writers would find its own balance between competitiveness and participation, manhood and boyhood, those conflicting values that seem to puzzle everyone, even Unitarians.

Later, at the tavern, watching foreshortened tv images of a truly miraculous game, I spilled almost as much as I drank. The Phils had been trailing 12–1 after three, but when we arrived (just in time for a seventh-inning stretch) they'd narrowed it to 13–7. Schmidt already had two homers. In the top of the eighth he lined another shot 440 feet to dead center, and then it was 13–12. The bar was exploding with noise, alive with boozy camaraderie.

> The force that through the green fuse drives the flower
> Drives shots to center. Nature hits with power.

In the top of the ninth when the Phils took the lead with three runs, the last on Johnstone's perfect suicide squeeze, some truck driver wearing a baseball-style cap with a "Massey-Ferguson" emblem bought beer for everyone. "Can you believe this shit?" he kept asking. We couldn't—especially when the Cubs came back with two off McGraw in the last of the ninth to tie it at 15. Next to me Clancy was making the bad mistake of eating tavern chili, but he was the only one sitting. In the top of the tenth, with Allen on first, Schmidt drilled Paul Reuschel's first pitch to left center. On the tv screen the ball hung for a moment over the beautiful ivy, then smashed into the stands as the bar erupted. Clancy knocked my beer over. In the din some stranger slapped me five; I slapped five back, unself-consciously, out of the rut and into the groove. I missed another run by the Phils, but finally sat still for the last of the tenth when the Cubs, down 18–15, scored one more incredible run before Lonborg, the eighth Phil pitcher, got a one-pitch save on a grounder to Schmidt. Team totals: 34 runs, 43 hits, and not a single error.

Nick elbowed me. "Maybe all that hitting'll inspire you."

"Yeah, well, I'd like to see Schmidt hit slow-pitch."

George danced up to the bar with a girl whose eyes were a little less glassy than his own. "Jeez," he said, "this is what I'd like to be doin' when I die."

The Massey-Ferguson guy laughed. "I know what I wanna be doin' when *I* die." He gave a big wink. "I'd be comin' and goin' at the same time. Har-har-har. Get it?"

I turned to Nick. "I think I get it."

"Me too."

"Yeah, but my fantasy's different. I'm ninety-some years old, see, and I'm in Florida, playing in one of those Geriatric Softball Leagues they have down there." Nick groaned. "Wait—listen: it's a tie game, last of the last, and I tear around third with the winning run. Halfway down the line the old ticker starts to stop. But on sheer effing will power alone I stagger six more steps and collapse into a perfect hook slide. Notice that I don't go straight into the catcher as some softballers have been known to do."

"You're dyin', for God's sake!"

"But not yet. Not before I see the umpire—he's a young guy, about fifty-seven—spread his arms like eagle wings. The last thing I hear is croaky cheers from fellow geezers, and canes tapping out appreciation in the stands."

"Oh, man, you know what your problem is? That's the kind of stuff you want to be doin' *after* you die."

"Now that you mention it . . . it's hard to imagine a real heaven without some ball games."

"Maybe by then you'll be able to hit."

"Oh yeah? Well, if I couldn't do better than you at beating Stormy around the bases, I believe I'd lay off sex before the next game."

Nick pointed to the Pabst smear on the bar in front of me. "Hey, you know what an Irish fag is? . . . That's a mick who prefers women to booze!"

> A drift of dandelions in shallow right
> Begins the season, shagging wind and light.

I rode back here with Gib Ruark, baseball-bitten poet. Compact and hefty, he claims never to have played much ball, even informally; and he's never tried a baseball poem. But the game seems part of the very weave of his life: he watched our loss today, rooting earnestly behind first base; at the bar he celebrated the tv game with a huge grin; and in the car he invited me, in his soft Southern voice, to drive down to Baltimore some Sunday for a doubleheader. "Memorial Stadium's a real park," he said, "in a real neighborhood. There's no big scoreboard, and there's natural grass, and they've got kosher hot dogs and Maryland crabs and cold beer—National Bo just poured from a bottle. And for three and a half bucks you get a great seat, right up close."

Well, why not? Gimme a kosher dog with relish and gusto. So what if the American League's inferior and bloated with designated hitters? Be nice to get a stereoscopic sense of the majors, and try again to see those fields as mandalas. All these versions of baseball feed off one another anyway; it's hopeless to try keeping them separate. I know that if the majors disappeared tomorrow the Game would remain alive and well—and I'd probably play more, just to take up the slack. But if I could keep it in focus, then spectating might still be a source of healthy energy. Because I can't play ball forever. Can I?

> Let this be what I am the day I die,
> And the day after: a pitcher in the rye.

Beer poetry, rough draft. Or it might have been Gib who encouraged this chatter; maybe someday when we're both sober we could collaborate on a baseball poem—a sexy pastoral: "Last Fungo in Paris, Kentucky." With that in mind, I reach for my wallet, fish out Pam's poem, shred it, toss the scraps on the compost pile, and shovel the words under.

In one shovel-load of compost I find a volunteer seedling (cuke? squash?), a mystery springing up from last year's rot, and I plant it gently next to the fence with as much awareness as I can muster, my own thoughts pyramiding with the soil around the stem. My father: dead eight years this week, who ran away from home at seventeen, bored with farm life, finally jumping ship in the New World, an illegal but unalienated alien. My son: that curly seedling, loose and alert, stretching toward the light. This space: this insulated middle landscape, now opening outward and arcing upward without end. I once considered buying a Whole Earth flag to fly over the garden and the field, but at this moment I swear even that would seem too parochial.

Ah, my brain cells have round heels. Too dark to play. I place all the tools in the barrow, and pick up the radio. (Got to get this honkey fixed: maybe bring it out here Sundays when I weed—even catch an occasional game.) At the edge of the kohl patch, this plot I'll seed again with rye around World Series time, my spikes unearth a small beetle larva. "Come back higher," I pray as I kill it and trundle out through the infield.

# RICHARD GROSSINGER

## Baseball Variants

In an *Io* baseball issue, I proposed a mythological origin for the game of baseball—as the merging of an English field sport with an American Indian board game. For England, I cited the actual pasture and cultivated green, with its fair and foul boundaries and its positioned players; the forerunners are club-ball, trap-ball, and cricket. Among the Amerindian contributions were an interior circle of occupiable bases, players making circuits and scoring, "painting of the sand" in symbols, and elements of strategy, chance, and gambling; its predecessors are Menominee snow-snake, Zuni tasholiiwe, and the Cheyenne basket/plum-stone game. If the bases were Indian, the ball and field were English. Of course, the Indians had sewn balls and open fields, games like lacrosse and ebesquamogan, so the English ball became more "animal" and earthier; the "green" became wilder and more wide-open, no hedges around the gardens. The prior English strategy (of stool-ball, bandy-ball, and their kin) was adapted for American Indian board rules and then projected back onto an open field.

All of this is apocryphal and undocumented, but it suggests the complex and obscure nativity of a game that was being played in local and bastard forms from New Jersey to Louisiana before it was ever schematized, standardized, and nationalized. The history it was given at that point, its Cooperstown history, is, in fact, far more misleading than the one I have made up.

Several years after the publication of *Io*/10, I realized how much my own interpretation was a Jungian one. That is, it bases an impossible chronological event on the psychological evidence of the archetypes, which are, by definition, eternal, transhistorical, and achronological. Impossible changes and mergers occur in the deep body-mind of humanity as the secular historical order is tugged into adjustment with a more basic psychic and cosmic order. Baseball as an American Indian/English game feels right. The seeds of this heterogamy were sown unconsciously in the North American blood and landscape; and where they fell, like the runaway cultigens of Mayan and Eurasian stock, grew up neighborhood games and raw regional variants. From a marriage that was never fully consummated or publicly announced, these hybrids sprang, the beans, tomatoes, and tubers of mixed agricultures, finally bred into a streamlined version that was made conscious for the nineteenth and twentieth century American psyche. The real game is archetypal and profound. As we play one version, we generate others, maddening in their insistence, in their competition with the waking familiar. By a true Freudian dream script, they demand expression too. Even now, as baseball is changing from within, there is no proof that the present framework of leagues or rules will survive much more than a trivial hundred years.

A re-reading of Jung confirms and enlarges my intuition. In his 1909 visit to Buffalo, he observed hundreds of factory workers suddenly in the streets, and remarked that he had never realized how much Indian blood there was in the European American. His companion was startled by this perception and assured him there was not one drop of Indian blood in the whole crowd; the workmen were pure Irish, Scottish, and German. Although chagrined at his naiveté, Jung pursued the intimation and later concluded that something lies deeper than pure genetics and cross-cultural exchange. "Certain Australian primitives," he writes, "assert that one cannot conquer foreign soil, because in it there dwell ancestor-spirits who reincarnate themselves in the newborn." These ancestor-spirits are partly human pagan, but also, in association with the land itself and chthonian principles, they embody a more original prehuman paganism. They demand Amerindian strains in baseball.

In my original model, I omitted one other obvious source: Africa. Jung finds it, curiously enough, in his visit to an American baseball game. This was not, he concluded, a public event of a Germanic town, a Roman crowd in witness, but the chattering, gathering, primeval jazz, and story-telling of an African village [my own version extends Jung's a bit here]. The African element of baseball is then the music and rumble of the crowd, the narrative and myth-motifs that link game to game throughout a cycle, or season. To an English ballfield and Indian bases, we add African fans: Zande witches, Zulu drummers, Hausas chanting spider-tales. And Dr. Jung concludes that "the American presents a strange picture: a European with Negro behaviour and an Indian soul" ["Mind and Earth," 1927].

In the daily newspapers we read the cumulative score and records of a Dogon creation myth, as if told by Ogotemmeli. On the city street-corners, singers and drummers gather, flipping cards of the ancestors and totem-beings, gambling on throws of Pima and Creek stones and otter's teeth. A ritual jam session precedes the pick-up game, everyone clustered, jiving, chorusing, then out in the field, guarding their positions, picking "roots and berries." In the stadiums of the city-states the big games are played, tribal ceremonies complete with totems and clan representation. We might actually believe that Willie Mays comes wild from the waterhole races and zebra hunts, tamed to the articulate skills of organized ball, via the dark vernacular of the Dixie slums.

In our outdoors inventions of baseball games, we try to recover the old asymmetrical fields and battered homemade balls. Everyone knows Bob

Feller honed his fastball, rocks against trees, and others fungoed them with sticks out into imaginary home run forests, translating an obscure radio image into a visible event. Two players, with a hardball, a base, and a boundary, can replace a whole eighteen-man quorum; on grounders the fielder automatically becomes the infielder; on flies, he is an outfielder. The distance and width of the zone in which he must stand re-enacts all the dazzling curve balls and sliders of the pitcher.

Baseball is contagious; it twists an environment, however large and undifferentiated or small and movable, to its uses. For instance, the whole field, even the transcontinental geography of major league baseball, is microscoped onto a sheet with numbers on it from which "players" generate whole seasons. The very real beings who participated in the games from which the formulas were drawn: disappear into number clusters that are the approximate cumulative result of their play. There is not only the infinite series of possible games generated by the sheets of numbers; there are also the infinite possible versions from different formulas and different transcriptions. The alternative seasons resemble faintly, but are startlingly different than, say, the 1948, or 1956, on which they are based. Although it is unlikely, Mickey Mantle may hit 25 homers instead of 52 and Minnie Minoso may lead the league with 49. This discrepancy is extremely interesting, perhaps more so than the relatively sterile season currently in progress and not subject to revision. Hence the groups that play these games publish their own league newspapers, writing *Sporting News* style articles about the teams, the players, and their weeks. Reading them, the "fans" have a dim or precise memory of how it actually was and how *this* is different. The image of that real season and those historical careers gives a significance, and existentiality, to the versions of what-didn't-happen. The season can be replayed hundreds of times, until, perhaps, a theme appears, and the different "seasons" cluster around it. It is not "Real," but the French, by calling it grammatology, remind us that even the real game is more a document and a trace than a permanent and indelible outcome.

Although board, card, and dice games interested me, they were contractive and menial. My fonder memory is of games invented in collaboration with particular landscapes of childhood. They are (with their places of discovery): Ocean Ball (Long Beach, New York), Roofball (Camp Chipinaw, Swan Lake, New York), and Sockball (Apartment 6B, 1235 Park Avenue, New York City).

My brother Jon and I made up Ocean Ball, modeling it after the old home run derbies on New York City television. We used a broomstick and a spalding high bounce (in later years in Maine, a hoe handle was the favorite bat). The hitter stands far up from the ocean at a line marked by cans and seaweed, and swings toward the fielder, who stands just short of the tideline. Any ball hit into the ocean on a fly is two runs; any ball rolling into the ocean is one run. Any ball fielded cleanly on the ground eliminates a run; any ball caught in the air eliminates two runs (with the exception that any ball caught in the ocean eliminates three runs). Nine innings of ten-swings-per make up a game.

In Ocean Ball, the various left- and right-field boundaries of a regular ballpark are topologically translated into a rhythmic temporal event: the general movement of the tide over nine innings, and the more dramatic in-and-out pulse of the waves. The "ocean" moves. In order to count, a ball must clearly splash; it cannot score in a wet spot from which the waves have retreated. The fielder must remain aware of where the water is. He may gaily field a grounder without realizing that the waves have come in under his feet: one run. If he is very alert, he may shift his feet at the last moment to catch a ball in the water rather than on land. Diving catches made out in the waves, with a five-run differential in the balance, are the guts of the game.

Although we had reasonable baseball scores, the verisimilitude was vague. A homer is a homer, but how is a two-run homer made with no one on base? How do you lose runs? The point, here and in other such games, is that we are dealing with a derivative of baseball, adapted in order to make use of geographical features rather than fight them. Major league baseball is racing in the opposite direction with its carpets and equilateral stadiums.

Roofball I found already flourishing in summer camp, but with friends and in different environments, we changed the game over time. Nowhere has it ever been better than in my present home in Vermont: there are four separate roofs, two of them corrugated, one slanted and leading directly back onto the field, the other horizontal and leading onto a lower roof, plus three chimneys and several ricocheting corners where the roofs meet.

If a roof leads onto a concrete surface, one can play single-double-triple-home run, based on the number of bounces from one to four. In rural environments, distances and locations determine hits. A home run is anything into the trees. A single is anything that drops in front of the fielder. A double is the clubmoss patch. The base runners advance the number of the hit (two bases for a double) with extra bases given for long singles and doubles (scoring a man from first, etc.). To discourage players from "swinging for the seats," especially with runners on, a double play is charged for any throw that goes over the roof or falls short and is caught. These result from throwing the ball either hard or high. Additional double plays and tag-ups can be included simply by marking a box on the side of the house and forcing the fielder to throw into it from where he fields the ball (putting the runner out or failing to).

The fielder stands in under the angle of the roof; the batter stands out beyond it. He can throw for corners or chimneys; he can put a spin on the ball; he can try a deceptive motion or path. If he gives it height for oomph, he also gives away placement, and the fielder can position himself more quickly. The fielder is not allowed to break until the ball hits the roof and re-enters his field of vision.

Jon and I invented Sockball also, and we played it in our room. A tennis racquet was the bat, and the ball was a tightly wound pair of socks. The pitcher lobbed the sock in, aiming inside or outside, high or low, and the batter swung for spots in the room. Singles were drives that bounced uncaught off a thin canopy around the far ceiling. Doubles landed on either bed; they had to stay, but no diving fielder could dislodge them. A clear catch resulted in a double play. A garbage can set before the radiator in "deep" center was a perfect triple because it was a rare poke. The left-field window had a glass guard set inside it at a forty-five-degree angle. It was a beautiful home run, either on a soft lob or a caroom. A lob could be defensed by a leap, with the ball sometimes batted down into a double, but there was one perfect arc, just over the pitcher and beyond his right arm, just soft enough so it didn't hit the window and bound past. With such a small "field," it was easiest to hit the canopy by pounding the ball down the right-field line, hard enough so it sank before its rebound was caught (meaning one out). A single had to be smacked. "Swinging for the seats," in delicious reversal, was the most delicate shot of the game. It called for a sharper stroke, in order to pull the ball, and yet a softer hit. One strategically went for homers in certain situations. One never swung for triples; they were accidents.

Our mother did not think much of this game, and she busted up many a contest before the fifth inning. When she was home, we were a bit like major league teams ordering their strategy around a possible rain-out. Sometimes you had to swing softly, even at the risk of outs, because if you slammed for singles, the racket might "bring down the rain." She thought baseball belonged outdoors, but, more poignantly, she thought socks were for wearing, not hitting, and she was convinced they went out the window, even though the window was closed. She never discovered, because of our game, that socks just disappear, without explanation. In fact, hers was a self-fulfilling prophecy because, after she inadvertently suggested the idea to us, we occasionally opened the window to add drama to the home runs. There was a garbage can out on 96th Street, and if you put it in that, you won the whole season. We never did. But it was sure nice to see a home run sail out of sight, and then watch it far down on the street below. After a homer-filled game, we would go and collect them. Contrary to belief, no one wanted our socks, and we rarely lost a one.

# 2

# Childhood Baseball

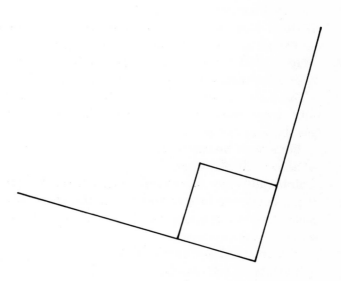

## *from* Pride of the Bimbos

Denzel wandered toward them with his glove under his arm. A few were in the outfield, crowding under liners and pop-ups that a tall boy threw them. "I got it!" they called in unison, "Mine, mine!" Off to one side a dark, barrel-chested kid was playing pepper with a boy who had a bandage over his eye. The rest milled around, joking, tossing gloves and hats in the air, fighting over the remaining bat to take practice swings. They all seemed to know each other.

Denzel squatted next to a thin boy who sat on his glove at the fringe of the action, watching expectantly. He was the only one there smaller than Denzel.

"Gonna be a game?"

"Uh-huh." The thin boy looked up at him, surprised.

"They got regular teams?"

"Nope. They pick sides."

Denzel nodded.

"Hope I get to play," said the thin boy. "When the teams don't come out even I got to sit," he said, "every single time."

He waited for a word of support but Denzel just grunted and moved several feet away. Might think we come together.

The ones on what seemed to be the field hacked around a little longer until a movement to start a game began. "Let's go," someone said. "Get this show on the road."

"Somebody be captains."

"Somebody choose up."

Gradually they wandered in and formed a loose group around a piece of packing crate broken roughly in the shape of a home plate. They urged each other to get organized and shrugged their indifference over who would be the captains.

"C'mon, we don't have all day."

"Somebody just choose."

"Big kids against little kids!" said a fat boy in glasses and they all laughed.

"Good guys against the bad guys!"

"Winners against the losers!"

"The men against the mice!"

"Okay," said the dark, barrel-chested kid, "Whynt we just have the same captains as yesterday?"

"Yeah, but not the same teams."

"Too lopsided."

"That was a slaughter."

"We got scobbed."

"Do it then," said the fat boy, "Bake and the Badger."

"Yeah, shoot for first pick."

"Let's go, choose up."

There was a sudden movement, everybody spreading in a semicircle around two of the boys, jostling not to be behind anyone, the thin boy hopping up and running to join them. Denzel got up slowly and walked to the rear of them. No sense getting all hot and bothered. No big thing. He drifted through hips and shoulders, quietly, till he stood in view of the captains.

They were shooting fingers, best four out of seven, like the World Series. The barrel-chested boy was one of the captains, the one they called the Badger, and the tall boy who had been throwing flies was the other.

Denzel slipped his glove on. It was an oversized Ted Kluszewski model his daddy had handed down to him. Each of the fingers seemed thick as his wrist and there was no web to speak of and no padding in the pocket. Orange and gunky.

The tall boy won on the last shoot and the Badger scowled.

"Alley Oop!" Bake called without even looking.

"Haw-raaat!" A wiry kid with arms that hung to his knees trotted out from their midst and stood by Bake. "We got it now, can't lose. Can not lose!"

"Purdy!" The Badger barked it like an order and a solid-looking red-haired kid marched out and took his place.

The two first picks began to whisper and nudge at their captains.

"Vernon," whispered the wiry boy, "get Vernon."

"Vernon."

Vernon came to join them and he and Alley Oop slapped each other's backs at being together.

"Royce," whispered the big redhead. "They get Royce, we've had it."

"Royce," said the Badger and Royce was welcomed into the fold.

"Pssssst!" called the fat boy with the glasses to Alley Oop and Vernon. "Have him pick me. You guys need a third sacker."

"Ernie," they said, on their toes leaning over each of Bake's shoulders, "Ernierniernie!"

"Okay, Ernie," he said and Ernie waddled out with his glove perched on top of his head.

"Gahs looked like you needed some help," he told them. "Never fear, Ernie is here!"

The captains began to take more time in their picking. They considered and consulted and looked down the line before calling out a name. The Badger pounded quick, steady socks into the pocket of his glove while beside him Purdy slowly flapped the jaws of his first baseman's mitt. Soon there were more that had been chosen than that hadn't. The ones who were picked frisked and giggled behind their captains while the ones who hadn't were statues on display. "You," the captains said now, still weighing abilities but unenthusiastic. Finally they just pointed. The Badger walked along the straggling line of leftovers like a general reviewing troops, stood in front of his next man and jerked his thumb back over his shoulder. When there was only one spot left for even teams Denzel and the thin boy were left standing. It was the Badger's pick.

Denzel stood at ease, eyes blank. It grew quiet. He felt the others checking him over and he smelled something. Topps bubble gum, the kind that came with baseball cards. He snuck a glance at the thin boy. His eyes were wide, fixed on the Badger, pleading. He had a round little puff of a catcher's mitt that looked like a red pincushion. There was no sign of a baseball ever having landed in it, no dent of a pocket.

Denzel felt the Badger considering him for a moment, eyes dipping to the thick-fingered old-timer's glove, but then he turned and gave a slight, exasperated nod to the thin boy. "We got him."

Before Denzel could get out of the way Bake's team streamed past him onto the field.

"First base!" they cried, "Dibs on shortstop!" Trotting around him as if he were a tree, looking through the space where he stood. "Bake?" they whined, "Lemme take left huh? I always get stuck at catcher or somethin." Denzel kept his face blank and tried to work the thing back down into his throat. They all knew each other, didn't know whether he was any good or not. No big thing.

He drifted off to the side, considered going back to the van, then sat beyond the third base line to watch. As if that was what he had come to do in the first place. Nice day to watch a ball game. He decided he would root for Bake's side.

"Me first," said the Badger, pointing with the bat handle, "you second, you third. Purdy, you clean up. Fifth, sixth, semeightnon." They had full teams so Denzel couldn't offer to be all-time catcher and dive for foul tips. You didn't get to bat but it kept you busy and you could show them you could catch. Denzel kept his glove on.

He could tell he was better than a lot of them before they even started and some of the others when the end of the orders got up. The pitching .was overhand but not fast. There was a rock that stuck out of the ground for first base and some cardboard that kept blowing so they had to put some sod clumps on it for second and somebody's T-shirt for third. Bake played shortstop and was good and seemed a little older than the others.

The one called Purdy, the big redheaded one, fell to his knees after he struck out. Everybody had backed way up for him. Alley Oop made a nice one-handed catch in center. Whenever there was a close play at a base, Badger would run over and there would be a long argument and he would win. The thin boy had to be backed up at catcher by the batting team so it wouldn't take forever to chase the pitches that went through. The innings went a long time even when there weren't a lot of runs because the pitchers were trying tricky stuff and couldn't get it close. Denzel followed the action carefully, keeping track of the strikes and outs and runs scored, seeing who they backed up for and who they moved in for, who couldn't catch, who couldn't throw, keeping a book on them the way his daddy and Pogo had taught him he should. When fat Ernie did something funny he laughed a little along with the rest of them. Once somebody hit a grounder too far off to the left for the third baseman or left fielder to bother chasing. "Little help!" they called and Denzel scrambled after it. He backhanded it moving away, turned and whipped it hard into the pitcher. No one seemed to notice. He sat back down and the game started up again.

The Badger's side got ahead by three and stayed there, the two teams trading one or two runs each inning. They joked and argued with each other while waiting to bat. They practiced slides and catches in stop-action slow-motion and pretended to be TV commentators, holding imaginary microphones and interviewing themselves. They kept up a baseball chatter.

"*Hum*babe!" said the team in the field, "Chuckeratinthere*iss*gahcantit-*iss*gahcantit! *Hum*babe! *Nostick*nostickchuckeratinthere—"

"*Lets*go!" said the team at bat, "*Big*innin*big*innin*we*gottateam*we*gotta-team*bang*itonoutthere! *Lets*go*lets*go!"

Late in the fifth inning a mother's voice wailed over the babble from a distance.

"Jonathaaaan!"

There was a brief pause, the players looking at each other accusingly, seeing who would confess to being Jonathan.

"Jonathan Phelps you get in here!"

The thin boy with the catcher's mitt mumbled something, looking for a moment as if he were going to cry, then ran off toward the camp.

Denzel squatted and slipped his glove on again. He wore it with his two middle fingers out, not for style but so he could make it flex a little. He waited.

The tall boy, Bake, walked in a circle at shortstop with his glove on his hip, looking around. "Hey kid!"

Who me? Denzel raised his eyebrows and looked at Bake.

"You play catcher for them."

Denzel began to rise but the Badger ran out onto the field. "Whoa na!

No deal. I'm not takin him. Got enough easy outs awriddy. Will play thout a catcher, you gahs just back up the plate and will have to send somuddy in to cover if there's a play there."

Denzel squatted again and looked to Bake.

"Got to have even teams," he said. "I got easy outs too. If you only got eight that means your big hitters get up more."

"I'm not takin him, that's all there is to it." The Badger never looked to Denzel. "We don't need a catcher that bad. Not gonna get stuck with some little fairy."

Bake sighed. "Okay. He'll catch for us and you can have what's his name. Hewitt."

The Badger thought a minute, scowling, then agreed. Hewitt tossed his glove off and was congratulated on being traded to the winning side.

"Okay," said Bake, "you go catch. You're up ninth."

Denzel hustled behind the plate and the game started up. There was no catcher's gear, so though it was hardball he stood and one-hopped the pitches. He didn't let anything get by him to the kid who was backing him up. He threw the ball carefully to the pitcher. There were no foul tips. Badger got on and got to third with two out. Bake called time. He sent the right fielder in to cover the play at the plate and Denzel out to right.

The one called Royce was up. Denzel had booked him as strictly a pull-hitter. He played medium depth and shaded toward center. The first baseman turned and yelled at him.

"What you doing there? Move over. Get back. This gah can cream it!"

He did what the first baseman said but began to cheat in and over with the delivery.

The second pitch was in on the fists but Royce swung and blooped a high one toward short right. Denzel froze still.

"Drop it!" they screamed.

"Choke!"

"Yiyiyiyiyi!"

"I got it!" yelled somebody close just as Denzel reached up and took it stinging smack in the pocket using both hands the way his daddy had told him and then he was crashed over from the side.

He held on to the ball. Alley Oop helped him to his feet and mumbled that he was sorry, he didn't know that he really had it. The Badger stomped down on home plate so hard it split in half.

"Look what I found!" somebody called.

"Whudja step in, kid?"

"Beginner's luck."

Denzel's team trotted in for its at-bats. While they waited for the others to get in their positions Bake came up beside him.

"That mitt looks like you stole it out of a display window in the Hall of Fame," he said, and Denzel decided to smile. "Nice catch."

The first man up flied out to left and then Ernie stepped in. Ernie had made the last out of the inning before.

"Hold it! Hold it rat there!" Badger stormed in toward the plate. "Don't pull any of that stuff, who's up? Ninth man aint it? The new kid?"

"We changed the batting order," said Ernie. "You can do that when you make a substitution. The new kid bats in my spot and I bat where Hewitt was."

"Uhn-uh. No dice."

"That's the rules."

"Ernie," said Bake, stepping in and taking the bat from him, "let the kid have his ups. See what he can do."

Bake handed the bat to Denzel and the Badger stalked back into the field. It was a big, thick-handled bat, a Harmon Killebrew 34. Denzel liked the looks of the other one that was lying to the side but decided he'd stay with what he was given.

The Badger's team all moved in close to him. The center fielder was only a few yards behind second base.

"Tryn get a piece of it," said Ernie behind him, "just don't whiff, kid."

"Easyouteasyouteasyout!" came the chatter.

Denzel didn't choke up on the big bat. See what he can do.

The first four pitches were wide or too high. He let them pass.

"C'mon, let's go!"

"Wastin time."

"Swing at it."

"Let him hit," said the Badger. "Not goin anywheres."

The next one was way outside and he watched it.

"Come *awn!*" moaned the Badger, "s'rat *over!*"

"Whattaya want kid?"

"New batter, new batter!"

"Start calling strikes!"

"Egg in your beer?"

"See what he can do."

The pitcher shook his head impatiently and threw the next one high and inside. Denzel stepped back and tomahawked a shot down the line well over the left fielder's head.

"Attaboy! Go! Go!"

"Dig, baby, all the way!"

"Keep comin, bring it on!"

By the time the left fielder flagged it down and got it in Denzel was standing up with a triple.

"Way to hit! Way to hit, buddy."

"Sure you don't want him, Badger?"

"Foul ball," said the Badger. He was standing very still with his glove on his hip. "Take it over."

This time Bake and half his team ran out to argue. The Badger turned away and wouldn't listen to them.

"Get outa here," they said. "That was fair by a mile. You gotta be blind."

He wouldn't listen. "Foul ball."

"Get *off* it," they said, "you must be crazy."

Denzel sat on the base to wait it out. The third baseman sat on his glove beside him and said nice hit. The Badger began to argue, stomping around, his face turning red, finally throwing his glove down and saying he quit.

"Okay," said Bake, "have it your way."

"Nope." The Badger sulked off but not too far. "If you gonna cheat I don't want nothin to do with it."

"Don't *be* that way, Badger, dammit."

"Hell with you."

"Okay," said Bake, looking over to Denzel and shrugging for understanding, "we'll take it over."

Denzel lined the first pitch off the pitcher's knee and into right for a single. Three straight hits followed him and he crossed the plate with the tying run. The first baseman made an error and then the Badger let one through his legs and the game broke open.

Denzel sat back with the rest of the guys. They wrestled with each other and did knuckle-punches to the shoulder.

They compared talent with a professional eye.

"Royce is pretty fast."

"Not as fast as Alley Oop."

"Nobody's that fast."

"Alley Oop can *peel*."

"But Royce is a better hitter."

"Maybe for distance but not for average."

"Nobody can hit it far as Purdy."

"If he connects."

"Yeah, he always tries to kill the ball. You got to just meet it."

"But if he ever connects that thing is gonna sail."

"Kiss it goodbye."

"Going, going, *gone!*"

Denzel sat back among them without talking, but following their talk closely, putting it all in his book. Alley Oop scored and asked Bake to figure his average for him and Bake drew the numbers in the dust with a stick till he came up with .625. That was some kind of average, everyone agreed. They batted through the order and Denzel got another single up the middle and died at second. It was getting late so they decided it would be last ups for Badger's team. The Badger was eight runs down and had given up.

Bake left Denzel in right for the last inning but nothing came his way. Purdy went down swinging for the last out and they split up. Bake and the Badger left together, laughing, but not before Bake asked Denzel his name and said see you tomorrow.

Denzel didn't tell him that he'd be gone tomorrow. That they'd have to go back to Jonathan Phelps.

## CHUCK SULLIVAN

### Stickball

In the middle
of the concrete heat
boys manning our
sneakered positions tarred
in the block's summer field

We hustled our
fates into shape
on the city's sweating face
in the lean, bouncing grace
of our broomstick, rubber ball game
bound by the sewers and parked cars
of our Outlaw Little League

While on the sidelines
dreaming in cheers
the old men watched
bleachered on brownstone stoops
and iron fire escapes
making small book on the shadowy
skills of stickball stars
lost in the late-inning sun
of the stadiumed street's
priceless, makeshift diamond

## *from* Doctor Sax

And yet despite all this rackety gray when I grew to the grave maturity of 11 or 12 I saw, one crisp October morning, in the back Textile field, a great pitching performance by a husky strangely old looking 14-year-older, or 13,—a very heroic looking boy in the morning, I liked him and hero-worshipped him immediately but never hoped to rise high enough to meet him in those athletic scuffles of the windy fields (when hundreds of less important little kids make a crazy army benighted by individual twitchings in smaller but not less tremendous dramas, for instance that morning I rolled over in the grass and cut my right small finger, on a rock, with a scar that stays vivid and grows with me even now)—there was Scotty Boldieu on the high mound, king of the day, taking his signal from the catcher with a heavy sullen and insulting look of skepticism and native French Canadian Indian-like dumb calm—; the catcher was sending him nervous messages, one finger (fast ball), two fingers (curve), three fingers (drop), four fingers (walk him) (and Paul Boldieu had enough great control to walk em, as if unintentionally, never changing expression) (off the mound he may grin on the bench)—Paul turned aside the catcher's signals (shake of the head) with his French Canadian patient scorn, he just waited till the fingers three (signal for drop), settled back, looked to first base, spit, spit again in his glove and rub it in, pluck at the dust for his fingertips, bending thoughtfully but not slowly, chewing on his inside lip in far meditation (maybe thinking about his mother who made him oatmeal and beans in the gloomy gray midwinter dawns of Lowell as he stood in the dank hall closet putting on his overshoes), looks briefly to 2nd base with a frown from the memory of someone having reached there in the 2nd inning drat it (he sometimes said "Drat it!" in imitation of B movie Counts of England), now it's the 8th inning and Scotty's given up two hits, nobody beyond second base, he's leading 8–0, he wants to strike out the batter and get into the ninth inning, he takes his time—I'm watching him with a bleeding hand, amazed—a great Grover C. Alexander of the sandlots blowing one of his greatest games— (later he was bought by the Boston Braves but went home to sit with his wife and mother-in-law in a bleak brown kitchen with a castiron stove covered with brass scrolls and a poem in a tile panel, and Catholic French Canadian calendars on the wall).—Now he winds up, leisurely, looking off towards third base and beyond even as he's rearing back to throw with an easy, short, effortless motion, no fancy dan imitations and complications and phoniness, blam, he calmly surveys the huge golden sky all sparkle-blue rearing over the hedges and iron pickets of Textile Main Field and the great Merrimac Valley high airs of heaven shining in the commercial Saturday October morning of markets and delivery men, with one look of the eye Scotty has seen that, is in fact looking towards his house on Mammoth Road, at Cow Field—blam, he's come around and thrown his drop home, perfect strike, kid swinging, thap in the catcher's mitt, "You're out," end of the top of the 8th inning.

Scotty's already walking to the bench when the umpire's called it—"Ha, ha," they laugh on the bench knowing him so well, Scotty never fails. In the bottom of the 8th Scot comes to bat for his licks, wearing his pitching jacket, and swinging the bat around loosely in his powerful hands, without much effort, and again in short, unostentatious movements, pitcher throws in a perfect strike after 2 and 0 and Scotty promptly belts it clean-drop into left over the shortstop's glove—he trots to first like Babe Ruth, he was always hitting neat singles, he didn't want to run when he was pitching.

I saw him thus in the morning, his name was Boldieu, it immediately stuck in my mind with Beaulieu—street where I learned to cry and be scared of the dark and of my brother for many years (till almost 10)—this proved to me *all my life wasn't black.*

## CHARLIE VERMONT

one day during fielding practice
while I was day-dreaming out in center field
the coach, Dick MacPherson
fungoed a pop-fly
I didn't even notice it

he stormed out to second base like a Mack truck
that was his name, what we called him, Mack

"Now wake up and die right!!! Charlie Vermont
or we'll get someone out there who'll hustle."

and, of course, any zen master
would be in complete agreement
and this is the meaning of

wake up and die right

## MIKE STEINBERG

### Ebbets Field Pilgrimage—A Memoir (1970)

Saturday mornings I would get up at 8 A.M.; my stomach was fluttering and churning so fast that I could not eat breakfast. My grandmother would hand me an oil-stained brown bag, the mayonnaise from the tuna fish already leaking through the wax paper. I would then walk through the dew-stained fields and shuttered Saturday morning streets up to 138th Street where I'd wake Sugar Carleson and nervously watch him eat his breakfast. Then we'd trudge up the block to pick up the other three fanatics. We'd be sweating and talking baseball from the minute we reached the bus stop to the time we got off the subway at Eastern Parkway. "Who do you think'll pitch for the Brooks today, The Preach, Ersk, or Newk?" "Do ya think Sal the Barber'll go for the Giants?" "I hope not. We can't ever seem to beat him except if we get him out of there in the first." "Who do ya think is the best center fielder, Duke or Willie?" It would go on like that for five hours. Between the bus ride and the first pitch, we'd play baseball initials, quote stats, mouth pennant-race-banter, and recall great games we'd seen. But most of all we'd luxuriate in the joy of knowing that we had a ticket to see the Dodgers play. I'd save the stubs and show them to the envious and unlucky urchins whose mothers wouldn't dare let them venture into Brooklyn unchaperoned. It was like belonging to some secret, elite fraternity. I wished that the games would go into extra innings so we could keep time at a stand still. And when the games did end, during the long, hot, crowded subway and bus rides home we'd keep the feeling alive by re-playing them over to one another complete with simulated crowd noises and sound effects.

Once home, my kid brother and I would put on Dodger hats and sneakers and we'd go outside and we would play stoop baseball. We reconstructed exact lineups, plays, and even the organ strains Gladys Gooding played as the Dodgers took the field. We pretended we were each one of the infielders in turn; Hodges, Robinson, Reese, and Cox. One of us would crouch down in simulation of Campy and the other would imitate the pitching motion of Newk, Preach, or Erskine. Then after we removed our caps and placed them over our hearts while we hummed the national anthem—right out there in the middle of the street—the game would begin. One of us would throw a Spalding high bouncer (good for two or three games) against the front stoop. The ball would spring off the wood and bounce into the road where the other pretender, posing as one of the fielders, would scoop it up and toss it back to the man at the stoop—easy out, short to first. At whim, we could produce line drive hits, pop-ups, bunts, and long flies. This madness would continue until the streetlights flickered on and all but obscured the flight of the ball. By that time the heat and humidity of the day had yielded to the evening's cool stillness, and as people sat around on their front stoops or guys gathered under the streetlights, we trotted off the field into the shelter of our imagined dugouts and waited for the next Saturday game when we could re-enact the ritual of childhood.

## LEWIS WARSH

### *from* Earth Angel

*Chapter Two*

My father bought his first car in 1954, a Chevrolet, and on June 5th of that year, my sister's twelfth birthday, we drove to Ebbets Field in Brooklyn to see the Dodgers play the St. Louis Cardinals. This was the only occasion the whole family went to a game and the only time I saw the Dodgers, my favorite team, play at home. Can you see? my mother asked. We were sitting in reserved seats behind third base and I could see everything perfectly, the players whose gestures I knew by heart, and the fans in the left-field grandstand without squinting. By the middle of game 2 some clouds passed bringing with them a feeling of hostility and thoughts of rain. The man next to my mother cursed into his beer. Kids ran into the outfield to shake Duke Snider's hand. A lady with gold earrings performed a belly dance number on her seat. Fistfights in the bleachers. It was time to leave.

When I was nine or ten I began going with friends to the Polo Grounds on Saturday afternoons, usually arriving as the Giants and the visiting team were taking batting practice, when it was still possible to hang out in the box seats and ogle the players, before returning to the grandstand— usually the first row in left. After the game we'd wait for hours outside the dressing room, surround the players, just a few ordinary guys in street-clothes, as they walked to their cars, shoving self-addressed post-cards into their hands with the hope, one day, bored, sitting around their hotel rooms on the road, they'd write their names, so highly valued, on the blank cards, and mail them, an act so simple I couldn't imagine any-one not doing it. That afternoon in Brooklyn Wally Moon, the Cardinal right fielder, hit a grand-slam homerun in the tenth inning to win the first game, 9–5. The ball just looped over the right field scoreboard, while Moon—rookie-of-the-year in '54—trotted around the bases, accepting his teammates' congratulations as he crossed the plate. In the second game the Dodgers recovered and led 10–3 by the fifth inning when we left and drove through Sunday afternoon traffic back to the Bronx, listening to the end of the game on the radio. Once I went by myself to an old-timers day game in Yankee Stadium and since it was crowded sat in the third deck along the right-field line while the miniscule figures whose names were just flashes of some weird sports page mythology were introduced on the field below, not really enjoying the game since I always disliked the Yankees, and knowing all the time my presence had been determined not so much by wanting to see the specific game but by a need to get out of my house, my apartment, and be anywhere—just to get away—if not out of my house then out of my head, which even at age 11 or 12 was becoming almost impossible. Following baseball, and playing it, was an activity I could lose myself in, at least most of the time, and there was a great feeling of security waking Sunday morning knowing the Dodgers were playing a double-header that afternoon, that I'd be free to spend the day alone in front of the TV. My sister was also a heavy Dodger fan during their most important years, '53 through '55; after they won their first Series it was all downhill as far as she was concerned, and in two years they'd be moving to L.A., anyway, as she herself would be doing some years later, though I don't think the coincidence had any bearing on her interest in sports (her first husband, a physicist, liked to race cars on Sunday). For a time Sue and I kept a scrapbook containing the Willard Mullin cartoons in the old *World-Telegram & Sun* which my parents bought because of the "News of the Schools" page; we also had secret favorite players whom we felt we could influence by magic, as if what we did determined how they performed on the field. The regular players like Snider, Furillo and Reese were beyond our powers; the marginal players, Billy Loes among them, who were having a hard time, or who if they lost a game or went into a slump would be sent to the minors or placed on the trading block, were the players we concentrated on. If Loes were pitching and we didn't, say, sip our milk between pitches, sure enough, he'd strike out the batter. Or if we directed our total attention to the screen while he pitched the game would invariably end in a shut out, for him, or at least a complete game. Most important we tried to communicate to him that in some way our futures hinged on the results of his performance, and in that way loaded a lot of responsibility on his shoulders. I don't want to turn this into a memoir about sports except to emphasize the effect that baseball, in particular, had on those hours, or moments, while I lay in bed trying to sleep, and on my waking hours as well, and that my first attempts at writing involved trying to notate play-by-play descriptions of games I'd invent in my head, much in the same way the early editions of *The Daily News* (which my father brought home from his late-night walks) reported games played too late to describe in a normal article. In minute typeface they'd give the barest details: "Gilliam flied out to Irvin in left. Reese walked on four pitches. Snider singled to right, Reese stopping at second." And that's how my stories would be. I'd take two teams and write out the entire game, keeping the score close to keep myself interested, and investing it with the weight of being the first game of the World Series or the deciding game of an also imaginary pennant race. My sense of the sports world, and of my own inner world in general, took a turn when I realized I could invent not only individual games but whole careers, starting with a rookie coming up with the Dodgers' farm team in Montreal, a 3rd baseman—that was their weakest position—and follow him through the trials of a few good years in the minors, making the team, winning rookie-of-the-year honors if I felt generous, having a salary dispute the next winter and then tailing off, victim of the sophomore jinx, there'd be a trade, possibly, and after a few mediocre years he'd suddenly blossom into a star, recover from an injury to make a big comeback in his later years, before finishing out his playing days as a pinch hitter on the team that first signed him. I never placed myself inside the image I created of the actual player, but as detached as I feel now thinking back on it, I realized that life didn't necessarily continue in one straight line but involved a series of jolts and bounces, and that the whole point was to recover from anything negative that happened, that's where I put my weight, on the blessing in disguise when a pitcher due to an arm injury lost his fastball only to return years later with a knuckler that kept his career intact for years past the time all the fastballers had lost their big pitch. And I knew that it was more than intelligence or luck that allowed a person to keep reviving himself, but the intuitive knowledge of what was the "right" thing to do at a given moment, a nameless attribute some people call will or inner strength but which is something I innately accepted as a fact of life, along with the prescience that was the way my life would eventually turn out.

## Season Wish

In turns of season
come exchanges,
transformations—daughters, even,
traded to gods for wheat or rain.
Rapunzel, before she was even born,
was traded away for cabbage leaves
on a risk her father took one night
for love. A man might think of dowry
on a night that pivots warmth and cold
during Indian summers, false
springs, sudden August cool.
A miller might say his daughter
can spin horses' straw to gold.
A man might offer in sudden hope
a crop, a dove, his youngest girl.

In spring, my father
took me out at dusk
to lots the boys had left,
seeing each year if I could spin
the winning curve ball back to him
and learn the catch, the grip and swing
of a missing son; hoping there was magic
in the glove or sneakers or wooden bat
like the power children found
in the legend in pauper's clothes
that created a man from balls of snow.
The cap, perhaps, might keep my hair
forever clipped; holding the glove
against my chest might stop
my breasts; and if I learned
the grip and stance, perhaps my wrists
would thicken, hard, around the bat.

My father made the diamond
out of stones he piled like altars
into three small mounds.
Pitching to him underhand,
sometimes I threw him winning runs
and watched him round our bases,
touch the stones and then
take home. He hoped
the season would never come
when something more important
would keep me on an April night
from trespassing with him into lots
till boys came back
to claim their ground
and kick our home and bases
into rocks again.

Year by year he built for me
the things he thought
a man one day would want me for:
investments, a name
the family business—stock
to insure a fair exchange
for a man who might try
to be a son. My father's
spring trades always failed:
I always came back being
still a girl who couldn't play
the way he'd hoped while he
built for me stone bases
on his knees there in the dirt.

# DONALD HALL

## Fathers Playing Catch with Sons (*excerpts*)

I started listening to the Brooklyn Dodgers in 1939 when I was ten years old. The gentle and vivacious voice of Red Barber floated from the Studebaker radio, during the Sunday afternoon drives along the shore of Long Island Sound. My mother and my father and I, wedded together in the close front seat, heard the sounds of baseball—and I was tied to that sound for the rest of my life.

We drove from Connecticut to Ebbets Field, to the Polo Grounds, to Yankee Stadium. When I was at college I went to Fenway Park and to Braves Field. Then in 1957 I left the East and moved to Michigan. At first, I was cautious about committing myself to the Tigers. The Brooklyn Dodgers had gone to Los Angeles, of all things, and whom could you trust? Al Kaline? Rocky Colavito? Jim Bunning? Norm Cash? I went to Tiger Stadium three or four times a year, and I watched Big Ten baseball frequently, especially in 1961, when a sophomore football player named Bill Freehan caught for Michigan, and as I remembered, hit .500. The Tigers signed him that summer.

All summer the radio kept going. I wrote letters while I listened to baseball. I might not know what the score was, but the sound comforted me, a background of distant voices. If rain interrupted the game, I didn't want to hear music; it was the sound of baseball-radio-voices that I wanted year after year.

Baseball is a game of years and of decades. Al Kaline's children grew up. Rocky Colavito was traded and left baseball and became a mushroom farmer and came back to baseball as a coach. Jim Bunning turned into a great National League pitcher and retired. Norman Cash had a better year, at thirty-five, than he had had in nearly a decade. And Kaline kept on hitting line drives.

And Janet and I met, and married, and in 1972 the sound of baseball grew louder: Janet loves baseball too. The soft southern sounds of announcers—always from the south, from Red Barber on—filled up the house like plants in the windows, new chairs and pictures. At night after supper, and on weekend afternoons, we heard the long season unwind itself, inning by inning, as vague and precise as ever. The patter of the announcer, and behind him always, like an artist's calligraphy populating a background more important than the foreground, the baseball sounds of vendors hawking hot dogs, Coke, and programs; and the sudden rush of noise from the crowd when a score was posted; the flat slap of a bat, and again the swelling crowd yells; the Dixieland between innings; even the beer jingles.

We listened on the dark screen porch, an island in the leaves and bushes, in the faint distant light from the street, while the baseball cricket droned against the real crickets of the yard. We listened while writing letters or reading newspapers or washing up after dinner. We listened in bed, when the Tigers were on the West Coast just hearing the first innings, then sleeping into the game to wake with the dead gauze sound of the abandoned air straining and crackling beside the bed. Or we went to bed and turned out the lights late in the game, and started to doze as the final pitches gathered in the dark, and when the game ended with a final out and the organ playing again, a hand reached out in the dark, over a sleeping shape, to turn off the sound.

And we drove the forty miles to Tiger Stadium, parked on a dingy street in late twilight and walked to the old green-and-concrete fort of Tiger Stadium. It is one of the few old stadiums left, part of the present structure erected in 1912, and the most recent portion in 1938. It is like an old grocer who wears a straw hat and a blue necktie and is frail but don't you ever mention it. It's the old world, Tiger Stadium, as baseball is. Hygrade Ball-Park Franks, the smell of fat and mustard, popcorn and spilled beer.

As we approach at night, the sky lights up like a cool dawn. You enter the awkward, homemade-looking, cubist structure, wind through the heavy weaving of its nest, and swing up a dark corridor to the splendid green summer of the field. Balls arch softly from the fungoes, and the fly-shaggers arch them back toward homeplate. Batting practice. Infield practice. Pepper. The pitchers loosening up between the dugout and the bullpen. We always get there early. We settle in, breathe quietly the air of baseball, and let the night begin the old rituals again. Managers exchange lineups, Tigers take the field, we stand for "our National Anthem," and the batter approaches the plate . . .

My father and I played catch as I grew up. Like so much else between fathers and sons, playing catch was tender and tense at the same time. He wanted to play with me. He wanted me to be good. He seemed to *demand* that I be good. I threw the ball into his catcher's mitt. Atta boy. Put her right there. I threw straight. Then I tried to put something on it. It flew twenty feet over his head. Or it banged into the sidewalk in front of him, breaking stitches and richocheting off a pebble into the gutter of Greenway Street. Or it went wide to his right and lost itself in Mrs. Davis's bushes. Or it went wide to his left and rolled across the street while drivers swerved their cars.

I was wild. I was *wild*. I had to be wild for my father. What else could I be? Do you want me to have *control?*

But I was, myself, the control on him. He had wanted to teach school, to coach and teach history at Cushing Academy in Ashburnham, Massachusetts, and he had done it for two years, before he was married. The salary was miniscule and in the twenties people didn't get married until they had the money to live on. Since he wanted to marry my mother, he made the only decision he could make: he quit Cushing and went into the family business, and he hated business, and he wept when he fired people, and he wept when he was criticized, and his head shook at night, and he coughed from all the cigarettes, and he couldn't sleep, and he almost died when an ulcer hemorrhaged when he was forty-two, and ten years later, at fifty-two, he died of lung cancer.

But the scene I remembered—at night in the restaurant, after a happy, foolish day in the uniform of a Pittsburgh Pirate—happened when he was twenty-five and I was almost one year old. So I did not "remember" it at all. It simply rolls itself before my eyes with the intensity of lost memory suddenly found again, more intense than the moment ever is.

It is 1929, a hot Saturday afternoon. At the ball park near East Rock, in New Haven, Connecticut, just over the Hamden line, my father is playing semipro baseball. I don't know the names of the teams. My mother has brought me in a basket, and sits under a tree, in the shade, and lets me crawl when I wake up.

My father is very young, very skinny. When he takes off his cap—the uniform is gray, the bill of the cap blue—his fine hair is parted in the middle. His face is very smooth. Though he is twenty-five, he could pass for twenty. He plays shortstop, and he is paid twenty-five dollars a game. I don't know where the money comes from. Do they pass the hat? They would never raise so much money. Do they charge admission? They must charge admission, or I am wrong that it was semipro and he was paid. Or the whole thing is wrong, a memory I concocted. But of course the reality of 1929—and my mother and the basket and the shade and the heat—does not matter, not in the memory of the living nor in the bones of the dead nor even in the fragmentary images of broken light from that day which wanders light-years away in unrecoverable space. What does matter is the clear and fine knowledge of this day as it happens now, permanently and repeatedly, on a deep layer of the personal Troy.

There, where this Saturday afternoon of July in 1929 rehearses itself, my slim father performs brilliantly at shortstop. He dives for a low line drive and catches it backhand, somersaults, and stands up holding the ball. Sprinting into left field with his back to the plate, he catches a fly ball that almost drops for a Texas leaguer. He knocks down a ground ball, deep in the hole and nearly to third base, picks it up, and throws the man out at first with a peg as flat as the tape a runner breaks. When he comes up to bat, he feels lucky. The opposing pitcher is a sidearmer. He always hits sidearmers. So he hits two doubles and a triple, drives in two runs and scores two runs, and his team wins 4–3. After the game a man approaches him, while he stands, sweating and tired, with my mother and me in the shade of an elm tree at the rising side of the field. The man is a baseball scout. He offers my father a contract to play baseball with the Baltimore Orioles, at that time a double-A minor league team. My father is grateful and gratified; he is proud to be offered the job, but he must refuse. After all, he has just started working at the dairy, for his father. It wouldn't be possible to leave the job it had been such a decision to take. And besides, he adds, there is the baby.

My father didn't tell me he turned it down because of me. All he told me, or that I think he told me: he was playing semipro at twenty-five dollars a game; he had a good day in the field, catching a ball over his shoulder running away from the plate; he had a good day hitting, too, because he could always hit a sidearmer. But he turned down the Baltimore Oriole offer. He couldn't leave the dairy then, and besides, he knew that he had just been lucky, that day. He wasn't really that good.

But maybe he didn't even tell me that. My mother remembers nothing of this. Or rather, she remembers that he played on the team for the dairy, against other businesses, and that she took me to the games when I was a baby. But she remembers nothing of semipro, of the afternoon with the sidearmer, of the offered contract. Did I make it up? Did my father exaggerate? Men tell stories to their sons, loving and being bored.

I don't care.

Baseball is fathers and sons. Football is brothers beating each other up in the backyard, violent and superficial. Baseball is the generations, looping backward forever with a million apparitions of sticks and balls, cricket and rounders and the games the Iroquois played in Connecticut before the English came. Baseball is fathers and sons playing catch, lazy and murderous, wild and controlled, the profound archaic song of birth, growing, age, and death. This diamond encloses what we are.

This afternoon—March 4, 1973—when I played ball and was not frightened, I walked with my father's ghost, dead seventeen years. The ballplayers would not kill me, nor I them. This is the motion, and the line that connects me now to the rest of the world, the motion past fear and separation.

Once I went to an old-timers game, a few innings of the great players of decades past, played before the regular game. The Cincinnati team from 1953—some fifteen members of it—played against a potpourri of retired players from other teams.

The generation of ballplayers slightly older than me, the ballplayers of my childhood and youth, magically returned in their old uniforms and joked and flipped the ball and swung at the slow pitches that the old pitchers lazed up to them. Mickey Vernon played first base, who had played major league ball in the '30s, the '40s, the '50s and the '60s. Carl Erskine pitched. Johnny Mize swung the bat again. Tommy Henrich at fifty-nine stood slim and erect in left field as he had stood for thousands of afternoons in Yankee Stadium. A ball sailed over Gus Bell's head in center field. He plodded after it, his gait heavy and ponderous and painful, while an old catcher dragged himself all the way to third and stood there puffing and gasping. It was grotesque, all of it, like elephants at the circus that waddle and trudge in ballet costumes while the calliope plays Swan Lake.

Yet there was an awkward and frightening beauty to the tableau, as the old men performed stiffly the many motions they had once done nimbly. An old third baseman underhanded the baseball toward the pitcher's mound, as he trotted into the dugout, so that the ball rolled to a stop on the dirt near the rubber; how many thousands of times had he made that gesture in the long summers when he was twenty and thirty?

And Peewee Reese played shortstop. I was stunned by Peewee, because I had known him the longest, from the summer of 1940 when he came up to Brooklyn, until he quit in Los Angeles in 1958. Now he stood at shortstop again, fifty-four years old, leaning all his weight on one slim leg, in a gesture almost effete and certainly graceful.

Suddenly I remembered a scene in grave detail, from the beginning of my baseball time. It is a Sunday afternoon, 1940 probably—possibly 1941—when the Dodgers will win the pennant and meet the Yankees in the Series and I will see the first game. My father and my mother are riding in the Studebaker, listening to Red Barber broadcast a crucial game between the Dodgers and the Giants. The Giants are ahead. Now the Dodgers begin to come close—maybe they tie the game; I don't remember the details—and the Giants stop, pause, confer. Then they summon Carl Hubbell from the bullpen.

My father explains how momentous it is, that Carl Hubbell should pitch relief. Things have not gone well for him lately. But King Carl is the greatest left-hander of all time, who in the 1934 All-Star Game struck out Babe Ruth, Lou Gehrig, Jimmy Foxx, Al Simmons, and Joe Cronin, all in a row; old screwballer who walks always with his left elbow turned into his ribs, his arm permanently twisted by his best pitch. The great man never relieved, and now he walked from the bullpen to the pitcher's mound and took his tosses; old man who had pitched since 1928, who couldn't have more than three or four dwindling years left in his arm; old man come in to save the game for his faltering team.

My father's face is tense. He loves the Dodgers and not the Giants, but he loves Carl Hubbell even more. My father is thirty-seven years old in 1940. So is Carl Hubbell.

Then the Dodgers send up a pinch hitter. It is Harold Reese, the baby shortstop, former marbles ("peewees") champion of Louisville, Kentucky, fresh from the minor leagues, and fifteen years younger than Hubbell. I sit in the front seat cheering the Dodgers on, hoping against hope, though I realize that the rookie shortstop is good-field no-hit.

Peewee hits a home run off Carl Hubbell and the Dodgers win.

Sitting there in the front seat, eleven years old, I clap and cheer. Then I hear my father's strange voice. I look across my mother to see his knuckles white on the wheel, his face white, and I hear him saying, "The punk! The punk!" With astonishment and horror, I see that my father is crying.

### 7 March

In the first exhibition game, at McKechnie Field in Bradenton, in the first game of the home season in the Grapefruit League, the Pirates play the Detroit Tigers. Al Kaline! Bill Freehan!

I am allowed to suit up for the game, and to sit in the dugout with the Pirates. I tell Luke Wrenn. He says, "You're going to sit in the dugout?" He shakes his head. "You're going to hear some language you've never heard before," he says. "I'll tell you. Last fall I was really surprised. I'd never heard anything like that before. Of course I suppose a lot of them had been playing all summer and they were pretty tired."

Listening to Luke, even watching his face, is like being in touch with my grandfather's America. One could think of Norman Rockwell—but there is nothing coy, and no kitsch about Luke. *He* is not nostalgic. He is Luke Wrenn, from Concordia, Indiana. And if we asked central casting for a "type" to play an eighteen-year-old rookie from a small town in Indiana, they would never find anyone who looked and acted the part this well. Luke is funny and gentle and honest and naive, and he is determined to be a major leaguer. He has read every biography of every baseball player in the Concordia library. He knows what they did. He is an outfielder, and he knows that the Pirates have good outfielders. If he can just *hit*. "If you have a good stick," he says, "they can't keep you down."

His face, even, is not like the face of a city boy, or a suburban boy. His face makes a sound like a train whistle heard in the middle of the night far away. It is a steam train.

When I get to the park I warm up with the ballplayers, throwing back and forth with Luke and with another rookie.

Also, I walk up and down a good bit, in front of the sellout crowd of thousands of fans, jammed in everywhere. Down to the bullpen, back to the Pirate dugout, over to the Tigers'. Somebody from the stands yells out, "When you going to get a shave?" They don't like Pirates; it's a rude Michigan crowd, the parking lot full of cars with Michigan plates.

I pass Billy Martin, who is talking animatedly to someone. Without thinking, I wave and smile at him and say "Hi." (I've seen him so much, on TV and at Tiger Stadium, that I am under the delusion that I know him.) He smiles back broadly and waves, apparently under a similar delusion. But the delusion cracks, horribly, in midsmile, as he realizes that he is waving at a fat Pirate with a beard and long hair. I hurry past, to get that one over with. Afterwards, I describe the incident to John Parrish. He advises me to use the line: "That phoney, Billy Martin! He's always pretending he knows me!"

It is permitted to fraternize with members of the opposing team before the game starts. I decide to fraternize with Bill Freehan, who is standing there doing nothing.

"Hi," I say, and rapidly introduce myself before he can get away. I have an angle, because Freehan attended the University of Michigan. When he was a sophomore, which was in 1960–61, I watched him play football in the autumn, and then in the spring I took my young son to the Michigan baseball games. He was extraordinary, that year, and signed with the Tigers for a big bonus at the end of the college season. I tell him that, as I recall, he hit .500 in the Big Ten.

No, he says. .585. In fact, .500 was the old record. It was Moose Skowron who set it.

Oh.

For five minutes or so we chat. He is most agreeable. Looking for something to say—and having been questioned all week about my physical condition—I complain about how horrible I feel when I try to get up in the morning.

"How old are you?" he says.

"Forty-four," I tell him. He nods. He does not make a joke. Freehan is thirty-two. He is lean, tan, and strong. He looks fine. His bat is lively. But I am sure that he feels old. He hears the cleats of the twenty-year-olds behind him. No matter what you do, no matter how hard you work to keep in shape, your body ages. The athlete at thirty-two begins to live in a pain that the athlete at twenty knows nothing about.

And what will he do when he grows up? Every day, I remember Steve Blass's remark. Of course, there is a lot they can *do*, but that is not the point. Growing up means ending what their lives have always aimed for.

Walking around, I talk to Bill Slayback, a young pitcher who came up from the minors, midseason 1972, and pitched several remarkable games. I congratulate him. With a modesty only slightly weary, he tells me that after all, it's a long season. I recall that his star dimmed, a bit, in the late going. He is not worried about what to do when he grows up. He is worried that he will not make the team. He is worried that he will grow up too soon.

I sit in the dugout, next to Luke, and wait for the game to start. I suspect I seek out Luke because he is the only person there as naive as I am.

We are at the far end of the dugout. At the end nearest home plate is the water fountain. The water fountain! I remember Red Barber in 1940: "Leo goes over to the water fountain, gets himself a drink . . ." Above the water fountain the day's lineup is Scotchtaped to the wall. Also against the wall there is a fierce NO SMOKING sign, by order of the National League. Still, all during the game, the players smoke. They lean back into the dugout when they smoke, so that fans (or Bowie Kuhn or somebody) won't see them. They pass the cigarette around like a joint.

Just before the game begins, the umpires climb into the dugout.

Explosive greetings, among ballplayers and umpires. "What you been doing all winter?"

"Oh, refereed a couple hockey games. Drank a lot of beer. You?"

"Yeah. Nothing much."

"And I moved. Left Toledo, Ohio, and moved to Syracuse, New York."

"You shouldn't of. Toledo is a good pussy town."

I find myself surprised: I thought that the players were fierce sons, the umpires gloomy and forbidding fathers. They're exactly the same.

After "The Star-Spangled Banner," and a tribute to the memory of Roberto Clemente, suddenly the dugout is all flurry and bustle. Everyone rummages among bats, pads, and gloves. People at work. The first game of the year.

Squatting for a while near the fountain, I put my glove down. Then I pick it up and move to the end of the dugout, to get out of the way. Suddenly a young man with a moustache approaches me. I recognize Richie Zisk, an outfielder. He snatches the glove from where I have it tucked under my arm, and turns away. I am flabbergasted. What does he want Luke's glove for? Then I realize I must have picked up the wrong glove by mistake. I follow him, babbling and embarrassed. "Is that your glove?" I say.

"That's right," he says.

"I must have picked it up by mistake," I say. He says nothing. "I put mine down on the ground," I say. "I must have picked up yours by mistake."

"Anybody can make a mistake," he says tersely.

"I'm sorry," I say. "I'm really sorry."

He says it again as if I hadn't heard him. "Anybody can make a mistake."

He sounds anxious. It is uncertain that he will make the team.

The game. Richie Hebner hits a home run. Everybody in the dugout shakes his hand, though I feel foolish when he looks up and sees it is me. "Jumbo," he says.

Bob Johnson gets hit. Bill Slayback is wild. Manny Sanguillen misjudges everything in right field. The Tigers win it. It's poor baseball, and nobody seems to care. As for me, I am perched in the center of a universe of bliss.

By the middle innings rookies are playing most of the positions. But not Luke. He keeps walking up and down in front of Bill Virdon, but the magic words go unspoken. Meantime, a Detroit Tiger eighteen-year-old has driven in a run, somewhat aided by Manny Sanguillen's fielding. And another outfielder throws to the wrong base. And in the dugout, no one offers criticism. In fact, the only chatter seems to come from Tony the trainer: "Strike his ass out!" When a rookie center fielder for the Pirates lets a fly ball by Rich Reese drop behind him for a double, Maz spits three times in rapid succession. That is about as emotional as we get.

I wander down to the bullpen where Bob Miller is warming up. "When I get in there," he says, "I want you to clear away all those photographers. Otherwise it'll be manslaughter."

One of the Pirate scouts, leaning against the bullpen wall in civvies, calls me Babe.

It is a lazy afternoon. Standing out by the bullpen I hear players talk slowly to each other, spitting, wondering what to do tomorrow. Back at the edge of the dugout, Bob Robertson is chewing and spitting magnificently. When the dugout is full, the arcs of spit are miraculous to behold. Look the length of the dugout at any given moment, and several brown wads of liquid tobacco will be rainbowing out. The cement floor, and the cement steps, are slimy with spit. When there are errors, or home runs by the Tigers, the only sign of vexation is an intensification of spitting.

On the other hand, there are the voices, like rain, especially the soft Spanish voices congregating in the center of the dugout. Ramon Hernandez, Vic Davalillo, Manny Sanguillen. The sound of Spanish softly droning, like a distant motor. Like a romantic mosquito.

In the shade of the manager's corner the field looks tranquil, the long lateral green stretching out forever in the afternoon, 342 to left field, 433 to center, 373 to right. But Bill Virdon stands with his foot up, and stares, and does not relent. He is terse. "Bob?" he says. "Left field." And Robertson picks up his glove and jogs out.

I decide to drink the water from this fountain of my youth. I lean toward the water, and experimentally twist the knob. A mighty jet stream vaults out, water that could have made the Olympics, and splashes all over Bill Virdon's right leg. He looks over his shoulder at me—and here I am apologizing again, awkward as a virgin—calmly and silently, and then turns back to the field.

I get the idea he thinks I am goofy.

All afternoon, off and on, I talk to Luke, sitting next to him in the dugout. He wants to know about my writing. Maybe I can help him, someday.

How?

Well, just in case . . . he is keeping a diary of his experiences, and perhaps if he is lucky, someday . . . Then he talks about how, last October, he watched the Pirates and the Tigers in the playoffs, and here he is.

He is another son. When you are a teacher, you get used to having extra sons. Baseball is fathers and sons playing catch, the long arc of the years between. Yet I also have my own son, who does not resemble Luke. My own son belongs to 1973, not 1923; reads Castaneda, not biographies of baseball players, frets over no one's dirty language, hitchhikes everywhere, and accepts everything except policemen, against whom he cherishes a firm and well-documented distrust.

Therefore Luke, if he is 1923, actually resembles my father more than he resembles my son. The moment I think of it, I realize that all along I have thought that he looked like photographs of my father.

### 8 March

The day after the Tiger game, the Pirates play Minnesota at 1:30. I am exhausted after my morning workout—it is almost the end of my brief career. I am prepared to hang it up; I am a broken man—and I decide not to come to the park for the game. It would be such a letdown, to sit in the stands, after I had been in the dugout the day before. Late in the afternoon, however, I wander down to the ball park anyway. Who can stay away?

The Pirates are down 2–0, going into the seventh. They score five runs to lead 5–2, and take the lead into the ninth, when Minnesota scores four more runs to go ahead 6–5. When a left fielder makes a good throw to third base, holding a runner to second after a single, I notice that it is Luke. Really, I am surprised. I didn't expect him to play, not even in the ninth inning of the second exhibition game of the spring. After all, even *he* keeps his ambitions modest and reasonable. He *expects* to play this summer in Bradenton, in the Gulf Coast League, the team lowest on the Pirate ladder. He *hopes* to be noticed enough to be sent a bit higher up, Class A, maybe to Salem, Virginia, in the Carolina League. He is in uniform, now, only because he lives at Pirate City all year long. The players practicing in Pirate City now will soon move to McKechnie Field, and Luke will stay behind at Pirate City with two hundred other minor leaguers.

So I'm surprised and pleased to see him in a game.

He comes to the plate in the last of the ninth, one out, and a man on second. He hits the ball cleanly, a line drive just out of reach of the second baseman. The ball goes into the alley in right center, and scores the tying run, and Luke stands on second base with a double after his first time at bat in a Pirate uniform. The next batter hits a ball on which Minnesota manages to commit two errors, and Luke comes home with the winning run.

In less than a minute, Luke is surrounded by cameramen and reporters, and by kids getting autographs. He keeps grinning. Eighteen years old.

### 9 March

This morning is my last. Heavy with fatigue and melancholy, I arrive at the clubhouse to find the rain starting. The team bus idles outside the entrance. In theory, the Pirates are driving to Lakeland, where they will play the Tigers again. Dock is going to pitch. He tells me that he always likes pitching against the Tigers. Good games, he says, grinning: lots of throwing at hitters.

But not today. It's raining in Lakeland, too, and the bus is waiting for word of a cancellation. The bus will never go. I look inside the bus. Smoke and card games. Some of the players, like Dock, wander around outside in the rain. A few run in the mud. Others start to take batting practice with the insane machine in the Quonset. There is an air of restless improvisation like summer camp when the rains come; what will we *do*?

I go inside to find Luke. He is dressing by his locker, and when he sees me—and he knows what I am going to say—his face loosens into a smile as broad as a barn. No ambiguities. The *Sarasota Herald-Tribune,* this morning, has taken full measure of his obscurity for journalistic purposes, and headlines the game:

BUCS CALL ON WRENN
FOR A 7–6 TRIUMPH

He accepts congratulations without pain, and can still talk about where the ball went.

The photographer Bob Adelman, unfamiliar as yet with the arduous path to the majors, asks Luke if this means that he will make the team. For someone of Luke's encyclopaedic knowledge of baseball, this is a stupid question. (Luke knows how long it took Ted Williams, where he played in the minors, and his batting average for the month of July 1936, in Class B ball.) But he answers the question politely. No, he says, it doesn't mean he'll make the team. Maybe it means he'll get to play in Class A, where he wants to play. Of course, he says, with his head vanishing under a sudden cloud of daydreams, if they took him on a road trip and he hit twelve for twelve . . .

I decide not to try to work out in the rain. I change from my uniform back into Bermuda shorts and sandals forever. I look for people to say good-bye to. Standing among the lockers, I feel a pinch on my calf. I look back. Ramon Hernandez looks innocently into space.

Oh, my teammates! How can I leave them!

Here is Dock, who shakes hands, and says with great formality and gentleness that it has been real good to know me, and that I should look him up at the ball park. I start to walk to the car, slogging through the instant mud. Then Luke runs up. One more thing! If he does make it, sometime, would we please write him for tickets? He sure would be pleased to see us again.

And I him, and my father and my son, and my mother's father when the married men played the single men in Wilmot, New Hampshire, and my father's father's father who hit a ball with a stick while he was camped outside Vicksburg in June of 1863, and maybe my son's son's son for baseball is continuous, like nothing else among American things, an endless game of repeated summers, joining the long generations of all the fathers and all the sons.

# 3

# Landscape

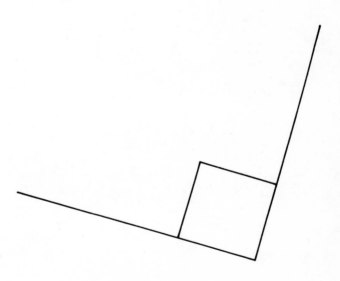

## Base-ball

The Ball once struck off,
Away flies the Boy
To the next destin'd Post
And then Home with Joy.

*Moral*

Thus Seamen for Lucre
Fly over the Main,
But, with Pleasure transported,
Return back again.

## Another Version of Pastoral

## (from an interview with Kevin Kerrane)

That picture is from 1950, when I was just back from China and teaching at the Kenyon summer school of English, organized by John Crowe Ransom.

Ransom once suggested that my book *Some Versions of Pastoral* could have included a section on games. He was thinking of baseball. He loved the game, and claimed that it embodied some of the qualities he associated with good poetry—a certain formality, a richness of texture, and so on—but I couldn't grasp what he meant. I was amused by his passion for the Cleveland Indians: he even had a scoreboard posted in his house to chart their wins and losses.

That summer I was finally introduced to baseball through softball, and I could recognize it as a form of rounders, which in England has remained a children's game, without the seriousness of cricket. The evening softball games at Kenyon were run by the students, but Robert Lowell sometimes came, and so did Delmore Schwartz. And somehow I became captain of a team called The Ambiguities; L. C. Knights' group was The Explorers. At first I was absolutely no good, and they often had to remind me to turn left at first base. It was all nonsense, really, but The Ambiguities usually won, and I began to like the special tones of American rounders. Your game is actually less pastoral than cricket, which spreads itself out even more in 360-degree space and endless time, but the Kenyon games were very much in harmony with the season, the weather, the Ohio landscape, the flowers and tall grass in that photograph. And all the cheering and jeering, and details that weren't cricket, were good natured in an easy American style. So perhaps Ransom was right in a way.

I haven't played since, of course. But I do like that photograph, and I once used it on the jacket of a record album of my poetry. I wish to hell I felt that vigorous now.

(September 26, 1976)

## From Altitude, the Diamonds

You can always spot them, even from high up,
the brown bulged out trying to make a circle
of a square, the green square inside the brown,
inside the green the brown circle you know is mound
and the big outside green rounded off by a round line
you know is fence. And no one playing.

You've played on every one. Second base somewhere
on the Dallas Tucson run, New Mexico you think,
where green was brown. Right field outside Chicago
where the fans went silent when you tripled home
the run that beat their best, their all-season
undefeated home town Sox. What a game you pitched
that hot day in the Bronx. You lost to that left hander,
Ford, who made it big, one-nothing on a fluke.
Who's to believe it now? Fat. Bald. Smoking your fear
of the turbulent air you are flying, remembering
the war, a worse fear, the jolting flak, the prayer.

When air settles, the white beneath you opens
and far below in some unpopulated region
of whatever state you are over (it can't be Idaho,
that was years ago) you spot a tiny diamond,
and because you've grown far sighted with age
you see players moving, the center fielder
running the ball down deep, two runners
rounding third, the third base coach waving hard
and the hitter on his own not slowing down
at second, his lungs filled with the cheers of those
he has loved forever, on his magnificent tiny way
to an easy stand-up three.

**ROGER ANGELL**

## The Interior Stadium

Sports are too much with us. Late and soon, sitting and watching—mostly watching on television—we lay waste our powers of identification and enthusiasm and, in time, attention as more and more closing rallies and crucial putts and late field goals and final playoffs and sudden deaths and world records and world championships unreel themselves ceaselessly before our half-lidded eyes. Professional leagues expand like bubble gum, ever larger and thinner, and the extended sporting seasons, now bunching and overlapping at the ends, conclude in exhaustion and the wrong weather. So, too, goes the secondary business of sports—the news or nonnews off the field. Sports announcers (ex-halfbacks in Mod hairdos) bring us another live, exclusive interview in depth with the twitchy coach of some as yet undefeated basketball team, or with a weeping (for joy) fourteen-year-old champion female backstroker, and the sports pages, now almost the largest single part of the newspaper, brim with salary disputes, medical bulletins, franchise maneuverings, all-star ballots, drug scandals, close-up biogs, after-dinner tributes, union tactics, weekend wrapups, wire service polls, draft-choice trades, clubhouse gossip, and the latest odds. The American obsession with sports is not a new phenomenon, of course, except in its current dimensions, its excessive excessiveness. What *is* new, and what must at times unsettle even the most devout and unselective fan, is a curious sense of loss. In the midst of all these successive spectacles and instant replays and endless reportings and recapitulations, we seem to have forgotten what we came for. More and more, each sport resembles all sports; the flavor, the special joys of place and season, the unique displays of courage and strength and style that once isolated each game and fixed it in our affections have disappeared somewhere in the noise and crush.

Of all sports, none has been so buffeted about by this unselective proliferation, so maligned by contemporary cant, or so indifferently defended as baseball. Yet the game somehow remains the same, obdurately unaltered and comparable only with itself. Baseball has one saving grace that distinguishes it—for me, at any rate—from every other sport. Because of its pace, and thus the perfectly observed balance, both physical and psychological, between opposing forces, its clean lines can be restored in retrospect. This inner game—baseball in the mind—has no season, but it is best played in the winter, without the distraction of other baseball news. At first, it is a game of recollections, recapturings, and visions. Figures and occasions return, enormous sounds rise and swell, and the interior stadium fills with light and yields up the sight of a young ballplayer—some hero perfectly memorized—just completing his own unique swing and now racing toward first. See the way he runs? Yes, that's him! Unmistakable, he leans in, still following the distant flight of the ball with his eyes, and takes his big turn at the base. Yet this is only the beginning, for baseball in the mind is not a mere returning. In time, this easy summoning up of restored players, winning hits, and famous rallies gives way to reconsiderations and reflections about the sport itself. By thinking about baseball like this—by playing it over, keeping it warm in a cold season—we begin to make discoveries. With luck, we may even penetrate some of its mysteries. One of those mysteries is its vividness—the absolutely distinct inner vision we retain of that hitter, that eager baserunner, of however long ago. My father was talking the other day about some of the ballplayers he remembered. He grew up in Cleveland, and the Indians were his team. Still are. "We had Nap Lajoie at second," he said. "You've heard of him. A great big broad-shouldered fellow, but a beautiful fielder. He was a rough customer. If he didn't like an umpire's call, he'd give him a faceful of tobacco juice. The shortstop was Terry Turner—a smaller man, and blond. I can still see Lajoie picking up a grounder and wheeling and floating the ball over to Turner. Oh, he was quick on his feet! In right field we had Elmer Flick, now in the Hall of Fame. I liked the center fielder, too. His name was Harry Bay, and he wasn't a heavy hitter, but he was very fast and covered a lot of ground. They said he could circle the bases in twelve seconds flat. I saw him get a home run inside the park—the ball hit on the infield and went right past the second baseman and out to the wall, and Bay beat the relay. I remember Addie Joss, our great right-hander. Tall, and an elegant pitcher. I once saw him pitch a perfect game. He died young."

My father has been a fan all his life, and he has pretty well seen them all. He has told me about the famous last game of the 1912 World Series, in Boston, and seeing Fred Snodgrass drop that fly ball in the tenth inning, when the Red Sox scored twice and beat the Giants. I looked up Harry Bay and those other Indians in the *Baseball Encyclopedia,* and I think my father must have seen that inside-the-park homer in the summer of 1904. Lajoie batted .376 that year, and Addie Joss led the American League with an earned-run average of 1.59, but the Indians finished in fourth place. 1904. . . . Sixty-seven years have gone by, yet Nap Lajoie is in plain view, and the ball still floats over to Terry Turner. Well, my father is eighty-one now, and old men are great rememberers of the distant past. But I am fifty, and I can also bring things back: Lefty Gomez, skinny-necked and frighteningly wild, pitching his first game at Yankee Stadium, against the White Sox and Red Faber in 1930. Old John McGraw, in a business suit and a white fedora, sitting lumpily in a dark corner of the dugout at the Polo Grounds and glowering out at the field. Babe Ruth, wearing a new, bright yellow glove, trotting out to right field —a swollen ballet dancer, with those delicate, almost feminine feet and ankles. Ruth at the plate, uppercutting and missing, staggering with the force of his swing. Ruth and Gehrig hitting back-to-back homers. Gehrig, in the summer of 1933, running bases with a bad leg in a key game against the Senators; hobbling, he rounds third, closely followed by young Dixie Walker, then a Yankee. The throw comes in to the plate, and the Washington catcher—it must have been Luke Sewell—tags out the sliding Gehrig and, in the same motion, the sliding Dixie Walker. A double play at the plate. The Yankees lose the game; the Senators go on to a pennant. And, back across the river again, Carl Hubbell. My own great pitcher, a southpaw, tall and elegant. Hub pitching: the loose motion; two slow, formal bows from the waist, glove and hands held almost in front of his face as he pivots, the long right leg (in long, peculiar pants) striding; and the ball, angling oddly, shooting past the batter. Hubbell walks gravely back to the bench, his pitching arm, as always, turned the wrong way round, with the palm out. Screwballer.

Any fan, as I say, can play this private game, extending it to extraordinary varieties and possibilities in his mind. Ruth bats against Sandy Koufax or Sam McDowell. . . . Hubbell pitches to Ted Williams, and the Kid, grinding the bat in his fists, twitches and blocks his hips with the pitch; he holds off but still follows the ball, leaning over and studying it like some curator as it leaps in just under his hands. Why this vividness, even from an imaginary confrontation? I had watched many other sports, and I have followed some—football, hockey, tennis—with eagerness, but none of them yields these permanent interior pictures, these ancient and precise excitements. Baseball, I must conclude, is intensely remembered because only baseball is so intensely watched. The game forces intensity upon us. In the ballpark, scattered across an immense green, each player is isolated in our attention, utterly visible. Watch that fielder just below us. Little seems to be expected of him. He waits in easy composure, his hands on his knees; when the ball at last soars or bounces out to him, he seizes it and dispatches it with swift, haughty ease. It all looks easy, slow, and, above all, safe. Yet we know better, for what is certain in baseball is that someone, perhaps several people, will fail. They will be searched out, caught in the open, and defeated, and there will be no confusion about it or sharing of the blame. This is sure to happen, because what baseball requires of its athletes, of course, is nothing less than perfection, and perfection cannot be eased or divided. Every movement of every game, from first pitch to last out, is measured and recorded against an absolute standard, and thus each success is also a failure. Credit that strikeout to the pitcher, but also count it against the batter's average; mark his run unearned, because the left fielder bobbled the ball for an instant and a runner moved up. Yet, faced with this sudden and repeated presence of danger, the big-league player defends himself with such courage and skill that the illusion of safety is sustained. Tension is screwed tighter and tighter as the certain downfall is postponed again and again, so that when disaster does come—a half-topped infield hit, a walk on a close three-and-two call, a low drive up the middle that just eludes the diving shortstop—we rise and cry out. It is a spontaneous, inevitable, irresistible reaction.

Televised baseball, I must add, does not seem capable of transmitting this emotion. Most baseball is seen on the tube now, and it is presented faithfully and with great technical skill. But the medium is irrevocably two-dimensional; even with several cameras, television cannot bring us the essential distances of the game—the simultaneous flight of a batted ball and its pursuit by the racing, straining outfielders, the swift convergence of runner and ball at a base. Foreshortened on our screen, the players on the field appear to be squashed together, almost touching each other, and, watching them, we lose the sense of their separateness and lonesome waiting.

This is a difficult game. It is so demanding that the best teams and the weakest teams can meet on almost even terms, with no assurance about the result of any one game. In March 1962, in St. Petersburg, the World Champion Yankees played for the first time against the newborn New York Mets—one of the worst teams of all time—in a game that each badly wanted to win; the winner, to nobody's real surprise, was the Mets. In 1970, the World Champion Orioles won a hundred and eight games and lost fifty-four; the lowest cellar team, the White Sox, won fifty-six games and lost a hundred and six. This looks like an enormous disparity, but what it truly means is that the Orioles managed to win two out of every three games they played, while the White Sox won one out of every three. That third game made the difference—and a kind of difference that can be appreciated when one notes that the winning margin given up by the White Sox to all their opponents during the season averaged 1.1. runs per game. Team form is harder to establish in baseball than in any other sport, and the hundred-and-sixty-two-game season not uncommonly comes down to October with two or three teams locked together at the top of the standings on the final weekend. Each inning of baseball's slow, searching time span, each game of its long season is essential to the disclosure of its truths.

Form is the imposition of a regular pattern upon varying and unpredictable circumstances, but the patterns of baseball, for all the game's tautness and neatness, are never regular. Who can predict the winner and shape of today's game? Will it be a brisk, neat two-hour shutout? A languid, error-filled 12–3 laugher? A riveting three-hour, fourteen-inning deadlock? What other sport produces these manic swings? For the players, too, form often undergoes terrible reversals; in no other sport is a champion athlete so often humiliated or a journeyman so easily exalted. The surprise, the upset, the total turnabout of expectations and reputations—these are delightful commonplaces of baseball. Al Gionfriddo, a part-time Dodger outfielder, stole second base in the ninth inning of the fourth game of the 1947 World Series to help set up Lavagetto's game-winning double (and the only Dodger hit of the game) off the Yankees' Bill Bevens. Two days later, Gionfriddo robbed Joe DiMaggio with a famous game-saving catch of a four-hundred-and-fifteen-foot drive in deepest left at Yankee Stadium. Gionfriddo never made it back to the big leagues after that season. Another irregular, the Mets' Al Weis, homered in the fifth and last game of the 1969 World Series, tying up the game that the Mets won in the next inning; it was Weis's third homer of the year and his first ever at Shea Stadium. And so forth. Who remembers the second game of the 1956 World Series—an appallingly bad afternoon of baseball in which the Yankees' starter, Don Larsen, was yanked after giving up a single and four walks in less than two innings? It was Larsen's *next* start, the fifth game, when he pitched his perfect game.

There is always a heavy splash of luck in these reversals. Luck, indeed, plays an almost predictable part in the game; we have all seen the enormous enemy clout into the bleachers that just hooks foul at the last instant, and the half-checked swing that produces a game-winning blooper over second. Everyone complains about baseball luck, but I think it adds something to the game that is nearly essential. Without it, such a rigorous and unforgiving pastime would be almost too painful to enjoy.

No one, it becomes clear, can conquer this impossible and unpredictable game. Yet every player tries, and now and again—very rarely—we see a man who seems to have met all the demands, challenged all the implacable averages, spurned the mere luck. He has defied baseball, even altered it, and for a time at least the game is truly his. One thinks of Willie Mays, in the best of his youth, batting at the Polo Grounds, his whole body seeming to leap at the ball as he swings in an explosion of exuberance. Or Mays in center field, playing in so close that he appears at times to be watching the game from over the second baseman's shoulder, and then that same joyful leap as he takes off after a long, deep drive and runs it down, running so hard and so far that the ball itself seems to stop in the air and wait for him. One thinks of Jackie Robinson in a close game—any close game—playing the infield and glaring in at the enemy hitter, hating him and daring him, refusing to be beaten. And Sandy Koufax pitching in the last summers before he was disabled, in that time when he pitched a no-hitter every year for four years. Kicking swiftly, hiding the ball until the last instant, Koufax throws in a blur of motion, coming over the top, and the fast ball, appearing suddenly in the zone, sometimes jumps up so immoderately that his catcher has to take it with his glove shooting upward, like an infielder stabbing at a bad-hop grounder. I remember some batter taking a strike like that and then stepping out of the box and staring back at the pitcher with a look of utter incredulity—as if Koufax had just thrown an Easter egg past him.

Joe DiMaggio batting sometimes gave the same impression—the suggestion that the old rules and dimensions of baseball no longer applied to him, and that the game had at last grown unfairly easy. I saw DiMaggio once during his famous hitting streak in 1941; I'm not sure of the other team or the pitcher—perhaps it was the Tigers and Bobo Newsom—but I'm sure of DiMaggio pulling a line shot to left that collided preposterously with the bag at third base and ricocheted halfway out to center field. That record of hitting safely in fifty-six straight games seems as secure as any in baseball, but it does not awe me as much as the fact that DiMadge's old teammates claim they *never* saw him commit an error of judgment in a ball game. Thirteen years, and never a wrong throw, a cutoff man missed, an extra base passed up. Well, there was one time when he stretched a single against the Red Sox and was called out at second, but the umpire is said to have admitted later that he blew the call.

And one more for the pantheon: Carl Yastrzemski. To be precise, Yaz in September of the 1967 season, as his team, the Red Sox, fought and clawed against the White Sox and the Twins and the Tigers in the last two weeks of the closest and most vivid pennant race of our time. The presiding memory of that late summer is of Yastrzemski approaching the plate, once again in a situation where all hope rests on him, and settling himself in the batter's box—touching his helmet, tugging at his belt, and just touching the tip of the bat to the ground, in precisely the same set of gestures—and then, in a storm of noise and pleading, swinging violently and perfectly . . . and hitting. In the last two weeks of that season, Yaz batted .522—twenty-three hits for forty-four appearances: four doubles, five home runs, sixteen runs batted in. In the final two games, against the Twins, both of which the Red Sox *had* to win for the pennant, he went seven for eight, won the first game with a homer, and saved the second with a brilliant, rally-killing throw to second base from deep left field. (He cooled off a little in the World Series, batting only .400 for seven games and hitting three homers.) Since then, the game and the averages have caught up with Yastrzemski, and he has never again approached that kind of performance. But then, of course, neither has anyone else.

Only baseball, with its statistics and isolated fragments of time, permits so precise a reconstruction from box score and memory. Take another date—October 7, 1968, at Detroit, the fifth game of the World Series. The fans are here, and an immense noise—a cheerful, 53,634-man vociferosity—utterly fills the green, steep, high-walled box of Tiger Stadium. This is a good baseball town, and the cries have an anxious edge, for the Tigers are facing almost sure extinction. They trail the Cardinals by three games to one, and never for a moment have they looked the equal of these defending World Champions. Denny McLain, the Tigers' thirty-one-game winner, was humiliated in the opener by the Cardinals' Bob Gibson, who set an all-time Series record by striking out seventeen Detroit batters. The Tigers came back the next day, winning rather easily behind their capable left-hander Mickey Lolich, but the Cardinals demolished them in the next two games, scoring a total of seventeen runs and again brushing McLain aside; Gibson has now struck out twenty-seven Tigers, and he will be ready to pitch again in the Series if needed. Even more disheartening is Lou Brock, the Cards' left fielder, who has already lashed out eight hits in the first four games and has stolen seven bases in eight tries; Bill Freehan, the Tigers' catcher, has a sore arm. And here, in the very top of the first, Brock leads off against Lolich and doubles to left; a moment later, Curt Flood singles, and Orlando Cepeda homers into the left-field stands. The Tigers are down, 3–0, and the fans are wholly stilled.

In the third inning, Brock leads off with another hit—a single—and there is a bitter overtone to the home-town cheers when Freehan, on a pitchout, at last throws him out, stealing, at second. There is no way for anyone to know, of course, that this is a profound omen; Brock has done his last damage to the Tigers in this Series. Now it is the fourth, and hope and shouting return. Mickey Stanley leads off the Detroit half with a triple that lands, two inches fair, in the right-field corner. He scores on a fly. Willie Horton also triples. With two out, Jim Northrup smashes a hard grounder directly at the Cardinal second baseman, Javier, and at the last instant the ball strikes something on the infield and leaps up and over Javier's head, and Horton scores. Luck! Luck twice over, if you remember how close Stanley's drive came to falling foul. But never mind; it's 3–2 now, and a game again.

But Brock is up, leading off once again, and an instant later he has driven a Lolich pitch off the left-field wall for a double. Now Javier singles to left, and Brock streaks around third base toward home. Bill Freehan braces himself in front of the plate, waiting for the throw; he has had a miserable Series, going hitless in fourteen at-bats so far, and undergoing those repeated humiliations by the man who is now racing at him full speed—the man who must surely be counted, along with Gibson, as the Series hero. The throw comes in chest-high on the fly from Willie Horton in left; ball and baserunner arrive together; Brock does not slide. Brock does not slide, and his left foot, just descending on the plate, is banged away as he collides with Freehan. Umpire Doug Harvey shoots up his fist: Out! It is a great play. Nothing has changed, the score is still 3–2, but everything has changed; something has shifted irrevocably in this game.

In the seventh inning, with one out and the Tigers still one run shy, Tiger manager Mayo Smith allows Lolich to bat for himself. Mickey Lolich has hit .114 for the season, and Smith has a pinch-hitter on the bench named Gates Brown, who hit .370. But Lolich got two hits in his other Series start, including the first homer of his ten years in baseball. Mayo, sensing something that he will not be able to defend later if he is wrong, lets Lolich bat for himself, and Mickey pops a foolish little fly to right that falls in for a single. Now there is another single. A walk loads the bases, and Al Kaline comes to the plate. The noise in the stadium is insupportable. Kaline singles, and the Tigers go ahead by a run. Norm Cash drives in another. The Tigers win this searching, turned-about, lucky, marvelous game by 5–3.

Two days later, back in St. Louis, form shows its other face as the Tigers rack up ten runs in the third inning and win by 13–1. McLain at last has his Series win. So it is Lolich against Gibson in the finale, of course. Nothing happens. Inning after inning goes by, zeros accumulate on the scoreboard, and anxiety and silence lengthen like shadows. In the sixth, Lou Brock singles. Daring Lolich, daring the Tiger infielders' nerves, openly forcing his luck, hoping perhaps to settle these enormous tensions and difficulties with one more act of bravado, he takes an excessive lead off first, draws the throw from Lolich, breaks for second, and is erased, just barely, by Cash's throw. A bit later, Curt Flood singles, and, weirdly, he too is picked off first and caught in a rundown. Still no score. Gibson and Lolich, both exhausted, pitch on. With two out in the seventh, Cash singles for the Tigers' second hit of the day. Horton is safe on a slow bouncer that *just* gets through the left side of the infield. Jim Northrup hits the next pitch deep and high but straight at Flood, who is the best center fielder in the National League. Flood starts in and then halts, stopping so quickly that his spikes churn up a green flap of turf; he turns and races back madly, but the ball sails over his head for a triple. Disaster. Suddenly, irreversibly, it has happened. Two runs are in, Freehan doubles in another, and, two innings later, the Tigers are Champions of the World.

I think I will always remember those two games—the fifth and the seventh—perfectly. And I remember something else about the 1968 Series when it was over—a feeling that almost everyone seemed to share: that Bob Gibson had not lost that last game, and the Cardinals had not lost the Series. Certainly no one wanted to say that the Tigers had not won it, but there seemed to be something more that remained to be said. It was something about the levels and demands of the sport we had seen—as if the baseball itself had somehow surpassed the players and the results. It was the baseball that won.

Always, it seems, there is something more to be discovered about this game. Sit quietly in the upper stand and look at the field. Half close your eyes against the sun, so that the players recede a little, and watch the movements of baseball. The pitcher, immobile on the mound, holds the inert white ball, his little lump of physics. Now, with abrupt gestures, he gives it enormous speed and direction, converting it suddenly into a line, a moving line. The batter, wielding a plane, attempts to intercept the line and acutely alter it, but he fails; the ball, a line again, is redrawn to the pitcher, in the center of this square, the diamond. Again the pitcher studies his task—the projection of his next line through the smallest possible segment of an invisible seven-sided solid (the strike zone has depth as well as height and width) sixty feet and six inches away; again the batter considers his even more difficult proposition, which is to reverse this imminent white speck, to redirect its energy not in a soft parabola or a series of diminishing squiggles but into a beautiful and dangerous new force, of perfect straightness and immense distance. In time, these and other lines are drawn on the field; the batter and the fielders are also transformed into fluidity, moving and converging, and we see now that all movement in baseball is a convergence toward fixed points—the pitched ball toward the plate, the thrown ball toward the right angles of the bases, the batted ball toward the as yet undrawn but already visible point of congruence with either the ground or a glove. Simultaneously, the fielders hasten toward the same point of meeting with the ball, and both the base-runner and the ball, now redirected, toward their encounter at the base. From our perch, we can sometimes see three or four or more such geometries appearing at the same instant on the green board below us, and, mathematicians that we are, can sense their solution even before they are fully drawn. It is neat, it is pretty, it is satisfying. Scientists speak of the profoundly moving aesthetic beauty of mathematics, and perhaps the baseball field is one of the few places where the rest of us can glimpse this mystery.

The last dimension is time. Within the ballpark, time moves differently, marked by no clock except the events of the game. This is the unique, unchangeable feature of baseball, and perhaps explains why this sport, for all the enormous changes it has undergone in the past decade or two, remains somehow rustic, unviolent, and introspective. Baseball's time is seamless and invisible, a bubble within which players move at exactly the same pace and rhythms as all their predecessors. This is the way the game was played in our youth and in our fathers' youth, and even back then—back in the country days—there must have been the same feeling that time could be stopped. Since baseball time is measured only in outs, all you have to do is succeed utterly; keep hitting, keep the rally alive, and you have defeated time. You remain forever young. Sitting in the stands, we sense this, if only dimly. The players below us—Mays, DiMaggio, Ruth, Snodgrass—swim and blur in memory, the ball floats over to Terry Turner, and the end of this game may never come.

## Baseball

*Keep your eye everlastingly on the ball while it is in play.*
—Complete Official Rules: General Instructions to Umpires, 9.00

Baseball is a pure game of continual action, which latter is not to be confused with movement, such as is displayed in football, basketball, hockey, etc. Since this action is often subtle, many think of the game as boring, or slow. So be it.

The game changes totally, and often invisibly, between each pitch.

Everything is gleaming space in baseball. One can *see* what happened.

Baseball games end in their own terms, they do not end because a clock runs out: one thus sees that anything can happen up until the time that last out is made. In football, if one team is four touchdowns behind with ten seconds to play, the football game is *over,* truly, although officially it is not. The players continue their movement, running out the clock in meaningless activity. Invented time imposes itself on the game and affects its patterns. Yet in baseball it is not at all rare to see teams tie and win games with two out in the 9th inning. Time has neither power nor meaning in this game. It works spatially: it is not "fair." No matter how good the pitcher has been, he must get the last out. His beautiful effort can be destroyed by a single mistake. In time games, the rules themselves often win for a team. The pitcher must pitch, in space, to each batter. What he *has done* has no effect on the batter he must face next. The eight men who assist him can only assist him after the ball is released.

It is the ball that controls the game.

Under its brilliantly simple surface, baseball is deeply complex, although this complexity is not arcane. The spectator can understand what happens on every play. There are no secret or bunched patterns. There is too much space between the players to hide anything.

The ball is pitched: something happens. The ball is hit: something happens. The detail is linear. Baseball is reading or painting, not film; it is strangely and elegantly still. The patterns change continually: a man on first with an o and 2 count on the batter is not the same thing as that man on first with a 3 and 2 count on the batter. The rests in the game seethe with potential action. The ball must be dealt with scrupulously: it must be played, not interfered with, nor blocked, nor intercepted, nor stolen, nor recovered, nor rebounded. The offensive or defensive player who addresses his skills to the ball in motion may not be tampered with by a player of the opposing team. It is this inevitable quality of the interaction of player and ball that may give the game its strange and calm magic.

It is a spare game of nouns and verbs, without the fussy adjectives of time games. Football, for instance, proffers dozens of plays in which the ball (which almost exists as an afterthought in the brutality of the professional game) moves not an inch, while 22 men smash and injure each other in the most fantastic and unintelligible patterns of mayhem. Time games are replete with penalties in order to control actions whose counterparts in baseball would be called "bush." It is a noble game: its players play against the ball.

It is not truly a game of specialists. Players substituted for are out of the game for its remainder. It is unsentimental.

Played within one rigidly prescribed area, which, in turn, is set within a large area whose boundaries vary astoundingly from park to park, this "carelessness" has given the game marvels of style. The Baseball takes place not only where the players are, but where they are not: it takes place where the ball is.

It exists outside of time.

GEORGE WRIGHT AND THE GOLDEN GATE
From a Painting by Carl Dahlgren, executed for S. R. Church

RICHARD GROSSINGER

## The Baseball Junkies
## (Codornices Field: August, 1977–September, 1978)

It's a secular country, so we forget: baseball contains primeval images, and
we return to the game because of them, not because we are athletes. We
go back to the memory of ourselves, throwing the ball, running after the
ball in the sun. The smell of grass brings it back. The pop of bat and ball,
and leather. The smell from within the pocket of an oiled glove is as dizzying as tomato leaves or lemon flowers. Who knows what skeleton it is.
The bones are alive; the flesh is a history of tidepools and animals of the
sea, animals of the plains. We re-enact a memory which is itself a memory
of something else. And baseball remains a wild New World dream. Which
it will be, until this world is the Old one and we look to China, Africa, and
the greater cosmic unknown. As simple and direct as the Snake River or
the Winooski.

Codornices is a hangout for baseball junkies. There's a regular group,
but it's difficult to say who it is. The players on the field change consistently
from week to week, month to month, season to season, but from one
Sunday to the next, the change is indiscernible. Anyone who's missing
might come back the following week, in a month, two years later, or never.
The first time I played up there, the opposition pitcher was a guy with an
EAT THE RICH tee shirt and a black scraggly beard that covered most
of his face. He played a rough angry game, hurling his bulk around the
basepaths. He left one Sunday in '75, came back in the spring of '78. He
had been in D.C. doing some sort of research on corporate dishonesty; he
left two weeks later to move to Pittsburgh.

The double-play combination of Jimmy and Janice were weekday production managers; they commuted to the games one whole season from
the set of "Close Encounters" in Alabama and Wyoming, later from
"Coming Home." Now they've been missing for months along with some
of the other old timers: Cisco the lawyer, Curry the draftsman and river
rafter, Judy the criminal anthropologist. 1978 has been a young man's
season, and most of the crowd comes from industrial league softball teams,
active or retired: Etch, Weed, Merlin, Anzalone, Reggie, Guy, Marty,
Curtis, Joe.

Also lost from the fall is Willy Riser, jazz musician from Chicago playing at Ivan Alexander's across the bay and entertaining us with his stubborn original genius, his weekly stories of searching for a gig. One unknown day he was gone, but we got a note: he was travelling in Europe with a group called Santa Esmeralda: "I don't want to be misunderstood."

Another "nonindustrial" irregular is Stacy, the travelling hippie and radical street actor with the propellor beanie. I caught him on t.v. at the Oakland Coliseum early in the spring, organizing the crazies in a crowd that looked like about two hundred twenty during the second game of a doubleheader. Every time Larry Wolfe of the Twins came up, they howled, until, in the extra innings approaching midnight, the ballpark reverberated like a hollow canyon. At Codornices, he played a game so slow and sleepy-headed that time itself seemed to wait for him and baseball slept on the streets like Rip Van Winkle, in week-old clothes and beads.

Eddie Detroit still pays us a visit sometimes. He's a brittle nervous guy, shirtless, in red shorts, thin legs, with a strutty chest, Elizabethan hair, and a sad formal face. He plays an intense, prancing game, with good basic rhythm, but some errors as complete and inexplicable as broken china. He's an absolute original, seeking on the field some vindication that goes well beyond baseball. His bit is to interrupt the game with soliloquies out of Shakespeare. Sometimes it won't happen for months, and then, after a crucial muff, he's down on his knees, and the quavery clarity of his voice booms: "O what a rogue and peasant slave am I!" or "Is it not monstrous that this player . . . ?" It's a game stopper. Once, after popping up for the second time in a row: "They trouble my sleep; they inveigh against my privacy." Scattering his team-mates with slashes of his bat.

Actually, there are two Sunday fields at Codornices, and they merge from season to season. One is the summer-in-the-city field; the other is the quieter fall and spring field which is marked by women players, kids, more eccentrics and characters, artists, older people, and intellectuals. There often aren't enough for two teams, and the wait for the field is, at most, a single game.

The California seasons themselves don't really decide baseball, but the first Raiders' t.v. game seems to mark the beginning of a decline which crests after the World Series. Few people brave the intermittent winter rains in January and February. I'd drive by to check out the field and see only a solitary jogger, or a man walking his dog, and it wasn't even late summer to my own New England nervous system.

The fall and spring are also times for organization picnics. One of the difficulties is that anyone who schedules their group for a Sunday thinks they own the field and should be able to kick us off. We're not a team or an institution. We're Sunday squatters. But we're the soul of that field.

The City of Berkeley doesn't agree. They will not issue us a permit, but then they will not issue one to anyone else, except in rare unjustifiable cases, like a bunch of little leaguers from fifty miles to the south, or a dog show from Marin County. Sometimes we fight for it, sometimes we leave. The City doesn't seem to have any ethics. They do not keep up the field, and, since Proposition 13, they do not even water. We complain about trailers of dogs dragging furrows, and they continue to issue only dog show permits. We offer to repair the field if they will supply some tools and materials, and they pass. So we are forced to do it anyway, freelance, bringing shovels and using the resident line-marker as a wheelbarrow. The outfield is developing sandpits, and the dirt part of the field has become marked with holes and, once the rains start, permanent puddles.

Occasionally we are able to turn a challenge into a game. One Sunday a bunch of black teenagers sat in the outfield hassling and diving at the women joggers, one of whom stole their ball and tossed it in the bushes leading to a confrontation. After peace was restored and the game resumed, their own women showed up, dressed for disco, three of them carrying enormous radios turned to the same station. They shuffled through the outfield, wagging their asses, and when people asked them to hurry they stopped right where they were and yelled, "Kiss my pussy." Another confrontation with the joggers led to the arrival of two bearded Berkeley policemen, but before the day was over, we had chosen everyone into the game.

One Sunday a fried chicken franchise had their annual solstice ceremony, and it became a game, in fact a triple-header, with free barrels of chicken afterwards. The following week, the Thai students organization of the Bay Area had a game and chose the six of us who were there onto their teams. They played by punching singles, and throwing for the lead runner, who himself never began running unless the ball was through the infield, even if there was a force. They were slick infielders, but utterly unable to judge pop-ups. We played our own game right on over theirs or under it, and they were at once delighted and oblivious; they ended abruptly in the middle of an inning as though it made sense, leaving us to hit hardball fungoes for the rest of the afternoon.

It's harder, though, when twenty-five people show up and want simply to take over. We had one squabble with a bar from Shattuck on their annual outing. It was mainly a clash in styles. They had a lot of fatter older players, one of whom was the bartender himself who played first, another the owner in rightfield. They had been talking up the game all week and brought a cheering section of women. They didn't believe women should play in the game. Judy was there ahead of them, so they had to include her on their team if they were to challenge us by the rules. After several long arguments, they went along with it, not without calling her sweetie (that was her name to them) and occasionally sitting down when the women on our team were at bat. At one point the game was held up for almost fifteen minutes when their red-headed pitcher refused to give a woman a good pitch. (We had the bases loaded and the game was tied.) I was on third, and shouted: "What the fuck are you trying to prove." He gave me a long stare, put it over, and she cleared the sacks with a triple. He stomped off the field, and the women on their side booed. When the centerfielder took a pop-up away from Judy in short center, she threw her glove at him and chased him back to his position shouting, "You stupid sexist bastard! What the hell do you think you're doing?" He giggled and looked to the sidelines for support. When they lost, they refused to leave the field, but that's another story.

The book itself came out in the fall of '77 and added a new level to the game. The week it arrived, Cisco brought champagne and, together with Jimmy, Janice, Curry, Sal, Merlin, we drank to it. Everyone stood around holding open a copy to the piece about the field. One person got the title page signed, like a big flattened out baseball.

A year later it is already dated. That's why I continue to write. Next season they will see themselves in the book and the match may be closer, and yet some utter mystery will still evade us—the soul of a pick-up field, with which our soul, insofar as our bodies are our souls, merges. They know it better than I, in their silence; and I know it too, better than them in another way. I'll bring a camera up next week and shoot some pictures to go with this. I can't resist the dialogue with baseball eternity.

Johnny Skeels was the hero of my first piece, but he moved north to Healdsburg the year I was away. I knew he heard about the book, but I didn't see him again until one day in March; he walked up beside me in centerfield and said, "Hi." At first I didn't recognize him; then we both stood there smiling. He had brought a team down from Healdsburg on motorcycles, and they sat on the edge of right field waiting their turn. He returned a number of other times during the season, sometimes with his team, sometimes alone.

"Hey Skeels, what's all this shit I'm reading about you?" someone asks. "You're not that good, man."

"Hey, you know, I didn't write it. He called it like he saw it, right?"

Another Berkeley boy is Curtis, a Baby Ruth slugger with a cherub face. About the only thing he does except play the game is comb out his hair in long blond tufts with tugs of a piece of metal; he also glugs down whole cans of beer. He has a total baseball consciousness, but he's not a team player. Very little can convince him to go for singles instead of homers. He does a lot of popping up and puts a few in the trees. He watches his drives with the seriousness of a cat. At shortstop absolutely nothing can convince him not to use his rifle arm, even in game situations. The first baseman can't always handle it.

When the game is over, even if he's on the losing team, he hustles his way into the next game. How can you turn down Babe Ruth? He just places his body there, and who's going to move that?

"What are you doing back out there, Curt?"

"I dunno. They wanted me to play, I guess."

He's as necessary as the ball, and he's perfected dumbness. You can't argue with him, you can't argue with fate. He can't conceive of not playing. He's baseball himself, and the rest of us are smaller beings, props to his deep breaths and power strokes. If Curtis wants to fire it through first, then Curtis does it, with absolute good nature and no guilt. He doesn't blame the first baseman either; he just happened to be there or not; instead he stares after the ball, watching where it goes, as though admiring a bad work of art.

Etch and Mike smile; they're baseball junkies who see the end of the line, but Curt's just beginning. He was born into a baseball body and comes up to the field to feed it, bask in it. Big Curt. He just swings the bat. It's a simple life.

A lot of the midseason regulars are laborers: gardeners, carpenters, postmen, mechanics, dishwashers; Curtis works for his mother in her International House of Pancakes franchises; Wolfman Dave, another Berkeley boy, mixes dough for Wonder Bread.

"My pappy grew up with Billy Martin," he says. "I went to school with Glenn Burke, Berkeley High, the no good sonofabitch."

They call him by his last name now, Anzalone. He no doubt has a heart of gold because I have seen him sneak a smile, but on a game to game basis there is not a meaner sonofabitch than the old Wolfman. He can control a game with his voice and edge of violence. He doesn't hurt anyone. He just agitates and agitates. He wears the other guys down. "Ain't no batter. Ain't no batter. Ain't no batter." Over and over, melodically.

"Dave, you're going to drive us crazy. Can't you say something else?"

"That's the point. It's meant to be irritatin'. You gotta be irritatin' or you're not distractin'."

He stands out in leftfield glaring, hunched over slightly, his hair thrown back from a bald spot. He shouts at the batters, daring them to hit it over his head. When he catches one, he responds big:

"Shut you up. Yeah, I shut you up man. You ain't got nothing, rookie. You ain't nothing but shit."

Called out at third, he starts to leave the field, then changes his mind and charges back. "Your man dropped the ball. He didn't field it clean. I'm not going to have you move me off the base, asshole." And he plants himself there with angry dignity, and takes off on the next hit and stamps on home plate as he scores. The other team may not like it, but they'll swallow it, and they may well find him on their side the next game.

"You ain't gonna get me out," he tells the pitcher. "I'm battin' .800 off you." He lines a single to right. "Take that, fucker."

When he pitches, he flicks up those big arcs and waits for the batter to hit one. A key hit off him, and he'll storm around the mound: "That's it. No more hits. You rookies ain't gettin' no more hits off me." And then he keeps them out of the strike zone, trying to bully the batter to swing. He'll call "Strike" each time, and "You're out," but, of course, he has to keep pitching.

And you don't win. I've gone up against Dave vowing to wait for a good pitch, and I've swung long before my time.

He arrives in a white Lincoln Continental, and when his game is over (if he's lost), he goes back to the parking lot and plays his tape deck, saunters up for the next game, the same chip on his shoulder.

"I'm gonna take you up the middle," Guy shouts at him.

"You take me up the middle, you're gonna be out. Ain't nobody takes me up the middle."

Etch says: "Why do you make them angry, Dave? You gotta play 'em next week."

Dave gives Etch a long look of disbelief, then says, "So I go out and beat their asses again next week."

One game we got a ten-nothing lead on his team in the first inning, so he came in from left to take over the pitching. He made us hit junk the rest of the game. He called out two of our runners at home for missing home plate (a ripped piece of newspaper no one took seriously); and he had several of his players beat out hits on routine groundouts. He demoralized us; our team had the wrong chemistry. They got four runs in the last inning when our shortstop, a man named Curtis, threw a bullet through the first baseman with the bases loaded and the batter having fallen down in the box. He gave it a long look, shrugged, walked off the field, and began hustling the next game.

I went home early that day, bitching about Dave, came back the next week, was made captain, and chose him first. Hell, he was worth three runs a game just for his jive.

The competitive tension reached its height in July. By then almost all of the fall-spring players left, Cisco weeping for his lost youth. The games became tough. I accepted a demotion from leftfield to right, and even caught a few times. There were often four teams waiting to take the field, and Curtis' hustle didn't always work. So one day he arrived at ten A.M. with some of his buddies; then he chose the best of those that were left and played the rest of us. It was blatantly against the rules, but the people on his team went along with it: Greg, and Mike, and Jeff Rhoda. I was on a team that was mostly unknowns, new players. I quit with the score fifteen–nothing.

Two weeks later I came back, and it was the same deal. Curt had been there early with his friends and had added Anzalone and a bunch of others. They were beating the first team badly, and we were to be the second.

It was one those Sundays when a whole lot of new players show up, people who stay. Many of them made up our team. Brian and Marty came from some other pick-up field; that late in history Al Robbins was the best shortstop Codornices had seen. Frampton stumbled onto thirdbase out of an Andy Warhol/David Bowie revue, and played it like an angel. Marty pitched. I went home to left, sullen and defeated, but I made a diving catch in the bushes on Anzalone, the first batter. Robbins and Frampton played perfect games; Brian hit a three run homer. We led seven to one going into the last inning, but, with two outs, they strung together a bunch of hits, three runs, and had the bases loaded. The last shot was a line drive to left I misjudged. I ran in, stuck my glove up, and it stuck in the webbing. Then Skeels and his boys arrived on their cycles and beat us ten to two.

## Berkeley Softball:   1979

This is the year everyone wants to play ball, tough pre-Vietnam West Coast baseball. Codornices is mobbed in March, as many as three teams waiting for the next game—chicanos in their undershirts and jewelry, fragments of ex-jock radio stations, rock bands and Berserkley Record leftovers (like Erik, the slugging Viking), the Minds themselves (in surly middle age trying to whip the kids), high schoolers with Expo and Cardinal caps (anything bright or loud), the Gentile brothers, and the earliest arrival of all, the angry slugging blackman called Mr. Steak after white letters on his red jersey, who hit fungos with me in the February rain when he couldn't wait for the season to start. Compared to what followed, those were pastoral days—looking for the ball in wet leaves among giant pink slugs, dodging mud puddles and football players.

The second edition of the baseball book was now out, with photographs of our field and cameos of the players. The first day I brought them up at 9 A.M., a familiar figure was catching batting practice, a man I hadn't seen for almost a year. "Is that . . . Willie . . . Riser?"

"Hey, man." Sticks his hand through a hole in the chicken wire and gives me a grip shake with extended thumb. Old Willie, back from playing Japan, Paris, Mexico, and, of course, Abu Dhabi and Kuwait, the oil and transistor disco circuit, riding around the desert in Cadillacs smoking Lebanese hash, back from hometown Chicago snows in the winter of light. Of course, it's all right now, Sam. He was born here; baseball makes it so.

"It's been a long time."

"Yessir." Followed by a moment of awkwardness and mute sentiment.

"Hey, let's play ball now. Let's play ball." The thing that lets us off the hook, forever.

Eddie Detroit is nervously snapping at the ball at third base, chanting rhymes with no apparent relationship to events. "Hipsecura. Hupsecura." He seems to be talking to the ball, repeating himself, as though curious with what he has mouthed. Skeels tosses his glove in the air, clips a line drive, and catches it barehanded off the glove. He casually throws it in, barest hint of a smile.

"Hey, did you hear about Merlin getting married today?" Mike asks.

"Sure did," John says. "Called him up when I got to town, said, 'Hey, John, what's new?' And he said, 'Nothin' much; gettin' married today.'"

Mike suggests we have Skeels run out onto the field and everyone will clap. "After all, isn't he supposed to be our hero?" John just smiles. He's grown a beard now; he's older and wiser.

Eddie Detroit sits on the bench reading and guffawing. "You got me. Yeah, you got me. There's no denying it. But tell me, what does 'inveigh' mean? I use it all the time." A little bit later he comes over and puts his arm around me. "Just one thing, though, one thing." He takes a silver flask out of his back pocket and gulps three times before capping it. "We're all waiting for the big moment. We're waiting to strike it rich, all our lives. The big contract. Any season now. And we're gettin' older too. So this year, it's not Eddie Detroit. It's Eddie Champagne." He walks away, nodding to himself, birdlike.

A few weeks later, as we are forced to sit out two games after losing, he comes up to me and says, "The name here is Arthur Edward Price, Mr. A. Edward Price. And anything else that appears in print is an extrasensory distortion."

When we finally take the field, the Mexican team has been defeated, and they occupy the third base bench. They tease and rattle Eddie, who is tipsy by now, flamboyantly missing most of them at the hot corner. "Anyone can be a sore sport," he lectures them from the stage. They roar at such an overt delicacy. They've got to wait two games now and they're going to enjoy it. After Eddie throws a couple of men out, he proudly holds his ground: "Attention, everyone." There is unexpected silence. "This game is being discontinued." Then he crouches for the next pitch. They are beside themselves, but no one begins to understand.

"California is real laid back compared to Chicago or Philadelphia," Willie says. "I played music in places I wouldn't dare to go except on business. I'd come out, you know, and find myself there on the street. Those guys plain hated you. For being white, nothing special. You had to be bilingual, and I don't mean a foreign language. To survive. You don't ever win those arguments. No way. But you survive. I'm here playing ball, aren't I?"

"You might as well argue with a comet," I say.

"You're damn right."

Codornices is the street too, Berkeley-Oakland-El Cerrito. It's a ceremonial plaza without kachinas or Aztecs. Nobody's taking it tough right now, and nobody's making any sacrifices like in uptown Africa or even Chico. The actors for the next event are here, but not in costume. The sun is so sharp and fine it's virtually on the ground. The blue of the Bay sky is equally indisputable. The energy is loose and crisp with static; it blows through like the wind, but never connects. The ritual colors are there. The representatives of the different communities are on hand. But we're not going to hassle politics or money, and we're not going to pray together. Just play ball.

A few motorcycles buzz in and park. Curtis appears over the hill for the first time in 1979. "Why here's Babe Ruth," says Anzalone. "Hey, what's up, Curt?"

Curtis reads briefly through the riff on him, puts the book down, saying, "Great, man," and is looking right away for how to get his name on the list for the next game though people are already signed up two games ahead.

"I've got a bad image up here," Wolfman says. "My mother's gonna think I'm picking on everyone again. Well, I'm gonna be a good boy from now on." And he has, with an occasional sly smile at me every time he would have blown up another season. "The press has reformed me."

One day in April we fought for the field with a bunch of law students who wanted to stay after losing the first game. They had gotten a bona fide permit, and they waved it around righteously. "Jesus," says Rhoda, "a bunch of assholes from New York and they want to take the field from us with a piece of paper. Seven of them and ten of us and fifteen more waiting to play. Hey, where you from, man?" he asks the most emotional of them.

He had guessed New York out of his own almost-racist provincialism, but they were enough of a cliché he was still right. These were stock pushy New Yorkers. "What does it matter?" the guy replied. "I've lived here eight years."

"Eight years, huh? Well, I was fucking born here. Twenty-five years."

"I suppose you think that gives you more protection under the law?"

"You got paper law. I got street law. Nothing fancy."

"Right. And I suppose you'll just go right ahead and build nuclear plants and cut down forests. You'll shove it down our throats."

"Hey, this is baseball. Don't hand me that shit. You got beat. Go wait on line behind the next people. We play fair around here."

The next team is one-half black, including two Caribbean players and a guy in a USC football shirt. By the time the game starts, a fine drizzle is blowing in across the Bay. The trees rustle and stir up cold forest smells. Then a steady rain begins to fall.

Their right fielder goes out for the third inning with an umbrella and stands there holding it, glove on his other hand. Anzalone is pitching; he gives him a long stare. "Don't worry. I'll catch it."

"You better."

In the fourth inning he gets his first chance. Rhoda pokes one to right; he throws down the umbrella, trips over it, and the ball rolls into Euclid Street for four bases. Etch puts the next one right on the line. He doesn't bother even to try for that one. He simply strolls leisurely after it, twirling the umbrella. "Play the line," is all Anzalone says.

"Don't you worry. They got those hits because I let them. Nobody else is getting one past me."

A few batters later, he lets a pop-up squib out of his glove. "This damn ball's too slippery. You guys are crazy playing ball out here. Now my new hairdo is ruined." Anzalone stands on the mound, motioning him into position. "I ain't going nowhere. The ball's coming right to me, baby."

"You get your wet ass over to the line." He doesn't move, so next inning Anzalone goes out to right field. "You're pitching now."

"But I lost my glove."

"You don't need no glove. You can't use one anyway."

His last at-bat, he puts money on the waterlogged piece of cardboard serving as home plate. "I put twenty dollars down," he says. "Then I'm going to hit the ball, run the bases, and come back and pick it up." But when the pitcher refuses to match it with another bill, he reclaims it.

"I just want to make back the twenty dollars I lost on this hairdo."

Everyone seems determined to go seven innings, though we lead by at least ten runs. Anzalone flies out to left to start the seventh. The rain is coming down in torrents. He grabs his gear and heads for his car out on Euclid. "Baseball junkies," he says to me. "See. Every one of them. Me included. Look at the fools, playing in the pouring rain."

Last batter hits a little pop to first. Etch is the first baseman, but he's playing on the other side of the foul line under the shadow of some high branches on the hill. He races over, grabs it, and then everyone simultaneously dashes for the bats and gloves on the bench, and their cars. On the radio, across the Bay, the sun is coming out and the Giants have just removed the tarp for their game with the Dodgers.

The one who tries Dave's patience the most is Steve Gentile, oldest son of the onetime Orioles' first baseman Jim. He's "Gentile"; his younger brother is Scott. Gentile has made a name for himself on the pickup diamonds of the Bay Area. He calls himself "The King," and he has been on many prominent local teams: bigtime softball, more than beer money and uniforms. He's even played for Campbell's Carpets, whose duffel bag he carries. The man defies description because he is so simple and paradoxical. He's a dreamer, an elegant goon, a professional ringer. He visits pickup fields like ours only to get ready for the real season. More than anyone else around, he's given his life to baseball, the best years, and all the rest, almost by birth, and not from any choice he knows of.

"What does your brother do otherwise?" I ask Scott.

"Otherwise? Not much. He puts up sheet rock if he needs money. But that's one day a month. He tends bar at Big Art's on Friday and Saturday. And he plays baseball, hustles baseball. As much as he can."

On the one hand, Gentile is conceited, self-enamored, and ruthless. On the other hand, he is lordly, gentle, and good-humored. Physically, he is big and red, hair and beard, like Bill Walton. He wears a blue baseball cap, goes shirtless, drinks a lot of beer, and slaps around a medium paunch. In the field he claims shortstop like an angry dog. No one else can go near it. He's also a lazy player, like a big soft lion bounding around. He plays in short left field, but with an arm that has first nailed almost by definition. He makes occasional errors on easy grounders, but that's clearly the beer. "Hey, that's my play," he tells the ball. It's all the beer—the beer, pot, and hanging out. That's why he's not in the majors—too much Aquarian Age debris in his blood. He knows it's going to be sour grapes from here on in. He plays with that attitude, like saying, "Look, man, you and I know I don't belong here, but if you think I'm going to go through the shit and training to be a big league ballplayer, or if you think I care about some fuckin' team . . ." And so on. He's twenty-five, looks older. And sometimes you feel he thinks there's still enough time to do it. Some part of him does.

Gentile is the stubborn right field pull hitter of all time. He plays with the rest of us, but he has his private set of arcs and azimuths. Everyone stands in right field, even the third baseman. The catcher would too if they'd let him. It's more than the Williams shift. It's the Gentile shift. Sometimes he beats it over the top, but not often. He yanks half a dozen towering pop-ups a game onto the rightside hill where there are too many trees and other obstacles for them to be caught with any frequency. When they are, he refuses to accept it. "Foul ball," he says, almost to himself. He doesn't shout.

"On this field, that's an out, Gentile."

"Get yourself a fence," he snaps, as though to the field itself, or as though we could instantly erect a fence for him if we wanted. Same thing he says when he hits a towering shot halfway up the hill to the reservoir at the limits of right field and the third baseman catches it because everyone's standing there as though it were fungo. "Home run," he announces, and breaks into a trot, terminating it about halfway to first, then gallantly striding back to the bench. It's a home run in his book.

"Big pop-up man. Can of corn," Anzalone shouts. He's pitching.

"Get yourself a fence."

The poke to left would be simple, and when the game is on the line, people plead with him and hint. "I guess they don't think he can go the other way." Loud enough for him to hear.

"I'm not gonna fuck with my swing. Not for any shitass game. There's still plenty of holes in right. Just because they got all those people out there, what makes you think there ain't holes too?"

One game he was on our team, and we beat Rhoda's resident all-stars who were trying to hold the field all day; we scored five in the bottom of the seventh: 8–7. Gentile got the last hit, with men on second and third. The game was ours if he poked it to left. Instead he squibbed it to first, and it spun under the first baseman's glove into right. "Sorry about that. Cheap single," he says, touching first as the winning runs score. In a key spot the next game, with left field teasing his vanity, he hits a gargantuan shot at the reservoir. He stands at home and watches it, sipping his beer while the ball's still in the air. "Got something on it." But there's an outfielder of some credentials there. "Deepest part of the ballpark," he sings, a mixture of pressbox lingo and reggae. "Oh, they get him out. Nice catch, man." All of it to himself, the giant. He sits on the bench singing his observations. "Let's see if you're going to be Mr. Ribbie today." Good hard "b's" for ribbie. He's grown up hearing it, and it's baby talk. "You're wrapping up for a . . . double," as someone puts on a batting glove. Men on base and he comes to bat. "They're ready for the big clean-up hitter." He stretches out his pectorals with three aluminum bats. Unself-conscious, as though everyone assumed him. He hits it straight up into the blue, grabs his beer off the backstop, and returns to the bench. "I'm leaving it up to you," he says to the next hitter, who might as well be Gus Triandos for all its resemblance to this game.

His critics sit on the hill. "He can tear up the league when there's a fence, five a game sometimes, but he doesn't give a shit for the team."

"Aw, he's probably supposed to play in the bigtime, but too much booze and smack. So now he's gotta be king shit of the pickup field."

"Just like his old man. Did you ever see him try to hit Whitey Ford? He came up slugging, but those little curve balls sat his ass down. In slow pitch they ain't got those curve balls, but the man beats himself all the same."

They miss the point. Gentile doesn't ever talk about the Orioles. He's a street man. *He's* Gentile. The first. No one came before him.

"Hey, too many dinners with Brooks Robinson, big shot," some miser yells from the hill. But the giant never hears that kind of stuff. He just continues his assault on right field. Others love him, like Rhoda, who dreams of playing on an all-star team that would hold the field for the rest of the century and whip everyone. It's a menial smalltown dream, but he's a blond native boy of this field. He lacks Skeels' zen antics and subtle undermining of victory. He could do without the scenery too. He parks his big bike and steps on the field to win—'79 is a tight year for everything.

One day Bob Pierce, the legendary slugger of Codornices, made a rare trip back, wearing his oldtime Pittsburgh Pirate cap. He took off his jacket in the batting circle. His shirt said: Marguarita's Mexican Lunch. Then he took off his shirt inside the cage. His tee shirt said: Total Spectrum. Then he slammed the first pitch so high onto the left field alley hill that the center fielder fell over just straining backward to see it. "What a one-two punch," said Gentile.

"The best righty and the best lefty hitters in the league," shouted Rhoda, his face gleaming like a mad scientist.

But the gentle giant bit shouldn't fool you. Gentile is a prime specimen of that new silent majority: the redneck hippie, the beer-drinking macho longhair. The Rhodas of the world come off surfboards to find his kind for buddies. It's country and western, and pure Berkeley. He's playing in the major leagues of his mind. Once, between games, he rearranged the batting order against field rules so that I lost a turn. I explained that to him, but I knew I was going to lose. I didn't even want to win, so far inside his jive had I come.

"What do you think this is: communist baseball? We don't do things fair. You're an eighth-place hitter, and you better learn to live with it. You're gonna be an eighth-place hitter all your life. Anyhow," he adds with a smile, "everyone wants to see the slugger. Everyone loves the slugger." And he heads up to bat.

He wanted to know why he wasn't in this book. So now he's here. Who said it isn't like a dream, all the way?

Even if we are just a bunch of street rabble playing ball in the sun.

# ROY BLOUNT, JR.

## Soil Is the Soul of Baseball

In the little bitty Massachusetts village where I live, white flecks like cold dandruff are sauntering arrogantly down from on high to join the heavy white topping that has glazed over everything for months. The only visible thing resembling dirt in this entire area is the sand in the roadways, and I am feeling an intense *nostalgie de la boue*.

My son plays hockey; in youth-hockey circles there is an almost panicky appreciation of a commodity known as "ice time." Got to get out there on that ice whenever it is unoccupied, from four a.m. to midnight; can't waste the ice's time. How about my time? And how about *dirt* time? It is good to know that elsewhere in this favored land spring training is under way and people are dusting their hands and bat handles with dirt or rubbing dirt into new balls to cut the slickness or digging into dirt with their spikes or scooping grounders up out of dirt or hurling themselves all out through the air to slide roughly but smoothly, to schuss, through dirt.

Ah. This column is a tribute to baseball's unbroken connection to earth. Baseball remains the only American sport that has not dispensed altogether, in any arena, with American soil. In seventeen of the twenty-six big-league stadia the grass is still real, and even the most thoroughly carpeted parks have patches of high-grade dirt at home plate and the mound, for pitchers and catchers and hitters to root in, and at the bases, for runners to slide in. There was, at a minor-league park in Portland, Oregon, in 1969, one game played on a completely fabricated surface, with vinyl "sliding granules" strewn at the approaches to the bases. But that experiment failed. Runners would hit those granules and keep on sliding, sliding, sliding, right on past the bases and sometimes as far as the stands. Good.

A football game, of course, is often played wholly on a rug, and consequently no dirt or grass stains appear on the players. Only smears of stickum, snot and blood, which can't be seen from the stands. By the fourth quarter, virtually pristine gridders look unreal, like mechanics sliding greaseless from under cars.

Football lore would be far poorer if games had always been played on carpets. Big Daddy Lipscomb, though a huge, fearsome tackler, had a dread of small creeping things. Once when he was playing on sod for the Steelers he bolted violently off side for no apparent reason. In explanation he pointed a great trembling finger at the ground: after he had taken his three-point stance a worm had come crawling up out of its hole right next to his knuckle.

Ten years ago, after the University of Tennessee's football field was covered with Tartan Turf, the U.T. football team had to have a dirt boy. One of its managers was designated to bring along a bucket of dirt for every home game because quarterback Bubba Wyche felt he threw better with a dry, dirty hand, and he insisted that rosin didn't help. Baseball today may need agents and stepped-up security and lawyers, but it doesn't need dirt boys yet.

I was a big fan of Dirty Al Gallagher, who played for the Giants and the Angels a few years back. "I really liked Montreal," he said once. "Montreal has some really funny dirt. You can really get filthy. The dirt is *dark* dirt." But he also liked the dirt in Anaheim Stadium, which was a mixture of red clay and brick dust that was prepared by the stadium's groundkeeper. "The great thing about the dirt here," Dirty Al Gallagher said, "is that you can't get rid of it. It comes through your uniform the next day."

One sunbaked August afternoon in Yankee Stadium, I was watching Vida Blue pitch Oakland to a good competitive 5–3 win. This was before A's owner Charlie Finley took the fun out of baseball for Blue, and before the designated-hitter rule took pitchers out of the offensive game. Pitching, hitting and running with a will on this parched day, Blue had worked up a wholehearted sweat. He had got so juicy by the eighth inning that he slid into third in a big cloud of dust and came up with his back covered with mud.

Ballplayers can't be afraid of getting a little dirt under their fingernails. And there are at least two other ways in which baseball is like farming.

One: Baseball's grass-roots popularity and local social importance, major leagues aside, have historically been greatest in rural areas, where open space and long, not to say vegetative, summer hours are most plentiful.

Two: Baseball buds in the spring, blossoms and ripens all summer and yields its harvest in the fall.

It is worth noting that even with the disappearance of flannel, all the essential elements of baseball—ball, bat, glove, rosin bag and player—are biodegradable. High-speed photos show the bat bending in its arc like a sapling. The glove is kept supple by application of neat's-foot oil, which is rendered from the feet and shinbones of cattle.

Granted, synthetics have had a great effect on the game. Man-made turf, a faster surface, puts a greater premium on baserunning and helps to improve batting averages. It also cuts down on the individuality of grounders. I remember talking to former *Sports Illustrated* writer and ex-bush-league second baseman Mark Kram about ground balls late one night in a Chinese bar. Old-fashioned treacherous grass-cutting bump-hitting grounders were what drove him out of professional ball, he said. He spoke gravely: "I can still see some of them coming toward me. Like certain snakes." On unnatural turf, grounders become more like rockets and less like animals.

Houston's Astrodome and Seattle's Kingdome, terrible places to watch a ball game because there is no sky, have artificial climates. But it seems far less certain today than it did a few years ago that in baseball synthetic elements are the wave of the future. Six different teams have appeared in the past six World Series, and only one of them, Cincinnati, had nonbotanical home turf. When Bill Veeck took over the White Sox a couple of years ago, he pulled out the artificial infield, whose chartreusishness clashed with the color of the outfield grass, and supplanted it with real grass and loam.

A person can make an *impression* on dirt. Dick Allen, who said about Astroturf, "If horses won't eat it, I don't want to play on it," also once expressed himself, and drew Commissioner Bowie Kuhn's wrath, by writing COKE, BOO, WHY, NO, WHY again and MOM in large letters in the base-path dirt with his foot as he played first base for the Phillies. Another time Campy Campaneris was playing for Oakland—he wrote a whole narrative in the dirt. It was in Seattle, in a cozy park called home by the now defunct (and even then unqualified) Pilots. Campaneris led off a day game by hitting a little squiggler down the third-base line. As several Pilots watched it squiggle, in hopes it would squiggle foul, Campaneris reached first and headed for second.

*A two-base squiggler?*

No. The Pilot third baseman snatched it up just before it exhausted itself and pegged it to first. Campaneris made a frantic circle and beat the throw back.

And there the whole play lay recorded in the fresh infield dirt: the first baseman's footprints coming straight to the bag and Campaneris describing three hundred sixty degrees and ending in still-unsettled dust. Like the ripples from the day's first dive into a swimming pool—except that these prints persisted, less and less distinctly in the company of others, until the whole palimpsest was dragged smooth by the grounds crew after the top of the fourth.

Dirt. Remember how it felt as a kid when, after fantasizing about such a thing for years, you actually made a *full-length diving stab of a wicked line drive,* and you got up and shed dirt from your glove and threw the ball with a puff of dust and shook the dirt off your entire person and found your cap and banged it against your leg to get the dirt off it and maybe there was even a little dirt in your shoes you had to shake out, and you sensed all over yourself a certain richly merited patina, and the other team was yelling in *terrible barefaced unvarnished envy,* "Okay, Mr. Hot Shit, play ball!"

# 4

# North America

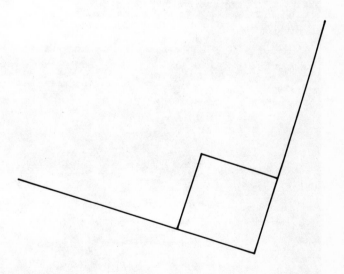

# PHILIP ROTH

## My Baseball Years

In one of his essays George Orwell writes that, though he was not very good at the game, he had a long, hopeless love affair with cricket until he was sixteen. My relations with baseball were similar. Between the ages of nine and thirteen, I must have put in a forty-hour week during the snowless months over at the neighborhood playfield—softball, hardball, and stickball pick-up games—while simultaneously holding down a full-time job as a pupil at the local grammar school. As I remember it, news of two of the most cataclysmic public events of my childhood—the death of President Roosevelt and the bombing of Hiroshima—reached me while I was out playing ball. My performance was uniformly erratic; generally okay for those easygoing pick-up games, but invariably lacking the calm and the expertise that the naturals displayed in stiff competition. My taste, and my talent, such as it was, was for the flashy, whiz-bang catch rather than the towering fly; running and leaping I loved, all the do-or-die stuff—somehow I lost confidence waiting and waiting for the ball lofted right at me to descend. I could never make the high school team, yet I remember that, in one of the two years I vainly (in both senses of the word) tried out, I did a good enough imitation of a baseball player's *style* to be able to fool (or amuse) the coach right down to the day he cut the last of the dreamers from the squad and gave out the uniforms.

Though my disappointment was keen, my misfortune did not necessitate a change in plans for the future. Playing baseball was not what the Jewish boys of our lower-middle-class neighborhood were expected to do in later life for a living. Had I been cut from the high school itself, *then* there would have been hell to pay in my house, and much confusion and shame in me. As it was, my family took my chagrin in stride and lost no more faith in me than I actually did in myself. They probably would have been shocked if I had made the team.

Maybe I would have been too. Surely it would have put me on a somewhat different footing with this game that I loved with all my heart, not simply for the fun of playing it (fun was secondary, really), but for the mythic and aesthetic dimension that it gave to an American boy's life—particularly to one whose grandparents could hardly speak English. For someone whose roots in America were strong but only inches deep, and who had no experience, such as a Catholic child might, of an awesome hierarchy that was real and felt, baseball was a kind of secular church that reached into every class and region of the nation and bound millions upon millions of us together in common concerns, loyalties, rituals, enthusiasms, and antagonisms. Baseball made me understand what patriotism was about, at its best.

Not that Hitler, the Bataan Death March, the battle for the Solomons, and the Normandy invasion didn't make of my contemporaries what may well have been the most patriotic generation of schoolchildren in American history (and the most willingly and successfully propagandized). But the war we entered when I was eight had thrust the country into what seemed to a child—and not only to a child—a struggle to the death between Good and Evil. Fraught with perilous, unthinkable possibilities, it inevitably nourished a patriotism grounded in moral virtue and bloody-minded hate, the patriotism that fixes a bayonet to a Bible. It seems to me that through baseball I was put in touch with a more humane and tender brand of patriotism, lyrical rather than martial or righteous in spirit, and without the reek of saintly zeal, a patriotism that could not so easily be sloganized, or contained in a high-sounding formula to which you had to pledge something vague but all-encompassing called your "allegiance."

To sing the National Anthem in the school auditorium every week, even during the worst of the war years, generally left me cold. The enthusiastic lady teacher waved her arms in the air and we obliged with the words: "See! Light! Proof! Night! There!" But nothing stirred within, strident as we might be—in the end, just another school exercise. It was different, however, on Sundays out at Ruppert Stadium, a green wedge of pasture miraculously walled in among the factories, warehouses, and truck depots of industrial Newark. It would, in fact, have seemed to me an emotional thrill forsaken if, before the Newark Bears took on the hated enemy from across the marshes, the Jersey City Giants, we hadn't first to rise to our feet (my father, my brother, and I—along with our inimical countrymen, the city's Germans, Italians, Irish, Poles, and, out in the Africa of the bleachers, Newark's Negroes) to celebrate the America that had given to this unharmonious mob a game so grand and beautiful.

Just as I first learned the names of the great institutions of higher learning by trafficking in football pools for a neighborhood bookmaker rather than from our high school's college adviser, so my feel for the American landscape came less from what I learned in the classroom about Lewis and Clark than from following the major-league clubs on their road trips and reading about the minor leagues in the back pages of *The Sporting News*. The size of the continent got through to you finally when you had to stay up to 10:30 p.m. in New Jersey to hear via radio "ticker-tape" Cardinal pitcher Mort Cooper throw the first strike of the night to Brooklyn shortstop Pee Wee Reese out in "steamy" Sportsmen's Park in St. Louis, Missouri. And however much we might be told by teacher about the stockyards and the Haymarket riots, Chicago only began to exist for me as a real place, and to matter in American history, when I became fearful (as a Dodger fan) of the bat of Phil Cavarretta, first baseman for the Chicago Cubs.

Not until I got to college and was introduced to literature did I find anything with a comparable emotional atmosphere and aesthetic appeal. I don't mean to suggest that it was a simple exchange, one passion for another. Between first discovering the Newark Bears and the Brooklyn Dodgers at seven or eight and first looking into Conrad's *Lord Jim* at age eighteen, I had done some growing up. I am only saying that my discovery of literature, and fiction particularly, and the "love affair"—to some degree hopeless, but still earnest—that has ensued, derives in part from this childhood infatuation with baseball. Or, more accurately perhaps, baseball—with its lore and legends, its cultural power, its seasonal associations, its native authenticity, its simple rules and transparent strategies, its longeurs and thrills, its spaciousness, its suspensefulness, its heroics, its nuances, its lingo, its "characters," its peculiarly hypnotic tedium, its mythic transformation of the immediate—was the literature of my boyhood.

Baseball, as played in the big leagues, was something completely outside my own life that could nonetheless move me to ecstasy and to tears; like fiction it could excite the imagination and hold the attention as much with minutiae as with high drama. Mel Ott's cocked leg striding into the ball, Jackie Robinson's pigeon-toed shuffle as he moved out to second base, each was to be as deeply affecting over the years as that night—"inconceivable," "inscrutable," as any night Conrad's Marlow might struggle to comprehend—the night that Dodger wild man, Rex Barney (who never lived up to "our" expectations, who should have been "our" Koufax), not only went the distance without walking in half a dozen runs, but, of all things, threw a no-hitter. A thrilling mystery, marvelously enriched by the fact that a light rain had fallen during the early evening, and Barney, figuring the game was going to be postponed, had eaten a hot dog just before being told to take the mound.

This detail was passed on to us by Red Barber, the Dodger radio sportscaster of the forties, a respectful, mild Southerner with a subtle rural tanginess to his vocabulary and a soft country-parson tone to his voice. For the adventures of "dem bums" of Brooklyn—a region then the very symbol of urban wackiness and tumult—to be narrated from Red Barber's highly alien but loving perspective constituted a genuine triumph of what my English professors would later teach me to call "point of view." James himself might have admired the implicit cultural ironies and the splendid possibilities for oblique moral and social commentary. And as for the detail about Rex Barney eating his hot dog, it was irresistible, joining as it did the spectacular to the mundane, and furnishing an adolescent boy with a glimpse of an unexpectedly ordinary, even humdrum, side to male heroism.

Of course, in time, neither the flavor and suggestiveness of Red Barber's narration nor "epiphanies" as resonant with meaning as Rex Barney's pre-game hot dog could continue to satisfy a developing literary appetite; nonetheless, it was just this that helped to sustain me until I was ready to begin to respond to the great inventors of narrative detail and masters of narrative voice and perspective like James, Conrad, Dostoevsky, and Bellow.

# WILLIE MORRIS

## *from* North Toward Home

Like Mark Twain and his comrades growing up a century before in an-other village on the other side of the Mississippi, my friends and I had but one sustaining ambition in the 1940s. Theirs in Hannibal was to be steamboatmen, ours in Yazoo was to be major-league baseball players. In the summers, we thought and talked of little else. We memorized batting averages, fielding averages, slugging averages, we knew the roster of the Cardinals and the Red Sox better than their own managers must have known them, and to hear the broadcasts from all the big-city ballparks with their memorable names—the Polo Grounds, Wrigley Field, Fenway Park, the Yankee Stadium—was to set our imagination churning for the glory and riches those faraway places would one day bring us. One of our friends went to St. Louis on his vacation to see the Cards, and when he returned with the autographs of Stan Musial, Red Schoendienst, Country Slaughter, Marty Marion, Joe Garagiola, and a dozen others, we could hardly keep down our envy. I hated that boy for a month, and secretly wished him dead, not only because he took on new airs but because I wanted those scraps of paper with their magic characters. I wished also that my own family were wealthy enough to take me to a big-league town for two weeks, but a bigger place even than St. Louis: Chicago, maybe, with not one but two teams, or best of all to New York, with three. I had bought a baseball cap in Jackson, a real one from the Brooklyn Dodgers, and a Jackie Robinson Louisville Slugger, and one day when I could not .even locate any of the others for catch or for baseball talk, I sat on a curb on Grand Avenue with the most dreadful feelings of being caught forever by time—trapped there always in my scrawny and helpless condition. *I'm ready, I'm ready*, I kept thinking to myself, but that remote future when I would wear a cap like that and be a hero for a grandstand full of people seemed so far away I knew it would never come. I must have been the most dejected-looking child you ever saw, sitting hunched up on the curb and dreaming of glory in the mythical cities of the North. I felt worse when a carload of high school boys halted right in front of where I sat, and they started reciting what they always did when they saw me alone and day-dreaming: *Wee Willie Winkie walks through the town, upstairs and downstairs in his nightgown.* Then one of them said, "Winkie, you *gettin'* much?" "You bastards!" I shouted, and they drove off laughing like wild men.

Almost every afternoon when the heat was not unbearable my father and I would go out to the old baseball field behind the armory to hit flies. I would stand far out in center field, and he would station himself with a fungo at home plate, hitting me one high fly, or Texas Leaguer, or line drive after another, sometimes for an hour or more without stopping. My dog would get out there in the outfield with me, and retrieve the inconsequential dribblers or the ones that went too far. I was light and speedy, and could make the most fantastic catches, turning completely around and forgetting the ball sometimes to head for the spot where it would descend, or tumbling head-on for a diving catch. The smell of that new-cut grass was the finest of all smells, and I could run forever and never get tired. It was a dreamy, suspended state, those late afternoons, thinking of nothing but outfield flies as the world drifted lazily by on Jackson Avenue. I learned to judge what a ball would do by instinct, heading the way it went as if I owned it, and I knew in my heart I could make the big time. Then, after all that exertion, my father would shout, "I'm whupped!" and we would quit for the day.

When I was twelve I became a part-time sportswriter for the *Yazoo Herald*, whose courtly proprietors allowed me unusual independence. I wrote up an occasional high school or Legion game in a florid prose, filled with phrases like "two-ply blow" and "circuit-ringer." My mentor was the sports editor of the *Memphis Commercial Appeal*, whose name was Walter Stewart, a man who could invest the most humdrum athletic contest with the elements of Shakespearean tragedy. I learned whole paragraphs of his by heart, and used some of his expressions for my reports on games between Yazoo and Satartia, or the other teams. The summer when I was twelve, having never seen a baseball game higher than the Jackson Senators of Class B, my father finally relented and took me to Memphis to see the Chicks, who were Double A. It was the farthest I had ever been from home, and the largest city I had ever seen; I walked around in a state of joyousness, admiring the crowds and the big park high above the River, and best of all, the grand old lobby of the Chisca Hotel.

Staying with us at the Chisca were the Nashville Vols, who were there for a big series with the Chicks. I stayed close to the lobby to get a glimpse of them; when I discovered they spent all day, up until the very moment they left for the ballpark, playing the pinball machine, I stationed myself there too. Their names were Tookie Gilbert, Smokey

Burgess, Chuck Workman, and Bobo Holloman, the latter being the one who got as far as the St. Louis Browns, pitched a no-hitter in his first major league game, and failed to win another before being shipped down forever to obscurity; one afternoon my father and I ran into them outside the hotel on the way to the game and gave them a ride in our taxi. I could have been fit for tying, especially when Smokey Burgess tousled my hair and asked me if I batted right or left, but when I listened to them as they grumbled about having to get out to the ballpark so early, and complained about the season having two more damned months to go and about how ramshackle their team bus was, I was too disillusioned even to tell my friends when I got home.

Because back home, even among the adults, baseball was all-meaning; it was the link with the outside. A place known around town simply as The Store, down near the train depot, was the principal center of this ferment. The Store had sawdust on the floor and long shreds of flypaper hanging from the ceiling. Its most familiar staples were Rexall supplies, oysters on the half shell, legal beer, and illegal whiskey, the latter served up, Mississippi bootlegger style, by the bottle from a hidden shelf and costing not merely the price of the whiskey but the investment in gas required to go to Louisiana to fetch it. There was a long counter in the back. On one side of it, the white workingmen congregated after hours every afternoon to compare the day's scores and talk batting averages, and on the other side, also talking baseball, were the Negroes, juxtaposed in a face-to-face arrangement with the whites. The scores were chalked up on a blackboard hanging on a red and purple wall, and the conversations were carried on in fast, galloping shouts from one end of the room to the other. An intelligent white boy of twelve was even permitted, in that atmosphere of heady freedom before anyone knew the name of Justice Warren or had heard much of the United States Supreme Court, a quasi-public position favoring the Dodgers, who had Jackie Robinson, Roy Campanella, and Don Newcombe—not to mention, so it was rumored, God knows how many Chinese and mulattoes being groomed in the minor leagues. I remember my father turned to some friends at The Store one day and observed, "Well, you can say what you want to about that nigger Robinson, but he's got *guts*," and to a man the others nodded, a little reluctantly, but in agreement nonetheless. And one of them said he had read somewhere that Pee Wee Reese, a white Southern boy, was the best friend Robinson had on the team, which proved they had chosen the right one to watch after him.

There were two firehouses in town, and on hot afternoons the firemen at both establishments sat outdoors in their shirtsleeves, with the baseball broadcast turned up as loud as it would go. On his day off work my father, who had left Cities Service and was now a bookkeeper for the wholesale grocery, usually started with Firehouse No. 1 for the first few innings and then hit Number Two before ending up at The Store for the post-game conversations.

I decided not to try out for the American Legion Junior Baseball team that summer. Legion baseball was an important thing for country boys in those parts, but I was too young and skinny, and I had heard that the coach, a dirt farmer known as Gentleman Joe, made his protégés lie flat in the infield while he walked on their stomachs; he also forced them to take three-mile runs through the streets of town, talked them into going to church, and persuaded them to give up Coca-Colas. A couple of summers later, when I did go out for the team, I found out that Gentleman Joe did in fact insist on these soul-strengthening rituals; because of them, we won the Mississippi State Championship and the merchants in town took up a collection and sent us all the way to St. Louis to see the Cards play the Phillies. My main concern that earlier summer, however, lay in the more academic aspects of the game. I knew more about baseball, its technology and its ethos, than all the firemen and Store experts put together. Having read most of its literature, I could give a sizable lecture on the infield-fly rule alone, which only a thin minority of the townspeople knew existed. Gentleman Joe was held in some esteem for his strategical sense, yet he was the only man I ever knew who could call for a sacrifice bunt with two men out and not have a bad conscience about it. I remember one dismaying moment that came to me while I was watching a country semi-pro game. The home team had runners on first and third with one out, when the batter hit a ground ball to the first baseman, who stepped on first then threw to second. The shortstop, covering second, stepped on the base but made no attempt to tag the runner. The man on third had crossed the plate, of course, but the umpire, who was not very familiar with the subtleties of the rules, signaled a double play. Sitting in the grandstand, I knew that it was not a double play at all and that the run had scored, but when I went down, out of my Christian duty, to tell the manager of the local team that he had just been done out of a run, he told me I was crazy. This was the kind of brainpower I was up against.

That summer the local radio station, the one where we broadcast our Methodist programs, started a baseball quiz program. A razor blade company offered free blades and the station chipped in a dollar, all of which went to the first listener to telephone with the right answer to the day's baseball question. If there was no winner, the next day's pot would go up a dollar. At the end of the month they had to close down the program because I was winning all the money. It got so easy, in fact, that I stopped phoning in the answers some afternoons so that the pot could build up and make my winnings more spectacular. I netted about $25 and a ten-year supply of double-edged, smooth-contact razor blades before they gave up. One day, when the jackpot was a mere two dollars, the announcer tried to confuse me. "Babe Ruth," he said, "hit sixty home runs in 1927 to set the major-league record. What man had the next-highest total?" I telephoned and said, "George Herman Ruth. He hit fifty-nine in another season." My adversary, who had developed an acute dislike of me, said that was not the correct answer. He said it should have been *Babe* Ruth. This incident angered me, and I won for the next four days, just for the hell of it.

On Sunday afternoons, we sometimes drove out of town and along hot, dusty roads to baseball fields that were little more than parched red clearings, the outfield sloping out of the woods and ending in some tortuous gully full of yellowed paper, old socks, and vintage cow shit. One of the backwoods teams had a fastball pitcher named Eckert, who didn't have any teeth, and a fifty-year-old left-handed catcher named Smith. Since there were no catcher's mitts made for left-handers, Smith had to wear a mitt on his throwing hand. In his simian posture he would catch the ball and toss it lightly into the air and then whip his mitt off and catch the ball in his bare left hand before throwing it back. It was a wonderfully lazy way to spend those Sunday afternoons—my father and my friends and I sitting in the grass behind the chicken-wire backstop with eight or ten dozen farmers, watching the wrong-handed catcher go through his contorted gyrations, and listening at the same time to our portable radio, which brought us the rising inflections of a baseball announcer called the Old Scotchman. The sounds of the two games, our own and the one being broadcast from Brooklyn or Chicago, merged and rolled across the bumpy outfield and the gully into the woods; it was a combination that seemed perfectly natural to everyone there.

I can see the town now on some hot, still weekday afternoon in midsummer: ten thousand souls and nothing doing. Even the red water truck was a diversion, coming slowly up Grand Avenue with its sprinklers on full force, the water making sizzling steam-clouds on the pavement while half-naked Negro children followed the truck up the street and played in the torrent until they got soaking wet. Over on Broadway, where the old men sat drowsily in straw chairs on the pavement near the Bon-Ton Café, whittling to make the time pass, you could laze around on the sidewalks—barefoot, if your feet were tough enough to stand the scalding concrete—watching the big cars with out-of-state plates whip by, the driver hardly knowing and certainly not caring what place this was. Way up that fantastic hill, Broadway seemed to end in a seething mist—little heat mirages that shimmered off the asphalt; on the main street itself there would be only a handful of cars parked here and there, and the merchants and the lawyers sat in the shade under their broad awnings, talking slowly, aimlessly, in the cryptic summer way. The one o'clock whistle at the sawmill would send out its loud bellow, reverberating up the streets to the bend in the Yazoo River, hardly making a ripple in the heavy somnolence.

But by two o'clock almost every radio in town was tuned in to the Old Scotchman. His rhetoric dominated the place. It hovered in the branches of the trees, bounced off the hills, and came out of the darkened stores; the merchants and the old men cocked their ears to him, and even from the big cars that sped by, their tires making lapping sounds in the softened highway, you could hear his voice, being carried past you out into the delta.

The Old Scotchman's real name was Gordon McLendon, and he described the big-league games for the Liberty Broadcasting System, which had outlets mainly in the South and the Southwest. He had a deep, rich voice, and I think he was the best rhetorician, outside of Bilbo and Nye Bevan, I have ever heard. Under his handling a baseball game took on a life of its own. As in the prose of the *Commercial Appeal's* Walter Stewart, his games were rare and remarkable entities; casual pop flies had the flow of history behind them, double plays resembled the stark clashes of old armies, and home runs deserved acknowledgment on earthen urns. Later, when I came across Thomas Wolfe, I felt I had heard him before, from Shibe Park, Crosley Field, or the Yankee Stadium.

One afternoon I was sitting around my house listening to the Old Scotchman, admiring the vivacity of a man who said he was a contemporary of Connie Mack. (I learned later that he was twenty-nine.) That day he was doing the Dodgers and the Giants from the Polo Grounds. The game, as I recall, was in the fourth inning, and the Giants were ahead by about 4 to 1. It was a boring game, however, and I began experimenting with my father's short-wave radio, an impressive mechanism a couple of feet wide, which had an aerial that almost touched the ceiling and the name of every major city in the world on its dial. It was by far the best radio I had ever seen; there was not another one like it in town. I switched the dial to short-wave and began picking up African drum music, French jazz, Australian weather reports, and a lecture from the British Broadcasting Company on the people who wrote poems for Queen Elizabeth. Then a curious thing happened. I came across a baseball game —the Giants and the Dodgers, from the Polo Grounds. After a couple of minutes I discovered that the game was in the eighth inning. I turned back to the local station, but here the Giants and Dodgers were still in the fourth. I turned again to the short-wave broadcast and listened to the last inning, a humdrum affair that ended with Carl Furillo popping out to shortstop, Gil Hodges grounding out second to first, and Roy Campanella lining out to center. Then I went back to the Old Scotchman and listened to the rest of the game. In the top of the ninth, an hour or so later, a ghostly thing occurred; to my astonishment and titillation, the game ended with Furillo popping out to short, Hodges grounding out second to first, and Campanella lining out to center.

I kept this unusual discovery to myself, and the next day, an hour before the Old Scotchman began his play-by-play of the second game of the series, I dialed the short-wave frequency, and, sure enough, they were doing the Giants and the Dodgers again. I learned that I was listening to the Armed Forces Radio Service, which broadcast games played in New York. As the game progressed I began jotting down notes on the action. When the first four innings were over I turned to the local station just in time to get the Old Scotchman for the first batter. The Old Scotchman's account of the game matched the short-wave's almost perfectly. The Scotchman's, in fact, struck me as being considerably more poetic than the one I had heard first. But I did not doubt him, since I could hear the roar of the crowd, the crack of the bat, and the Scotchman's precise description of foul balls that fell into the crowd, the gestures of the base coaches, and the expression on the face of a small boy who was eating a lemon popsicle in a box seat behind first base. I decided that the broadcast was being delayed somewhere along the line, maybe because we were so far from New York.

That was my first thought, but after a close comparison of the two broadcasts for the rest of the game, I sensed that something more sinister was taking place. For one thing, the Old Scotchman's description of the count on a batter, though it jibed 90 percent of the time, did not always match. For another, the Scotchman's crowd, compared with the other, kept up an ungodly noise. When Robinson stole second on short-wave, he did it without drawing a throw and without sliding, while for Mississippians the feat was performed in a cloud of angry, petulant dust. A foul ball that went over the grandstand and out of the park for short-wave listeners in Alaska, France, and the Argentine produced for the firemen, bootleggers, farmers, and myself a primitive scramble that ended with a feeble old lady catching the ball on the first bounce to the roar of an assembly that would have outnumbered Grant's at Old Cold Harbor. But the most revealing development came after the Scotchman's game was over. After the usual summaries, he mentioned that the game had been "recreated." I had never taken notice of that particular word before, because I lost interest once a game was over. I went to the dictionary, and under "recreate" I found, "To invest with fresh vigor and strength; to refresh, invigorate (nature, strength, a person or thing)." The Old Scotchman most assuredly invested a game with fresh vigor and strength, but this told me nothing. My deepest suspicions were confirmed, however, when I found the second definition of the word—"To create anew."

So there it was. I was happy to have fathomed the mystery, as perhaps no one else in the whole town had done. The Old Scotchman, for all his wondrous expressions, was not only several innings behind every game he described but was no doubt sitting in some air-conditioned studio in the hinterland, where he got the happenings of the game by news ticker; sound effects accounted for the crack of the bat and the crowd noises. Instead of being disappointed in the Scotchman, I was all the more pleased by his genius, for he made pristine facts more actual than actuality, a valuable lesson when the day finally came that I started reading literature. I must add, however, that this appreciation did not obscure the realization that I had at my disposal a weapon of unimaginable dimensions.

Next day I was at the short-wave again, but I learned with much disappointment that the game being broadcast on short-wave was not the one the Scotchman had chosen to describe. I tried every afternoon after that and discovered that I would have to wait until the Old Scotchman decided to do a game out of New York before I could match his game with the one described live on short-wave. Sometimes, I learned later, these coincidences did not occur for days; during an important Dodger or Yankee series, however, his game and that of the Armed Forces Radio Service often coincided for two or three days running. I was happy, therefore, to find, on an afternoon a few days later, that both the short-wave and the Scotchman were carrying the Yankees and the Indians.

I settled myself at the short-wave with notebook and pencil and took down every pitch. This I did for four full innings, and then I turned back to the town station, where the Old Scotchman was just beginning the first inning. I checked the first batter to make sure the accounts jibed. Then, armed with my notebook, I ran down the street to the corner grocery, a minor outpost of baseball intellection, presided over by my young Negro friend Bozo, a knowledgeable student of the game, the same one who kept my dog in bologna. I found Bozo behind the meat counter, with the Scotchman's account going full blast. I arrived at the interim between the top and bottom of the first inning.

"Who's pitchin' for the Yankees, Bozo?" I asked.

"They're pitchin' Allie Reynolds," Bozo said. "Old Scotchman says Reynolds really got the stuff today. He just set 'em down one, two, three."

The Scotchman, meanwhile, was describing the way the pennants were flapping in the breeze. Phil Rizzuto, he reported, was stepping to the plate.

"Bo," I said, trying to sound cut and dried, "you know what I think? I think Rizzuto's gonna take a couple of fast called strikes, then foul one down the left-field line, and then line out straight to Boudreau at short."

"Yeah?" Bozo said. He scratched his head and leaned lazily across the counter.

I went up front to buy something and then came back. The count worked to nothing and two on Rizzuto—a couple of fast called strikes and a foul down the left side. "This one," I said to Bozo, "he lines straight to Boudreau at short."

The Old Scotchman, pausing dramatically between words as was his custom, said, "Here's the pitch on its way—There's a hard line drive! But Lou Boudreau's there at shortstop and he's got it. Phil hit that one on the nose, but Boudreau was right there."

Bozo looked over at me, his eyes bigger than they were. "How'd you know that?" he asked.

Ignoring this query, I made my second prediction. "Bozo," I said, "Tommy Henrich's gonna hit the first pitch up against the right-field wall and slide in with a double."

"How come you think so?"

"Because I can predict anything that's gonna happen in baseball in the next ten years," I said. "I can tell you anything."

The Old Scotchman was describing Henrich at the plate. "Here comes the first pitch. Henrich swings, there's a hard smash into right field! . . . This one may be out of here! It's going, going—*No!* It's off the wall in right center. Henrich's rounding first, on his way to second. Here's the relay from Doby . . . Henrich slides in safely with a double!" The Yankee crowd sent up an awesome roar in the background.

"Say, how'd you know that?" Bozo asked. "How'd you know he was gonna wind up at second?"

"I just can tell. I got extra-vision," I said. On the radio, far in the background, the public-address system announced Yogi Berra. "Like Berra right now. You know what? He's gonna hit a one-one pitch down the right-field line—"

"How come you know?" Bozo said. He was getting mad.

"Just a second," I said. "I'm gettin' static." I stood dead still, put my hands up against my temples and opened my eyes wide. "Now it's comin' through clear. Yeah, Yogi's gonna hit a one-one pitch down the right-field line, and it's gonna be fair by about three or four feet—I can't say exactly —and Henrich's gonna score from second, but the throw is gonna get Yogi at second by a mile."

This time Bozo was silent, listening to the Scotchman, who described the ball and the strike, then said: "Henrich takes the lead off second. Benton looks over, stretches, delivers. Yogi swings." (There was the bat crack.) "There's a line drive down the right side! It's barely inside the foul line. It may go for extra bases! Henrich's rounding third and coming in with a run. Berra's moving toward second. Here comes the throw! . . . And they *get* him! They get Yogi easily on the slide at second!"

Before Bozo could say anything else, I reached in my pocket for my notes. "I've just written down here what I think's gonna happen in the first four innings," I said. "Like DiMag. See, he's gonna pop up to Mickey Vernon at first on a one-nothing pitch in just a minute. But don't you worry. He's gonna hit a 380-foot homer in the fourth with nobody on base on a full count. You just follow these notes and you'll see I can predict anything that's gonna happen in the next ten years." I handed him the paper, turned around, and left the store just as DiMaggio, on a one-nothing pitch, popped up to Vernon at first.

Then I went back home and took more notes from the short-wave. The Yanks clobbered the Indians in the late innings and won easily. On the local station, however, the Old Scotchman was in the top of the fifth inning. At this juncture I went to the telephone and called Firehouse No. 1.

"Hello," a voice answered. It was the fire chief.

"Hello, Chief, can you tell me the score?" I said. Calling the firehouse for baseball information was a common practice.

"The Yanks are ahead, 5–2."

"This is the Phantom you're talkin' with," I said.

"Who?"

"The Phantom. Listen carefully, Chief. Reynolds is gonna open this next inning with a popup to Doby. Then Rizzuto will single to left on a one-one count. Henrich's gonna force him at second on a two-and-one pitch but make it to first. Berra's gonna double to right on a nothing-and-one pitch, and Henrich's goin' to third. DiMaggio's gonna foul a couple off and then double down the left-field line, and both Henrich and Yogi are gonna score. Brown's gonna pop out to third to end the inning."

"Aw, go to hell," the chief said, and hung up.

This was precisely what happened, of course. I phoned No. 1 again after the inning.

"Hello."

"Hi. This is the Phantom again."

"Say, how'd you know that?"

"Stick with me," I said ominously, "and I'll feed you predictions. I can predict anything that's gonna happen anywhere in the next ten years." After a pause I added, "Beware of fire real soon," for good measure, and hung up.

I left my house and hurried back to the corner grocery. When I got there, the entire meat counter was surrounded by friends of Bozo's, about a dozen of them. They were gathered around my notes, talking passionately and shouting. Bozo saw me standing by the bread counter. "There he is! That's the one!" he declared. His colleagues turned and stared at me in undisguised awe. They parted respectfully as I strolled over to the meat counter and ordered a dime's worth of bologna for my dog.

A couple of questions were directed at me from the group, but I replied, "I'm sorry for what happened in the fourth. I predicted DiMag was gonna hit a full-count pitch for that homer. It came out he hit it on two-and-two. There was too much static in the air between here and New York."

"Too much *static?*" one of them asked.

"Yeah. Sometimes the static confuses my extra-vision. But I'll be back tomorrow if everything's okay, and I'll try not to make any more big mistakes."

"Big mistakes!" one of them shouted, and the crowd laughed admiringly, parting once more as I turned and left the store. I wouldn't have been at all surprised if they had tried to touch the hem of my shirt.

That day was only the beginning of my brief season of triumph. A schoolmate of mine offered me five dollars, for instance, to tell him how I had known that Johnny Mize was going to hit a two-run homer to break up one particularly close game for the Giants. One afternoon, on the basis of a lopsided first four innings, I had an older friend sneak into The Store and place a bet, which netted me $14.50. I felt so bad about it I tithed $1.45 in church the following Sunday. At Bozo's grocery store I was a full-scale oracle. To the firemen I remained the Phantom, and firefighting reached a peak of efficiency that month, simply because the firemen knew what was going to happen in the late innings and did not need to tarry when an alarm came.

One afternoon my father was at home listening to the Old Scotchman with a couple of out-of-town salesmen from Greenwood. They were sitting in the front room, and I had already managed to get the first three or four innings of the Cardinals and the Giants on paper before they arrived. The Old Scotchman was in the top of the first when I walked in and said hello. The men were talking business and listening to the game at the same time.

"I'm gonna make a prediction," I said. They stopped talking and looked at me. "I predict Musial's gonna take a ball and a strike and then hit a double to right field, scoring Schoendienst from second, but Marty Marion's gonna get tagged out at the plate."

"You're mighty smart," one of the men said. He suddenly sat up straight when the Old Scotchman reported, "Here's the windup and the pitch coming in . . . Musial *swings!*" (Bat crack, crowd roar.) "He drives one in to right field! This one's going up against the boards! . . . Schoendienst rounds third. He's coming on in to score! Marion dashes around third, legs churning. His cap falls off, but here he *comes!* Here's the toss to the plate. He's nabbed at home. He is *out* at the plate! Musical holds at second with a run-producing double."

Before I could parry the inevitable questions, my father caught me by the elbow and hustled me into a back room. "How'd you know that?" he asked.

"I was just guessin'," I said. "It was nothin' but luck."

He stopped for a moment, and then a new expression showed on his face. "Have *you* been callin' the firehouse?" he asked.

"Yeah, I guess a few times."

"Now, you tell me how you found out about all that. I mean it."

When I told him about the short-wave, I was afraid he might be mad, but on the contrary he laughed uproariously. "Do you remember these next few innings?" he asked.

"I got it all written down," I said, and reached in my pocket for the notes. He took the notes and told me to go away. From the yard, a few minutes later, I heard him predicting the next inning to the salesmen.

A couple of days later, I phoned No. 1 again. "This is the Phantom," I said. "With two out, Branca's gonna hit Stinky Stanky with a fast ball, and then Alvin Dark's gonna send him home with a triple."

"Yeah, we know it," the fireman said in a bored voice. "We're listenin' to a short-wave too. You think you're somethin', don't you? You're Ray Morris' boy."

I knew everything was up. The next day, as a sort of final gesture, I took some more notes to the corner grocery in the third or fourth inning. Some of the old crowd was there, but the atmosphere was grim. They looked at me coldly. "Oh, man," Bozo said, "*we* know the Old Scotchman ain't at that game. He's four or five innings behind. He's makin' all that stuff up." The others grumbled and turned away. I slipped quietly out the door.

My period as a seer was over, but I went on listening to the short-wave broadcasts out of New York a few days more. Then, a little to my surprise, I went back to the Old Scotchman, and in time I found that the firemen, the bootleggers, and the few dirt farmers who had short-wave sets all did the same. From then on, accurate, up-to-the-minute baseball news was in disrepute there. I believe we all went back to the Scotchman not merely out of loyalty but because, in our great isolation, he touched our need for a great and unmitigated eloquence.

Joe's American Legion Junior team actually amounted to an all-star squad from all the country towns surrounding ours; it was easier to make the high school team first. On Tuesday and Friday afternoons we would ride in our red and black bus through the heavy green woods to the small crossroads towns to play the locals. The crowds would sometimes be in a foul frame of mind, especially if the farmers had got hold of the corn gourd early in the day. Since we were the "city boys," with our pictures in the *Yazoo Herald* every now and again, we were particularly ripe for all that boondocks venom. The farmers would stand around the field shouting obscenities at the "slickers," sometimes loosening up their lungs with a vicious organized whoop that sounded like a cross between a rebel yell and a redneck preacher exorcizing the Devil and all his family. More often than not, to compound the injury, we got beat. Yet far from being gracious in victory, those sons of dirt farmers rubbed our noses in our own catastrophes, taunting us with threats to whip us all over again in the outfield pasture, while their elders stood around in a group as our coach chased us into the bus and shouted, "You ain't such hot stuff, slickers!" or "Go on back to town now, boys, and get your *photos* took some more." One afternoon when I ruined the no-hitter the best pitcher in the county had going (he later made Double-A), with a broken-bat fluke into right field in the eighth inning, I thought those farmers might slice me in pieces and feed me to the boll weevils. "You proud of that little skinny hit?" one of them shouted at me, standing with his nose next to mine, and his companion picked up the broken bat that had done the evil deed and splintered it apart against a tree trunk. When we beat the same team two or three weeks later on our home field, I ran into their shortstop and catcher, two tough hardnoses, on Main Street the following Saturday. They sidled right up to me and waited there glowering, breathing in my face and not saying a word for a while. We stood nostril-to-nostril until one of them said, "You think you're somethin' don't you, bastid? Beat us at home with your crooked umpires. Next time you come see us we'll whup you 'til the shit turns green." And they did.

The next summer, when I made the Legion team, I finally came under the tutelage of Gentleman Joe, a hard taskmaster of the old school despite his unfamiliarity with "stragety," as he called it. Gentleman Joe would always have us pray before a game, and sometimes between innings when the going got rough. He was a big one for church, and began to remind me more and more of my old fourth-grade teacher. But his pep talks, back behind the shabby old grandstand of our playing field, drew on such pent-up emotions, being so full of Scriptures and things of God's earth, that I suspected we were being enlisted, not to play baseball, but to fight in the Army of the Lord.

That was the team which won the Mississippi championship, beating almost everybody without much trouble. Before the final game for the championship in Greenwood, with 4,000 people waiting in the stands, Gentleman Joe delivered the best speech of all. *"Gentlemen,"* he said, using that staple designation which earned him his nickname, "I'm just a simple farmer. Fifteen acres is all I got, and two mules, a cow, and a lot of mouths to feed." He paused between his words, and his eyes watered over. "I've neglected my little crop because of this team, and the weevils gave me trouble last year, and they're doin' it again now. I ain't had enough rain, and I don't plan to get much more. The corn looks so brown, if it got another shade browner it'd flake right off. But almost every afternoon you'd find me in my pickup on the way to town to teach you gentlemen the game of baseball. You're fine Christian gentlemen who don't come no finer. But I saw you gettin' a little lazy yestiddy, showin' off some to all them cute little delta girls in the bleachers. We didn't come way up here to show off, we come up here to *win!*" Then, his pale blue eyes flashing fire, half whispering and half shouting, he said: "Gentlemen, I want us to pray, and then . . . I want you to go out there on that field and win this Miss'ippi championship! You'll be proud of it for the rest of your lives. You'll remember it when you're ole men. You'll think about it when you're dyin' and your teeth are all gone. You'll be able to tell your grandchildren about this day. Go out there, gentlemen, and *win this ball game for your coach!*" After we prayed, and headed for that field like a pack of wild animals, the third baseman and I shouted in unison, and we meant it: "Boys, let's get out and win for our *coach!*" That fall they gave us shiny blue jackets, with "Miss. State Champions" written on the back; I was so happy with that jacket I almost wore it out. And when my old dog Skip died of a heart-attack trying to outflank a flea that had plagued him since the Roosevelt Administration, looking at me with his sad black eyes and expiring in a sigh as old as death, that is what I wrapped him in before I took him in my arms and put him in the ground.

Two or three years later, when we were past the age for Legion competition, I had my last confrontation with baseball. The owner of the tire store organized a semi-pro team, made up of college and high school players from around the state. There was a popular tire that year called the "Screaming Eagle," and thus we were the Yazoo "Screaming Eagles," the pride of the delta. Out of a roster of fourteen, one made it to the major leagues, one to a Triple-A league, and two to Double-A. That team won the Deep South championship, and at the national tournament in Wichita beat the U. S. Navy and ended up close to the top.

The state league we played in, making $25 or $30 apiece a game, was composed of both delta and hill-country towns, and we played to big Saturday night crowds who had heard about the Screaming Eagles, under lights so faulty that it was difficult to see a ball coming at you in the outfield. Insects bigger than fifty-cent pieces caromed off the bulbs and zoomed around us in our isolated stations in the field, and the ground was full of holes, ruts, and countless other hazards. Playing center field one night in one of the hill towns, I went back to examine a sloping red mound of earth that served as the outfield fence; I discovered a strand of barbed wire eight or ten feet long, an old garbage can full of broken beer bottles, and a narrow hole, partially covered with Johnson grass, that looked as if it might be the home for the local rattlers. The most indigenous field of all was near a little delta town called Silver City. It was built right on a cottonfield and was owned by the two young heirs to the plantation on which it sat, one of whom later made it all the way to the New York Yankees. The grandstand would seat close to 2,000 people, but the lights were so bad you had to exert all your finer perceptions to discriminate between the bugs and the balls; this took genius, and tested one's natural instincts. It was here, in the state finals, that a sinking line drive came toward me in right field, with the bases loaded and two out in the first inning; I lost track of that ball the moment it came out of the infield. A second later I felt a sharp blow on my kneecap, and then I saw the ball bouncing thirty feet away over by the bleachers. "*Get* it boy! Stomp on it! Piss on it!" the enemy bleacher section shouted gleefully, and by the time I could retrieve it three runs had scored. Between innings our pitcher, who soon would be pitching in the major leagues for the Pittsburgh Pirates, looked at me wordlessly, but with a vicious and despairing contempt. Right then, with the world before me, I promised myself that if I ever made it to those mythical cities of the North, the ones I had dreamed about in my Brooklyn cap, it would have to be with a different set of credentials.

## The Anxious Fields of Play

By the mid-'30s, when I was 10 or 11, baseball had become such an obsession that I imagined ball parks everywhere. In the country, I visualized games in progress on the real grass cattle were eating. In the city as I rode down Fourth Avenue on the bus, the walls of warehouses became outfield fences with dramatic doubles and triples booming off them. Hitting was important in my fantasies. Pitching meant little except as a service necessary for some long drive far beyond the outfielders. I kept the parks small in my mind so home runs wouldn't be too difficult to hit.

The lot across the street from my grandparents' house was vacant and whenever I could get enough neighborhood friends to join me we'd have a game there. In center field a high board fence bounded the west side of the Noraines' backyard. It was about 100 feet from the worn spot we called home plate. The right field fence, a good 40 feet away at the imagined foul line, ran east and bordered the north side of the Brockerman's yard. "Over the fence," I yelled, "is a home run." "Over the fence," said Mr. Brockerman from his yard, hoping to keep his windows intact, "is out." "It's our game and we can make the rules, and besides you can't even get a job," I yelled back. It was a cruel remark. The depression was on and my grandfather was the only man in the neighborhood who had steady work. A few years later when I was old enough to realize the hopeless state of things for men during the depression, I wanted to apologize to Mr. Brockerman, but he had long since moved away. No left field fence. Just some trees and the ground of the Burns' yard, looking more trampled than the ferns and grass of the vacant lot.

One evening the men in the neighborhood joined us for a game. I was so excited, I bubbled. Growing up with my grandparents, I missed the vitality of a young father. I ran about the field loudly picking all the men for my team. My hopes for a dynasty were shattered when a grown-up explained that we might have a better game if we chose even sides. Days after, I trudged about the neighborhood asking the fathers if they would play ball again, but no luck.

When my grandparents had the basement put in, a concrete full-sized basement replacing the small dirt cave where Grandmother had kept her preserves, a pile of gravel was left on the north side of the house. Our house was the only house on that side of the block and in my mind the woods to the north became a baseball field. The rocks—smooth, round, averaging about the size of a quarter—were perfect for my purpose.

I fashioned a bat by carving a handle on a one-by-four and I played out entire nine-inning games, throwing the rocks up and swatting them into and over the trees. Third base was a willow tree. Second base was (I knew exactly in my mind) just beyond the honeysuckle and the giant hollow stump that usually held a pool of rainwater inside its slick mossed walls. Many times that pool reflected the world and my face back at me in solitary moments. First base, not really important because I seldom hit rocks that way, was vaguely a clump of alders.

I knew exactly how far a rock had to sail to be a home run. It had to clear the fence I dreamed beyond the woods. My games were always dramatic and ended with a home run, bases loaded, three runs down, two out, the count three and two, bottom of the ninth. How did I manage that? It was easy. I could control my hits well enough to hit three singles to load the bases because my notion of what constituted a single was flexible. Then I'd select a rock whose size and shape indicated it might sail well, and clobber it. If, for some reason, it didn't sail far enough to be a home run, I simply tried again.

Inning after inning, I swatted rock outs, rock singles, rock doubles, rock triples, and rock home runs. I was the Yankees and also my opponents, the Giants. The only major league ball I heard was the World Series. It was carried on the radio and the Yankees were usually playing. The Yankees also had the most glamorous stars. Sometimes I played out the entire series, all seven, letting the Giants win three. The score mounted. The lead changed hands. Then the last of the ninth, when Babe Ruth, Lou Gehrig, or Joe DiMaggio broke it up. I don't remember now if Ruth still played with New York when DiMaggio joined the team but on my Yankees they were teammates.

One game, the dramatic situation in the ninth, a strong wind was blowing, as usual from the south. I tossed a flat round stone, perfect for sailing and caught it just right. I still can see it climb and feel my disbelief. It soared out over the trees, turned over once, and started to climb like a determined bird. I couldn't have imagined I'd ever hit one that far. It was lovely. It rose and rose. I thought it might never stop riding that high wind north. It crossed the imaginary left field fence before its flight became an aesthetic matter, and it disappeared, a dot, still climbing, somewhere over Rossner's store on the corner of 16th and Barton. I believe that rock traveled about two blocks. Why not? Joe DiMaggio had hit it.

I couldn't see the neighborhood beyond the trees. I simply drove the rocks out over the woods and imagined the rest, though sometimes I heard doubles rattle off the sides and roof of the community hall in center field just beyond the woods. A few years later I realized how dangerous my Yankees had been, spraying stones about the neighborhood. During my absence in World War II, the woods were wiped out by new housing.

One Sunday I left the house to play off somewhere and so was gone when my Uncle Lester from Tacoma showed up without warning to see if

I wanted to go with him to watch the Seattle Indians play in the Pacific Coast League. When I got home and found I'd missed the chance, I wept bitterly and whined against the fates. I was still whining and sobbing when my uncle returned on his way back home. He must have been touched by my disappointment because he returned the following Sunday and this time I was ready. It was kind of him. He saw that I was a bored, lonely boy. Grandfather had few passions outside of the house and the yard, and no interest in baseball.

When I was old enough and had some money, I went to the Sunday doubleheaders alone, catching a bus downtown and transferring to a trolley—an hour-long trip from White Center. I was there by 10 o'clock when the park opened and waited for the players to arrive. I collected autographs of course and saw several stars on their way to the big leagues, including Ted Williams who was hitting around .260 with San Diego. I took it all in, hitting practice, infield practice, then the two games. I went filled with anticipation, heart pounding, but I sat, untypically for someone my age, quietly in the stands watching the game. Recently my Aunt Dol, Lester's widow, told me that in church I would sit so quietly for a small boy that people remarked on it. I can remember that despite my nervousness and anxiety, I also had moments when I was unusually patient and quiet. I could wait for hours with nothing to do. Given the drabness of life with my grandparents, I had developed ways of entertaining myself in my mind.

In 1936, I was a seventh grader and a substitute on the Highland Park Softball Team. That was something. Seldom did anyone but an eighth grader make the team, even as a sub. "You can beat eggs. You can beat cream. But you can't beat Highland Park's Softball Team." That was our yell, and the vowel repeat of "beat cream" intrigued me even then. The last game of that season, Mr. Fields, the coach, sent me in to pinch hit. I was 12 and had never been in a league game before. I was excited and frightened and people seemed to swirl, the other players, Mr. Fields, and Miss Shaefer, our other coach. My hero, Buss Mandin, our star pitcher, was watching. The world was watching. The pitcher was no longer another boy, he was a stranger from another universe. The ball came, surely too fast for any mortal to hit, yet as slow as if dreamed. I don't remember swinging. The bat seemed to swing itself and I saw the ball lining over the shortstop hole into left field, a clean single. Mandin, Fields, and Shaefer smiled approval from the sidelines as I held first. I had found a way of gaining the attention and approval of others and I was not to let it go for nearly 30 years.

In the eighth grade next year, I was the softball team catcher. Ralph Lewin, a short thick powerful boy, was the pitcher. He was good. I was good too and not afraid of the bat—a consideration at that age. I crouched quite close to the hitter and didn't flinch when he swung. Actually, the closer you squat to the batter the easier catching is.

One night Ralph and I were at Betty Moore's house. She was the cutest girl in school and somehow I was supposed to be "with her." We were on a sun porch, the three of us, all 13 years old. Betty's older brother and another boy his age had girls in the darkened front room and were necking. Ralph urged me to kiss Betty but I was far too scared. He said to me, with disdain, "This is what you do," and he kissed her. I tried to keep my composure and I said, "Oh, is that it?" or something like that and humiliation flooded my stomach. They went on necking. I had never seen a man kiss a woman before except in the movies, and I'm not putting anyone on when I say that I really thought people kissed only in films. I can never remember being kissed as a child nor did I ever see any show of affection between my grandparents. I walked out, my face flushed with shame, through the dark living room where one of the older boys yelled some insult at me, and finally after years of groping, into the fresh air outside, free and alone. I walked the mile home, degraded and in anguish, and as I cried my tears created a secondary glow around the streetlights. I wanted to be like Ralph Lewin, like Betty Moore's brother, like anybody else. At home, my grandparents were already asleep, and I sat alone, as I did so many times in that still house, and stared into the solitary void I was certain would be my life.

But on the ballfield, Ralph and I were social equals. One day we played the alumni, now freshmen and sophomores in high school, and I struck out, fooled badly on a change of pace. The fans laughed. Maybe I couldn't do anything about the humiliation I'd suffered in Betty Moore's house, but I could do something about it on the ballfield. I promised myself no one would ever fool me again on a change of pace, and I kept my promise. I developed a technique of hitting late, of starting my swing at the last possible moment to avoid being tricked. Nearly all my hits for the next 30 years were to my off field, right field. Over the years whenever players asked me why I hit to right and never pulled the ball, I told them a half truth. I said I hit better to right field. That was true. When I hit to left, I tended to grind the ball into the dirt. But I never told them the real reason.

That final year in grammar school we won the championship of our league in an extra inning game against E. C. Hughes. They had beaten us out of the soccer championship in an overtime game just a few months before and the softball win felt good. I looked to the city play-offs with confidence. In my small world, how could any team be better than ours? Our first play-off game we were defeated by a team of seven Orientals, two blacks, and a tall Jewish short fielder by the score of 14 to 0. Despite my working-class background I was lucky to grow up knowing prejudice was wrong, but I remember thinking then that minority people possessed some sort of magic.

My hitting was my ticket to acceptance. That first summer out of grammar school, I spent with my mother in Bremerton and I joined a softball team. The opening game was played in a pasture, very like the pastures I'd imagined into ballfields years before, and I hit a single, a double, a triple, and two home runs. My standing with the other boys, strangers just a few days before, was insured. The summer was mine.

After that I turned to hardball for several years. In the Park League I began as a pitcher but one day a shower of triples and home runs convinced me that either second base or the outfield was where I really belonged. The summer I was 14 I played second base on the Boulevard Park Merchants. All the other players were adults except for my buddy, George Zimmerman, who lived in Boulevard Park and had me try out for the team. I also made the American Legion Team in West Seattle and hit around .350 for the season.

Often a ball game gave me confidence I could find nowhere else. Once, playing center field in a Park League game when I was around 15, I memorized the lineup of the opposing team, and in the last inning, score 2 to 1 in our favor and the other team threatening with men on base and two out, I detected a player batting out of turn. The umpire checked and called the batter out.

In high school, though I made the squad all four years, I spent three of them on the bench. I knew the coach, Lloyd Doty, was reluctant not only to cut pitchers but even to try to distinguish between pitchers and players who called themselves pitchers. So I hung in there calling myself a pitcher and became a batting practice ace. Park League experience had taught me three things about my pitching. One, I had exceptional control for a boy; two, I was easy to hit; three, when I was hit, the ball went a hell of a long way. I was indispensable to the morale of the starting hitters. "Just throw your fast ball, Richard," Coach Doty said.

In my senior year, a starting outfielder was caught burglarizing a clothing store and was sent up for a year. I declared myself an outfielder and played every game in right field. I had a miserable season, made errors, failed to hit consistently. My desire for acceptance was so overwhelming in high school that out in the field or at bat I was dizzy with tension and fear of failing in front of the students. I remember I played better when we were away at other schools.

I played semipro ball in the city leagues after that and did well. Just after I turned 19, I was called into the service. In the army, the chances to play were few, and I seized them when they came. I remember playing second with some sharp players, one of them a professional, at Logan, Utah, where we held infield drills on the Utah State campus quadrangle. I put everything into it, whipping the final throw of each infield round from second to home in a taut rope that sang through the thin mountain air as the spectators gasped. I remember playing third base in a monastery courtyard at the Army Air Corps rest camp on Capri, while the monks and a Red Cross girl with gorgeous legs looked on. I did not relax on a ballfield. I always played my best no matter how makeshift the game.

I was discharged in June of '45, and I immediately joined a semipro team in the city league. It was clear to me by then that I was fouled up sexually and I was drinking more and more. I even played a game drunk and hit a triple far over the right fielder's head. I ended up at third base gagging. The run had made me sick and the manager took me out.

I turned out for the University of Washington team in the spring of '46, and made the squad for a few weeks until I was caught playing intramural softball and cut. That summer I played on another semipro team but was told to get out by the grim manager after the fourth game when I made the mistake of trying to joke with him after we'd lost a close one. That hurt, the sudden hostile and permanent rejection when I was only trying to be friendly. I remember saying good-bye to one of the players, and though I barely knew him, I was close to tears. I felt I was losing something I loved, and with my life so void of satisfaction, the loss seemed monumental. The good-bye I was saying to whoever that player was seemed a big good-bye to many things.

I went to school, off and on, majoring in creative writing but tiring badly after three or four quarters. Then I'd go out and find a menial job somewhere. I worked in warehouses and at a steel mill, then in California at an ammunition magazine. In the summer of '47, I went back to softball, to a team in West Seattle. Several members were old friends from high school, and they were good players. I came to the team after the season started and it took awhile before I got into the lineup but by the end of the season I was the catcher. It felt good, crouching close to the batter as Jimmy Gifford's pitches broke past the batter into my glove for the third strike, and I wheeled the ball down to Ed Schmidt at first base to start the infield throw around.

For the next 13 years, I played softball in the West Seattle Class A League. The first year we lost the championship to a veteran team, the West Seattle Auto Dealers, in a play-off game. But we had the nucleus of a good team, as well as the camaraderie of young men who had known each other for several years, and in 1948 we became the power of the league. By then, I had studied two quarters with Theodore Roethke and was working on poems at home in the evening, when I wasn't out drinking. I was still living with my grandparents who were nearing the end. With no sex life, there seemed little reason for me to move out. I was frozen, a perpetual 15, but after a bad two or three years, I was playing ball again and loving it. My appetite for acceptance, for the approval of others was satisfied on the ballfields, if nowhere else.

Ken Gifford, Jim's brother, and one of my high school chums, played third base. John Popich, four or five years younger than Gifford and myself, played shortstop, and his cousin, Walt, about my age, played second. Ed Schmidt, also a high school friend, played first. That was the nucleus of the team. When Jim Gifford went to Seattle University to play basketball and pitch softball, Mimo Campagnaro, a strange hypochondriac who threw best on those days he complained of a wrenched back or a devastating headache, became our pitcher. Stinkey Johnson, another high school friend, was the backup pitcher to Mimo. For years, it was like we were still kids, or so it seemed to one of us.

The last scheduled game of the season in 1948, we found ourselves again playing the West Seattle Auto Dealers. We were tied in the standings for first place, so again the championship was on the line. With two out and the tying run on second in the last of the seventh, I drilled a single up the middle to send the game into extra innings. (Oh, Joe DiMaggio.) Ed Schmidt was managing and, though not a demonstrative man, he couldn't hide his delight in the first base coaching box. We won in the bottom of the eighth.

I remained after the others went home. Dark clouds were moving in from the southwest. The field seemed lonely and forlorn, abandoned to the dusk. I luxuriated in the memory of the game just completed, and in some odd way I felt at one with the field deserted to the wind. Several times, I visited ballfields in the fall and winter and sat alone in the car remembering some game I'd played there, as the rain fell or leaves blew across the empty grounds.

I cultivated a casual, joking attitude on the field to hide the seriousness with which I took each game. But I betrayed that seriousness by showing up earlier than the others and sitting around the park alone waiting for the equipment to arrive. Whenever players were late, I kept an anxious lookout. (Two more and we'll have nine and won't have to forfeit.) I took that anxiety into the batter's box. I doubt that in those nearly 30 years of ball, I ever batted relaxed. Because hitting was so important, I developed ways of countering my anxiety. I managed to remove any idea of competition from my mind by ignoring the pitcher as a human being until he vanished and only the ball remained. If I was aware of the pitcher as a man, I was finished.

John Popich was just the opposite. He had to hate the opposition. "Let's beat these bastards," he would say without one touch of humor. He grew up in Riverside, where West Marginal Way parallels the Duwamish River, the son of Yugoslavian immigrants, and life for him was an endless fight. Like most of those who grew up in Riverside, he had moved to middle-class West Seattle. I think he suffered conflicts that many children of immigrants do: the society pulling him one way, his loyalty to his heritage pulling him the other. He often spoke with fondness of Yugoslavian dishes his mother prepared. And he insisted, perhaps too much, on poking fun at the Italians on the team—Mimo and his brother Freddie; Robert Rimpini, an outfielder; and Morrie Capalato, another outfielder, Italian-Jewish by background, who owned a small grocery in Alki. Popich's remarks usually implied the superiority of Yugoslavs. His cousin Walt, from the same area and circumstances, but emotionally far less complicated, suffered little conflict. When he spoke of Riverside, which he had left behind for good, it was usually as "those people."

Physically, John was easily the most gifted player on the team—fast, unusually strong, well coordinated. From his shortstop position, he fired accurate cannon shots at Schmidt who took them easily in his cool, unhurried way as if they were easy tosses. Popich had one failing that prevented him from realizing his potential. He couldn't adjust his aggressive instincts to conditions. One game, he flew out every time up trying to power the ball against a hopelessly stiff wind. With Schmidt's cool, he could have played professional baseball.

One game, at Alki Field, I was run over in a play at home. That was the one play I hated. It is always open season on the catcher, and later, during my last four or five years, I gave up blocking the plate and started tagging runners like a third baseman, flashing in once with my hands and getting out of there. This time, I made the mistake of taking Popich's streaking relay squatting on my haunches. The ball and runner arrived at the same time and the runner, seeing how vulnerable I was, ran me down. His knee crashed into my head and I rolled back, green stars exploding. I remember lying there on the plate, holding the ball for a moment before my right hand involuntarily relaxed and the ball dribbled out. I was taken out, of course. I had double vision and my right arm ached from a stretched nerve trunk, a neuritis that stayed with me for three months. The run tied the game.

In the last of the seventh, Popich hit the longest home run I've seen in softball. The bases were loaded at the time, and the ball went far over the head of Jack Marshall, a fast young left fielder. It must have landed 150 feet beyond him as he ran back and he had already been playing deep. I believe it would have cleared many left field fences in baseball parks. With my double vision, I saw two unbelievable drives sailing over two Jack Marshalls, and eight runners scoring.

Popich's home runs were raw power, shots that seemed to take less than a second in flight. Schmidt's were just the opposite. In one game, he unloaded two home runs and with his classic swing the balls didn't seem hard hit at all. They soared slowly like lazy birds, beautiful to watch, like the rock I'd hit that day. Popich batted third, Schmidt fourth, and I followed, swinging the bat like I was swatting off demons, driving the ball late into right field. Despite our hitting, we were primarily a defensive team. In a typical game, we would grab an early lead, then play flawless defensive ball. Once we got the lead we seldom added to it. We concentrated on defense as if we considered the game already won. Usually, it was.

Most of the others were married and getting on with their lives. I took the score book home and computed averages. When I listened to professional games on the radio, I often lined out a score sheet on a piece of paper, using the blunt back edge of Grandmother's bread knife for a rule, and scored the entire game sitting alone at the table in the kitchen. I watched my dissolute life passing. Sometimes with anger and resentment that exploded into verbal abuse of friends when I was drunk and filled me with shame the next day when, terrified I'd end up friendless and alone, I made embarrassed apologies. Sometimes with frustration when I refused to admit my defeat and sought out women only to find myself unable to conquer my timidity. But mostly with sadness and the intense love of simple compensations like softball and fishing.

One day, before a game, at Lincoln Park, I'd come early as usual, and was sitting in the grass near some boys in their middle teens. They were talking about girls and chewing the tender root ends of grass blades. "Sharon's easy," one of them said, "Jesus, she's easy." He was smiling. Ten years younger than I was, and already they knew more about life than I believed I ever would. I looked away through the trees at the sea. Somewhere out there beyond me was a life of normalcy and I was certain I would never be a part of it. It was farther than the islands I could see. It was beyond reach. It was a sad moment and I wanted the players to come and the game to begin.

Within a few years we had become a smooth, balanced team. Jim Gifford came back. He was now one of the best throwers in Seattle and could have pitched AA ball. Gordon Urquhart replaced Walt Popich at second base and we formed the best team I've ever played on. Urquhart and I managed the team, or rather I should say Urquhart managed the team on the field and I planned strategy with him over a beer at our sponsor's place, the Blew Eagle Cafe. The strange spelling occurred during the depression. Gino, the original owner, first named it the Blue Eagle Cafe, but when the Roosevelt administration launched the National Recovery Act in the early '30s, it adapted as its symbol a blue eagle. Every time a radio announcer said, "Look for a blue eagle," Gino got free advertising. The government insisted he comply with some law by changing the name, but Gino complied only by changing the spelling. The possibilities for obscenity were too good to pass up.

We went through the league undefeated, the first team to do it since the '20s, and that season I played in the most perfectly played game I can remember. Neither side made a mistake. Jim Gifford threw a no-hitter. The opposing pitcher threw a two-hitter. We won late in the game on a triple by our center fielder, Jim Burroughs, and an infield out. I remember it well because it again reflected the way I felt about things in general and my poems in particular. If something was good in itself, well done, it made no difference whether it was important or not, nor whether it had an audience. Here was a game in a Class A softball league at Alki Field in a city in the Far West, one of thousands of such games going on all over the country with practically no one watching, and yet the game itself had been played with a perfection that to me made it important. I was constantly looking for perfection in my poems. It was a handicap really, because in my drive for perfection I rewrote poems completely out of existence. I was blind to all the mistakes I can see there now, but had I seen them then, I would have rewritten again and again until the mistake was gone. And while I didn't realize it then, the reason I had to rewrite so much was that making real changes was so difficult. Each rewrite was almost the same thing over, done with the hope something would change and that, in turn, would trigger other changes that would finally result in a perfect unit of sound. My perfectionism was really a symptom of stagnation. No matter how I tried, my poems, like my life, were going nowhere. Later I tried to handle this theme in a long poem called "Duwamish Head." That's where the Duwamish is backed up by the sea and no longer seems to flow.

Gordon Urquhart was the most interesting person I played ball with. By lucky accident we found ourselves working together at Boeing and I got to know him well. He surmounted setbacks and adversity with a resiliency I found monumental and he had a great sense of humor. He had been a marine NCO in Korea in an outfit overrun by the Chinese. He found himself one night standing in the dark, firing wildly as Chinese soldiers in bewildering numbers rushed by all around him. He was hit in the leg and, typical of him, took charge of the survivors he could find the next morning and led them back to safety, hobbling on his wounded leg.

He loved his wife and she died, strangled in an asthmatic seizure while he held her, help on the way too late. I remember the voice over the intercom at work telling him to call home and his hurried departure. I offered my awkward condolences a few days later when he returned. "Yes," he said, "it was a shock." He was most composed and his grief never surfaced, despite his emotional honesty. Later, he remarried and went on his undestructible way. An alder. A catfish. Those were my two private nicknames for masters of survival.

Gordon loathed the idea of privileged people, people on top. He used to say sarcastically, "What's happening to your precious Yankees?" when they were losing. He also hated Sugar Ray Robinson, and was outraged when Robinson got a championship fight against Bobo Olson, while Tiger Jones, who had beaten Robinson, was ignored. Of course, I loved Robinson and the Yankees because they had class, which, to paraphrase Henry Reed, in my case I had not got. Like my grandfather, who identified with Henry Ford, I appreciated the most successful, especially those who had what I thought of as style—those who won and looked good doing it. Urquhart was a winner who identified with the underprivileged, but only those who tried. (In my poems, I was on the side of the losers who lived their defeat.)

Urquhart's hatred of privilege was so intense, I think his own drive for success must have involved some conflict. I even imagine he may have disliked himself for it. The first time I met his father, he told me with undisguised bitterness that Roosevelt had broken him. I didn't get the story clear, but it seemed to involve large holdings of beef Mr. Urquhart had had in Montana in the '30s, a situation sure to profit him considerably until the federal government had made beef available at low prices or for free to the poor. Something like that, as I remember. This seemed to have ruined him for good, because he still dwelled on it with considerable anger despite the years that had gone by. I remember I was bewildered by it because my world was so small and immediate that to hate Roosevelt years after his death seemed a little like being pissed off at Xerxes.

Whatever Urquhart's relation was with his father, it must have involved intense attitudes about success and failure. When Robinson knocked out Gene Fullmer, I was delighted. Urquhart, of course, was furious and suggested at lunch the next day that New York money had bought Fullmer to take a dive. Fullmer was Urquhart: without style or grace, tough and aggressive, and probably most important, from a remote area where he could not benefit from the New York publicity centers. Urquhart had moved to Seattle from eastern Montana. Like Fullmer, he was a fighter from the moon. Urquhart was assailing Robinson, when I said, unexpectedly (even I didn't expect it and had I thought about it probably wouldn't have said it), "Isn't what you really don't like about him is that he is a success?"

I might have accused him of murder. He was stunned and flashed into anger. I could have crawled away and died. I apologized later for the obvious hurt he had felt but he was still angry and accepted my apology with something less than graciousness. Some people may think it odd that I would apologize when his anger demonstrated I was probably right. Let them. One of my favorite quotes is Valéry's: "I can't think of anything worse than being right."

Urquhart had little natural ability. He looked terrible in practice. He booted grounder after grounder. Made bad throws. He could never have made any team as good as ours had we not known how good he was once the game started. I never remember Gordon making an error in a game, and although not a consistent hitter, he seldom failed when it counted. Unlike most softball players he took his competitive instincts to his job and I've heard he has risen quite high in the Boeing company. I dare say he did it on plenty of hard work and guts, clawing away, refusing to be beaten. He lacked the physical gifts of Popich, the fast reflexes of Ken Gifford, or the cool smoothness of Schmidt. Yet, more than anyone on the team, he was responsible for the best season we had. I find it hard to think of him in a high executive position. He was never good at hiding his feelings, an honesty not usually found in corporate executives. I can't imagine him as cold or manipulative, or anything really but a nice, tough, and resilient man. I remember him vividly because we played ball together. That was our link. We both loved playing, he with his honest intensity, and I with my intensity hidden behind my jokes because I knew if it surfaced it would ruin my ability to play.

Years after I was finally able to have sexual relations with women, I continued to play ball, both in the West Seattle League and in the Boeing League (employees only). Our West Seattle team got old, like that team we had first beaten out for the championship, and we found ourselves coming in second more often than first in the league. I published some painting poems in *Contact*, one of the best of the early West Coast magazines, and for the picture on the cover sent in a photo of myself in a Boeing All-Star softball shirt. I took a kind of perverse delight (still do) in not looking like a poet, and I enjoyed appearing on the cover looking like a jock alongside the pictures of the other contributors, some of them terribly affected shots (face half hidden by smoke in the coffeehouse gloom), when inside the magazine my poems, with reproductions of the paintings that had triggered them, were by far the artiest items there.

Bob Peterson, the San Francisco poet and now a good friend, was poetry editor. He is also a baseball nut and, I think, entertains fantasies of himself as a star pitcher. When, for the contributor's notes, I sent in my Boeing League-leading batting average of .541 he reduced it to .400. "No one," he said, "would believe .541." "They would if they had seen the pitching," I wrote back. There were younger and much better players on our Boeing team, several of them top players in the city leagues, but they didn't take our games seriously and tried only to see how far they could hit the ball. I was still hitting as intensely as always to right field no matter how absurd the score or weak the opposition.

A friend named Bill Daly pitched for that Boeing team. Bill made a remark one day to Dick Martin, the third baseman, that had a lot of wisdom: "Dick, I was thinking the other day how much time we've put into this game all these years. What if we'd put that time into work, making a living. We'd probably be rich." Bill also pitched against us in the West Seattle League, and though I knew his stuff well, he struck me out one game. He did it with a drop, not too much on it, that came in high and outside and dipped into the strikezone. I'd seen it all the way, saw it drop into my favorite spot, and I never pulled the trigger. (Good-bye, Joe.) I walked away, the message clear, remembering many times I'd slammed that pitch deep into the right center field gap, had seen the outfielders turned and running as I rounded first on my way to a triple or home run. My reflexes were going and I knew it as I sat down and waited for the inning to end. I didn't feel sad. I didn't feel any sense of loss. I didn't feel humiliated at striking out as I once would have, though I was still intensely trying to avoid it. More than just the reflexes had gone.

The only good sports poem I can remember reading was one called "Cobb Would Have Caught It" by Robert Fitzgerald. Whenever I tried to write about baseball or softball, I found myself thinking about the game itself and the poem kept turning into a melodramatic sports story with the winning hit coming at the crucial moment. (Oh, Joe DiMaggio. Oh, beautiful rock sailing downwind high over 16th and Barton.) I was interested in the score, not the words.

In the summer of '72, two of my students were playing softball in Missoula and I started going to the games. I foolishly put my name on the roster one night at the last minute to avoid a forfeit and before the season was over I played four games, a fat middle-aged man standing in the outfield, being eaten by mosquitoes and wishing he could lose 20 years for an hour and a half. My first time at bat in a serious game (serious because the pitcher was throwing hard) I lined a double over the right fielder's head. Anyone else would have had a home run. I hobbled into second just as surprised as the spectators. The last game I played I pulled off a running one-handed catch before a large crowd that went wild. I couldn't believe it when the ball, blurred by sweat and fear, hit my glove and stuck there as I ran full tilt toward the foul line. But now only luck was on my side and luck has a way of running out. I loved those late triumphs but I could also laugh at them.

I took interest in the whole scene, not just the game. Except for those times I was obliged to play to prevent forfeits, I sat in the stands and took note of the spectators as well as the game, of the players' wives and children, of the players from teams not on the field. One night I watched a player's wife play with a small child. It was beautiful. *She* was beautiful, a full, warm woman who radiated affection. I imagined myself coming home to her from work tired and putting my head in her lap. Another wife kept score with intense dedication, marking each play in the book, always with the score, inning, and number of outs ready for anyone who would ask. Though in her 30s and the mother of three children, her flesh looked soft and virginal like that of a high school girl.

The player-spectators who interested me were working people of the old cut, posturing, clowning, awkward, self-conscious, never quite accepting themselves, kidding the players in the field with loud, sometimes crude, always good-natured insults. They drank lots of beer. They also turned me through parts of my life I'd neglected for a long time and I suppose I loved them for that.

I thought again about those tiny worlds I'd lived in with far more desperation than I hoped any of them would ever know. I thought of Ingmar Bergman's film *The Naked Night* (sometimes called *Sawdust and Tinsel*) where the degraded protagonist and his wife have finally only each other with whom to face an arrogant humiliating world. How the crutch we once needed to hobble through life remains in our closet long after our leg has healed. How Gordon Urquhart could fight through his setbacks and his complicated attitudes about life to a kind of success while my best hope of avoiding defeat was to turn values around with words, to change loss into victory. How John Popich came to the field with his physical gifts, hoping in seven innings to win the battle he would probably never win. How failures are in many ways successes and how successful people, those who early in life accepted adult values and abandoned the harmless fields of play, are really failures because they never come to know the vital worth of human relationships, even if it takes the lines of a softball field to give them a frame. How, without play, many people sense too often and too immediately their impending doom. After nearly 30 years of writing, I was ready to try a softball poem.

### Missoula Softball Tournament

This summer, most friends out of town
and no wind playing flash and dazzle
in the cottonwoods, music of the Clark Fork stale,
I've gone back to the old ways of defeat,
the softball field, familiar dust and thud,
pitcher winging drops and rises, and wives,
the beautiful wives in the stands, basic, used,
screeching runners home, infants unattended
in the dirt. A long triple sails into right center.
Two men on. Shouts from dugout: go, Ron, go.
Life is better run from. Distance to the fence,
both foul lines and dead center, is displayed.

I try to steal the tricky manager's signs.
Is hit-and-run the pulling of the ear?
The ump gives pitchers too much low inside.
Injustice? Fraud? Ancient problems focus
in the heat. Bad hop on routine grounder.
Close play missed by the team you want to win.
Players from the first game, high on beer,
ride players in the field. Their laughter
falls short of the wall. Under lights, the moths
are momentary stars, and wives, the beautiful wives
in the stands now take the interest they once feigned,
oh, long ago, their marriage just begun, years
of helping husbands feel important just begun,
the scrimping, the anger brought home evenings
from degrading jobs. This poem goes out to them.
Is steal-of-home the touching of the heart?

Last pitch. A soft fly. A can of corn
the players say. Routine, like mornings,

like the week. They shake hands on the mound.
Nice grab on that shot to left. Good game. Good game.
Dust rotates in their headlight beams.
The wives, the beautiful wives are with their men.

It struck me as a crude poem and for a while I didn't like it. It seems to be discussing its own meaning. But one day, I came to believe that the crudeness was right, at least for that poem.

The summer of '73 I returned again to watch a few games. It was pleasant saying hello to a lot of nice people, most of whom ask little from life or from others. A few inquired if I was going to play again and I told them not a chance, but I felt a little proud that they had asked. One night a big husky girl, who played on one of the women's teams in town, brought a group of handicapped young people to watch one of the men's games. Some of them seemed retarded, others afflicted with physical and neurological problems. From all I've written here, I should not have to explain the following villanelle I finished a few months ago.

### The Freaks at Spurgin Road Field

The dim boy claps because the others clap.
The polite word, handicapped, is muttered in the stands.
Isn't it wrong, the way the mind moves back.

One whole day I sit, contrite, dirt, L.A.
Union Station, '46, sweating through last night.
The dim boy claps because the others clap.

Score, 5 to 3. Pitcher fading badly in the heat.
Isn't it wrong to be or not be spastic?
Isn't it wrong, the way the mind moves back.

I'm laughing at a neighbor girl beaten to scream
by a savage father and I'm ashamed to look.
The dim boy claps because the others clap.

The score is always close, the rally always short.
I've left more wreckage than a quake.
Isn't it wrong, the way the mind moves back.

The afflicted never cheer in unison.
Isn't it wrong, the way the mind moves back
to stammering pastures where the picnic should have worked.
The dim boy claps because the others clap.

I think when I played softball I was telling the world and myself that futile as my life seemed I still wanted to live.

# 5

# Rhythms and Forms

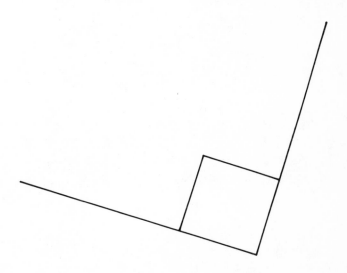

A BASE BALL GAME IN FULL SWING

**RICHARD HUGO**

## Letter to Mantsch from Havre

Dear Mike: We didn't have a chance. Our starter had no change
and second base had not been plugged since early in July.
How this town turned out opening night of the tournament
to watch their Valley Furniture team wipe us, the No-
Name Tavern of Missoula, out. Remember Monty Holden,
ace Havre pitcher, barber, hero of the Highline, and his
tricky "catch-this" windup? First inning, when you hit that shot,
one on, the stands went stone. It still rockets the night.
I imagine it climbing today, somewhere in the universe,
lovelier than a girl climbs on a horse and lovelier than star.
We lost that game. No matter. Won another. Lost again
and went back talking fondly of your four home runs,
triple and single in three games, glowing in the record book.
I came back after poems. They ask me today, here in Havre,
who's that player you brought here years ago, the hitter?
So few of us are good at what we do, and what we do,
well done or not, seems futile. I'm trying to find Monty
Holden's barber shop. I want to tell him style in anything,
pitching, hitting, cutting hair, is worth our trying even
if we fail. And when that style, the graceful compact swing
leaves the home crowd hearing its blood and the ball roars off
in night like determined moon, it is our pleasure
to care about something well done. If he doesn't understand
more than the final score, if he says, "After all, we won,"
I'll know my hair will not look right after he's done,
what little hair I have, what little time. And I'll drive home
knowing his windup was all show, glad I was there years back,
that I was lucky enough to be there when with one swing
you said to all of us, this is how it's done. The ball jumps
from your bat over and over. I want my poems to jump
like that. All poems. I want to say once to a world that feels
with reason it has little chance, well done. That's the lie
I cannot shout loud as this local truth: Well done, Mike. Dick.

## Gentle Reader

*for Larry Eigner*

(out the window)    (across the street)

there is this kid this spade kid
        running, away from me, running a-
cross the asphalt, his keds landing
        on the lines painted on it to
contain the games—over which he
        runs: 250 ft away when
I started this poem & moving
        farther with every word—he runs
without looking
        where he's going; he's looking over
his left shoulder & his left hand is
        rising
on the end of his arm which is
        rising in front of him till he
sticks it out straight & the ball
        which wasn't even headed in his direction
when I started this poem, the ball is
        in his glove, there where he runs, &
I'm there, too, in his glove, & you,
        too, gentle reader, there in his glove,
& he doesn't stop

## Curve Ball

That curveball,
that terrible hummingbird,
dropped over the plate
so soft, *so real,*
like a pear or breast,
striking me out.

I love the pitcher.
I sit on the bench cursing him.

That curveball was the wheel,
was wine, was cooked food,
was Stonehenge.

## Third Base Coach

He commands as mysteriously as
the ghost of Hamlet's father.

Shuffles & tugs & yawns & spits.
Like a steeplejack he itches weirdly and continually.

Dances on his grave plot.
Prophetic flame at the wiped lip.

The fouls go by him like tracer bullets.
Writes runes with his toe, healthy spells.

Like an Aeschylan tragedy he's static; baffling;
Boring; but.

                                        Urgent with import.


## Fast Ball

### for Winthrop Watson

The grass raw and electric
as the cat's whiskers.

3 and 2.

At second the runner: loiters:
nervous as the corner
junkie: loitering for a connection.

Hunched like the cat, the batter;
his prehensile
bat he curls and uncurls.

The pitcher hitches & hitches.

At last the hitcher pitches.

"It gets about as big," Ty
Cobb said, "as a watermelon seed.
It hisses at you as it passes."

The outfielders prance like kittens
back to the dugout.
They've seen what they're glad *they*
don't have to worry about.

## Spitballer

A poet because his hand goes first
to his head & then to his heart.

The catcher accepts the pitch
as a pool receives a dripping diver;
soaks up the curve like
cornflakes in milk.

The hitter makes great
show of wringing out his bat.

On the mound he grins, tiger
in a tree, when the umpire
turns round & round the ball
magically dry as alum.

He draws a second salary as maintenance man.
Since while he pitches he waters the lawn.

## Junk Ball

By the time it gets to the plate
it's got weevils and termites.

Trying to hit Wednesday with a bb gun.

Sunday.

Or curves like a Chippendale leg or
flutters like a film unsprocketed or
plunges like Zsa Zsa's neckline or
sails away as coy as Shirley Temple

(or)

Not even Mussolini could make
the sonofabitch arrive on time.

## Strike Zone

*for Joe Nicholls*

Like the Presidency its size
depends upon the man.

Paneless window he doesn't want to smash,
the pitcher whittles at the casement.

The batter peers
into it like a peeping tom.
Does he like what he sees?

The limits get stricter
as they get less visible:

throwing at yards & yards of McCovey,
an inch or so
of Aparicio,
the pitcher tries not to go
bats.

The umpire knows a secret.
But he gives no sign.

Ball 2.


## JONATHAN HOLDEN

### Hitting Against Mike Cutler

One down. I step into the narrow,
dust-floured shooting gallery, glance
out where the tall right-hander's squint
aims in to size things up. If it were up
to him, he'd take all afternoon he looks so
lazy—a gunslinger who just sauntered
into town, his jaw working over
a forgotten scrap of gum. He spits,
feels up the ball like a small, hard hornet;
and I hear the catcher settle in creaking
leather harness. He clucks contentedly,
does something dirty in his groin. Far
out there on the bright, bare, heat-rippling
hill the big guy nods. The hornet in his hand
begins to buzz. He bows. Slowly he
revolves away, then whirls, draws. I fire back.
The hornet hisses, vanishes with a BANG.  STEE-RIKE!
The catcher grins. Good chuck, good chuck, he clucks.

## How to Play Night Baseball

A pasture is best, freshly
mown so that by the time a grounder's
plowed through all that chewed, spit-out
grass to reach you, the ball
will be bruised with green kisses. Start
in the evening. Come
with a bad sunburn and smelling of chlorine,
water still crackling in your ears.
Play until the ball is khaki—
a movable piece of the twilight—
the girls' bare arms in the bleachers are pale,
and heat lightning jumps in the west. Play
until you can only see pop-ups,
and routine grounders get lost in
the sweet grass for extra bases.

**ROBERT FRANCIS**

## Catch

Two boys uncoached are tossing a poem together,
Overhand, underhand, backhand, sleight of hand, every hand
Teasing with attitudes, latitudes, interludes, altitudes,
High, make him fly off the ground for it, low, make him stoop.
Make him scoop it up, make him as-almost-as-possible miss it,
Fast, let him sting from it, now, now fool him slowly,
Anything, everything tricky, risky, nonchalant,
Anything under the sun to outwit the prosy,
Over the tree and the long sweet cadence down,
Over his head, make him scramble to pick up the meaning,
And now, like a posy, a pretty one plump in his hands.

## The Base Stealer

Poised between going on and back, pulled
Both ways taut like a tightrope-walker,
Fingertips pointing the opposites,
Now bouncing tiptoe like a dropped ball
Or a kid skipping rope, come on, come on,
Running a scattering of steps sidewise,
How he teeters, skitters, tingles, teases,
Taunts them, hovers like an ecstatic bird,
He's only flirting, crowd him, crowd him,
Delicate, delicate, delicate, delicate—now!

## Pitcher

His art is eccentricity, his aim
How not to hit the mark he seems to aim at,

His passion how to avoid the obvious,
His technique how to vary the avoidance.

The others throw to be comprehended. He
Throws to be a moment misunderstood.

Yet not too much. Not errant, arrant, wild,
But every seeming aberration willed.

Not to, yet still, still to communicate
Making the batter understand too late.

# 6

# Skinned Infields

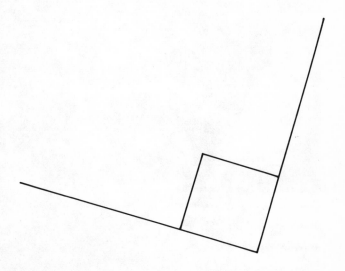

## Big Sky, Big Dream
### *from* A False Spring

I remember first the land. It was flat. Between it and the sky there was nothing—no buildings, no trees, no hills, no shadows—nothing as far as the eye could see but the sun and the sky and never-ending fields of wheat and corn and alfalfa. It was a land of horizons. Occasionally a thin black road parted the fields. The road went straight for miles. There was nothing on either side of it but the fields. As the road and the fields stretched ahead they grew closer and closer together until they converged at a point on the horizon. It was an illusory point that was never reached. It remained always the same distance ahead. Perpetually approaching it, one felt all movement was illusory, too. Only the fields moved, flashing by like scenery in a cheaply made movie. Finally, the illusion was broken by some scraggy trees growing alongside a water hole a few yards off the road. A cow, standing motionless in the shade of the trees, gazed blankly at the road. Beside her lay another cow, her tail switching off flies. Beyond the water hole was a dirt road that branched off from the paved road and led through the fields to a red barn and conical silo. Farther back from the barn, almost a mile from the paved road, was the farm house. It was small and white and cellarless. Each corner of the house rested on cinder blocks. From the paved road a passer-by, were he to look, could see underneath the farmhouse to the thin line of blue horizon visible on the other side.

I had been riding in the taxi for two hours and had seen nothing but an occasional farm and the fields. I had begun to lose all sense of place and direction, of where I'd come from and was going to, had become almost transfixed by the monotony of the land when I saw a sign flash by, *McCook City Limits* and another *Pop. 7687* then, one after another, the welcome-to-McCook signs put up by the Chamber of Commerce and the Masonic Lodge and the Kiwanis and Lions and Elks and Eagles and Rotary clubs. Then nothing for a while until the Calvary Cemetery and the Drive-In Theater, and then a little ways to the A-and-W Root Beer stand and the Phillips 66 Station and, quickly now, the wood-fronted pool hall, the bar, the M-and-E Diner and, turning left onto Main Street, the city of McCook. Inexplicably built on a hill. Main Street rose ahead of us at a 30-degree angle. It was a broad street on which cars were parked diagonally to the curb, still leaving plenty of room for traffic. It was lined on both sides by one- and two-story brick buildings—drugstores and shoe stores and hardware stores—and, moving up the hill, three- and four-story brick buildings—J. C. Penney's and Modrell's Cafe—and, almost at the top where I got off, the tallest building in McCook—the six-story Keystone Hotel. From its entrance I could see down the hill past the stores to the edge of the city about five blocks away. I could see beyond where Main Street stopped, too, out over the city to the surrounding plains. Main Street was a north-south road, and if it had not stopped at the edge of the city but had continued south for about 14 miles, it would have crossed into Kansas. Eighty miles west of Main Street was the Colorado State line. I had come to McCook by way of North Platte, Nebraska, which was 75 miles due north. North Platte was the only city of any consequence within 150 miles of McCook, and it possessed the only commercial airport within 230 miles.

A few yards up the hill from the Keystone, I could see the Fox Movie Theater, and a little further north the McCook YMCA. At the top of the hill was a small, tree-shaded park. There was an old band shell in the middle of the park. Beyond the park were houses. The business section of Main Street stopped at the park and the residential section fanned out east and north and west from there for about half a mile in each direction. Included among its white frame houses were a few churches, three grammar schools, a high school, McCook Junior College, St. Catherine's Hospital, the Municipal Swimming Pool, the McCook Fair Grounds where each July the Red Will County Fair and Rodeo was held, the National Guard Armory that also served as a dressing room for the McCook Braves' baseball team and, about half a mile north of the armory, Cibola Stadium. The city's only lighted baseball park, it was part of the McCook County Fair Grounds. The fair grounds was a flat open field about one-quarter of a mile square located at the northern edge of the city. Beyond it, the plains began. Cibola Stadium was in the southern part of this field closest to the city. It faced north across the fair grounds toward the plains. Its playing surface was separated from the fair grounds only by an unpainted wooden picket fence that curved around the outfield. The field inside that fence was an extension of the field outside. It consisted of rock-hard dirt and scattered clumps of tall dried grasses. Surrounding the playing surface were about a dozen or so telephone poles, on top of which were 20 hooded light bulbs aimed down at the diamond. A 10-foot-high fence of chicken wire separated the field of play from the temporary stands along the firstbase line, behind home plate and along the thirdbase line. All told, the stands seated about 900 people. They were a mere skeleton of permanent stands, consisting of metal supports and 10 inclining rows of long wooden planks. The planks clattered and groaned when stepped or sat on. They were warped and splintered from use and from constant exposure to the elements, the wind and rain and hail and snow, all of which could be seen, at times, forming across the fair grounds on the plains. There was a much smaller section of stands along the left field foul line directly behind a single picnic bench that served as the home team bullpen. Unlike seats in the other stands, which cost 75 cents, the left field seats cost only a quarter. They were reserved for the Mexican and Indian migrant workers who lived in shacks on the outskirts of McCook because they were prohibited from living in the residential section. Behind the left field stands was a small wooden building. This was boarded up during the day, but at night, with a game in progress, it became a refreshment stand on one side and rest rooms on the other. The rest rooms were directly below the highest part of the left field stands and so were always in shadows. The refreshment side was well-lighted and faced an open gravel space that was the stadium's parking lot. This could be entered and exited through only one gate, over which was strung a banner proclaiming Cibola Stadium the home of the McCook Braves of the Nebraska State League.

I have described McCook in detail, not because it was distinctive in any way but because it was distinctive in no way. There was nothing there, really, certainly nothing one couldn't find in hundreds of similar towns throughout the country. Over the next few years I would live in many such towns—Eau Claire, Waycross, Palatka, Bradenton—and for longer periods of time than the two months I spent in McCook. And yet, I remember none of those towns with the clarity of detail I do McCook. Even as I write this, I can see Main Street, the Keystone, the band shell, Cibola. Possibly because McCook was the smallest town in which I would ever play. Since I had no car, I walked everywhere, and within two months I knew every street and store, and even a few people, as one soon does in such a small, isolated town. And it was isolated. No matter where I walked, I came quickly to the town's limits. There was so much openness beyond those limits, so many horizons almost suffocating in their possibilities. The townspeople were confronted daily by this. It had intimidated them. There was too much out there; too many possibilities they would never grasp. And so for them there was nothing out there, nothing beyond the limits of their town, nothing to do, no place to go—except after a two-hour drive across the plains—to another town exactly like the one they'd left.

Living in their town, as I did, I got to know its limits very well. At times I felt, like the townspeople, bound by them. But only at times. Those horizons still had meaning for me, indicated direction. McCook was the first point on the map of my career. It would be a small but important part in my life that would be fulfilled someplace else, at a point further up ahead that would not elude me. I was as positive of this as only a self-absorbed 18-year-old can be. I knew that in years to come McCook would be important as the point where my career began.

Ironically enough, I was right, although for reasons other than I'd anticipated. McCook was a very important part of my life. It still is. In fact, its importance grows in my mind as I write this. It was the first place I lived alone. The life I built there was my own responsibility. I was confronted each day with myriad possibilities—when to eat, what to do, whom to befriend—from which I had to choose. For a brief time I made a pretense of looking to my past for help. I tried to remember what had been expected of me in similar situations. But sometimes the situations I met in McCook were new to me. Nothing from my past applied. So increasingly I turned out of desire and necessity to my own inclinations. What did I think? What did I feel? What did I want? I began to see things—myself and others—through my own eyes. What I saw and what I was is still clear to me today. Much of it is what I am today. The person I was in McCook, however, bore little resemblance to the one I'd been under my watchful and protective family. And yet that new person, whether I liked it or not, was more consistent with my nature than the other had ever been.

It was a warm night, my first in McCook. From my seat on the top row of the stands behind home plate, I saw the McCook Braves run onto the field and the first batter for the North Platte Indians emerge from his dugout. Under Cibola's faint lights, each player was trailed by his shadow. There was a smattering of applause from the fans who filled almost every seat in the park.* It was exciting to know that tomorrow I would be part of this.

As yet, no one knew I was in town. Surrounded by strangers, my anonymity was exciting, too. It allowed me to watch the game with an objectivity that would soon be denied me. Sitting on the plank in front of me was a farmer in bib overalls. He wore a stiff, straw cowboy hat with a tightly curled brim. Through the crown of his hat I could see the curve of the top of his head. Beside him sat his wife and two young sons, their hair

---

* It was Tuesday evening in early July and almost 800 people had come to watch the McCook Braves in their third game of the season. (The NSL, being a rookie league, operated only in July and August of each year. It consisted of six teams: Holdrege (White Sox), Kearney (Yankees), Hastings (Giants), North Platte (Indians), Grand Island (Athletics), McCook (Braves). It was designed specifically for high school and college graduates who had not signed contracts until their classes had been graduated in June.) The Braves were the major source of entertainment for the townspeople and farmers alike. All of the Braves' weekday games were played at night to allow fans to put in a day's work, eat supper and still get to the ball park. Over the summer the Braves would have an average attendance of 700 people per game, about 10 percent of the town's population. This was comparable to the New York Yankees drawing over 700,000 people to each of their games.

dampened and flattened by their mother's hand. She, like her husband, was of indeterminate age. She wore her hair in a ponytail, and when she turned to speak to her husband I could see that the skin at the back of her neck was creased and leathery, like his, although whether from the sun and hard work or age was not clear. She wore a white sleeveless blouse and a long cotton skirt fluffed out by crinolines and resting high on her lap. Every so often she would fold her hands over it and press down gently. The stands were filled with such families, and with teenage girls in Bermuda shorts and teenage boys in Levi's and football jerseys and prosperous-looking merchants in white shirts and ties and sharp-toed cowboy boots. Throughout the game the fans gossiped and talked business and crops and the teenagers flirted in the shadows behind the stands. Occasionally someone clapped at a fine play on the field or shouted at the umpire to the delight of their friends. People were constantly moving up and down the groaning planks, going to the rest rooms or returning from the refreshment stand with hot dogs and cokes.

From my high seat I could see into the left field corner where four Braves' relief pitchers were slouched on the picnic bench in the bullpen. Two of them had turned their backs to the playing field and were talking to some of the Mexicans in the left field stands. Behind those stands I could see the shadows of people waiting in line to get into the rest rooms. Others, mostly children, milled around the refreshment stand. The parking lot was filled with cars, older Fords and Chevys with fender skirts and lowered rear ends. There were some pickup trucks, too, and on their flat beds were dark bundles of dried alfalfa that gave off a sickly-sweet odor.

By the fifth inning the Braves were losing 8–6. It was a typical Class D minor league game, I would learn, filled with energetic but erratic play. A shortstop charged a ground ball and kicked it past the pitcher's mound, then followed with a diving catch in the hole of a line drive. An outfielder got down on one knee to field a ground-ball single and then turned around and ran wildly toward the outfield fence to retrieve the ball, which had rolled through his legs. On the next play that very same outfielder would catch a line drive over his shoulder after having run so deep into the centerfield corner, 420 feet away, that he had outrun the range of the lights and had momentarily disappeared into the darkness. The fans had to wait until the umpire, who had run into the darkness with him, emerged with his fist in the air before they could applaud the catch. The pitchers on both sides were wild and filled the night with bases on balls and wild pitches, and none of them, I noted with satisfaction, threw as hard as I did. When the Braves tied the game in the sixth inning, the fans cheered lustily.

In the seventh inning I felt a cool breeze and heard the sound of gears changing in the parking lot. I noticed that some of the fans had already left. Others were gathering their children, who had been playing underneath the stands, and were herding them toward the parking lot. Soon the breeze grew colder and more forceful, and with it came the hiss of gas escaping from a stove. The hissing came from the fair grounds and was, I discovered, only the rustling of the tall grasses in the wind. I looked out over the darkened fair grounds and saw on the plains an even darker swirling mass rising like a horn of plenty into the sky. The sky was a translucent purple, and the swirling mass was solid and black against it and seemed to be growing larger as it moved toward us. By the time it hit, the stands were all but deserted. Instantly, it rippled the players' uniforms, whirled dust everywhere. Batters stepped out of the box and turned their backs on it. Infielders flattened their gloves against their faces and peeked through the spread fingers until a split-second before the pitcher delivered the ball. At one point a pitcher reared back to throw and a gust of wind blew him off the mound. Both managers stormed out of their dugouts toward the homeplate umpire, and an argument ensued as to whether or not the pitcher should be charged with a balk. Such incidents must not have been rare in the Nebraska State League, for the umpire rendered his decision promptly and the game resumed in the midst of the wind and dust and it did not even stop when the first rain fell. Big, heavy, widely spaced drops, they hit the deserted planks in front of me with a loud splat. Dark splotches appeared in the wood.

In the ninth inning, with the score still tied, I heard a gunshot, and another, and still others coming quickly now, and it wasn't until I heard the tinkling of broken glass and saw thin ribbons of smoke unraveling from the lightpoles that I realized the bulbs were exploding. The growing number of black spaces in the rows of lights that ringed the field began to resemble missing teeth in a huge, gaping mouth. Each time a bulb broke there was a flash and a loud pop and a ribbon of smoke, and below the players shrugged their shoulders about their ears to avoid being cut by falling glass. By the tenth inning the field had darkened considerably, and in the darkness the Braves managed to push across the winning run and the game was over.

It wasn't until the following afternoon when I saw Cibola in the light of day that I realized how far I'd come from County Stadium in Milwaukee. Its shabbiness disheartened me. It was beneath me, I thought. I arrived at the park at noon after having walked almost a mile from town. The sun was high over the fair grounds and my teammates were in the midst of their afternoon workout. The pitchers were playing catch along the third-base line while the other players underwent fielding drills on the diamond.

They wore Milwaukee Braves' uniforms similar to the one I'd worn recently. Six years ago those uniforms had been worn by players on the Milwaukee Braves, five years ago by the Wichita Braves of the Triple-A American Association, four years ago by the Austin Braves of the Double-A Texas League, three years ago by the Jacksonville Braves of the Class A Sally League, and so on down the line until they'd settled, the thinned and yellowed residue of the system, on the backs of the McCook Braves. The uniforms were patched in spots where someone from Austin or Jacksonville or maybe even Milwaukee had broken up a double play or made a diving catch. Many of the tomahawks and numerals had been torn off and not replaced. All that remained to indicate a player's number was a dark shadow on his shirt where the numeral had been. Still, they *were* major league uniforms. Stitched inside the waistband of each pair of pants and on the tail of each shirt was the last name and number of the man who'd first worn them—Spahn 21, Aaron 44, Mathews 41. We always fought for the uniform of the major leaguer we most admired. It didn't matter whether an 18-year-old third baseman was a 40-extra-long and his idol, Eddie Mathews, a 46-stocky. The minor leaguer would tolerate the uniform's ill fit for the sake of whatever talent remained in those dark sweat stains that could never be laundered out. I was the last player to arrive in McCook and I would discover later that someone had mistakenly given Spahnie's uniform to a skinny left-handed pitcher named Dennis Overby. Vernon Bickford's uniform had been saved for me. It was in better condition than the others—almost new—and it fit perfectly.

I stood by the dugout for a while, aware of my teammates' curious glances, and watched my manager, Bill Steinecke, as he stood near home plate and hit ground balls to his fielders. He had been a catcher in the minors for years but had never made it to the major leagues. He had also played professional basketball with "The House of David," a touring team supposedly made up of Orthodox Jews but actually comprised of Gentiles, like Steinecke, who wore a false rabbinical beard for games.

Steinecke, who was in his late fifties, stood about five feet, five inches tall and weighed over 200 pounds, most of which had settled in his stomach and strained against his uniform shirt. He had a pink, shining, hairless face with small blue eyes devoid of eyebrows. He resembled Nikita Khrushchev except for the mouth, which, in Steinecke's case, was a lipless slit. His missing lip line had been redrawn with a brown stain, the result of 30 years of tobacco chewing. There were tiny tracks, like bird tracks, down the front of his uniform shirt. They were made by the tobacco juice that dribbled down his chin whenever he got so excited during a game that he forgot to spit.

Steinecke stood at home plate with a fungo bat in one hand and a baseball in the other. He tossed the baseball into the air in front of him and, grunting fiercely, swung the bat. The ball landed, untouched, at his feet. The infielders, who had hunched forward in anticipation of a double play, relaxed, kicked dirt and resumed their stance. Steinecke's catcher, Joe Shields, picked up the ball and handed it to him. Shields, clean-cut and handsome, had recently been graduated from an Ivy League college and, in the fall, would begin his first year of medical school. For Shields, professional baseball was simply a summer job that would someday enable him to become a doctor. His back-up, who was catching one of the pitchers on the sidelines, was Elrod Hendricks, a black, very limber native of the Virgin Islands. He spoke a rhythmic calypso English that amused Shields, as it did most of the American players. But whereas Shields had received a $20,000 bonus from the Braves, who were ignorant of his future plans, Hendricks had got practically nothing from the Braves, and in fact was released by them within a year. Eventually, he signed with the Baltimore Orioles, for whom he played in two World Series. Shields became a doctor.

Steinecke tossed the ball into the air again, grunted and missed it. The infielders sighed. Steinecke glared at the ball at his feet. "Mother-fucker," he said to it. Shields attempted to pick it up, but Steinecke brushed him aside. Laboriously, the manager got down on one knee and picked up the baseball. He righted himself, using the bat for leverage. He threw the ball into the air again, only this time he swung timidly and the ball trickled toward third base. It stopped before Ron Hunt, a 19-year-old third baseman from St. Louis, Missouri, could reach it. Still, Hunt scooped up the dead ball with the great earnestness that would become his trademark and threw it toward second base. Chuck Carlin snatched it from the air and, in the same motion, flipped it across his chest to first base.

Carlin, a recent graduate of the University of Alabama, was pale and thin and unusually slow-moving off the diamond. He had fine yellow hair and the delicate features one associates with the decadent Southern aristocracy in a Faulkner novel. His wife too, was pale and thin and slow, and only their four-month-old baby seemed to have flesh and vitality. Carlin came to McCook directly from his college campus, and the first person he saw in the Braves' locker room was Bill Stevens, a black outfielder recently graduated from the University of Connecticut. Carlin handed his spikes to Stevens and told him to polish them. "I didn't know," said Carlin later. "I'd never played with them or against them. The only ones I'd ever seen in a locker room were the clubhouse boys."

Carlin's relay was low and had to be scooped out of the dirt by Frank Saia, the 23-year-old first baseman. Saia, also married and a recent father, was a student at Harvard Law School in Cambridge, Massachusetts. Like Shields, he would play professional baseball this summer only as a means to furthering his education. Saia shook the dirt from his glove, spun toward home plate and threw the ball to Shields, who caught it and immediately threw to second. Carl Derr, a shy 20-year-old shortstop from Pennsylvania, caught the ball on the infield grass in front of second and returned it to Shields. Derr, a $22,000 bonus boy as was Hunt, would prove to be one of the most talented of the McCook Braves. And yet, like many such players, he never reached the major leagues, for reasons not apparent to anyone who'd seen him play.

When Steinecke finished with his infielders he waddled out to a spot between second base and the pitcher's mound and began hitting fly balls to his outfielders. Bill Stevens was in left field. He was a muscular, handsome, light-skinned black from Norwalk, Connecticut. Off the diamond he dressed in button-down shirts and crew-neck sweaters. He had been one of the most popular athletes at the University of Connecticut and had often dated white girls at college, which in the late 1950s was still something one took notice of at a movie theater or restaurant. When Stevens first arrived in McCook he had had difficulty finding a room to rent because of the town's ordinance prohibiting nonwhites from living in the residential section. An exception was made in his case, however, and he moved into an old house with five of his white college-educated teammates. Stevens played professional baseball for only two seasons. He decided to quit one night as he sat in an empty Trailways bus outside a roadside restaurant and waited for a teammate to bring his food.

Stevens' teammate at the University of Connecticut had been Ken Cullum, who, like Stevens, had been signed for a modest bonus by Jeff Jones. Cullum was now standing only a few yards away in center field. He was one of the most vicious left-handed pull hitters I would ever see. Short and mildly stocky, he had piercing blue eyes, a broad, high forehead and wavy hair that he combed straight back. Cullum was an immaculate man who always smelled of cologne and often walked the streets of McCook wearing a paisley sportshirt, open at the throat, and a neatly pressed garbardine suit. His conversation was sparse and sprinkled with non sequiturs and sly grins. He spoke seriously and in comprehensible sentences only when discussing an article he'd read in *Playboy* magazine. He was reputedly a heavy drinker, and this fact had discouraged many major league scouts from offering him a bonus commensurate with his talent. Even Jeff Jones was not sure he'd done the right thing in signing Cullum, and he told me to avoid him when I reached McCook. "He's too mature for you," said Jeff.

Cullum was flanked in right field by two South Carolinians, Barry Morgan and Tim Strickland. Morgan, a $30,000 bonus baby, was only 18, but by virtue of his bonus he had been made the starting rightfielder. He was red-haired, freckle-faced and resembled a young Mickey Mantle. His batting swing was powerful like Mantle's, but as yet undisciplined. Over the years he would never quite discipline it enough to bring him to the majors, although he would have a fairly successful minor league career. Morgan was the youngest married player on the team. He'd married his high school sweetheart a few weeks before leaving for McCook. His wife had remained in South Carolina, however, and he never talked about her except to describe their wedding night.

Strickland, two years older than Morgan, stood almost six feet, four inches tall. He had a long nose stuck in the middle of a tiny head, an incredibly long neck and sloping shoulders. When he charged fly balls his elbows flapped like the wings of a terrified goose. In the midst of

McCook's many bonus babies, Strickland was self-conscious about having signed with the Braves for practically nothing.† He was also self-conscious about his meager education and the fact that the second and third fingers of his right hand had been fused together, like Siamese twins, since birth. He shook hands with his left hand, in the manner of an Italian film star, until two years later when minor surgery separated the two fingers. Strickland kept to himself in McCook, and the only words I remember him speaking were to an umpire who had called him out on strikes. With eyes bulging, he stuck his homely face against the umpire's mask and said, "You gook, you couldn't call a donkey fight!"

When Steinecke had concluded his outfield drills he dismissed everyone but his 10 pitchers. The other players returned to the armory in cars while the pitchers formed a line behind the mound and took turns fielding bunts. Each pitcher would step up on the mound, pantomime his motion without actually delivering a ball, and then wait in his follow-through until Steinecke bunted a ball down one of the baselines. Whenever Steinecke missed a bunt, the ball landing at his feet, he would kick it down one of the base lines. Occasionally, out of eagerness or maybe a desire to impress, one of the pitchers would charge the plate before Steinecke had bunted the ball. In response, Steinecke would surprise even himself with a vicious line drive at the pitcher's head. Such instances were rare but they seemed to delight the manager. While the offender lay quaking on the ground, Steinecke would cackle (a little madly, I thought) and tobacco juice would dribble down his chin.

Of the 10 pitchers on the mound that day, four were starters (I would be the fifth), and each of them had received a bonus between $30,000 and $40,000. The least impressive and yet the one who would be most successful during the season was Dennis Overby, a frail 18-year-old with a milky complexion and a seriousness beyond his years. Overby, a left-hander, delivered a baseball with such nonchalance it seemed to arrive at the plate simply by the force of his pulse. Because most of the bonus pitchers threw harder than Overby, we would watch in disbelief as he struck out batter after batter, achieving by savvy and pinpoint control what none of us could achieve by firing the ball with all our strength. The secret to Overby's success escaped me that year and I envied him. It was not fair, I thought, as I sat in the corner of the dugout and watched him coast from one victory to another, all of which he treated with a slighting indifference. Of course he was successful, he seemed to say. What else

---

† The McCook Braves were one of the wealthiest minor league teams in history, and certainly the wealthiest Class D team that ever existed. Its players had been given almost $500,000 in bonus money, and many of them were drawing monthly salaries in excess of $1500. True, there were those among us, like Hendricks and Strickland, who had received nothing and were drawing only $300 per month, but they were in the minority.

could he be? He never missed mass on Sunday, did he? And because I hungered for those achievements, I threw harder and harder, and still they came infrequently. And when they did come, they were muted in comparison to his. Secretly, I began to root against him. I had discovered, finally, that every victory he achieved, every strikeout, had been snatched irrevocably from my preordained allotment. Those were *my* successes! He was stealing them! It was unjust. I consoled myself with the knowledge that one day justice would prevail, things would right themselves as I'd been taught they always did.

And they did, for both of us. It began the following spring. I had been assigned to the Braves' minor league spring training camp at Waycross, Georgia, while Dennis had been invited to the major league camp at Bradenton, Florida. Each week I would pick up *The Sporting News* to read of his progress. In one intra-squad game he struck out Hank Aaron, Eddie Mathews and Joe Adcock in succession. He was the sensation of that camp, and the sportswriters at camp voted him the Braves' most-likely-successor to Warren Spahn. He was given a watch. Then one day after a heavy rain, he slipped on a muddy mound and tore the muscles in his left shoulder. Doctors who examined him said he would never pitch again. But because the Braves had given him a bonus whose payments were spread out over four years, they refused to let him quit.

If he quit before his contract expired he would lose his bonus money. Each spring Dennis would be assigned to Waycross and immediately put on the disabled list.‡ While the rest of us worked out with various teams in the system, Dennis remained teamless. His shirt bore no number. Often as I warmed up to start a game I would see him on some empty diamond running wind sprints in the outfield. He ran them in a half-hearted way, sensing, I'm sure, the idiocy of having to keep himself in shape for the game he'd never pitch. But still, it must have helped him pass the time— running from left field to center field and walking back again. Sometimes, too, I would see him throwing a baseball against a screen. Not throwing, actually, but pushing a ball in that funny, straining way a shot-putter does, his head inclining toward his left shoulder as if to hear the pain.

Whenever I passed Dennis that first spring, I saw in his eyes the dazed, unfathoming expression of an accident victim, one who has been struck down senselessly from the blind side. Each year his expression would change a little. It became one of resignation the following spring, an uncomprehending resignation touched with cynicism. But then that look changed, too. Resignation gave way to acceptance, and with it understanding. It was as if Dennis had been forced to acquire a certain knowledge very quickly, a knowledge the rest of us would acquire only much

---

‡ All of the Braves' minor league teams from Class AA to Class D trained at Waycross, Georgia. The camp was located on the outskirts of town and consisted of five army-type barracks, a recreation building, a large clubhouse and five baseball diamonds.

later, if at all. It was a knowledge whose acquisition became increasingly painful as it was prolonged. Seeing him then, I knew things no longer bothered him. He'd been the victim of an accident a while ago, but now he saw it all from a slight distance, standing on the curb with the others, looking at himself—the victim—with curiosity and understanding and even a certain amusement. There had been no blood, just a sudden jolt, more wrenching in its surprise than its injury. The pain had diminished considerably—not because the accident hadn't mattered, hadn't affected his life, because it had. Everything mattered. But with a little distance it didn't matter quite so much anymore. He knew if he could always be a spectator as he was being a victim, then he would not have to wait for time to pass. Even at the moment of impact he would know that the pain would be diminished with time, and so the pain would be diminished then, even as he was feeling it.

In my final season with the Braves, when things were going bad for me (not as bad as they'd gone for Dennis, but bad enough), I began to recognize in a most superficial way that look of his and I realized that what I was beginning to glimpse only as a faint shadow, he'd already seen in detail. One day at Waycross I asked him if he wanted to have a catch. We tossed the ball back and forth in silence for a while. I wanted to say something to indicate I sympathized, but I didn't know what to say. He was distracted, his mind elsewhere as he threw. I thought he seemed indifferent to me, that he still remembered McCook.

Although Dennis Overby was the most successful pitcher at McCook in 1959, it was not by a wide margin. Paul Chenger, a 20-year-old physical education major from West Chester State Teachers' College in West Chester, Pennsylvania, was almost as effective and a great deal more impressive. Chenger possessed a superior fastball and a curveball of such speed and sharpness that Steinecke called it "the unfair one." Chenger was short and built like a weight lifter. He prided himself on the condition of his body and went to extremes to tap its resources. Between innings of a game he was pitching, he sucked honey from a plastic bottle. On the hottest nights he wrapped his arm in towels and wore a heavy windbreaker to ward off imaginary chills. Unlike Overby, who won effortlessly, Chenger's victories were carved from granite. On the mound he sweated and fidgeted and took deep breaths and stretched his arm overhead and twitched his shoulders and, in fact, seemed to feel his performance would be lacking unless he filled every second of it with a physical gesture. Work was his value and he cultivated it. With runners on base, Chenger simply worked harder, sweating more, twisting his arm a bit more strenuously for a sharper curveball. One day, a few years later, he twisted his arm a bit too strenuously and loosened bone chips in his elbow, ending his career.

One of Chenger's mound opponents in college had been Bill Marnie, a 20-year-old left-hander also from Pennsylvania. Marnie had signed a bonus contract with the Braves, too, and was one of McCook's starting pitchers.

He was tall and gawky-looking, with a horsey, Lee Marvin face. He would have great success in the minors and within three years was pitching in the Double-A Texas League. However, he felt he should be pitching for Louisville of the Triple-A American Association. So, to teach the Braves a lesson for not promoting him quickly enough, he enlisted in the Navy for four years—and never pitched again.

Bruce Brubaker, a 17-year-old right-hander from Harrisburg, Pennsylvania, was the youngest starting pitcher at McCook. He had a handsome face dominated by thick brows, and a large body that tended to baby fat. He was such a languid youth in both speech and movement that at times he seemed literally somnambulent. One spring training he was stricken with mononucleosis and continued to function for two weeks before he or anyone else discovered it. He treated his career with the same indolence and seemed to arouse enthusiasm only for such favorite pastimes as hunting deer and driving his souped-up Corvette. One day he wedded both pleasures when he gunned his Corvette to a speed of 126 miles per hour on a deserted road and ran straight into the stomach of a large deer who was crossing that road with an indolence equal to his own. Bruce stayed in professional baseball for 14 years. He reached the major leagues only once, in 1967, appearing in one game for the Los Angeles Dodgers before they returned him to the minors. In 1⅓ innings he allowed three hits, struck out two batters and accumulated an earned run average of 20.25. He is still pitching in the minor leagues, and there is talk that someday he will be made a pitching coach.

Only Raymond Orlikowski, of all the relief pitchers, was occasionally given a starting assignment. Orlikowski, a 17-year-old southpaw from Stevens Point, Wisconsin, was as physically talented as any of the team's bonus pitchers. However, he had been cursed (blessed?) with an unbelievable naïveté that had permitted him to sign the first major league contract offered him. He had no conception of his talent, nor how to use it to bargain for a large bonus. So the Braves had acquired him for a few thousand dollars. Shortly after he signed with them, the Cincinnati Reds offered him $30,000. Because he was not a bonus baby, the Braves treated Orlikowski with none of the pampered deference accorded the rest of us.* Ultimately this would embitter him and affect his career. He never became the major league pitcher his talent prophesied; instead, he returned to Stevens Point and became a baker.

---

* The term "bonus baby" is usually applied to any player receiving more than $10,000 upon signing a contract. Naturally, whenever a team invests such money in a player they treat him more tenderly than they would a player in whom they invested little money. A bonus baby had only to hint at improvement in order to advance in the minors. But a non-bonus baby had to fashion a record of unquestionable success before he advanced. Les Bass, for example, a non-bonus pitcher, once won 15 games in a Class C league only to be returned to that league the following year. Tony Cloninger, a $100,000 bonus pitcher once finished with an 0–9 record in Class B league and the following year pitched at Austin in the Double-A Texas League.

Most of the remaining relief pitchers were considerably less talented than Orlikowski and few of them lasted longer than a season in professional baseball. Dennis Taijchman was a hulking Kansas farm boy with the square jaw and thick eyeglasses of a Clark Kent. He once single-handedly lifted a tractor out of a ditch to the amazement of his teammates. His strength disappeared magically whenever he tried to throw a baseball, however, and the following spring training he was released. Bobby Joe Wade, a 24-year-old Southerner, often boasted to his teammates that he would have sexual intercourse with a rattlesnake if only he could find someone to hold the snake. One day in the bullpen he offered to disclose the secret of his curveball if I would give him $10,000 of my bonus. A week later he was given his unconditional release.

Dave Breshnahan, a puckish, red-haired Northern Irishman, also failed to finish the season at McCook. During his stay, however, he delighted his teammates by reading to them from the erotic love letters of his 16-year-old sweetheart, who expressed a desire to resume their love-making at the bottom of her parents' swimming pool.

During the 1959 season more than 15 pitchers would appear in a McCook Braves' uniform, although never more than 10 at a time. Only one, Phil Niekro, a 20-year-old knuckleball pitcher from Blaine, Ohio, would ever have a major league career. In 1969 Niekro won 23 games for the Atlanta Braves and became the first knuckleball pitcher in major league history to win 20 or more games in a season. He is still the ace of the Atlanta staff. In 1959, however, the Braves had given him a $500 bonus and sent him to McCook as the tenth pitcher on the staff. At first he appeared only in the last innings of hopelessly lost games. He was ineffective because he could not throw his knuckleball over the plate and preferred, instead, to deal up one of his other pitches, all of which were deficient. He seemed deficient. He was tall and blond and affected a deferential slouch. I dismissed him as a timid man. Years later I would realize that what I'd mistaken for timidity was actually a simple nature. Phil Niekro was the least complex man I'd ever met. He devoted his life to mastering a pitch. He had been taught that pitch by his father when he was six years old and had still not mastered it when he reached McCook. It is a capricious pitch. It has no logic. Even its name is illogical, since knuckles have nothing to do with its performance. To throw one, a pitcher digs the nails of his first two fingers into the seams of the ball and then pushes it toward the plate with the same motion he would use to close a door. Once released, the ball has no spin. It is caught immediately by air currents. (A spinning ball cuts through such currents and takes a direction of its own.) The vagaries of these currents may cause a knuckleball to rise or dip or flutter left and right, or maybe all these things at once, or just some of them, or none at all as it just floats lazily plateward. The ball's behavior is as erratic as the flight of a hummingbird. A knuckleball is as impossible to hit when thrown over the plate as it is to throw over the plate. A pitcher has no control over the peregrinations of the ball. He imposes nothing on it but simply surrenders to its will. To be successful, a knuckleball pitcher must first recognize this fact and then decide that his destiny still lies only with the pitch and that he will throw it constantly no matter what. It was at McCook that Niekro first surrendered to the whims of this pitch and, shortly thereafter, where his first success began. It is a surrender a more complex man could never make, but one that eventually brought Niekro a success none of his teammates at McCook would ever approach.

I stayed to myself at first. I lived in a room at the Keystone Hotel. In the afternoons I walked to the Armory, where I dressed with my teammates and then sat in the back seat of one of their cars for the short ride to Cibola. I stared out the window and said nothing. Until I pitched my first game (and awed my teammates with my talent) I would not feel a part of the team. After the games I returned to town and sat on the bench in front of the hotel until midnight. I was fascinated by the cars "dragging main." It was a ritual I'd never seen back home and which, I learned, was indigenous to small, isolated towns like McCook. They were mostly older cars—rectangular Chevy Nomads and boxy Ford coupes with front ends indistinguishable from the backs and, occasionally, a low-slung and ponderous black Mercury with narrow windshield and hump back that crawled up Main Street looking as sinister as an alligator. The cars were filled with teenagers. They beeped their horns and gunned their motors and, half-hanging out of their windows, shouted recognition to passing cars filled with other teenagers they saw daily. Some of the cars were filled with girls in their early twenties who worked the night shift at the telephone company and who dragged main on their midnight lunch break. Others were filled with Mexicans who used the darkness and the obscurity of their moving cars to peer out at the town they seldom saw in the daylight. Even families dragged main, I noticed, and one night I saw the farmer and his wife whom I'd first seen sitting in the stands at Cibola. They were sitting in the cab of a pick-up truck, their two young sons between them, and staring out at the stores and the shouting teenagers and me. When they reached the bottom of the hill they turned right onto U.S. Highway 6 and returned to their farm somewhere beyond the city hills.

One night I was standing on the curb in front of the hotel when I saw Ron Hunt walking up the hill toward me. As he approached, a car filled with teenage girls drove by. I waved to them. They waved back and the car continued down the hill. Hunt noticed my gesture and came over to talk to me. He was a shy, earnest youth with a very short crew-cut that made his large ears look even larger. He was the first of my teammates with whom I'd had a conversation. We talked about our hometowns and our ambitions and hinted at the size of our bonuses. He seemed reticent to reveal the amount of his bonus but eager to discover mine. I told him off-handedly it was a lot more than $20,000. "Gosh!" he said.

While we talked the cars kept moving past us, and eventually the car with the girls came back up the hill. I stepped into the street and called out, "Hey, pull over!" The car slowed considerably, but when its occupants saw Hunt remain on the curb, his hands stuffed in the pockets of his khaki pants, it picked up speed again.

"Do you know them?" he asked.

"Of course not," I said, and yelled after the disappearing car, "Come on back!"

"Jeez!" He shook his head and smiled at my audacity. He seemed impressed with it, as if it were a kind of sophistication he knew he lacked but, nevertheless, still admired from afar. He was a lot like a friend I had in Connecticut. Doug was shy, too, especially around girls. Whenever we saw two good-looking girls he would say, "Why don't you go talk to them?" I always did. While he hung back I would approach the girls and often make a fool of myself. Occasionally, though, I'd be warmly received and then I would turn and motion for Doug to catch up—which he did in his sheepish way. One day I approached two girls on the midway of an amusement park. After a little coaxing ("You can trust us, we're not dirty.") the girls agreed to go for a ride in the House of Horrors. Doug and his girl sat in the cart behind ours. It was pitch black inside, and when the first cardboard skeleton leaped out the girl beside me grabbed my arm. The darkened tunnel was filled with enough leaping skeletons and horrifying shrieks to keep her clinging to me throughout the ride. Near the end of it, however, I heard a loud slap that did not seem connected with any of the witches or skeletons popping up around us. When we finally emerged into the daylight, I looked back and saw Doug rubbing his cheek, his girl beside him, her arms folded tightly across her chest.

Ron Hunt reminded me of Doug, so when he asked me to be his roommate that night I gladly accepted. I moved in with him the following morning. We lived in a small gray house a few blocks north of the hotel. It was owned by a tiny, stooped lady with steel-gray hair. Ron first introduced her to me as "Mom," which momentarily confused me until I realized she wasn't actually his mother. She was a woman in her late sixties whose children had married and left McCook. She charged us eight dollars a week to sleep in a small room with two cots and one bureau. For another dollar she would serve us breakfast and allow us to watch television with her at night. I declined but Ron didn't, although I'm sure she never got around to charging him that extra dollar. When I woke each morning I'd hear them in the kitchen. "Have another piece of toast, son," she would be saying. And he'd laugh in that boyish way of his and tell her that she treated him even better than his mother did. I always waited until they left the kitchen before I slipped out the door and walked downtown to eat my breakfast. After the games at night I continued to spend my time in front of the Keystone Hotel. I would stay there until midnight, by which time I knew both Ron and she had finished watching television and gone to bed.

I envied the easy intimacy they shared. I was alone for the first time in my life and would have been happy to find in McCook a remnant of the familial warmth I'd left behind. But I could never call her "Mom." It embarrassed me to do so. Their intimacy embarrassed me, too. It was too easily acquired, like a new glove broken in by someone else. No matter how comfortably it fit the hand, it would never feel quite right because it was someone else's glove. The oils that had softened and molded it had come from someone else's palm. Its comfort, then, was unearned. The intimacy Ron Hunt and that old woman shared was unearned too, and actually not an intimacy at all. It was impossible to acquire such intimacy in only a week or even two months, and what they'd settled for were its superficial trappings. ("It's cold, son, don't forget your sweater.") Yet this simple manner would serve Ron Hunt well in the years to come. I did not have it, nor did I think it worth acquiring, although I know now it would have made things easier for me. I chose distance instead. I never spoke more than a few perfunctory words to her as I entered or left the house. She told Ron I was aloof, unfriendly. I do not remember what she was, other than an old woman in whose house I once slept for eight dollars a week.

Ten days after I arrived in McCook, Bill Steinecke told me I would pitch the second game of a night doubleheader against the Holdrege White Sox in Holdrege. The first game went 15 innings. In the eleventh Steinecke told me that if the game didn't end shortly there would be no second game. A town ordinance prohibited any game from beginning after 11 P.M., and it was already 9:30. "You'll get your chance some other day," he said. In the twelfth the White Sox got a runner to third base and I prayed he would score. He didn't, and in the following half-inning I prayed the Braves would score a run, but they didn't. My allegiance skipped back and forth between the two teams after each half-inning until finally the Braves won it in the fifteenth. It was 10:30 P.M.

"We'll start as soon as you're warmed up," Steinecke said to me. My warm-up catcher was Elrod Hendricks, who had caught all 15 innings of the first game and would sit out the second. He had just unbuckled his shinguards and was resting in the dugout when I told him I had to warm up.

"Oh, mon! Got plenty time," he said with a smile.

"I gotta start now," I said, and I walked down to the bullpen along the right field foul line. He followed, shaking his head sadly. He was very black, and in the dimly lighted bullpen I could barely see his face. I began to throw hard almost at once. Hendricks was standing, catching the ball with a carefree snap of his glove. Before he returned each pitch he spoke to the fans standing alongside the fence. I could see his white teeth as he smiled. "Hurry up," I shouted, but he did not seem to hear me. He lobbed the ball back in a lazy arc. He was still standing a few minutes later when I began to throw full-speed. I motioned for him to get down in a crouch and give me a target. He did so slowly, as if with great pain, and

I heard the fans laughing. I fired the next pitch over his head. He made a half-hearted swipe at it with his glove. The ball rolled to the dugout.

"You coulda had that!" I kicked the dirt in front of me. "Shit!"

I saw his teeth again. "You don't like it, mon, get 'nother catcher."

"I will, goddamn it!" I ran to the dugout and got Joe Shields. When Hendricks saw me return with Shields he said, "Hey, mon, whey you won do thot? Make Elrod like bod to moniger. Shouldn't do thot. We talk 'bout it in McCook, eh?" He was shaking his head sadly as he spoke, yet I could see his teeth so he must have been smiling, too.

My performance in that first game would typify my career. It was brief and resolved nothing. I pitched 2⅓ innings before Steinecke relieved me with the score tied 2–2. I proved I had potential by striking out four of the seven batters I retired, but I also proved that that same talent was undisciplined by walking five batters in less than three innings. I allowed no hits and, in fact, refused to let the White Sox batters make contact with the ball. In the third inning, after I had struck out one man and walked two others in succession, Steinecke trotted to the mound.

"You're trying to throw the fuckin' ball by everyone," he said. "Relax, let the bastards hit it. We'll help you out." He looked over his shoulder at the next batter, a skinny, spectacled little infielder named Al Weis (he would star for the New York Mets in the 1969 World Series, the same one in which Hendricks would star for the Baltimore Orioles.)

"This little bastard is gonna bunt the runners over," Steinecke said. "You let him. If he bunts toward first base, you to first with the ball. But if he bunts down third, try to nail the lead runner. You understand?" I nodded, but as soon as he left the mound I decided to strike out Weis. I walked him on four pitches, then walked the next batter to force in a run. This time Steinecke walked slowly out to the mound, and as he did so he pointed to our bullpen where Orlikowski was warming up.

"That's it," he said and reached for the ball. I put it behind my back.

"What for?" I asked. "They're not hitting me."

"No, they're not," he said, smiling that maniacal smile of his. "But you're not gettin' the fuckers out, either." He spit tobacco juice and wiped the excess from his chin with the back of his hand. "No siree, Podner, you are certainly not getting them fuckers out, are you?"

I walked off the mound and sat in the dugout. I didn't know what to feel at that moment. I'd expected to strike out 18 batters and pitch a two-hit shutout or perhaps even be hit unmercifully. I had not precluded the second possibility. But this confused me. It was so inconclusive. What did it mean? I was still sitting there stunned when my teammates came in from the field at the end of the inning. As they did I heard Ron Hunt say to someone, "Man, my roomie throws bullets, don't he?" Then he lowered his voice a little and said, "He got a big bonus, you know. *Really* big!"

I relaxed considerably. It hadn't been a total loss after all. Thanks to Ron, they knew. That was enough to satisfy me, for at the time I still preferred those pure, isolated and transitory moments of success—a point

proved—that stood out clearly and did not require the effort a more substantial success demanded.

The following morning I was sitting on the bench in front of the Keystone
reading a newspaper when I heard a voice say, "Hey, mon, been looking
for you." I looked over the paper to see Elrod smiling at me.

"What for?" I said. Still smiling, he hit me on the side of the head and I
fell off the bench. I landed in a sitting position on the sidewalk, my legs
spread out in front of me. I was still holding the newspaper, more dazed
than hurt. I did not yet believe what had just happened. I looked around
to see if there were any witnesses. But it was Sunday and the streets were
deserted. Then I remembered the night before. Was that why Elrod had
hit me? It was not enough, I thought, not enough for *me* to hit someone,
anyway. There must be more. I had been shoved into the climax of this
melodrama without having played the first act. And he was still smiling at
me! I got up and he swung again. This time I blocked it with my arm. We
circled each other warily. To the death, I wondered? But I wasn't even
angry. I just hoped he would suddenly put down his arms and walk
away and all would be forgotten. But he didn't. I decided to go out
heroically. I lowered my head like a bull and charged his stomach. He
grabbed me around the neck with one arm and began punching me in the
stomach with his free hand. He punched me a number of times but none
of the blows hurt; they just took my breath away in stages—punch by
punch—until I had none left. When his arms got tired he let go and I fell
down again. I took a deep breath but nothing came up. I took another but
still nothing. My mind went into hysterics! I would never catch another
breath! I would die here, on the streets of McCook, thousands of miles
from nowhere! *My career!* It flashed before my eyes—2⅓ innings? Was
that *it?* I felt a little breath come and I gasped for it, then a bigger one
and a still bigger one, until finally I was panting heavily on the sidewalk.
Elrod must have decided I'd had enough, because when I looked up he
was gone. I got up and sat on the bench for a few minutes. My stomach
began to feel sore so I decided to walk home. By the time I reached the
band shell in the center of the park my temple was throbbing and I could
feel a large lump there. I walked faster, and when I reached my house my
stomach began to convulse. I opened the front door and ran through the
house. I passed Mom in the kitchen. She looked over her shoulder at me
just as I burst into the bathroom and began to dry-heave into the toilet.
Nothing came up (I hadn't eaten yet), but every time I made a God-aw-
ful noise. When I finally stopped I was soaked with perspiration. I dried
myself off and went into the bedroom and lay down. I slept through that
afternoon's ball game and into the night. When I awoke it was dark. Ron
was sitting on his bed in his underwear looking at me. He had a very serious expression on his face.

"You look terrible," he said.

"I don't feel so good," I replied. My stomach was sore and my temple was throbbing. I touched it. There was a large welt on the side of my head, as if I'd grown a frog's popeye while I'd slept.

"Mom's awfully upset," Ron said.

"I'll be all right."

"It's not that," he said. "She told me to speak to you. She said to tell you she won't tolerate no drinkers in her house. She never took in drinkers before and—"

"What? I wasn't drunk! I got into a fight with Elrod in front of the hotel."

"I know. I heard. I told Mom, but she just shook her head and said she wouldn't tolerate no drinkers and that's final!"

"But I wasn't drinking!" I began to shout. "I don't even drink beer!"

"Shh! Mom's sleeping. She was so upset she went to bed early. She's not used to this kinda thing, you know? I think you oughta apologize anyway. Promise her you'll never do it again."

"Do what again?"

"Get drunk," he said. "Otherwise she'll have to throw you out, and that would bother her something awful. She's been like a mother to us, you know?"

"Go to hell!" I said, and I left the house. Ron forgave my outburst, however. He said it was typical of me. That was typical of him, I said. Anyway, the next morning he spoke to Mom. She would let me stay, he said, because he'd given his word I'd behave myself. But his word was not quite enough for Mom. Whenever I walked past her, my eyes lowered in shame, she would fix me with a wary and ominous gaze that hinted at dire consequences for any future transgressions.

Once the initial excitement of my arrival in McCook the start of my career had worn off, I discovered it was a dull life. The mornings and afternoons were free and seemingly endless. Only the hours from 6 to 11 P.M., when the games were played, held any excitement. Those games were our only reality. Our lives were lived within their nine innings and were greatly affected by what took place during them. The rest was nothing but dead time somehow to be filled. There was a pool hall that opened at noon and a bar that served those over 21. There were two movie theaters, both of which opened at 7 P.M. and closed at midnight. After a night game we could rush to see the final minutes of the same movie two weeks running. So we had only ourselves to alleviate the boredom. Most of the players drifted into cliques and shared the boredom as if its weight would lessen in proportion to the number of shoulders bearing it. For instance the Spanish-speaking players from Cuba, Puerto Rico and the Dominican Republic stayed to themselves on the outskirts of town where they lived. There were never more than a few of them in McCook at any one time. And it was seldom more than a game or two before they were released, so I don't remember their names (except Elrod's, of course). I saw them at the armory and at Cibola and, occasionally, at a restaurant in town where they sat together and spoke in rapid Spanish, which they'd abandon only to order "Ham'n egg, over easy, orange juice," a meal that served for breakfast, lunch and dinner.

The older American players—Ken Cullum, Joe Shields, Bill Stevens and others—shared a large house in the residential section, while the families of Chuck Carlin and Frank Saia lived close by. Often the two married players visited their single teammates, as they were united by the common bonds of age and maturity (all were over 21 and had graduated from college) that the rest of us lacked. These men were not so single-minded about their baseball careers and so, unlike most of us, did not live or die with each base hit or strikeout. Instead they approached the game, outwardly at least, with a cool and mocking cynicism that confused the younger players and served only to reassure us they would never make the major leagues with such attitudes. They even doubted themselves, and were not reluctant to speak disparagingly of their talents, or lack of them. They preferred to regard baseball as simply an extension of their college life that would lead to a more meaningful career. I'm sure they secretly harbored the same fantasies as we did—of someday making "the bigs" and becoming "a star"—but if they did they considered it bad form to admit to such romanticism. They looked with annoyance on our open and unabashed enthusiasm toward baseball, our only topic of conversation. They had other interests. They discussed politics and literature and existential philosophy. And when they discussed women (not girls) their conversation was foreign to the rest of us, who treated girls as simply "clean" or "dirty." They spoke on a different level than we did; they were more analytical, more introspective, and were, in short, adults. This bond was so strong as to eventually unite Bill Stevens, a black, and Chuck Carlin, who had once thought of him as a clubhouse boy. Before the season was over, Mrs. Carlin would have Bill Stevens to dinner many times.

These older players seldom ventured into town, preferring to spend their mornings and afternoons sleeping off the effects of large quantities of beer they'd consumed the night before. In my mind there was always an aura of mystery surrounding their lives in McCook, and I was fascinated by them. I'd heard, for instance, that Stevens was dating a white girl who worked at the telephone company—although only his roommates had seen them together. I'd heard also about night-long parties and the strange girls entering and leaving their house at all hours of the day and night, and about garbage cans filled with nothing but empty bottles. There was a rumor, too, that after Ken Cullum drank 20 or so bottles of Falstaff, he'd go outside on particularly hot nights and fall asleep on the lawn waking in the morning to find himself covered with dew and still wearing only his white boxer shorts emblazoned with red cupids.

Word also got around that Lois Steinecke, our manager's 21-year-old daughter, had come to McCook to visit her father and promptly fallen in love with Cullum. I remember seeing her once after I'd heard that rumor and wondering just what Cullum saw in such a plain-faced girl. Of course, I never noticed her spectacular body at the time, nor was I aware of her impressive I.Q. and disposition so gentle as to draw anyone. They carried on their romance throughout his minor league career, and often Lois would appear in Boise, Idaho, or Eau Claire, Wisconsin, or Davenport, Iowa, just to be with Ken for a short time. Never during those years did she make the slightest demand on him. Finally, sensing he would not marry her, she left for South America one day, where she taught English to Indian children.

One night, walking home from the armory, I passed the town's bar. Through its dusty window I could make out the figures of Cullum, Stevens, Shields and Carlin. The bar was dimly lighted, but their faces were illuminated in an eerie way by the flickering colored lights of the pinball machine around which they stood. They held bottles of beer, and every so often one of them would raise a bottle to his lips, tip his head back and take a long swallow. They took turns playing the pinball machine. As the silver balls richocheted underneath the glass top, they laughed and pointed at the lights jumping on the scoreboard. At one point Cullum walked over to the bar and returned shortly with four more bottles, which he passed out to his teammates. I watched for a while, not daring to go inside and suffer the humiliation of being denied service because I was under 21. Besides, I had not yet acquired a taste for beer, or for pinball machines either for that matter, although I longed for the camaraderie they seemed to be sharing.

A few nights later I got up the nerve to walk over to their house after a game. They were all sitting around in their underwear talking and swearing, and drinking beer, in that effortless natural way. They offered me a beer, too, and I sat down with them. I didn't say much at first, but after a few sips I began to talk loudly and slur my words. I was not drunk, really, just showing off, and it wasn't until I saw the disgusted look on Stevens' face that I realized I had done the wrong thing. But I was undaunted, and a few days later made another attempt to befriend them. I saw Cullum and Shields standing in front of a drugstore talking with two pretty girls. I walked over to them and said in my most blasé tone, "Hi, who're the cunts?"

The girls turned to me with looks more startled than shocked. For a split second they could not believe what they'd just heard. When it finally did register, they were at a loss to respond. Cullum and Shields ignored me. They moved closer together so that their backs formed a barrier between me and the girls. They continued talking to the girls as if nothing had happened, as if *I* had not happened, and when the girls turned back to them I went away.

I lacked something, I decided after that experience. But what? I gave up trying to befriend the older players. Still, I did not spend much time with my roommate either. Despite Ron's intercession with Mom, I had grown more and more estranged from him over the weeks. We had little in common. I was restless and preferred to spend my free time downtown. He would rather stay at home with Mom or else walk over to the house where most of the younger players lived—Bruce Brubaker, Dennis Overby, Ray Orlikowski, Phil Niekro, Dave Breshnahan and others. I went there once but found little to interest me. They spent most of their time writing long letters to their moms or girl friends, from whom they were forever receiving cookies or snapshots. The latter were treated with great reverence no matter how unpretty the girl might be. Each player was faithful to his snapshot during his stay in McCook. ("It's been 32 days since I last saw her.")

To display the seriousness of his intentions toward his girl friend, Dennis Overby went so far as to bring her to McCook for a few days. I saw them together once. They were holding hands while walking up and down Main Street one hot sunny afternoon. They looked serious, did not speak much and paused frequently to look into store windows. They lingered especially long in front of the jewelry store and its display of engagement rings. She was a thin, ordinary-looking girl with a complexion as pale as his own. She pointed to a ring. He nodded once. That night, a Saturday, Dennis struck out 17 batters, and the following morning he and his girl friend were at eleven o'clock mass. They went to Holy Communion, too, before she flew back to Fond du Lac, Wisconsin.

I had a girl friend "back home" also. She is now my wife, and has been these past 12 years. She says my letters from McCook were rare, never more than a few lines scrawled in large script across one side of a piece of notepaper. She kept one.

> Dearest Carol,
>
> I miss you so much. I love you an awful lot. I can't wait to see you again. How are you? Fine I hope. I pitched yesterday but was wild. My arm didn't feel real good. But I still throw harder than anyone on the club. And I'm learning lots about pitching and lots of other things, too.
>
> Love and Kisses XXXX<br>Pat
>
> P.S. Please don't
> worry about my arm!

And I was faithful to her, at least for a while. But unlike the celibacy of my younger teammates (which earned them one another's respect), mine was due more to circumstance than inclination.

On those rare occasions when players like Overby, Niekro and Hunt ventured downtown it was usually in groups of five or six, either to watch the last half-hour of a movie at the Fox Theater, where they sat in the balcony and tossed popcorn at the seats below, or to eat at Modrell's

Cafe. Modrell's served the best food in town and had the prettiest waitresses. There were three of them, all blonde and in their late teens. The players flirted with them in an antiseptic, brotherly way, and the girls responded like sisters. They gave the players advice about their girl friends and commiserated with them over their careers. They all promised to keep in touch when the season was over. And they did, too. They wrote letters every month at first. Then every few months or so. Then only an occasional card at Christmas or Easter. Then nothing.

The cashier at Modrell's was a beefy woman with a booming voice. The waitresses called her "Mom," which was only natural since she was their mother. She, too, treated the players affectionately (some of them, anyway), and it was only a matter of time before I walked into Modrell's one day to hear Ron Hunt call her "Mom."

One afternoon I returned to our house to find Ron standing on the front lawn with one arm around a middle-aged man in a business suit and the other around a middle-aged woman with a corsage pinned to her dress. Our landlady was peering at all three of them through a Brownie camera. After she snapped their picture, Ron introduced the man to me as "My dad," and the woman as "My mom." I got over my initial confusion quickly and realized that this was his real mom, his mother, the woman who'd given birth to him. Somehow the knowledge that such a person existed, that like the rest of us he had a "real" mother, not just surrogates, restored a portion of sanity to the world. However, a few weeks later I returned home to find the same scene being played out once again. Ron, smiling, his arms around a man and a woman. Only they were different. Not the same as the last two. Mom snapped their picture. Ron called me over. "I want you to meet my dad," he said. "And this is my mom."

Later I learned his parents had been divorced and had remarried, so that Ron had two sets of moms and dads, not counting all the others he could pick up here and there throughout his career.

By mid-July I no longer ate at Modrell's. (Actually, I had made a less than antiseptic pass at one of the waitresses and had been soundly rebuffed. Ron was very upset with me. I hadn't followed the rules, it seemed.) Instead, each morning I walked to the bottom of Main Street and then right for a few blocks to the M-and-E Diner. The M-and-E had only one waitress, a silent, 28-year-old Indian girl with a pockmarked face and lumpy white scars on her dark arms. She kept a knife in her teased hair. Only its handle showed, and at first I thought it was simply an odd-shaped barrette. But one day a cowboy patted her behind and the next instant the knife was quivering in the tabletop inches from his hand. Unlike Modrell's, which catered to businessmen during the day and families at night, the M-and-E served mostly truck drivers (it was on U.S. 6) and drifters and rodeo cowboys from the Red Willow County Fair. Every so often Ken Cullum would eat there, too. He would come in at about 3 P.M., his eyes red from a night of drinking, and order a breakfast of eggs and sausage and pancakes and a quart of orange juice. He always ate at the M-and-E after such a night, he said, so Steinecke wouldn't find out about it. I discovered what he meant one night when Steinecke came up to me before a game and, grinning, said, "So, you wanna get in the pants of that waitress at Modrell's, eh, kid?"

After breakfast I walked back to the Keystone and sat on the bench out front and read the newspapers. I read *The Sporting News* first, beginning on the last page which was nothing but tiny columns of statistics on every minor leaguer. I checked these for all the pitchers in the Braves' farm system and then turned to the front page to learn about Whitey Ford and Warren Spahn. I always had a paperback book with me, too, although I seldom read one. I'd just lay it on the bench beside me hoping that one of the college-educated players might come along and see it. "What's that you're reading?" he would ask, and I would shrug and say, "Nothing much," and hold up my new copy of *The Greatest Story Ever Told*. But the only person who ever noticed my book was Lois Steinecke. She stood in front of me one day and pointed to the book. "What are you reading?" she said, and the moment she said it I was struck dumb, saw instantly what a fool I was, my little ruse! She picked up the book and looked at its cover painting of a finely-featured man with long blond hair, blond beard and sorrowful eyes. She looked at it for a long second and I knew she was going to laugh, was going to humiliate me, but all she did was nod her head seriously and say, "It's a good book." Then she looked at me. "I like to read a lot, too."

When I finished with the newspapers I spent the rest of the morning walking around town, looking into store windows, occasionally going inside a store, wandering up and down its aisles without the slightest intention of buying anything until a salesman would step in front of me. "Can I help you, sir?" I would panic, snatch the closest thing, buy it and escape. One morning, the third in a row of 100 degree heat, I grabbed a woolen sweater and thrust it at the salesman. He looked at it and then at me. "It's cold back home," I said, as if "back home" was the North Pole.

I also spent a lot of time drinking coffee in drugstores. I often hit two or three drugstores in one morning. I liked to sit at the long formica counters, drinking my coffee and watching the waitresses. They were husky farm girls with thick bodies that strained against their nylon uniforms as they reached and stooped and knelt. The sound of those moving bodies, their nylon slips and stockings rustling, never failed to excite me. I was fascinated by the off-hand way they glided through their routine—tapping huge stainless-steel urns, balancing cups and saucers halfway up each arm, cleaning a counter with one swipe of a damp cloth and pocketing their tips in the same motion—and, upon seeing a familiar face enter the store, had coffee on the counter before that person even reached it. I fantasized that one day I would walk through the door and, before I had mounted my stool, before I had swung my leg over it, there would be a cup of coffee waiting for me, too. I stayed in those drugstores for hours, nursing my coffee and waiting for mid-morning when businessmen and farmers and housewives and secretaries would pour in for their coffee breaks and the counter would grow crowded and noisy around me. I liked the feeling of being in the midst of such a crowd, in the midst of people moving through familiar lives, meeting familiar faces, while my life, at the time, was so unfamiliar to me and all the faces in it were those of strangers. Sitting at the counter, eavesdropping, I shared in their lives. But I never once abandoned my anonymity, never once turned to my left or right and reached into one of their lives. I just took comfort from being near them, and poured more and more milk into my coffee until it was nothing but milk. I preferred my anonymity. It gave me freedom and a certain distance from those lives, which, if entered, I might discover to be oppressively familiar to their possessors in a way I did not care to see. They could never escape them as I could, by simply standing up and walking outside into the daylight of my unknown and myriad possibilities.

At noon I walked up U.S. Highway 6 and waited outside the poolroom until its proprietor, Shorty, came by to open up. He was a neat little man with wavy red hair and a handlebar mustache. He wore fancy cowboy shirts with snap buttons and new dungarees that were always pressed to a knifelike crease. He rolled up the cuffs of these until they were 12 inches wide and exposed his pointed cowboy boots branded with elaborate scrollwork.

The poolroom was as small and neat as its proprietor. The walls were paneled in light pine and stacked with dozens of new cuesticks. The Brunswick pool and snooker tables were of dark wood polished to a mirrorlike finish, their green felt tops bright and unscratched. After Shorty had cleaned his spotless room—swept the floor, waxed the wood tables, brushed the chalk dust from the green felt—he took his accustomed position behind the counter, where he could survey the room through narrowed eyes, and began to wax his mustache. This he'd wax for hours on end, pausing only to dispense bottles of beer and cellophane packages of beef jerky or bags of Red Man chewing tobacco to his infrequent customers. There was a brass spittoon in front of the counter, and any man who failed to hit it was promptly ushered out the door. Shorty also kept two guns behind his counter—a 12-gauge shotgun as well as a .38-caliber pistol—and both were loaded. When he found out I was a baseball player he asked me to get him a bat, a 38-ounce Louisville slugger, and when I did he kept that behind the counter, too. Possibly this is why I never saw more than three or four men in his poolroom at any one time. Most of the town's cowboys and farmers preferred to shoot pool at the bar next door, whose proprietor was not so fastidious as Shorty.

The first few times I came into his establishment Shorty watched me carefully for signs of slovenliness. Finding none, he took a liking to me. He taught me how to hold a cuestick and the basic rules of nine-ball, eight-ball and rotation, and then left me alone to shoot pool most of the afternoon. I loved the game. It was simple and orderly and not difficult to master. During my years in professional baseball I spent lots of time shooting pool. The game was an excellent refuge from the frustrations of my career. And when I left baseball in 1962, having no trade, no education and no ambition, the first thing I turned to was the cuestick. It supported my wife and me for two years. It also helped assuage the demands of my ego, which, without baseball, was shrinking daily. Pool was still a refuge, only by then from other frustrations.

At Shorty's one afternoon I met a teammate, Julius French. He was a year older than I and supposedly a great troublemaker. Most of the players on our team avoided him. He had an air of self-destructiveness about him that threatened to carry down those in his wake. A few days before I arrived in McCook, the players were invited to a party at the home of one of the girls who worked at the telephone company. Soon that girl was huddled in the corner with Julius, rapidly succumbing to his courtly southern manners (he could light a woman's cigarette as if it were an inherited gesture) and his exquisite good looks. He had fine, almost delicate features, deeply-colored lips and a mole on his cheek. His blue eyes were always half-lidded and when he spoke to women his lashes fluttered. They were fluttering then, as he spoke to this girl at her party. Her finance noticed and protested to Julius. Julius invited him into the bathroom to discuss the matter privately. The door closed. When it reopened Julius's right hand was wrapped in a towel and the fiancé was unconscious in the bathtub.

As we shot pool that afternoon, I asked Julius about the incident. He showed me his hand. Its knuckles were hardened scabs. He was used to fighting, he said. He had been a Golden Gloves boxer in Georgia before his career had been terminated one night. He was in a bar with his girl when a sailor made an obscene remark to her. Julius knocked him down. The sailor got up and rushed Julius with a chain. The next few minutes were a blank. Julius could only remember five men pulling him off the unconscious body of the sailor. He had continued to beat the sailor, it seemed, long after the sailor had collapsed. Eventually the sailor died. Julius said he had never gone to prison for that killing but he had had to leave Georgia, and playing minor league baseball in McCook, Nebraska, was a more tempting offer than the possibility of playing for the Georgia State Penitentiary.

Julius signed a contingent bonus contract with the Braves. He was promised $10,000 if he remained on the McCook roster for 40 days. If he was released within 40 days he would get nothing. Julius had already passed 21 days in McCook, and, though he was as talented as most of our pitchers, had done little more than pitch batting practice before each game. He threw with a vengeance. The hitters groaned when he took the mound. They complained to Steinecke. They feared for their lives, they said. Steinecke only laughed. "It'll do the fuckers good," he said. "If they can hit that red-ass they can hit anybody." Steinecke loved to sit in the dugout and watch Julius throw. Whenever one of our players did hit the ball solidly off Julius, Steinecke would get excited and start elbowing whoever was next to him. "Watch this! Watch this!" he would say. Invariably, Julius would fire the next pitch at the offending batter's head, and the batter would sprawl in the dust. "Heh! Heh! Heh! That's a nasty little fucker out there!" Steinecke would cackle to no one in particular. "Yes siree, Podner, that's a nasty fucker!"

Why did I become friendly with Julius French of all people! I often wonder. Obviously, neither of us quite fit in anywhere on the team, and so perhaps naturally we seemed to fit in with each other. Yet that's a shaky foundation on which to build a friendship consisting primarily of sullen silences. At best, we shared a common moodiness, a dissatisfaction, but with what we did not know. We met every afternoon at Shorty's to play pool. Our games began jovially enough, but always turned sour. We released our private frustrations in those games. The day's loser stalked out of Shorty's determined never again to speak to the winner. Those resolutions lasted a few hours, sometimes even a day, but never longer. We were both parted and reunited by our murky dissatisfactions and the grudging admittance that we needed someone with whom to share them. Yet, even as we befriended one another we held something in reserve. We *were* strangers! Our situation had thrown us together for the moment (we never saw each other after McCook) and to act as if we'd become intimate friends on such short notice would be false. We sensed this in McCook, and so we shared our tenuous friendship just at odd times and at a certain level.

Julius and I watched our home games from the bullpen in the left field corner. We sat on the picnic bench and chewed tobacco. We stretched our legs out in front of us, dug the heels of our spikes into the ground and pushed back slightly so that the bench tottered on two legs and we rested against the wire fence that separated us from the Mexican and Indian fans behind us. We held this pose for innings, hats pulled down over our eyes, hands folded on stomachs, stirring ourselves only to spit tobacco juice high into the air, part our legs quickly and close them again before we lost our precarious balance. The bullpen was in the shadows and so far from home plate that we could see the ball in the catcher's glove a split second before we heard its "crack." We watched the games with but faint interest. They were being played by someone else and so influenced their careers, not ours. We rarely found ourselves a part of those games, and then only by accident.

One night a base hit skipped over the foul line and hooked under our bench. We were so surprised at this intrusion into our solitude that we didn't move until we heard the cursing and pounding feet of the opposing team's left fielder. We dove off the bench just before he grabbed it and flung it into the air. He picked up the ball and fired it to third base. Im-

BASEBALL DIAMONDS

mediately, his shoulders sagged. He muttered to himself as he walked back to his position. Julius dusted himself off with mock solemnity, "God-damn, fella, show some manners!" Without looking back, the left fielder gave us the finger. The fans behind us laughed as we righted our bench and resumed our pose.

Such intrusions were rare, however, and often the closest we came to the action was when Phil Niekro sprinted to the bullpen to warm up before going in to save yet another game. Most of the time we just sat there, chewing our tobacco (getting slightly drunk on it) and cursing Overby's luck. To help pass the time there were always a few young boys rattling our fence. They pleaded with us to show them our gloves. Like prisoners, they reached their hands through the wire mesh to try on the gloves. They pounded their fists into their gloves, and shouted, "Fire it to me, Babe!" And when we turned our backs they tried to pull the gloves through the fence, but they were too big and the openings too small. They lost interest in the gloves and asked for us to give them a baseball. Often we did, but only in return for a hot dog or hamburger, which we ate behind our upraised gloves so that Steinecke would not see us from his spot in the third base coach's box. Every so often we asked the boys if they had an older sister. They always did and she was always good-look-ing. They ran off toward the homeplate stands and returned minutes later towing a 14-year-old girl wearing glasses. While their sister, or who-ever she was, giggled and blushed, the boys began shouting for their baseball—"You promised! You promised!"—and we tossed it over the fence just so they would go away before Steinecke heard the commotion and looked down at us.

When not pitching (which for Julius was frustratingly frequent) we preferred to sit in the bullpen rather than the dugout. In the dugout, alongside our teammates who were playing those games, we would be ex-pected to show an enthusiasm and interest in their outcome that we did not feel. It's difficult to sustain such enthusiasm when not in games (even when your team is winning regularly, as ours was), and perhaps even more so considering the number of games we played in two months. We played six night games a week and one afternoon doubleheader, usually on Sunday. Rarely was a game rained out, and even then only after we had sat much of the night in the dugout and watched the field turn into a swamp before the umpires finally rendered their decision. The game would then be rescheduled as part of a twi-night doubleheader the follow-ing day. We had no open days, even for travel, because none of the Ne-braska State League's six towns was farther than a three-hour bus ride. Our road trips were one-night stands. We arrived in time for batting prac-tice, played that night's game, ate supper at midnight and were back in McCook by 4 A.M.

Because we never stayed overnight, I have retained no sense of those other towns. I remember only that to reach Hastings and Holdrege and Kearney and North Platte and Grand Island we had to pass through miles of flat land that smelled of sweet alfalfa, and occasionally through a quick town like Funk or Indianola or Wellfleet or Juniata or Arapahoe that was simply a few stores, a railroad crossing, a huge grain silo and a population sign that read less than 1000 people.

I remember specifically only one afternoon. We had stopped to eat at a roadside cafe outside Holdrege when it began to rain. The drops splattered against the restaurant's plate glass window. While eating I became conscious of a pinging sound and looked up to see hailstones. They grew larger and larger before my eyes until they were the size of a paperback book. They were flat, jagged chunks of ice that looked as if they were being torn from an iceberg and hurled against the window by some savage and unseen god. The sound was deafening. The ice struck with a "clang" and the window rippled like a tissue-thin sheet of aluminum. Everyone in the cafe—players, patrons, waitresses—left their seats and huddled against the far wall away from the window. We stared in disbelief and waited for it to shatter. But the hail stopped as suddenly as it had begun, and seconds later the sun was shining. We hung back a few minutes more and then, like stone age savages, ventured outside. The hot sun had now melted most of the hailstones to the size of rock salt. We searched for the large pieces but could find none. We even began to doubt our senses until one of the waitresses pointed to some parked cars, their windshields shattered and bodies pockmarked.

The sun stayed out for the rest of the afternoon, and that night we played a doubleheader against the White Sox. I don't remember how those games turned out. In fact, I don't remember much about any of the games we played on the road (or at home, either, for that matter) except those I pitched in, which affected my career.

I remember in detail, for instance, a game at Grand Island in mid-July. I defeated the Athletics 1–0, for my first victory in professional baseball. My mound opponent was José Santiago, a tall, lean Puerto Rican with stiletto sideburns. Santiago would one day become a successful pitcher for the Boston Red Sox. However, that night in 1959 I was the better pitcher by a slight margin. I threw harder. We matched serves for eight innings. Then Ron Hunt scored from third base on a fly ball to shallow center field, diving headfirst past the lunging catcher. I hugged him when he entered the dugout. I ended the game by striking out the last batter on three pitches. In nine innings I had struck out 11 batters, walked 3 and given up 2 singles. It was the kind of performance that would hound me throughout my career. I would produce such games about once every four starts. After them, my manager would say, "It shows you can do it." But those games had a will of their own. I could never summon them on command, and, in fact, the harder I tried to duplicate them the more they eluded me. In my next three starts I would fail to last beyond the fourth inning. Then, when I was about to despair of ever duplicating such a game, everything would return in a whoosh—speed, curve, control, savvy, luck—and I would pitch a game of both blinding and maddening brilliance.

I was standing in the lobby of the Fox Theater waiting for Julius to buy the popcorn. We had rushed over after the ball game to catch the last 30 minutes of an Elvis Presley movie. It was a Saturday night and the theater was packed. From inside I could hear the teenage girls screaming at Elvis. A girl walked by me. I thought she smiled. She started up the stairs that led to the balcony.

"Heh, wait up!" She stopped halfway up the stairs and turned around. She had long brown hair that flipped up at the ends. She was wearing a white blouse and very tight black shorts. The blouse was tucked into her shorts in such a way that her smallish breasts strained against it. She wore a wide belt that made her waist look unbelievably small for such a big girl. She must have been about five feet, seven inches tall. Her face was pretty. I remember a broad, white forehead.

"Where you goin'?" I said.

"To the balcony."

"Want some company?" I smiled but my heart was pounding.

"Sure. Come on." I followed her up the stairs.

"My name is Sally." She looked back at me and smiled. "It isn't really. It's Sarah. That's a biblical name, you know. I hate it. Everybody calls me Sally."

"Sure," I said. "My name is Pat."

"I know."

The balcony was crowded and noisy. Hunt, Overby, Niekro and a few others were sitting in the first row. They were slouched low in their seats and their feet dangled over the railing that kept people from falling into the orchestra. When they saw me with a girl they turned around and stared. I made believe I didn't see them. Sally led me up the steeply inclining balcony until we were only a few rows under the bright, conical light coming from the projection room. She turned into a row and sat down. I sat beside her. The light from the projection room fanned out over our heads, grew wider and fainter as it approached the screen far below us. Suspended in the light were particles of dust. I put my arm around the back of her seat and she moved close to me. We stayed that way for a long moment, both of us staring at the screen. I let my hand drop onto her shoulder and she pressed her head against mine. I could feel her soft hair against my cheek. I breathed its sweet fragrance and closed my eyes and kissed her. She opened her mouth and breathed in deeply. I began to tumble slowly through space, spinning and falling faster and faster until I feared I would pass out. I opened my eyes and saw overhead a whirling prism of color. I focused hard on the prism and it began to spin more slowly, and finally it stopped. I saw it was only the cut-glass chandelier. We parted. I took a deep breath and became conscious again of the darkened theater and the conical light and the people around us. Down below, I caught a glimpse of Ron Hunt turning back toward the screen. My head filled quickly now, with thoughts of my unbelievable luck.

Sally and I kissed throughout the movie. Each kiss was less dizzying than the last. We pressed our lips together so tightly that our teeth cut into them. We tried to press our bodies together, too, but the arm rest between us bruised our ribs. Still we strained and pressed and began to sweat. Her blouse was wet and it stuck to her back. When the movie ended and the lights came on, I saw that her hair was damp and thick strands of it were matted to her forehead. Her lips were red beyond the lip line and looked swollen. My lips were sore. I left her in the lobby after we had made plans to meet at the band shell in the small park across from the Fox after tomorrow night's game. She did not seem surprised to find out I was a ballplayer. Julius was waiting for me outside the theater. "You look like shit," he said and began to laugh. He was not the least bit upset over my having deserted him for Sally. "Those are the rules," he said. "I would have done the same thing." We both laughed and he offered to keep me company while I waited for Sally the following night. "I don't exactly have any pressing appointments of my own," he said.

After the ball game, Julius and I bought a fifth of gin and a quart of lemonade and walked over to the band shell to wait for Sally. It was 11 P.M. and the park was dark and deserted. We sat inside the shell, after we had drunk most of the gin and lemonade we began to sing to an imaginary audience. We walked to the edge of the stage and took profuse bows. Julius accepted roses with his usual grace. When Sally finally drove up in her '50 DeSoto, we were both deliriously drunk and I was beginning to feel sick. I introduced Julius to her as "a fine Southern gentleman" as we both grinned like idiots and swayed beside her car. She did not get out of the car at first. She looked at each of us, a flicker of doubt passing over her eyes, and then smiled. She shook her head in mock disgust the way women do. I moaned. "I don't feel so hot," I said. She made me get into the back seat and then she got out of the car and into the back with me. She told Julius to drive. We headed down Main Street and turned right onto U.S. 6 toward her home. She lived with her parents and three brothers on a farm on the outskirts of McCook. I lay my head in her lap and closed my eyes. Everything began to spin wildly, and when Julius turned off the highway onto the bumpy dirt road that led to her house, I vomited. "Jeezes!" said Julius and jammed on the brakes. I opened the door and rolled out of the car into a field. I threw up again. Sally wiped herself off, and then she and Julius got out of the car and picked me up. They both supported me while I continued vomiting. When I stopped, they put me back in the car, which had a horrible stench, and we drove the rest of the way to her house.

It was after midnight and everyone was asleep. Sally told us to be quiet and not to turn on any lights. They deposited me on the couch in the living room and, while Julius watched television without sound, Sally cleaned me up by its faint light. She washed my face with a wet cloth and then rinsed it out in cold water and folded it across my forehead. She took off my shirt and brought me one of her brother's t-shirts. I heard her washing mine in the kitchen sink and then I passed out. I woke to the sounds of whispered shouts. Sally's 21-year-old brother was standing in the living room and she was pleading with him. I could make out only their shadows. She grew adamant. "I don't care," she said. "I won't throw him out the way he is." Her brother's shadow moved toward me. Julius suddenly appeared and grabbed him by the shirt. He grabbed Julius's shirt. Sally pleaded with them to stop. They held tight to one another, neither one moving. I raised my head and moaned. Sally began to cry. I saw the shadow of her brother's head turn toward her and then back at me, and then his hands flew up into the air in disgust and he left the room. It was almost four in the morning when we got back to town. Sally dropped Julius off first, then drove me to Mom's house. "Are you all right?" she said. Nodding, I stumbled out of the car into the house.

I did not see Sally for the next few days, nor did I ever expect to see her again.

I started my third professional game a week later, the first game since my two-hitter in Grand Island and my first ever at Cibola Stadium. The *McCook Gazette* carried an article about me. It described me as one of the brightest of the McCook Braves' pitching prospects and mentioned I was a bonus baby. I was very nervous before the game and was determined to impress the 1000 fans with at least a repeat of my performance against Grand Island. I walked the first three men I faced and then struck out a batter. The fans cheered. I saw myself striking out the side with all those runners stranded on base. I walked the next man and the next, and when Steinecke came out to the mound and I saw Niekro walking toward me from the bullpen, I made no attempt to dispute Steinecke's decision. On the contrary, I breathed a sigh of relief. When the inning was over Steinecke told me I could return to the armory and take a shower. "You're through for the night," he said. I stepped out of the dugout and walked through the fence into the parking lot. Sally was waiting for me.

"I read about you in the paper," she said. "I wanted to see you pitch."

"You didn't see much," I said.

"Oh, it's only one game. There'll be others." She laughed as if embarrassed. "I even dressed up for the occasion." She was wearing a white blouse with a scooped-out neck and short, puffy sleeves. It was tucked into a long, full skirt. She wore white socks and loafers.

"Are you going back to the armory now?" I nodded. "Come on, I'll give you a ride."

We drove the short distance in silence. I was so disconsolate over my pitching that I forgot to apologize to her for my performance of a week ago. She seemed to have forgotten it, or at least to have forgiven me. She parked in front of the armory. "I'll wait for you," she said. I went inside, showered and dressed, and returned to the car. She drove aimless through McCook. I stared out the window at the darkened streets and thought of home. I scarcely listened as she spoke about herself. She had just turned 18, she said. She had been graduated in the top quarter of her high school class. "Which wasn't much," she added with a laugh, "since there weren't 50 kids in my senior class. Still, I thought I might go on to college. I wanted to go to college. Are you going?"

"What?"

"Are you going to go to college?"

"Yeh, in the fall."

"I wanted to go a lot," she said. "But my mother took sick and someone had to take care of her and do the chores. I don't mind it much, really. I kind of like it, even. But someday I want to get away. I'd like to work in Denver or even go to school there. McCook is okay but it's so small. You don't know how small it is until you get older. Every year it gets smaller." She laughed. "That sounds stupid, doesn't it? Is Fairfield a small town?"

"Kinda," I said. "But it's close to New York City so it doesn't matter much."

"I'd love to go to New York City," she said, and then she was quiet for a long time. I looked across at her. She sat erect in her seat. From the waist up she was rigid and leaning forward to see over the huge steering wheel of the ponderous old DeSoto. Her chin—I remember now—was slightly squarish and, at that moment, it was thrust forward as if she were trying to peer over the top of bifocals. With her eyes still on the road she said gaily, "Come on, don't be so glum. Cheer up! We could go to the drive-in, if you want."

"Sure, let's go."

She turned the car onto U.S. 6 and drove past Shorty's and the M-and-E Diner and the A-and-W Root Beer stand, which was filled with cars and carhops in black shorts rushing back and forth with their orders. When we reached the Drive-In Theater at the edge of town, she drove past its entrance.

"Heh, you passed it," I said.

"Uh-huh. We'll go in the exit. We won't have to pay." She drove behind the theater's towering screen, which leaned forward, away from the road and toward the cars that were facing it on the other side. Sally flicked off the headlights and turned into the exit. We were on a bumpy dirt road that first led past the screen and then past row after row of parked cars. Sally drove even more carefully now, her back very rigid.

"Do you do this all the time?" I asked.

"Lots. There's a place!" She turned right into one of the rows and passed behind three or four cars before coming to an open space. She backed the car up and then tugged on the steering wheel with great effort and guided the car forward in little spurts. She turned off the engine and reached out the window for the sound box. Hooking it over her half-opened window, she clicked it on. "See, I told you," she said, turning toward me. "Nobody ever catches us."

I don't remember what the movie was—gigantic images on an overwhelming screen—because the moment Sally turned toward me we began to kiss as we had in the Fox Theater. There was no arm rest between us now, and we pressed our bodies together as tightly as we could. Our tongues touched. I put my hand on her breast. She did not move away. After awhile I said, "Let's go sit in the back seat."

Breathing heavily, she pulled away and sat up. "No," she said.

"Why not?"

"I don't know. Let's stay here. Please!" She tried to kiss me. I pulled away.

"All right," I said. "We'll watch the movie."

We sat apart in silence and stared at the screen. Finally she said, "I'll be right back." She got out of the car and I saw her darkened form moving between cars toward the small shack that served as refreshment stand and rest rooms. I breathed a sigh of relief. What if she'd said yes! But she hadn't. My heart stopped pounding. By the time she returned to the car I was no longer scared. I was relaxed even, and unbelievably confident. When she sat down I began to kiss her again and she responded. She responded feverishly, more feverishly than I, in fact. My mind was clear. With confidence, I renewed my protestations.

"Let's go in the back."

"No, please!" She did not stop kissing me.

"Come on!" I said when I could.

"We shouldn't."

"Yes!"

"All right." She opened the door and got out of the car. I was alone in the front seat. I looked at her standing there, and for a split second I wondered what she was doing. Then I opened my door and got out, too. We both slammed our doors at the same instant and the sound of those slamming doors still echoes in my mind. I felt the eyes of every person in that drive-in on me. My God! They all knew! I grabbed the handle of the rear door and pulled. It was locked. Sally was sitting in the back seat waiting for me. I grinned through the window and pointed at the lock. She pulled it up. I opened the door and got in beside her. I shut the door carefully so as not to make a sound. The door did not fully close. She reached across me, opened it again and slammed it hard. That sound wilted the last remnants of any passion I'd had. It seemed to renew Sally's however, and she began to kiss me with even more fervor. We kissed wildly as she lay back in the seat, pulling me down on top of her. The car's upholstery smelled stale and faintly sour. I propped my elbows on the seat so not to crush her with my full weight. The seat was not long enough. When I tried to stretch my legs out my shoes banged against the door window. I thought for a moment and then pulled them up under my stomach, so that now, like crouching cat, I looked ready to spring.

"Your knees," she rasped. "They're in my stomach."

"Oh, I'm sorry." But what to do with them? Should I open the window and stick my feet out?

"Bend your legs backward," she suggested. "Behind you." When I did, my legs folding like a jackknife behind me, I felt much more comfortable. We began to kiss again, and within seconds were as passionate as before.

"Aaaggghhh!"

"What happened?" she cried.

"My leg! Charley horse!" I began to shake my left leg violently, and my shoe banged against the door window until I thought it would shatter. Gradually the muscles in my calf relaxed and the cramp subsided. I folded my legs behind me again and, as we resumed our kissing, felt only a slight soreness. Would it affect my follow-through?

We had been kissing a long time before I finally reached my hand under her skirt. It froze.

"I took them off in the ladies room," she said, and so, after more fumbling with my pants, we made love. A euphemism, perhaps. Maybe she made love. I never thought of it at the time, though over the years such a possibility has, with distressing frequency, crossed my mind.

It was over quickly. When I was finished, I stopped. She looked up at me with wide, mad eyes that momentarily frightened me. "What's the *matter?*" her voice was like glass.

"Nothing," I said and sat up. I zipped up my pants. She lay there on the seat, breathing heavily, then less heavily, and at last, with a deep breath, she pulled herself up beside me. We sat in silence. I remembered something I'd read once. I tried to recall what it was.

"Did anything move?" I asked.

The following morning, sitting on the bench in front of the Keystone Hotel, I was assailed by unbearable guilt. Surely God would strike my arm dead! At the very least He would give me a disease as my mother had warned me. I would go insane. My flesh would rot as my black soul already had begun to. I waited for lightning to pin my charred and shriveled corpse to the wall. Nothing happened. It occurred to me that I had also betrayed my girl back home, but that guilt was assuaged quickly by knowing she would never find out. I cursed Sally. It was her fault. How could she let me do such a thing? She'd seemed okay at first. But now—after she'd let me do *that* . . . No girl had ever let me do *that* before! I resolved never to see her again.

She was waiting for me in the parking lot after that night's game. I told her.

"But why?" she said.

"It wouldn't be fair. I have a girl friend back home."

"I know," she said. "But I won't let myself think about it."

"I don't want to hurt her," I said, and, immediately I began to feel much better.

"Oh! I understand."

A few days later I was scheduled to start my second game at Cibola. It was a chance to redeem myself in the eyes of the McCook fans. I sat in the dugout after my warm-ups and waited for the game to begin. Steinecke was at home plate with the umpires and the opposing team's manager. Bill Marnie sat beside me.

"I hear you've been messing with that Sally broad."

"I might be," I said.

"Don't waste your time. She's flakey." He tapped his head with his finger.

"What do you mean?"

"You should know. She won't let anyone touch her. She thinks she's a goddamn princess or somethin'."

"Oh, you think so?" I said, and I gave him my best cat-that-swallowed-the-canary smile.

He grinned back. "I know so."

I didn't pitch much better than I had the game before. I lasted a few innings, at least, before I was tagged for two hits and began firing the ball like a madman. Finally Steinecke came out to the mound. "What a fucking exhibition!" he snapped. "Go take a shower!"

"Fuck you, too!" I stormed off the mound.

"That'll cost you," he yelled after me.

I kept walking past the dugout, through the fence, into the parking lot and beyond to the road that led to the armory. I was furious, and only after I'd walked a few minutes in the darkness did I realize what a long way I had to go. I could see the low, flat silhouette of the armory far in the distance. I passed a few houses, my spikes clicking on the sidewalk, and then the paving ended and I was on the dirt shoulder beside the road with only the crickets for company.

The houses were behind me now and I was walking between the road and a darkened field. My rage became despair as I walked, and finally self-pity. Not until I was half-way to the armory did I realize that someone was following me. I looked back and saw overhead the lights of Cibola. On the road below I saw the headlights of a car. It was about 100 yards behind me and barely moving. As I began to walk faster I heard the car drawing closer. Its headlights caught and illuminated me and then they were shining ahead of me.

"Hello," she said.

"Hi." I continued to walk, and Sally drove slowly beside me.

"How've you been?"

"Okay, and you?"

"Okay." She laughed a little, and I looked at her for an instant. She was steering with one hand and leaning across the seat, facing me. Every few seconds she would glance quickly at the road and then back at me. "Can I give you a lift?"

"That's all right. I'd rather walk."

"It's a long walk."

"I don't care!" She must have taken her foot off the gas just then because the next instant I was bathed in the car's headlights. They grew fainter and fainter as I walked. I did not look back until I reached the armory. When I did the car was stopped by the side of the road, its lights still on.

That night I woke from my sleep with a thought. Why me?

Before the next night's game, I waited until Steinecke was alone in the dugout before I apologized.

"It'll still cost ya," he said, without taking his eyes off the playing field where our team was having batting practice.

"I know. I deserve it." Then I said in a rush that surprised even me, "But I don't deserve to be starting games the way I'm pitching. I know you're just starting me because I got a bonus and all."

"That's my problem."

"But I don't feel right. It's not fair. Guys like Julius aren't even getting a chance and I am."

He leaned forward and spit tobacco juice onto the wooden planks of the dugout floor. "Well, Podner, I might just agree with you there. Yessir, I might." Then he looked at me and grinned—a fat, bald, lecherous old man. "But did it ever occur to you I might not have a fucking choice in the matter?"

"Oh!" I nodded.

"So until I get different orders you will start every five days whether you deserve it or not." He watched batting practice for a few seconds, then said, "How's it feel, Podner?"

"What?"

"That first thought."

But I'd had another, I wanted to tell him.

I was fascinated by Bill Steinecke from the first moment I met him. I introduced myself to him and said, "You must be my coach."

"Coach, my ass," he said. "That bastard who put flowers in your hair in high school was your coach. I am your manager. Your skipper. Skip. Steinecke. Steiny. Bill, Anything, but your fucking coach." And he walked away from me.

He was right, of course. He was not like any coach I'd ever had. My high school coach led us in prayer before each game. We knelt on the ground in a circle, lowered our heads, put our hands in the center of that circle and prayed to St. Jude for victory. Steiny did not lead us in prayer. He led us in other ways. One night, sitting on the top step of the dugout, he was berating the homeplate umpire. All the while a woman fan screamed epithets at him. Steiny ignored her for a time. She cast aspersions on his manhood.

"Can't cut the mustard anymore, you old fart!"

He shouted back at her. "Not with an old piece of meat like you."

At the end of the inning he returned to the dugout bench out of the woman's vision. He was cackling to himself. Julius Overby, Brubaker and I thought he was mad. "That old whore!" He shook his head, as if in admiration. "Used to be one helluva lay in her day. Yessiree. But so did we all, I guess. Well, she got the change and now she's just a nasty old bitch. Don't wanna do much of anything anymore. Ha! 'Cept let you do all the work." He looked across at us, at our pink and puzzled faces, as if discovering our presence for the first time. "I don't suppose any of you know what I'm talkin' about? No, I expect not. You think it's just push-push and good-bye, huh? Well, Podners, it's time you got educated. With a woman you gotta do things. Make them happy, too." And then, while we listened with rapt attention—and the opposing team loaded the bases—Bill gave us our first course in sex education. His course was very thorough, touching all the bases: physical (various positions, unusual acts), anatomical (a description of the female body); medicinal (prevention of disease), and psychological ("Make them happy, too.") It was very graphic and, at appropriate moments, punctuated by darting little gestures of his tongue, while his eyes, no bigger than Le Suer peas, gleamed.

Throughout most of each game Bill sat on the top step of the dugout, from where he could easily torment the umpires. He began the moment they walked past him toward home plate. "Hello, girls," he would say in a falsetto voice. They would look at him—skinny, pink-faced youths like ourselves—and smile weakly. Bill said it was his job to torment them. "Keeps the bastards on their toes, know what I mean?" But secretly, I think he took pleasure in it, and, in fact, viewed each game as a dramatic production that would be incomplete until he found an excuse for his entrance. When he did, when some poor 22-year-old umpire called Barry Morgan out on a close play at the plate, Bill would stand, hitch up his pants, mutter "Show time" and step out of the dugout. The McCook fans clapped and roared their approval as he waddled with agonizing slowness toward the plate. The umpire would take off his mask, his shoulders sagging, and stand there for what seemed like an eternity while Bill, a crusty old rhino, took his sweet time amid the fans' growing cheers.

"Now, Bill! Don't get hot! You know . . ."

But it was no use. The umpire's logic and even his person were superfluous to Bill's performance. The umpire was needed only as a playwright needs a butler—"Madame, the Archduke." Once Bill had made his entrance, the umpire, like the butler, might just as well have vanished. Since he didn't, Bill used him as a foil.

Bill's monologue began rationally enough, with him explaining in pantomime (elaborate gestures of the arms) and using the simplest logic (which even such a dunce as this umpire could understand) how Barry Morgan had successfully evaded the catcher's tag. Eventually, of course, Bill would have to become indignant when the umpire did not accept his account of the play. Bill's eyes bulged in disbelief. His face bloated. He cursed the umpire's ancestry, expressing some doubt, at first, that he had any, but then deciding it was surely of the foulest kind—horse thieves and highwaymen and ladies of the night. His rage spent, Bill turned his back to the umpire, banished him to the wings and, with outspread arms, addressed the audience behind the homeplate screen. They cheered every word and gesture. The umpire, relieved that his ordeal was past, stooped over to dust off the plate. He bent low to the ground, his tail to the wind. So flustered was he that he forgot to face the homeplate fans (as he had so recently been taught in umpire's school) and, instead, was facing the centerfield fence. Bill turned instinctively back to his victim and pointed to his upraised rump. The fans laughed uproariously. Bill shook his head in disgust, and with just a bit of pity, and then left the stage.

One night in Grand Island, the fans behind home plate interrupted his monologue with a shower of popcorn, beer, boxes, cups and hot dog remnants. Bill did not flinch, but turned toward our dugout and exited with the greatest dignity. Debris rained down upon him. Once inside, his eyes glistened with pleasure. "Gave them fuckers their money's worth, didn't I?" After that game, as we walked across the parking lot to our dressing room, the Grand Island fans tried to run us down with their cars and trucks.

Needless to say, I worshipped Bill Steinecke. I spent hours learning how to chew tobacco without getting sick. I cursed the umpires, called Julius "Podner," would do anything Bill asked. But he asked nothing. He demanded nothing, explained nothing (other than sex). He assumed all. When I figured out the real reason for his starting me every five days, he did not congratulate me on my perception as I'd expected. I should have had it sooner. An adult would have. He was the first adult ever to treat me as an equal. Whether I was or not seemed no concern of his. That was my problem. What he assumed at the time was often vague to me. I struggled to discover what it was, wondered if that was not his intent.

"Is your arm sore?"

"No."

"Can you throw about 10 minutes of batting practice?"

"Sure, Skip."

No matter how much I grimaced on that mound, clutched my aching arm, indicated to him that I was pitching in pain, for him, for his admiration (and pity, too), he ignored me. After 10 minutes he sent in another pitcher. He did not ask how my arm was. He assumed it was fine. So the next time he asked me such a question, I answered truthfully. Still I got nothing for it.

"Did you do your running today?"

"No. Should I?"

"It's up to you."

Perhaps I am giving Bill more credit than he deserves, that in retrospect I am imparting to his indifference intents and reasons he never had. Possibly, as I've always felt of W. C. Fields, he really did hate dogs and little children and wondered to his dying day, why the laughter? Whichever is true, the effect on me then and now remains the same.

I pitched well for the rest of the season. I won my next game 4–3 (at Cibola, finally) and, even though I lost the one after that in Kearney, I pitched a beautiful game. I was leading 1–0 in the bottom of the ninth inning. A walk and an error put runners on second and third with two outs. I induced the next batter to loft a routine fly ball to Ken Cullum in center field. I started off the mound, but saw Cullum circling the ball oddly. He staggered, and the ball dropped at his feet. He picked it up and threw it over Ron Hunt's head at third base, and both runners scored. When Cullum reached the dugout, his face had a pixie smile and I knew he was drunk.

My mound opponent that night in Kearney was a chunky right-hander named Jim Bouton. He was only one of a number of players in the Nebraska State League who would achieve fame in the majors—and, in Bouton's case, beyond. Bill Hands, once a 20-game winner with the Chicago Cubs, was, in 1959, a seldom-used pitcher for the Hastings Giants. Duke Sims, who helped the Detroit Tigers reach the 1972 American League play-offs, was a second-string catcher with the North Platte Indians. José Santiago pitched for the Grand Island A's and Al Weis played second base for the Holdrege White Sox. These future major leaguers were far from the most talented players in the NSL in 1959, however. In fact, Bouton was the fifth fastest pitcher on the Kearney Yankee team. He was surpassed by Hub King, Ralph Scorca, Jack DePalo and Jim Lasko. They all looked as if they had brighter futures than Bouton, but none ever reached the major leagues. Al Weis, a .200 hitter in 1959, played in the majors for over 10 years, while Woody Huyke, who led the NSL in home runs and RBIs and batted over .300, never reached the majors and, in fact, at 35, is presently a second-string catcher with the Sherbrooke Pirates in the Double-A Eastern League.

At the time, the most talented player in the NSL was a tall, handsome, light-skinned black named Jim Hicks. He could do everything well—run, hit with power, throw, field—and do it all with uncommon grace. He once played basketball for the Harlem Globetrotters and looked as if he could master any sport within minutes. He led the league in almost every hitting department during the first month of the season. Then one night some pitcher threw a fastball at his head and Hicks ducked a little too soon. Word spread through the league. Everyone took a shot at him. His average dipped below .400. I remember sitting in the dugout one night and watching as he rapped out three hits against our best pitcher. When he came to bat in the ninth inning of the hopelessly lost game, Steinecke brought in Julius to pitch to him. When Hicks stepped into the batter's box, Steinecke yelled, "Give him a little pierce arrow, Podner." Julius's first pitch caught Hicks on the ankle. He limped toward first base, could not make it (he'd already stolen two bases against our catcher) and was taken out of the game. "That'll slow the bastard down a little," said Bill. Hicks finished the year with a batting average below .300.

Despite the presence of such talent on other teams, the McCook Braves had the most talent of all. Bill Marnie pitched so well for us that he was promoted to a Class C league in mid-season, and Paul Chenger was eventually voted MVP. Dennis Overby won the league's strikeout crown with ease, and Phil Niekro was far and away the best relief pitcher. The rest of our team had almost as much ability and, at times, it seemed that Bruce Brubaker and myself alone, of all the bonus players, made only modest contributions to the success of the Braves. We assumed the league lead in mid-July and by the first week of August had an even firmer grasp on it. We eventually won the NSL title.

Julius French was given his unconditional release in August, a few days before his $10,000 contingent bonus was due. He had pitched sporadically and then only indifferently. He *seemed* to be a major league prospect but, to the Braves, not worth the money they would have to pay to find out for certain. If the decision had been Steinecke's, he would have kept Julius. But Steiny had little say in the matter. Julius did not get a cent from his hypothetical bonus, except for the money he'd been paid as a salary. I learned of his release when I arrived at the armory one afternoon. He'd left McCook without saying good-bye. I was glad. I don't like good-byes, never have. I distrust the emotions that rise from them, which are magnified and distorted by them. This indeed had been the basis for our brief friendship. We both distrusted emotion, saw in its external show hints of false sentiments.

I never heard from Julius again, though I saw his name once—on the roster of Triple-A team in the Cleveland Indians organization.

Julius French was not the only player to vanish suddenly that August. Dave Breshnahan, our freckle-faced relief pitcher and reader of erotic love letters, disappeared even more mysteriously. One day, after the team cuts had been made, he was gone. None of his rommates—Niekro, Derr, Overby, Orlikowski—would admit to any knowledge of his disappearance, beyond saying that Breshnahan had not been released. It wasn't until 12 years later that Niekro, then a star with the Atlanta Braves, revealed the reasons behind Breshnahan's disappearance. It seems at McCook, the personable redhead had organized games of nickel-and-dime poker with his roommates. He always won—10, 15, 20 dollars a night. He won every night for a month and none of his roommates grew suspicious—surely, they were the most trusting gamblers in all Christendom. One evening, Breshnahan won three consecutive hands by virtue of his possessing the ace of spades. A strange coincidence, thought Niekro, and he counted the deck of cards before dealing the next hand. The ace of spades was missing. Niekro asked everyone to stand up and look for it. They found it under Breshnahan's left thigh. Niekro's roommates wanted to banish Breshnahan from their house forthwith, but Niekro pleaded Breshnahan's case. "It was too late at night for him to find a place to sleep," said Phil. His roommates grudgingly let the culprit stay the night, after they had herded him, the black sheep, into his bedroom and locked the door.

"Later that night in bed," said Niekro, "I remembered that Davey kept a gun under his pillow. He was always showing it to us and bragging about his marksmanship. I couldn't sleep at all. I kept waiting for him to come blasting into my bedroom before wiping out the rest of the household. But he didn't. The next morning he packed his things and left McCook. We all made a vow not to tell anyone what had happened."

Without Julius during those final weeks, I was left to my own devices—drugstores and pool and the bench in front of the Keystone. I saw my teammates only during the games and occasionally, by accident, downtown. Ron Hunt and I seldom spoke anymore. We passed each other with faint nods as we entered or left Mom's house. Our final break had come over my brief friendship with Sally. "I thought you had a girl friend back home?" he said. "So what?" I said. But I was shamed by his faithfulness to his girl. She was more than that, he said, she was his fiancée. He missed *her* a lot. She must have missed him a lot, too, because one day she surprised him with a visit to McCook. That first evening as the engaged couple drove through town a car forced them off the road. The car was driven by one of the blond waitresses at Modrell's, who, it seemed, had been sharing Ron's affections these many weeks. The thought of the following scene, how it must have played out, more than sustained me during the final weeks of the season.

Walking home from the armory one night, I was given a ride by a 21-year-old Mexican named Anthony. I never learned his last name. He was short and fat with black shiny hair and a tan complexion. He spoke with a lisp. He knew little about baseball, seemed to have no interest in it. Yet he contented himself with picking me up after each game and commiserating with me over my pitching as we drove the town's streets until early in the morning. We drank beer, which he bought, and he taught me certain Spanish words that I should never use in mixed company, he warned. We laughed. He was unlike any friend I'd ever had. We had little in common. He was much more intelligent than I and, I realize now, possessed an adult sensitivity. He was repulsed by my crude talk (in imitation of Steinecke), and yet he often tried to imitate it, to curse and swear, it seemed, for my benefit alone. But the effort pained him. I liked him well enough, as one likes someone who does them small favors, but I never thought about him, never once wondered why he shared his beer and time with such a dull, single-minded youth as myself. The depths of his loneliness escaped me then. We often drove the streets in long silences (we had nothing really to say to one another), during which I would gaze blankly out the window and think of home or my pitching. When I woke from these reveries and turned toward him, saw him sitting behind the wheel, his small feet barely reaching the pedals, I sometimes caught him looking at me. He would then turn immediately back to the road and, flustered, make one of his infrequent coarse comments, at which I would laugh and be distracted from what I had just seen.

It was because of Anthony that Sally and I were reunited two days before I left McCook. I had mentioned her name to him a few times, hinted crudely at our intimacy, and he said he knew her. Then, one night when he picked me up at the armory, she was sitting in the front seat beside him. It surprised me—how glad I was to see her. I wondered why. She was very nervous when I got in beside her. "I hope you don't mind," she said. "I wanted to say good-bye." I put my arm around her and she put her head on my shoulder and smiled. Anthony drove us through the darkest of the city streets and, while he did, we kissed—the three of us sitting in the front seat, Sally between us, Anthony drinking beer while he drove. At one point, as I was kissing Sally, I looked across and saw him staring intently at the road ahead. Sweat glistened on his forehead, which shone white as we passed under a street lamp. His eyes never left the road. The can of beer was resting on the seat between his legs. He picked it up, took a long swallow and, still without taking his eyes from the road, replaced it.

We would end the season with a game in Kearney, and from there I would fly to Omaha and then home. Before I left with the team I called Sally.

"Meet me in Kearney," I said. "We can stay the night there."

She said she couldn't. Her mother was too sick for her to leave even for a day. Then she was silent for a long moment.

"I think I'm in trouble," she said finally.

"What?"

"It's been two weeks," she said. "You know . . . since I should have gotten it . . ."

I was stunned, unwilling to believe her. "Are you sure?"

"Pretty sure."

My only thought was to escape. To get off that telephone, onto the team bus and as far away from her as possible. Then it would all vanish like the bad dream it was. I knew, now, what she had wanted from me. She wanted to use me to escape McCook. She wanted my bonus. She wanted to ruin my career. My future. My life.

"That's impossible," I said. "It can't be."

She didn't answer right away, and then she said, "Maybe you're right."

I finished that first season with a 3–3 record and a 3.54 earned run average. I gave up 41 hits in 56 innings. I walked 55 batters and struck out 56. I obtained these statistics from a back copy of *The Sporting News*. I'd forgotten them. I'd forgotten much about those games, which, at the time, were so important to me. Small fragments, like the hailstones in Holdrege, they have melted in the warm waters of my memory. There are some fragments, however, that have not melted but have surfaced, hard and cold and sharp, from my subconscious. They seldom concern those games ("my only reality"), but deal instead with all that "dead time" I passed in McCook. These float about, knocking against one another in a disturbing way, until two at length fit together to form a larger piece and, repeating that process, a still larger one, until they have taken on a shape I now can recognize.

I called Sally a month ago. It had been almost 14 years since our last conversation. I'd gotten the telephone number from a relative of hers who still lives in McCook, and then, for days, I stared at it on the desk in my attic room. Downstairs, my wife of 12 years was moving through her day, making breakfast for our five children, cleaning the house, preparing lunch, while I sat transfixed by that accusing number. Finally, I dialed it. A woman answered. I asked for Sally by her maiden name.

"This is she," she said, adding that now she was Mrs. — and I did not catch the last name. I told her who I was, and then blurted out that she would not remember me probably, that it was stupid of me to call, after all these years, I'd had a whim, and so . . ."

"Yes, I remember," she said. "How are you?"

We talked for a while. I was nervous, laughed a lot, spoke quickly in a loud voice. She seemed strangely calm, assured even, as if she had been waiting for this second call all those years.

She told me she had married shortly after I left McCook. Her husband sold farm equipment. They moved from one small town in Nebraska to another and were now living in a town even smaller than McCook. "I'll never escape small towns, I guess," and she laughed. I wondered what she looked like now, at 31. I tried to remember but saw only a broad white forehead.

"Do you remember Anthony?" I asked. "The Mexican fella? What was his last name?"

"Oh, yes," she said. "He was a nice person. I never knew his last name, either. He wasn't part of our group, really. I knew him only in that casual way everyone in a small town knows everyone else. But, yes, he was such a nice person."

I reminded her of the night I had gotten drunk, the first time I had ever been drunk, and how she had taken care of me and I had never thanked her. I remembered, too, that night in the drive-in, but said nothing about it. "It's so embarrassing to remember such things," I said. "To remember what a fool I was. Why did you bother?"

"You weren't so bad," she said. "We were all foolish at that age, weren't we? I don't remember it being as bad as you do. In fact, I miss those days. It's hard sometimes living in such a small town as we do now. I won't ever get used to it. I reminisce a lot. It passed the time. Sometimes I wish I could go back to those days. They were exciting—for me, at least."

"They were horrible days for me," I said. "I don't remember much of anything nice about them. That's why I called. You were one of the few people in McCook I remember fondly."

"Really! I'm glad." Then she asked how many children I had. She knew I was married, of course. Our generation always married.

"I have five. And you?"

SKINNED INFIELDS

"Three."

"That's great." There was nothing else to say. There was an awkward silence during which I tried to think of some way to say good-bye. Her suddenly flat voice intruded upon my thoughts.

"We have a daughter," she said. She paused a moment, as if, for a second time, waiting for me to respond. I said nothing, wondered curiously why she did not mention her other children. "Our daughter will be 13 years old soon."

## Two Baseball Poems

### *from* The Wrong Season

*I*

john g. "scissors"
mcilvain, described by
the sporting news as
remarkable, died
in charleroi, pa.,
recently. he was
88. he pitched for
22 minor league teams
in 15 different leagues
and was still in semi-
pro ball in his seventies.
when he won a 4–3 ball
game at seventy-five he
said: i don't see anything
to get excited about. i
think a person should feel
real good when he does
something unexpected.
i expected this. his
big disappointment was
that he never made the
majors, although he won
26 for chillicothe
one season, and 27 the
next. he was, however,
a bird-dog scout for
the indians for several
years. he had been
deaf since 1912.

*II*

andy the paperman at
bleecker and eleventh
is grungy, his paunch
and stubble offending
even me. he played
shortstop in the pennsylvania
league in 1941 and
believes "kids today
don't love the game
any more like we did."
he played against the
best of his time, major
leaguers and all, babe
dahlgren, sibby sisti,
you name 'em, he played
them all. he once
safely stole third through
a slough of mud, soaking
all through his shirt.

(Left to right): Maury McDermott, Richard Grossinger, Don Larsen.

# 7

# Ou Sont les Garçons de l'Été Dernier?

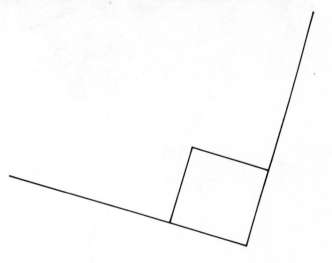

ROCKY COLAVITO

## Willie Miranda

*for Barry Weiner*

Marshall and I went into Donohue's on 72nd Street to have a beer. It was a cold night, November, but I felt like a beer in an Irish bar and Donohue's was on the way home. Marshall said they served good dinners but I wasn't hungry yet, I wanted to eat at La Maravilla anyway, so we figured we'd have a couple then walk up to 85th and have some ropa vieja.

We were about to leave when a guy midway down the bar began talking Cuban-English loud enough for us to hear. He was telling baseball stories, but I couldn't tell who he was, I'd missed his name if he'd said it.

He was wearing a belted trenchcoat, all lapels and buttons, and used a high-pitched Desi Arnaz laugh to punctuate his speedy patter. He ordered vodka with an orange juice chaser. I went over and asked him his name.

"Willie Miranda!"

"Oh sure, I remember you," I said.

He smiled and nodded rapidly. "Sure you remember me, Willie Miranda, you remember me."

"I saw you when you were with the White Sox, and with Baltimore. You were a great fielder."

Still nodding and smiling he said, "I was pret' goo' heeter, too. I drove een only ron when Weel-helm peetch hees no-heet gen New York. I know McDougal' at thir' take too moch time throw to firs' so I heet groun' ball to heem weeth man on thir' and beet eet out."

"That was in 1956," I said.

"Haha!" He slapped me on the back. "He know more than you guys," he said to the others at the bar. "Nineteen feefty-seex, you remember!

"But no more Cuban ballplayers now," he said. "Minoso, Luis Aloma, Arroyo."

"Sandy Consuegra," I added. "He won 16 one year for the Sox."

Willie nodded. "Tony Taylor the las' one lef'."

He took a sip of the vodka. "I leev now een the Bronx weeth Cepeda's seester. I look for chob as maitre d'. Everyone know me, I make good maitre d'. I bin work at Playboy Club, checkin' keys. But I was fire'. I'm wait now for check, thousan' dollar, after tha' nothing, but I ain worry. People remember Willie Miranda."

He finished off the vodka. His stiff black pompadour was streaked with gray. He was about twenty pounds overweight for his five feet six inches.

"Castro ruin Cuba," he said. "Ain nothin' for people there now."

"They're eating," I said. "They're healthier, the literacy rate is up. And Castro was a ballplayer, they have a great amateur team."

"Sure, Cubans the best ballplayers! But they ain nothin' there." He shook his head. "No money, no decen' life."

He ordered another drink. Marshall was moving toward the door. I zipped up my jacket.

"Nice to have met you, Willie," I said. "Good luck."

He drank half the vodka quickly and nodded. "Sure, sure," he said, as we shook hands, "I be all ri', everybody remember Willie Miranda."

—New York 1975

## Of Kings and Things

What happened to Joey on our block
Who could hit a spaldeen four sewers
And wore his invisible crown
With easy grace, leaning, body-haloed
In the street-lamp night?

He was better than Babe Ruth
Because we could actually see him hit
Every Saturday morning,
With a mop handle thinner than any baseball bat,
That small ball which flew forever.
Whack! straight out at first, then
Rising, rising unbelievably soaring in a
Tremendous heart-bursting trajectory
To come down finally, blocks away,
Bouncing off a parked car's
Fender, eluding the lone outfielder.

Did he get a good job?
Is he married now, with kids?
Is he famous in another constellation?
I saw him with my own eyes in those days
The God of stickball
Disappearing down the street
Skinny and shining in the nightfall light.

## All

Nothing that came before
was as tight as the All-Connie Mack Team
my 12 and under year
   had a third baseman at third
   a right fielder in right
2 good athletes had to look
towards second
for a spot in that lineup.

The closest I ever got
to the power of God
was being shortstop on that team.
just calling "play to third"
was an out,
and holding upstretched arms for relays
was
like pouring liquid outs
thru a funnel.

## The Knuckler

We knew your stooped figure in Astoria Park,
knuckle-baller, your hand slow & disdainful
on the diamond beneath the TriBoro Bridge,
fingers forking behind your back. Whatever you
threw wobbled in the air like a soap bubble.
Your mother was the nicest woman in a yard
full of cukes & tomatoes. She bought you aquariums,
little oxygen pumps, a Schwinn, blow-ups of father.
She thought you too thin. She bought you huge
mittens, big-shoulder coats, while the McDonald
brothers spit on the metal doors of grocery cellars
where you slipped. Anyone at all could find
you in Mendel's, at the magazine rack, slipping
girlies between the pages of *Sports Illustrated*.

All those years, you waited for a fast sign:
a wave from the blonde divorcee in her bedroom
across the driveway. Through Woolworth binoculars,
webbing of blinds, you learned the moles & fine
track of her spine, the rayon slide of her buttocks:
her hands behind her back unhooking a fullness
in your head, behind your eyes, in your throwing hand
that had only a knuckler, only an odd way of holding on.
We couldn't hit you at all in those days,
the gray & muggy afternoons when the ball should
have carried into the East River. We popped up,
we grounded out, the boys from Seymour's Hardware,
& Baker's Garage, & Queeco's Beer, we whiffed in
sunlight, or under cumulus, in the shadow of a long bridge.

But she died suddenly, thirty-eight, a bad heart:
released from your grip, writhing in a midnight glare.
It was obviously your fault. You stopped going

to Mendel's. Sold your Schwinn. Gave up fishing
for minnows in the bay near La Guardia: that airport
built on garbage, carriage wheels, father's shoes.

You stopped catching killies in bent window-screens,
stopped bringing them home alive in tomatoe cans,
& pouring them into the tank with your tropical fish,
like common children among angels, while your guppies
with the bulbous eyes gave birth & ate their young
beneath the 25c pink plastic bridges. You took apart
the pumps. You began to focus on empty windows, sparrows.
All morning, all afternoon, we hit you, O we hit you.

# 8

# Paleo-Baseball

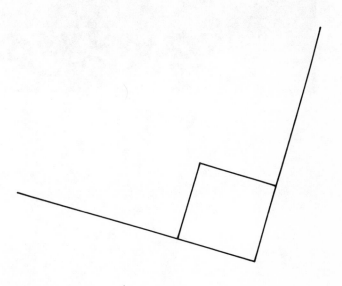

# DONALD HALL

## The Country of Baseball

Baseball is a country all to itself. It is an old country, like Ruritania, northwest of Bohemia and its seacoast. Steam locomotives puff across trestles and through tunnels. It is a wrong-end-of-the-telescope country, like the landscape people build for model trains, miniature in distance and old age. The citizens wear baggy pinstripes, knickers, and caps. Seasons and teams shift, blur into each other, change radically or appear to change, and restore themselves to old ways again. Citizens retire to farms, in the country of baseball, smoke cigars and reminisce, and all at once they are young players again, lean and intense, running the base paths with filed spikes.

Or they stay in the city, in the capital of the country of baseball. At the mouth of the river, in the city of baseball, young black men wear purple leather maxicoats when they leave the ball park. Slick dressers of the twenties part their hair in the middle and drive roadsters. In old *barrios* everyone speaks Spanish. Kids playing stickball, and kids running away from cops, change into fierce adults rounding third base in front of fifty thousand people, and change again into old men in their undershirts on front stoops.

Though the grass transforms itself into a plastic rug, though the players speak Arkansas or Japanese, though the radio adds itself to the newspaper, and the television to the radio, though salaries grow from workingmen's wages to lawyers' compensations, the country remains the same; everything changes, and everything stays the same.

The players are white and black, Cuban and Welsh and Mississippi farmers. The country of baseball is polyglot. They wear great mustaches and swing bottle-shaped bats, and some of them dress eccentrically. John McGraw's Giants play two World Series wearing black uniforms. Now the citizens' hair shortens, their loose uniforms turn white, their faces turn white also, and the white world cheers—while on the other side of town, black crowds cheer black ballplayers. Now the hair returns—beards, handlebar mustaches, long locks hanging beside the catcher's mask; now brightly colored knickers cling close to thick legs; now bats are scooped out at the thick end; now black and white play together again.

In the country of baseball the magistrates are austere and plainspoken.

Many of its citizens are decent and law-abiding, obedient to their elders and to the rules of the community.

But there have always been others—the mavericks, the eccentrics, the citizens of independent mind. They thrive in the country of baseball. Some of them display with Lucifer the motto, "I will not serve." Some of them are known as flakes, and unless they are especially talented bounce from club to club, to retire from the active life sooner than the others. Left-handed pitchers are reputed to be craziest of all, followed by pitchers in general, and left-handers in general. Maybe forty percent of the population in the country of baseball is flaky, at least in the opinion of the other sixty percent.

When Al Hrabosky meditates hate, in his public solitude behind the St. Louis mound, he perpetuates a great tradition.

The country of baseball begins to take shape at the age of six. Earlier, sometimes. Dock Ellis's cousin gave him a baseball to hold when Dock was in his crib. But Little League starts at six and stickball and cowpastureball at about the same age. At seven and eight and nine, the players begin to reside wholly in the country of baseball. For the people who will live there forever, the long summers take on form—time and space shaped by the sharp lozenge of the base paths. Then high school; maybe college, maybe rookie league, Class A, Double A, Triple A—the major leagues. In the brief season of maturity, the citizens of this country live in hotels, watch movies, pick up women who lurk for them in lobbies, sign autographs for kids, and climb onto the team bus for the ride to the ball park at five in the afternoon.

In their brief season, they sit for a thousand afternoons in front of their lockers, pull on archaic stockings, set their knickers at the height they affect, and josh and tease their teammates. Tony the trainer measures a tender elbow, tapes an ankle. Then the citizens saunter without urgency onto the field, gloves under arms, and pick up a ball.

Richie Hebner sees Richie Zisk. "Hey," he says, "want to play catch?"

Baseball, they tell us, is part of the entertainment industry.

Well, money changes hands; lawyers make big money; television people and their sponsors make big money. Even the citizens make big money for a while. But like actors and magicians and country singers and poets and ballet dancers, when the citizens claim to be in it for the money, they are only trying to be normal Americans. Nothing is further from the country of baseball than the business life. Although salaries grow and contract clauses multiply, the business of baseball like the business of art is dream.

In the cardboard box business, a boss's expectations rise like a plateau gradually elevated, an infinite ramp leading to retirement on the ghost plains of Arizona. And in the country of cardboard boxes, the manners of

Rotary proliferate: the false laughter, the bonhomie of contracts, the golf played with boss's boss. Few flakes survive, in the country of cardboard boxes.

But in the country of baseball, men rise to glory in their twenties and their early thirties—a garland briefer than a girl's, or at least briefer than a young woman's—with an abrupt rise, like scaling a cliff, and then the long meadow slopes downward. Citizens of the country of baseball retire and yet they never retire. At first it may seem that they lose everything—the attention of crowds, the bustle of airplanes and hotels, the kids and the girls—but as they wake from their first shock, they discover that they live in the same place, but that they live in continual twilight, paler and fainter than the noon of games.

Dock visits an old friend, Alvin O'Neal McBean, retired to his home in the Virgin Islands. In the major leagues, McBean was *bad*. The language of Rotary does not flourish in locker rooms or dugouts; the citizens' speech does not resemble the honey tongued *Reader's Digest;* eccentricity breeds with outrage. "McBean would as soon curse you as look at you," Dock says—even if you were his manager or his general manager; and he could *scream.* He was therefore not long for the major leagues. Now Alvin O'Neal McBean supervises playgrounds, the old ballplayer teaching the kids old tricks, far from reporters, umpires, and Cadillacs. "He's made the Adjustment," says Dock. "He doesn't *like* it, but he's made the Adjustment."

The years on the diamond are fantasy. The citizens *know* they live in fantasy, that the custom cars and the stewardesses and the two-inch-thick steaks belong to the world of glass slippers and golden coaches drawn by unicorns. Their fathers were farmers and one day they will be farmers also. Or their fathers loaded crates on boxcars for a hundred dollars a week and one day they too will load crates on boxcars for a hundred dollars a week. Just now, they are pulling down two thousand.

But for them, the fantasy does not end like waking from a dream or like a transformation on the stroke of midnight. They make the Adjustment, and gradually they understand that even at a hundred dollars a week, or even on top of a tractor, they live in a crepuscular duplicate of their old country.

And most of them, whatever they thought, never do just what their fathers did. When they make the Adjustment, they sell insurance or real estate to their former fans, or they open a bar in the Missouri town they came from. They buy a restaurant next to a bowling alley in their old Oakland neighborhood, and they turn paunchy, and tilt a chair back behind the cash register, remembering—while they compute insurance, while they pull draft beer—the afternoons of August and the cold September nights under the blue lights, the pennant race at the end of the dying season.

The country of baseball never wholly vanishes for anyone once a citizen of that country. On porches in the country of baseball old men are talking. Scouts, coaches, managers; car salesmen, manufacturers' representatives, bartenders. No one would let them exile themselves from that country if they wanted to. For the kids with their skateboards, for the men at the Elks, they remain figures of youth and indolent energy, alert at the plate while the pitcher fidgets at the mound—a young body always glimpsed like a shadow within the heavy shape of the old body.

The old first baseman, making the final out of the inning, in the last year he will play, underhands the ball casually toward the mound, as he has done ten thousand times. The ball bounces over the lip of the grass, climbs the crushed red brick of the mound for a foot or two, and then rolls back until it catches in the green verge. The ball has done this ten thousand times.

Basketball is not a country. It's a show, a circus, a miracle continually demonstrating the Newtonian heresy that muscle is lighter than air, bodies suspended like photographs of bodies, the ball turning at right angles. When the game is over, basketball does not continue; basketball waits poised and immobile in the locked equipment room, like the mechanical toy waiting for a hand to wind it.

Football is not a country. It's a psychodrama, brothers beating up on brothers, murderous, bitter, tender, homosexual, ending with the incest of brotherly love, and in the wounds Americans carry all over their bodies. When the game is done, football dragasses itself to a bar and drinks blended whiskey, maybe seven and seven, brooding, its mouth sour, turned down, its belly flowing over its angry belt.

In the country of baseball days are always the same.

The pitchers hit. Bunting, slapping weakly at fat pitches, hitting line drives that collapse in front of the pitching machine, they tease each other. Ken Brett, with the fireplug body, lifts one over the center-field fence, as the big hitters emerge from the dugout for the honest BP. "Did you see *that*?" he asks Wilver Stargell. "Did you see *that*?" he asks Al Oliver.

The pitcher who won the ball game last night lifts fungoes to a crowd in left field—outfielders, utility infielders, even pitchers who pause to shag flies in the midst of running. When they catch a ball, they throw it back to the infield by stages, lazy arcs linking outfielders to young relief pitchers to coaches. Everyone is light and goofy, hitting fungoes or shagging flies or relaying the ball. Everyone is relaxed and slightly self-conscious, repeating the motions that became rote before they were ten. Some citizens make catches behind their backs, or throw the ball from between their legs. Behind the mound, where a coach begins to throw BP to the regulars, Paul Popovich and Bob Moose pick up loose baseballs rolled toward the mound, and stack them in the basket where the BP pitcher retrieves three at a time. Now they bounce baseballs on the cement-hard turf, dribbling them like basketballs. Moose dribbles, fakes left, darts right, jumps, and over Popovich's jumping body sinks a baseball in a wire basket for a quick two points.

Coaches slap grounders to infielders, two deep at every position. Third, short, second, first, a bunt for the catcher. The ball snarls around the horn. Third, short, second, first, catcher. At the same time, the rubber arm of the BP pitcher stretches toward the plate, where Bob Robertson takes his turn at bat. Two balls at once bounce toward Rennie Stennett at second. A rookie up from Charleston takes his cuts, and a shortstop jabs at a grounder from Bob Skinner, and Manny Sanguillen leaps to capture a bunt, and the ball hums across the infield, and Willie Stargell lofts an immense fly to center field. Behind the cage, Bill Robinson yells at Stargell, "Buggy-whipping, man! Buggy-whipping!"

Stargell looks up while the pitcher loads himself with balls, and sees that Joe Garagiola is watching him. Tonight is Monday night. "Hey, man," he says slowly. "What are the rules of this bubble gum contest?" He whips his bat forward, takes a cut, tops the ball, grimaces. Willie has two fractured ribs from a ball thrown by a forty-one-year-old Philadelphia relief pitcher. Philadelphia is trying to catch Pittsburgh and lead the Eastern Division.

"What rules?" says Garagiola. "I don't have them with me."

Willie whips his bat forward with accelerating force. "How many pieces?" He hits a line drive off the right-field wall.

Garagiola shrugs. "Four or five," he says. "Something like that." He laughs, his laugh a little forced, as if he felt suddenly foolish. "Got to have a little fun in this game."

Nearer to game time, with the pitchers running in the outfield, the screens gone from the infield, five Pirates are playing pepper between the dugout and the first-base line. Dave Giusti holds the bat, and fielding are Ramon Hernandez, John Morlan, and Daryl Patterson. Giusti hits miniature line drives back at the other relief pitchers. Everyone laughs, taunts, teases. Giusti hits one harder than usual at Hernandez. Another. The ambidextrous Puerto Rican—who tried pitching with both arms in the same inning until they stopped him; who pitches from the left side now, and strikes out the left-handed pinch hitter in the ninth inning—Ramon drops his glove, picks up a baseball in each hand, winds up both arms as he faces Giusti head on, and fires two baseballs simultaneously. Giusti swings laughing and misses them both.

In the outfield, big number seventeen lopes with long strides, then idles talking to fans near the bullpen for ten minutes, then fields grounders at second base, says something to make Willie Stargell laugh, and walks toward the dugout. Seeing Manny Sanguillen talk with Dave Concepcion and Pedro Borbon, soft Spanish fraternization with the enemy, he throws a baseball medium fast to hit Manny in the flesh of his thigh. Manny jumps, looks around, sees who it is, laughs, and runs with gentle menace toward him. But Dock has turned his back, and leans on his folded arms at the top of the dugout, scanning the crowd for friends and for ladies, his high ass angled up like a dragster, his big handsome head solemnly swiveling over the box seats—bad Dock Ellis, black, famous for his big mouth, suspended in 1975 for a month without pay, the suspension rescinded and pay restored, Dock, famous for his Bad Attitude, maverick citizen in the country of baseball.

At Old Timer's Day in Cincinnati, Edd Roush is an honorary captain, who hit .325 in the Federal League in 1914, .354 in the National League in 1921, and played eighteen years. Lou Boudreau plays shortstop. His gut is huge, but he breaks quickly to his left and scoops a grounder from the bat of Pee Wee Reese, and throws to Mickey Vernon at first. I saw Lou Boudreau, player-manager for Cleveland, hit two fly balls into the left-field screen at Fenway Park in the one-game American League pennant play off in 1948. I discovered Pee Wee Reese eight years earlier, when I was twelve, and the soft voice of Red Barber on WOR chatted about the new shortstop up from the Louisville Colonels. Joe Nuxhall pitches, who pitched in the major leagues when he was fifteen years old, and still pitches batting practice for the Cincinnati Reds. And Carl Erskine pitches, and Harvey Haddix. Harvey Kuenn comes to the plate, and then Dixie Walker—who played right field for the Brooklyn Dodgers, and confessed to Mr. Rickey in the spring of 1947 that he could not play with a black man. Dixie Walker flies out to a citizen who retired last year, still limber as a squirrel, playing center field again—Willie Mays.

In the country of baseball, time is the air we breathe, and the wind swirls us backward and forward, until we seem so reckoned in time and seasons that all time and all seasons become the same. Ted Williams goes fishing, never to return to the ball park, and falls asleep at night in the Maine summers listening to the Red Sox on radio from Fenway Park; and a ghostly Ted Williams continues to play the left-field wall, and his flat swing meets the ball in 1939, in 1948, in 1960. In the country of baseball the bat swings in its level swoop, the ball arcs upward into the twilight, the center fielder gathers himself beneath it, and *Dixie Walker flies out to Willie Mays.*

## The Frenchman

Once there was an ump
Of French descent
Still knew a few words in
His native tongue.
In conference one day
On a disputed double steal
He was asked if he
And all his kind
Were blind.
He was heard to reply,

"Oui um peu!
Oui um peu!
Oui um peu!"

Later that season
In the hulking
Five o'clock shadows of
Old League Park
His body was found
A gash in his forehead
(Broken beer bottle)

At his side these two volumes
were neatly placed:
A French/English Dictionary
An American League Rulebook

Pinned to his chest protector were
These words on a slip of paper:
"Napoleon Lajoie, 2B Cleveland."

Next afternoon, from his office
Judge Kenesaw Mountain Landis
Acknowledged that the protest
Had been properly filed
And was legally binding.


## STEPHEN CORMANY

---

### Big Six and Alexander the Great


*I.*

On Labor Day of 1916
Matty pitched his last game
Locking up with his ancient foe
Mordecai "Three-Finger" Brown of the Cubs
In the second game of a twin-bill.
Matty's fadeaway was a mere crook by now, and
Neither old-timer was baffling,
But with nothing hanging in the balance
Both stayed around until the end,
Matty picking up the win, 10–8.


*II.*

Thirteen years later, in 1929
Grover Cleveland Alexander
Was nearing immortality, and
The St. Louis chapter of A.A.
Was having a field day
Keeping him off the wagon.
Drunks in every corner of Missouri
And Southern Illinois
Were dropping by the local headquarters

With home remedies.
One more victory, and
Pete would break Matty's
National League record of 372.


### III.

On a somber day in August
Pete accomplished just that.
Though weaving, all the same
He had receded sufficiently from the tremens
To make out in the shadows
Shoulders gingerly affixed to bats.
Those who saw him that day say
He pitched as if the world were a drop of wine
Clinging to the bottom of a slender necked bottle.
To retrieve it, all he had was
A coat hanger and a sponge.


### IV.

Fifteen years later,
Give or take a year,
A figure filbert discovered an error
In the National League records of 1902.
A victory by Matty had accidently been recorded
A defeat.


### V.

Out on the prairie near St. Paul, Nebraska
Ol' Pete was too drunk to know, or care
Or even differentiate the difference
If anybody had cared to explain it to him.
Matty's case was another.
In 1925, almost a year to the day before
Pete's infamous whiffing of Lazzeri,
Matty was dead at forty-five
At Saranac Lake, New York
After a bout of spinal meningitis,
An erroneous number imprinted on his brain.

## Judy Johnson Remembers

When veterans of the Negro Leagues were recently polled by Art Rust, Jr., they chose William "Judy" Johnson as their all-time third baseman. Johnson's former teammates and opponents recall a slender, stylish player, blessed with speed and finesse, who was respected for his intelligence and class everywhere he played. "He was like a rock," says ex-outfielder Jimmy Crutchfield, "a steadying influence on the club. Had a great brain, could anticipate a play, knew what his opponents were going to do." Newt Allen of the Kansas City Monarchs describes Johnson as "a gentleman all through those baseball years when baseball was as rough as could be. He was the type of fellow that didn't try to hurt anyone. He just went along and played the game. You have to respect a man like that."

Born in 1900, Judy Johnson began his Negro League career with the Philadelphia Hilldales in 1918 and ended it with the Pittsburgh Crawfords in 1936. During those years he played in more than 3,000 professional games—including League contests, championship series, barnstorming tours, and winter ball in Mexico and the Caribbean. Fragmentary records give Johnson a lifetime batting average of .349, but no statistics can measure the qualities that distinguished him, even among the best black players of his era: marvelously graceful fielding, clutch performance, and field leadership.

Johnson was renowned as a fine teacher of baseball. In 1930, as manager of the Homestead Grays, he discovered and helped to develop the great Josh Gibson. He later served as field captain for the Pittsburgh Crawfords, probably the best black team ever assembled. After his retirement Johnson worked as a scout for the Philadelphia Athletics, and he remembers trying to persuade the front office to sign such players as Larry Doby, Minnie Minoso, and Hank Aaron. If he had succeeded, Johnson says, "The A's would still be in Philadelphia." Later, as a scout for the Phillies, he was instrumental in signing Dick Allen. "Judy was a scout," says ex-Crawford teammate Ted Page, "but he could have done the major leagues a lot more good as somebody who could help develop ballplayers. He should have been in the majors fifteen or twenty years ago as a coach."

In 1975 Judy Johnson was inducted into baseball's Hall of Fame in Cooperstown, New York.

The following transcript, edited by Ron Beaton and Kevin Kerrane, includes additional material provided by John Holway and Sherry Weiss. Holway's recent book, *Voices from the Great Black Baseball Leagues* (1975), contains commentaries by nineteen Negro League veterans.

I used to steal third base a lot, because if you're on second base, the pitcher will get into his stretch, look back twice, and then when he turns his head, all you've got to do is start running, because that's his pattern. I'm over seventy years old and I bet I could steal on some of those pitchers they've got now. Just let me practice a few days.

You see, we were daring. Negroes can run—we had to run—and we kept that up. We'd run, drag, push. If we'd catch a shortstop playing back, we'd push it to him and he'd have to come in fast and field it with one hand. Why, it would be too late. Jackie Robinson brought all that stuff back into the big leagues.

I love to teach baseball. And I watch a lot of major league athletes playing now, and I know they're not putting out what they should, what they're getting paid for. They're getting a lot of money, but they're not extending their ability. I get so disgusted looking at the boys play, I really do, because outfielders will take their time and give an extra base. They're sluggish. And I don't like to see an outfielder going down on one knee— they do that in the big leagues. But can he throw from down there? Why, of course not. And by the time he gets straightened up, the man has two steps on him. These are the things that help you lose ball games. You make that little extra step, it helps you to win. That's the training they should get in the minor leagues, but they just don't.

We talked baseball day and night. I've seen the time when if we lost by one run, after we had our showers we'd have a meeting, and we'd sit in there a couple of hours going over the plays and seeing where we lost the ball game. I could tell you every play through the ninth inning. Today some of the players beat the crowd out of the park; they're in the shower and they're gone.

Baseball is like anything else: you've got to study every angle to win. Sometimes, when I thought I could get away with it, I'd have a bottle cap hidden in my glove. While the ball was tossed around the infield, the pitcher would start motioning the outfielders this way and that. Everybody's watching him, but I've got the ball and the bottle cap, and I'm going scrape-scrape-scrape. When the pitcher got the ball back, you couldn't hit it with a board that wide!

But it was hard to pull that stuff in regular League games, because they'd look for it. Most of our tricks came from out-thinking the other guy. If a man's on third base and it's the winning run, nowadays you catch the fly ball up high for a quick release. We'd pretend we were going to do it, then shift our hands and catch it down low. The player would leave the base before the ball was caught, so we'd put him out at third. We would always do things like that. When a man was on third base I'd get a big conversation going with him. And before he'd know it, the play was over and he was just realizing what was happening. Whoever they had coaching third, he'd say: "Don't talk to Judy, don't talk to him, he's trying to get your mind off the game."

Or a man's on second base, and he's going to score on a single. I stand like this, near the inside corner of the bag, but giving him room to get by. Now he can't cut that corner. I would make them take that wide turn. Well, they were losing three or four steps and a good outfielder would throw them out at the plate. They'd get back, the manager might say, "What the hell did you take that big swing around for?" They'd say, "Why, Judy was standing there. . . ." "Knock him *down!*" I've got knocked down many times.

We had more trouble with violence in the Negro Leagues than playing with white boys. My leg's all cut up. They would take files and sharpen their spikes. When they were sliding into third base, they often came in high with one foot up. I had to have five stitches put in my lip right here where a guy cut me. As I went to tag him, he put his foot out and ripped my face to the teeth. And he didn't even say "Excuse me!" I never got a chance to get him back. You just have to learn to protect yourself . . . in anything.

I was born in Maryland, though we moved to Delaware when I was quite young. We lived on Wilmington's West Side, right near a ball field. Nowadays it's called Judy Johnson Park. But back then it was part pasture, and we had to clean it off because both cows and horses grazed on it. It never bothered us, though, and we'd play until dark.

I used my father's glove. Compared to the big mitts today, that one would look like a dress glove. Eventually I could hardly hold it in my hand, there was so much dry rot. I turned a regular pair of shoes into my first set of spikes. A shoemaker cut down the heel for me and tacked on some metal spikes, and I felt like a real big-leaguer.

Baseball was my first love. I even kept score for a six-team league, including Harrisburg, Wilmington, Newark, and other towns. My teacher let me slip out of school five minutes early so that I could get my ten cents a game. I used a nickel of that money to buy a fishcake sandwich on the way home.

My father was the athletic director of the Negro Settlement House. Our yard had everything that you'd find in a gym. I worked with the equipment, but he wanted me to prizefight. My sister was my sparring partner. When she whacked me all over the place, I knew fighting wasn't for me.

High school wasn't for me either. I never finished at Howard High. Since my father couldn't afford the clothes I would have liked, I got a job for three dollars a week. When I look at kids now, things are different. Everything comes so easy for them. They don't do any chores. They need a ride to get around the block. I think it's a shame. We had to work hard. I thank God for it because it made me a better man.

One thing I worked hardest at was playing ball. When I became good-sized, I joined a Wilmington team called Rosedale. We played on Saturdays against other white and Negro teams from around town. All of us, whites and blacks, played every chance we got at the ballpark at 2nd and Du Pont. People came early with crates to sit on. By game time they'd be packed around that square field. We also played in Marshallton, and at Eden Park at 2nd and Adams. We walked to all the games.

I thought I was pretty good. There were a lot of fine ballplayers in Wilmington then. Like Eddie Stone: he was a home boy, like some of the other really good players—just didn't want to leave Wilmington and travel. But I figured I was the best around, and I just wanted to move up. So I signed on with the Stars in Chester. They were a good team with a good park, and I was paid a couple of dollars and trolley fare for each game. That was my first professional club. But I must have impressed the manager of the Philadelphia Hilldales, because he asked me to play with them on Thursdays and Saturdays at their Darby field. Sundays they'd go to Atlantic City as the Bacharach Giants—same club, just different suits on. I got five dollars a day, and in those days that was really good money. There was an old-time player named Judy Gans on the team. He said I looked so much like him I could be his son. So they started calling me Judy.

The next year they arranged to play every day. The manager said, "You work hard this winter, come back in the spring, and we'll sign you on as a regular." I worked hard all winter. I would get anybody to hit me a ball, or have a catch. In 1921 I joined the Hilldales full time. We had our own park in Darby, and our crowds got so big we had to enlarge the park—not just for Negroes, for white fans too. The Athletics and Phillies weren't doing very well then, and people were getting season tickets to see us. You couldn't buy a box seat.

By 1923, when the Eastern Colored League was formed, we had Biz Mackey catching, and John Henry Lloyd played shortstop and managed the club. Lloyd was a great teacher; he'd make you play your head off, and he was always full of encouragement: "You can do it. You can do it." And at shortstop Lloyd just looked like he was sliding over to the ball—you could hardly see his feet move. According to Connie Mack, Honus Wagner and John Lloyd were the best shortstops ever. "If you put Wagner and Lloyd in a bag," he said, "you wouldn't go wrong whichever one you picked first."

If we had an open date, I'd go up to Philadelphia, and Connie Mack would let me sit near third base for free. I watched Jimmy Dykes every chance I got. At that time he was considered the best third baseman in baseball. I'd study his movements, and later I'd try to execute his plays.

Our season never really ended. In the spring we'd travel all the way to Hot Springs without stopping. After ten days training there, we'd move on to New Orleans for a big doubleheader, and then start back North playing every day. We'd only have fifteen or sixteen guys on our traveling squad. Our season ran on into September, and then right after the big-league season ended we'd go barnstorming. Connie Mack's son, Earl, would assemble a team of white all-stars to play us.

Later, when I played third base for the Pittsburgh Crawfords, we played Dizzy and Paul Dean's all-stars fifteen times. We won nine times. We played the champion Philadelphia Athletics five times, winning three. Playing against the best players or teams in the white leagues we always managed to equal them, or better.

I remember once when we came to Wilmington to play a team of white stars. This was on Harlan's Field at Market Street Bridge—and, you know, the fans almost tore the stands down trying to get in to see the game. But most of the black-white games were played in major league parks because we knew they would be jammed. The only big-league field we couldn't use was in St. Louis. Out there they had a Jim Crow section. We weren't allowed to play, just watch from behind chicken wire.

On our tours, if we traveled to where we couldn't get back to our home, we'd go to a hotel. We stayed at Negro hotels, but if they were crowded, we'd go to individual homes. People would offer to take in two or three players. But we would try to get back. One time we played a Sunday doubleheader in Chicago. We put all our clothes on top of the bus. After the games, we drove to Philly without stopping. There wasn't any interstate highway in those days. We only stopped at stores for our cheese and baloney, or sardines—anything but a decent meal. Finally, we reached Philly on Tuesday afternoon and played another doubleheader right away.

Playing conditions were often bad, poor lights and tiny dressing rooms. And after a tough doubleheader we usually had a cold shower. But we still had fun, clowning a lot. Our infield practice would be a game in itself, and in a pepper game we'd pass the ball between our legs, doing tricks like the Globetrotters. People loved it. In one town everything would close up when we came to play.

And we always gave the public their money's worth. We never dogged a game. Any place we went to play, we played.

I played with the best. Martin Dihigo, a Cuban, may have been the greatest all-around player I knew. You could put him at any position and he'd look like he'd been playing there a lifetime. And nobody had an arm like Dihigo; only Clemente came close. If a fly went up, he'd go all the way to the left or right to get it instead of letting another fielder make the catch, because he could fire that ball on a dead line to home plate. Then he'd get on the ground and laugh: "You no run on me, boy, you no run on me."

Oscar Charleston was another great all-around player. He just made the Hall of Fame, but he's dead now; he should have been voted in a lot sooner. He could beat you with his hitting or his baserunning, and I never saw anyone cover the outfield like he did. He played a very shallow centerfield, which is what made him great. You still couldn't hit a ball over his head. He could really go back on the ball, like Willie Mays, but

Mays didn't play as shallow as Charleston. You couldn't score from second on a single when Charleston was out there.

But when I played for Pittsburgh with the Crawfords, we were a real powerhouse. Satchel Paige, Josh Gibson, and Cool Papa Bell were teammates. Cool Papa was so fast that if he chopped down on the ball and it bounced high, there was no way you could throw him out at first. He was the fastest man I've ever seen in baseball spikes, and a great baserunner too. When he'd steal a base, which was quite often, he was a gentleman. He wouldn't push a guy out of the way; he didn't have to.

You know, Babe Ruth was part black. That isn't just a rumor: I can't pinpoint them, but I've heard very good reports that he was. But *nobody* could hit a ball farther than Josh Gibson, nobody that I ever saw. And I started him off at the first night game in Pittsburgh. This was in 1930, when I was managing the Homestead Grays. The Kansas City Monarchs had this big bus. They took all the seats out and put a dynamo in to generate the electricity. I couldn't see the outfielders out there. If the ball went up above the lights, you had to watch out it didn't hit you in the head. Smokey Joe Williams was pitching. Buck Ewing was catching. Buck got down to give the signal—why Joe couldn't see his hand! I guess if we'd had some lime or something to put on it we'd have been better off. Ewing split his hand right down. My sub catcher was in right field. He wouldn't catch! Here we are: Forbes Field was packed. Josh Gibson was sitting in the stands, him and a bunch of little boys who played sandlot baseball. I asked if he would catch. "Yes sir, Mr. Johnson!" I had to hold up the game, let him go in the clubhouse and put on a suit. When he got back, Joe and him got together on the signals. I never saw a man get hit so much in the chest, and the shin guards, and the mask. Josh was back there trying to catch those balls. He was determined! We finished the game, and I felt so sorry for the poor boy. He said, "Mr. Johnson, how did I look?" I said, "You looked fine." I said, "If you want to continue playing baseball, we'll sign you tomorrow."

He wasn't a great catcher. But he wanted to learn. He used to catch batting practice for me and then catch the ball game. A lot of times after the game I'd have papers I was trying to get straightened out for the next day or something, and he'd come in. "Jing"—he used to call me Jing—"how'd I look today?" I'd say, "You looked fine, except . . ." He'd say, "Well, I'll try to freshen up on that tomorrow." He really wanted to learn.

He was the biggest kid you ever saw in your life. Like he was just 12 or 13 years old. Oh, he was jolly *all* the time. When he got sick, it hurt me, it hurt me bad. I couldn't get around to help him. I only wished I could. I think I could have helped him a whole lot. Because he thought the world of me. And anything I'd say: "OK, Jing . . . OK, Jing." But he got sick. I never got the right story about his illness. I don't know what started his decline. It might have been trouble with his wife: I know he loved her dearly, but he was a touchy guy. I could almost make him cry just talking to him. That's the truth—I could. He'd just sit there, never say a word, never argue back, he'd just sit there and listen.

I used to warm Satchel up a lot. His fastball was hard, and straight like a string, and I could take that box that the ball comes in and put it down for a plate, and I could just give him a target and I wouldn't have to move my glove that far. He was a professional, a perfect pitcher.

We were playing in Yankee Stadium, a play-off game against the Phil Stars. They got the bases loaded with nobody out and we were leading by one run. So I called time and I went over to Satchel Paige and I said, "You know, the boys were down the barbershop yesterday and they said they're gonna make a so-and-so out of you today if they got you in a crack like this." I said, "I know you don't want to be showed up." I took the ball and threw it over there and I walked away. When I got half way back to third base, he said, "Did they say that?" I said, "That's right, they talked about you." He threw nine balls and they didn't even touch a foul! He walked over by the dugout, he says, "Now go back to the barbershop and tell them *that!*" He threw nine balls and struck the side out. That's the way he was: he was a master in pitching. If a hit would mean a run or maybe two runs, he wouldn't deliberately walk you, but he would throw you balls so if you got four balls it was all right. But they would be so close to the plate that if you were anxious to hit, nine out of ten times you would go for a bad pitch. They looked so good they would almost draw the bat there, you know?

And Satchel did that every day. He could throw the ball through the eye of a needle. He had that kind of control because he used his arm every day. The guy that starts a big-league game today, if he's shelled, he has to wait 5 days before he starts again and all that time his arm is there and he's not doing anything with it. I never remember any of our pitchers stop pitching because his arm went dead. They used it. Like a pair of shoes. If you wear them and put them in the closet and don't wear them till next week sometime, they're going to feel a little snug on you. If you use them every day, finally they'll get so that you hardly know you have them on. Well, that's the way with using an arm. If you use your arm a little every day, the muscles look for it. Then they don't get tight.

Our league had a lot of good pitchers. Smokey Joe Williams threw harder than Dizzy Dean or even Satchel: he could really zoom the ball. He could have been a real star in the big leagues. His father was a full-blooded Indian, but they never tried to pass him off as one to get him in. Several of our guys did try to pass as Cubans to play.

Later, when I was scouting for the Athletics, I asked Connie Mack why they would never let Negroes into the big leagues. He said, "Judy, there's just too many of you boys to go at once." Well, I'm not bitter that I couldn't play in the majors. I'm proud of my career. I was just born too soon.

But when they were talking about having a separate wing in the Hall of Fame for players from the Negro Leagues, I didn't approve. If you're a professional in a certain thing, you're supposed to be as good as the next guy. Why should you come in the back door while he uses the front? As it is, too few of our players will make the Hall. The committee to select players from the Negro Leagues will dissolve in a couple of years, and it's a shame.

Just look at black major-leaguers today and see how well they stack up, in every phase of the game. And is there any reason to think we wouldn't have stacked up as well forty or fifty years ago? Sure, there are seven of us now in the Hall of Fame—but what about Dihigo, or Lloyd, or Smokey Joe? And that's just the tip of the iceberg: there are plenty of others who ought to be considered for the Hall.

I'm going to write about all this. There are a lot of things I want to say. But, you know, my real regret is that more people couldn't see the great black players of those days. I guess I'm a loner now. There's very few of us left, very few and far between.

## TOM CLARK

### And You Are There

Wearing the familiar Yankee pinstripes
With the heraldic      NY      elegantly covering the heart
Over a longsleeve white sweatshirt
Babe Ruth sits on a hardback chair in front of his locker
It is locker No. 3

The photographer has caught him in the act of
Reaching across his body with his large and powerful right hand
To untie his left shoe

His long slim legs in black knee socks are crossed
And his body hunches forward over them
With his left hand dangling in his lap

His head is moon-shaped and seems much too big for his body

He cocks his head up to the left as if someone there is speaking
His eyes are intelligent and wary
His nose is broad
His ears are enormous
They are pinned back flat against the side of his head

In its cowish amplitude his face
Slightly resembles Severn Darden's

The Babe is saying something we can't hear
To a person whom we do not see
Probably a reporter since the whole scene looks strictly posed

Three doors down the row of lockers
On a Persian strip rug
Which covers the board floor of the clubhouse
There is a pair
Of two-tone Oxfords—brown and white?—
The kind golfers used to wear

Maybe they're Wally Pipp's

## White River Spools

The photograph shows them posed in the far left field corner, in front of the snow fence. Oldtimers say that Inez Wilson once fell on that fence stepping after a sure home run and poked a row of 1½-inch-by-¼-inch holes in her middle part, but that was before that lead paint scare and she was okay, her brain was okay. Had another boy.

In back of that is the Royal Crown scoreboard, and that was the year somebody had blacked out "Home" and took and wrote in chalk "White River Spools" overtop of "Visitors," as it was their town. "Visitors," look there, is followed by a string of zeros that didn't very often have to come down or be played with. Spiders lived in them; their paint scaled.

Out there past the scoreboard is the White River. You don't see it here, but if you look close through Betty Sturgess's armpit, you can see a small boy on the far bank, next to a lazy old bluetick dog on its back in the hay. That's me.

They're all posed around two bats crossed in front of them, and there's a ball or two down there. They all have gloves on. They look like the dime store kind, flat and no pocket, and the fingers curl this way and the other, but that's the way things were back then. There's Ethel Gribbus smiling down there in front. Three or four in the back row are half looking up at the same place in the sky, and I can't think why they would of been doing that. There's a hole where Mabel Wheelwright would have been, so this picture must have been taken along toward the middle of the season. Isn't it funny how around 1930 something happens to pictures. They get gray, not old gray but bright, steely, rocky gray, like the whole thing was painted on an airplane wing. They're all like that, look.

Now hand me that one, the one with the writing. Yeah. You can't make it out real well, but it says "To My Big Leaguer, Love and Kisses, Sweetie." That's Eleanor Zufall, Sweetie, because her husband called her that. She'd come up to bat in a real tight game and you could hear him start behind the bench. "Hey Sweetie! *Hey* Sweetie! Get poppy a hit or he's gonna take that catcher home!" Course that was Betty Sturgess, so we'd all laugh. She'd make three of him, and only four or five teeth in her head besides. Poppy was a case. He'd be with a bottle of beer in his hand there behind the bench, and maybe in his house slippers. He was one of the last to take sick, in August or so, but by then nobody could catch the White River Spools. "*Hey* Sweetie!"

That one there you just ran your hand across, that's the mill. Now let me show you how things were laid out. As I said, left field sat right up close to the edge of the river just so. The Royal Crown scoreboard was so close to the edge. Finally, in that bad spring of '47, the river came up and got it one night, took all the ground right up from neath that snow fence and washed the scoreboard about ten or eleven miles downstream, folded it all up like in an accident. After that the Army came in and fixed the river, sifted it down, and the young kids at the mill laugh when we talk about the river running mean enough to swallow up ground. That's all over.

But in those days, that summer in particular, people would come out to the games and send the younger ones off down to the water to play, then settle in behind the backstop, in the bleachers. There were six–seven rows, and down behind the older ladies had their hot dogs and RC cola to sell, in a little green booth no bigger'n a minute. I recall the sound of the grease dropping down on the fire, that ratchety noise, and the way how, by the fifth inning or so, all things seemed to be swallowed up in a green light that was soft as quiet water.

Out past right field was the mill. It's all concretized now, but it used to be that it was brick, and it bent over the river like an old roan horse. One or the other of the girls would get a hit, you see, and we'd go up on our feet to root it through the infield, and that brick wall would catch the hit and the yell, and they would come back to us so true that you could pick out the Presbyterian Reverend Warren shouting "Send 'em on back, ladies!" and we'd all laugh. Or that echo could catch you by surprise, and you'd look over, thinking real quick that there was another game going on *inside* the mill, some secret game, and they'd given it away with their yelling. Then you'd remember, and know it was just you.

But that green time of day made me feel so good. I'd pretend we were all underwater, cool and slow. Or you could stand up against the backstop and press yourself to the wire and grab your hands around it, till the umpire saw you and told you. He'd say don't you know that Tommy Mooney lost a finger that way boy? Everybody knew that Tommy Mooney lost his finger at the mill, but it was just his way of saying, so you went on somewhere else.

Now there you got a picture of Jeannie Pottus. She was so pretty. Some few of the women at the mill said she was from gypsies. I know for certain that a gypsy caravan came through town back around the ought-hundreds, and some stayed and raised children. She looks like one, doesn't she? That hair and skin and eyes. She's not wearing a hat in that picture because she never would. She was fast as an animal, and when she'd run after a ball in that hot summer her black hair would be crazy with sweat and wind, all around her head. My uncle always said she was a Jew, but if she was she didn't let on.

But let me tell you. Once, I was twelve, I called her up. That was the summer that I sat in left field putting the numbers on the scoreboard. My father was a foreman at the mill, so that's why I got to do it, even after he died with fever. And my mother sat upstairs in mourning and grief with her door closed, so I got hold of the phone one night and called up Jeannie Pottus. I told her I'd been keeping my eye on her at the mill, to fool her as to who I was. She laughed in an easy way and said was this Bucky, that she'd been wondering about my intentions. Just like that, she said it. I didn't know a Bucky at the mill, and my head went blank. "Meet me at the field." I said. That's all.

But at first it was just a few of us came to the games. It was girls' softball, you know, not like the legion games even. Some of them had been at the mill for twenty years, and their skin was white like powder from no sun. The uniforms were old gray legion hand-me-downs with ghosts where the lettering had been torn away: John Deere, Amos Tool and Dye, the Flying A. When the women ran, the old clothes flung around them like they were filled with air instead of bodies. Even the young pretty ones looked past their better years. So there would just be me working the scoreboard, and some of the older women from the mill, and maybe Orville Coon to take a picture for the paper. Orville drank from an early age due to his name, though, so he got a lot of pictures of feet, even his own. He'd wait down along first base and when play came his way he'd reach the camera up to his face with one hand and the bottle with the other. Orville Coon tried to take more than one picture with a half-pint of Johnny Walker.

Now I can only recall some of the games, but if you'll look in the mill bulletin you'll see the scores. That one. The first one comes back plain, of course. Walton Bedecker, he was vice-president in charge of shipping and distributing, and kind of a team coach. He threw out the ball. The Spools were playing Westover Hospital and Emergency. A bunch of big tough nurses, and that was so many letters printed on their blouses that when they ran it looked like food had run all down their front parts. They beat the Spools, 14–2. Was it 3? Well, Miriam Hart pitched for the Spools. She'd had a husband run off with a little senorita, so she whipped her kids and wanted to pitch. Those nurses just bounced her around. Four runs, five runs, without an out. She cried from the second inning on, just out of pure hurt I guess, and Westover Hospital and Emergency kept putting balls in the White River. But Miriam Hart kept coming out, inning after inning, finally not even crying, and then with a spooky kind of half-smile. It got dark, and even the few that were in the bleachers had begun to grab up stray young ones to go home, when she struck the last nurse out. Everybody stood up and gave her a hand, just due to her spunk and all, and she got halfway to the bench, her face all blistered and shrunken, then stopped and screamed "Kiss my rosy red ass!" And course the mill wall picked *that* up and sent it back first class. Walter Bedecker like to messed himself, but even he could see that she was as surprised as anybody at what had come out of her mouth, and besides there was no man in her house, so she even got to stay on the team.

Walter Bedecker's in that nursing home down route 404 now. His head went all bad, he doesn't know his children and they got to cart him to the johnny, but regular as rain, once or twice a week, he'll sit up in bed and say "Did I hear right? Did she say 'Kiss my rosy red ass?'" Then he'll go back to that other place, and his eyes drift away.

But it started after that first game. Four or five of the White River Spools called in sick at the mill, and one day Amy Simmons and Betty Sturgess never came back from 10:00 whistle. Jeannie Pottus came to work in packaging. My daddy would come home from the mill and put the paper on his lap. My momma would be sitting in the chair across, with a pile of sewing or potatoes. She'd say "So how's it there?" My daddy would say "Same."

The afternoon sun fell through the crack of window beneath the curtain onto the floor, and I'd take the sports pages down there and fix it so that the column I was reading just caught that piece of light and held it, all the dust falling, like a church. I'd read a page, and in a minute my daddy would say "I'm going to turn it over. Pick up my check on Friday. I'm too old," he'd say. "Time to turn it over." It meant he was quitting. He was going to turn it over when Amy Simmons and Betty Sturgess never came back from whistle. I looked at Orville Coon's picture of Miriam Hart's feet, and Momma laid down her potatoes and called my daddy upstairs and shut the door.

My daddy stayed at the mill, and the White River Spools beat the North Corner Wives of Firemen, 8 to 0. They beat Worthy Brothers Lumber 12 to 0. You can check these scores to make sure. Miriam Hart pitched again and again, and something happened to the way she threw. No one could say what. Things just took Miriam over. Now she moved like soft rain. The sweat curled the hair around her ears. Her arm came up and went down under; her hand hung behind the ball like a lover letting go. I was young then, of course, but there were times I stood behind the backstop and saw her as part of a woman's body, hair or breast or hand. Or I would keep the scoreboard, and Jeannie Pottus would clean left field.

A fireman's wife sent her to the snow fence with a fly ball. She hit the fence full stride. She caught it, bent over the fence in a picture that was never taken. It would show me covering my crotch, my eyes, reaching for the ball, clapping, on my feet, falling, fearful, dreaming, drinking Daddy's whiskey in the cellar. Jeannie Pottus would be a woman in the night sea, a burning branch in her hand, her hair leaping past her head.

And then the White River Spools won and won. The games disappear in my mind; the scores go. Stokely Canneries, Philadelphia Dirigible Incorporated, the Eastern Shore Daughters of Shipping. A man from Philadelphia came down to write the White River Spools up in the newspaper. He watched them beat the South Jersey Lady All-Stars, 8 to 0, then got

Betty Sturgess in his Packard after everyone had gone home and I was taking the row of zeros off the RC scoreboard. His stockinged feet hung out the door.

Northeast Dairy Workers. A team of secretaries from Baltimore called the Depression Sinners. The town began to empty of a night, and the people wash out toward the mill on a tide. First the families, and then the young men. They came and stood along the foul lines with their beer, and parked their cars along the road, in the ditches.

There was a fellow who had had a shot with the Red Sox, but was of otherwise suspicious circumstances. He kept a room in town and roamed at night, looking to tell his stories. Curtie. He worked at the filling station in his Red Sox cap, and when he talked he'd push it back on his head, or if it was back he'd shove it down on his eyes, and after weeks of pushing and shoving it all across his head the bill turned black from grease on his hands, and smelled like a train. "Fella named Alexander," he'd say. "Fella named Jolley." And so on and so forth. But it was the wrong story for our town that summer, and he soon knew it. He'd pump your daddy's gasoline and say two dollars or three dollars or whatever it was. Your daddy'd pay. Curtie'd rock back on his heels, rubbing the money. Back goes the hat. "Course I was with the Sox," he'd say, looking off down the street. Then he'd spit, and squat down so his face was in your daddy's window. "But the White River Spools is the-best-I-ever-SEEN." Down comes the hat. "Damn right."

The year the Sox sent Curtie packing they lost 111 games. They lost 46 of their first 57. One of the worst teams in the history of the majors. They couldn't win to save their tail. Curtie was probably glad to be in White River, talking up a winner. But a couple years later a fellow named Joe Cronin took over the Sox, gave one-way tickets to seven starters, and brought the Sox back. Cronin was a feisty little sonofabitch who went after the pennant like it was planted on top of a mountain. The Sox went 80–72 in '37, then 88–61, then 89–62. Up the ladder, an inch here, a place to put your foot. Then he'd fall back a bit, circle, look for a better way up. 82–72. Get rid of the bums and go again. 84–70. 93–59 in '42, where the air got thin. Fall back. Wait it out. We beat Hitler and the Japs in '45, and '46 Joe Cronin and the Sox won the pennant, with a machine's patience. Joe Cronin did for baseball what the war effort did for this country, I'd say. You did your job, or the crazy stranger came and got you in the night. There was a need to produce. Carry a flashlight instead of a candle. Eveready made their fortune in World War II. In 1946 the Sox won the pennant, and they put in a time clock at the mill.

But in that hot summer, the teams came and went, Miriam Hart disappeared behind her cat hands, Jeannie Pottus flew at the fences, Betty Sturgess crawled in with every fast-talking lover and hit like bricks, and the young mill men stood along the foul lines in their white t-shirts, jitterbugging like clothes on the line.

Then, on Fourth of July day, against the Methodist Ladies Auxiliary,

Mabel Wheelwright, the Spools' first basewoman, went to her right for a ground ball. She got it, took a step back to the base, and fell down. She got up. The Methodist lady came on and was safe. Mabel got halfway to the bench and fell down. That's in my mind, seeing her across the field in the white hot afternoon, getting up and collapsing like in a cowboy picture in the sudden dead silence, with the rest of the women frozen, legs straddled, fists in gloves, then moving toward first base, slow at first, pushing through the thick air, gaining speed then, a scream coming through the mouth of the crowd. Walter Bedecker had been off in the woods for business, and came back running through the maze of cars, no more than half attached to his pants.

Somebody took Mabel Wheelright to the doctor, though, and it grew cool. The game went on without much talk, the sweat clung to your back like ice, and the Methodist Ladies drove home shut out.

The sun let up a little after that hot spell, and people left the shade and talked on the streets again. "Well," and "Whew," and "I declare," laugh and grab each other's arms like after a long bad time, like after being trapped without air. "I guess it wasn't all that bad," we said. Everybody's grandpa had seen worse, and talked about ought-7 and '94 like they were years for good wine. It was as if—what do I mean?—Mabel Wheelwright had taken care of things there, crawling toward first base. People were grateful. Flowers came in.

Of course it turned out that Mabel Wheelwright did nothing, because a week later the heat rushed back and people in White River started kicking over like mad dogs. In July came the fever. The river went down from no rain, and the sky was like glass. Children stopped from their playing and stood in yards, their heads hanging like cattle. Mrs. Beatrice Hannan, a good mother, went wild in the afternoon and beat her baby with a stick.

My daddy died at the mill, thank the good Lord, and they never even brought his stuff home, so as far as I was concerned he just caught a bus out of this world. That was a handy way to think of it. But the White River Spools, now that was a problem. First off, Doctor Willis, he was everybody's doctor, quarantined all those families suspected of the fever. Then they closed down the mill. And worst of all, it got so they couldn't get a team of ladies to come to White River for fear of disease. Why, there are pictures of Main Street bare, the stores closed up, the cars collecting dust and bugs. They closed the bars, and Orville Coon would pace the streets like a blind man, picking at himself and shouting "A man can't get a drink for love nor money!" to whoever would come to their porch rail to listen. If no one did, he'd stand shaking his fist at the sky, his dirty coat up around his shoulders. We'd watch, behind our windows.

The team that did come, when we were locked in our houses, was the Bluebees. They had that scripted in white across blue blouses, but we just called them the colored team, or the coloreds. They travelled across the country in four cars worn down to their prime coats, leaving a player in one town, picking one up in the next. They had no town. They played whoever would take the field on them, fifteen women black as ashes, their ratty hair wrapped in stained bandannas or tied with loose pieces of shoelace. Only some five or six of them had gloves. They were managed by an old white man whose one shirt had dried blood or tobacco spit all down its buttons. The story goes that he'd walk into a bar and line drinks up for the biggest men in the place. When they got around to talking sports, he'd tell them he could get them a game against the best ball-players in the country. Bullshit, they'd say. You're an old dead man. They're women, he'd say. They're black women. He'd lean close, and the talk would go down. Filthy-rotten-dirty-nigger women. And I'll bet you ten dollars a man they stomp your balls.

So drunken, reeling white men would play the Bluebees in empty lots, under the prism of car headlights, digging for taped-together softballs among the weeds and broken glass, falling on asphalt, overcome with nausea in the dark corners, wondering what in the name of God they were doing there, in games their wives would never hear about. The Bluebees would give them a respectable first game, losing 6 to 2 or so, then raise the stakes for the second and beat them by fifteen or twenty runs, and back out of town with knives drawn on these poor assholes who were coming out of this strange dream to find their wallets missing.

They backed into White River, and the old man peered in the windows of closed down bars, and walked the streets looking for loud-mouthed men. He found Walton Bedecker, wandering home from Mabel Wheelwright's funeral.

I'd been to the funeral, and that was the night I called Jeannie Pottus. "Meet me at the field," I said, a pillow wrapped around my head and the phone so my mourning mother wouldn't hear. I went upstairs and picked up my bat and ball on legs that were stiff with fear.

Maybe the little white man in the dirty shirt knew that this was the right town for a crowd, that they'd come to gawk at these raw black women who'd scrubbed floors in Fayetville or shot their no-good men in Chattanooga and run into the night, leaving their snot-nosed, crying children with sleepy sisters, stuffing a second dress into a paper sack and climbing into this shit-brown old Hudson with a crazy white fella says he's got a map to the River Jordan!

And crazy white man, for the first time he can remember, will get him some real bleachers in this town, and a crowd to play for! He walks past the black women throwing a softball around the dead grass, onto the pitcher's mound. "Ladies and gentlemen," he says, turning on his rotting shoes. "First, let me pay my thanks to your lovely town for hosting the young ladies and myself. I am having the understanding that you pride yourself on your own assemblage of players that is quite powerful in the varied aspects of the game. But the world famous Bluebees"—here he dreams of waving his arm around the diamond, at the tight-lipped black women—"politely but with due firmity dispute your judgment. They appear here this evening in order to demonstrate their remarkable prowess. Watch them work . . ."—and here his voice will be amplified by the thousand and one radio microphones thrust in his face—". . . their black magic . . ."

I reach home plate in the blackness, the bat on my shoulder, the ball in my hand. When I see the first edge of shadow cross the infield, I toss the ball up and swing. The ball skates across the dirt toward her. A moment later it bangs into the backstop behind me, and ripples down the wire.

I am twelve years old. I line the numbers on the scoreboard, and there is the noise of the river that the crowd must drown. The ball is white against the evening grass.

The old white man meets Walton Bedecker wandering home from Mabel Wheelwright's funeral. Imagine them standing in the empty town in the beautiful summer night, paper drifting down the street. One of them in a shirt crusty with spit, the other in a suit as stiff as stone. "I've got a team," the old man says. They walk.

# 9

# Players

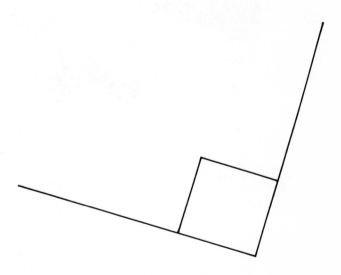

## Ty Cobb Poem

*For Leo Connellan*
*who also fights hard*

*1.*

where there are two or three
are gathered together
are sitting around
quizzing each other
on statistics
listing who was the greatest this
and who was the greatest that
calling up all the more important
baseball players of today and yesterday

where there are any there
is one question that usually
never gets to be asked:

> who was the greatest major league
> baseball player of all time
> the first man who was voted into
> the Hall of Fame
> whose mother took a shotgun
> and killed his father during
> the first week of this player's
> major league career?

where there is a stunned silence
and the question hangs unanswered:

> who was born December 18 1886
> in Narrows, Banks County, Georgia
> who during his playing days

weighed 175 pounds and stood
six foot one

whose mother took a shotgun
and blasted his father's head off
when this player was only
18 years old?

where the more one lives with the question
the more one tries to imagine
a lifetime of trying to fight
the knowledge of it:

who played in the American League
who was a left handed hitter
who was a right handed fielder
who played for the Detroit Tigers 1905–1926
who played for the Philadelphia Athletics 1926–1927
whose mother took a shotgun and
blasted his father backwards
in the grass during this player's
first week of playing the outfield
for the Detroit Tigers?

2.

Tyrus Raymond Cobb
the Georgia Peach

who in this day
of almost daily record breaking
still lays claim to more records
than any other man
in the history of baseball

he has the highest lifetime batting average
(.367)
he is still first in total runs
(2244)
he is still first in total at bats
(11429)
he is still first in total games played
(3032)

he is still first in total stolen bases
  (892)
he is still first in total outfielding games
  (2943)

he is still second in total triples
  (297)
he is still second in total stolen bases one season
  (96)
he is still second in total double plays
  (107)
he is still third in total outfield chances
  (7024)
he is still fourth in total runs batted in
  (1959)
he is still fourth in total put-outs
  (6361)
he is still fourth in total bases
  (5863)
he is still sixth in extra base hits
  (1139)
he is still seventh in total hits one season
  (248)
he is still eighth in season batting average
  (.420)
he is still seventeenth in total bases on balls
  (1249)

he won the batting title 12 times
9 times in a row from 1907–1915
(Tris Speaker beat him out in 1916)
Cobb came back to win it in 1917, 1918, 1919

he hit .300 or more
for 23 straight
years

he stole
home
34 times

for 8 years
he stole more
than 50 bases

5 times
he made 5 hits
in one game


3.

what was it like to see Ty Cobb play
in those days of Tris Speaker the Grey Eagle
Napoleon LaJoie
Honus Wagner the Flying Dutchman
the Kentucky Colonel Earle Combs
the Big Train Walter Johnson
and the Bambino, the Sultan of Swat, Babe Ruth

what was it like
in those 1920s the Golden Age of Sports
what was it like to see Ty Cobb play
in those days of Red Grange the Galloping Ghost
the Four Horsemen of Notre Dame
Jim Thorpe the Fabulous Indian
tall Bill Tilden in tennis
the Manassa Mauler Jack Dempsey
the Fighting Marine Gene Tunney
and little Bobby Jones in golf

what was it like to see Ty Cobb play

Casey Stengel
the ole perfesser
sums it up this way:

    i never saw anyone like him
    it was like he was superhuman


4.

never mind about the records
just say i was on base more often
than anyone else
and that i scored more runs
than anyone else

that will always stand
and that will say it all

i hold the bat this way
like it is a long
strong part of me

i have one hand
on the thick of the throat
and i have the other hand
on the other end

my hands are far apart
so when the pitch comes over
i can make a quick switch
either up or down
and hit the ball
to any field i please

if i ever get
into a batting slump
i hit the ball
right back at the pitcher
make him feel foolish
fumbling all over the place

that way i never worry
about a batting slump
for very long

      Ty Cobb
      why did you fight
      so hard?

today when kids play on a team
that is on its way to a pennant
they usually say:

      it's a chance
      at $25,000
      extra

but when you were playing
it wasn't a matter
of money

Ty Cobb
why did you fight
so hard?

for all my trying
i only won the Tigers
3 lousy pennants


5.

Ty Cobb
why did you fight
so hard?

"My father was the greatest man
I ever knew. He was a scholar,
state senator, editor, and philosopher.
I worshipped him."

he didn't want me
to go into baseball
he wanted me
to be a doctor
or a lawyer

but in April 1904
i sat myself down
i wrote off a lot of letters
to every club in the
South Atlantic League
asking them for a try-out

i only got one reply
from Augusta
they said they would
try me out
but i had to pay my own way
to the ballpark

okay so i go
and they put me in the outfield
i hit a double and a home run
in 4 times at bat
and i score 4 runs

one game later
their regular
center fielder shows up
so they release me

i go down to Anniston
in the Southeastern League
and i play there awhile
until Augusta asks me back

opening game of spring 1905
i am playing the outfield for Augusta
it is a peaceful day
we have a shut-out going for us

everything is so free and easy
i am eating pop corn in the outfield

    someone hits a pop fly
    catches me off guard
    it drops in a few feet away from me

the shut-out is spoiled
and all because
Ty Cobb is eating pop corn
in the outfield

    the Augusta manager
    is furious at me
    he sells me off the club
    for $2 cash on the spot

later i rejoin Augusta
and later Augusta sells me again
this time to the Detroit Tigers

it is my first week
in the major leagues
i am 18 years old
it is August 1905
i am playing the outfield
for the Detroit Tigers

meanwhile
back home in Georgia
my father is walking up
to our house
it is late at night
and he has come back home
without telling my mother
he is coming back home
because he suspicions
that my mother is seeing
someone else on the side
and so my father
has come back home
and he is walking up
to our house
it is late at night
and he has come back home
without telling my mother
my mother hears him
walking around
outside the house
and so she goes
and loads the shotgun
and she walks over
to the door
and she throws it open

    and there is my father

and my mother pulls the trigger
and the shotgun blasts
my father backwards
in the grass
rolls him up against the hedge
his head is blown completely off
and as he lies there
what is left of him
lets out a long low moan

    later on my mother tells the police
    she thought my father was a burglar

it is August 1905
i am 18 years old
it is my first week
in the major leagues
i am playing outfield
for the Detroit Tigers

and as i stand there
in the outfield
i am thinking:

> my mother is my mother
> and my father is my father
> and my mother took a shotgun
> and she blasted my father
> backwards in the grass

6.

> Ty Cobb
> why did you fight
> so hard?

> "I had to fight all my life to survive
> they were all against me
> tried every trick to cut me down"

was always so afraid
i would go down
before the fans

would have to hear
their jeering
in my ears

would have to feel
the rush of blood
humiliation

was why i fought so hard
to win was all that mattered
to stay one step ahead

of whatever it was
blasting my ass
backwards in the grass

May 1912
there is this fan in the stands
who began riding me

    calling me faker
    calling me fraud
    calling me weak-kneed sissy coward

and i come over to the stands
and i yell up for him to shut his mouth
and i shake my fist at his face

    but he keeps on
    calling me no good lousy Southern
    weak-kneed fairy son of a bitch

so i jump up in the stands
and i knock this guy down
and i stand up on top of him
and i walk all over him
me with the cleats on my feet

and the park police
refuse to arrest me
but the umpires put
me out of the game
and the baseball commissioner
who happens to be there that day
says he has to suspend me

    later on in Philadelphia
    when they say that i can't play
    the entire Detroit team
    walks off the field
    May 16 1912

## 7.

when i go to different cities
i stay in lonely hotel rooms
and look in bathroom mirrors
say to myself:

    my name is
    Ty Cobb

then walk out on streets at night
i always carry a loaded revolver with me

i like to be all alone in the starlight
and sometimes i find my way
out to the empty ballpark
and i go on in
stand there in the empty center field
feel the emptiness of all
those deserted bleacher seats
and think of all those people
who aren't there
think of all the noise and excitement
of the next day
and see myself the next day
fighting for my life
down there in the dust
spilling whoever gets in my way
sliding spiking
chasing line drives
catching pop flies in the outfield
hurling the ball to first

see all these things
while i stand there all alone
in the empty center field

then i shrug and turn away
walk through the infield
out through the stands
onto the streets again
see if i can pick up
some young girl somewheres

hi there
i'm Ty Cobb

take her with me
back to my hotel room
keep her up all night
try to find out
why is it Ty Cobb
always has to fight
so hard

who knows how many wives
and mistresses
i run through

who knows why i once
broke a woman's nose
with a baseball bat


8.

was always the Tiger

would claw      snarl
        brawl       tear
        cheat       cut
        steal       swear
        rip         shout
        hit         gouge
        spit        beat
        bitch       scream

was called a hothead
                conceited
                arrogant
                a petty villain
                maniacal
                borderline psychotic

                    i was the most
                    cordially hated
                    man in the game

9.

yesterday May 5 1925
i got myself 2 singles
one double
three home runs
for a total of 16 bases

a good day

but today is today
and i got to go out
and do it all
all over again

so god help anyone
gets in my way
on the base path

i fight so hard
and run so fast
the catchers have to throw
one base ahead to cut me off

    if i'm stealing second
    they throw to third
    if i'm stealing third
    they keep the ball
    and try to guard home plate

sometimes i deliberately
get myself entrapped
between bases to enforce
a run-down

once i get on base
i take my lead
and i crouch down
and stare at the pitcher
for the slightest thing
will tip me off
on when he is about
to commit himself
to a pitch

whether it is
a twitch of shoulder
or a ripple of muscle
or a gesture of the neck

and once the pitcher
begins his motion
is the moment i wait for
is the exact instant
i break for the next base
racing down the base line
like a pacing horse
both hands out like flippers
not lifting my knees
swaying from side to side
with my head over my shoulder
so i can keep my eye on the ball

as soon as i see
the face of the baseman
is when i begin my slide
spikes high
cleats out like teeth
ready to bite
i slam down hard on the ground
digging in dirt
hurtling forward feet first burning the earth
in a sweeping hook slide
clenching my teeth against impact
which is the shotgun
blasting the baseman backwards
spilling him head over heels in the air
as i touch the tip of my toe to the bag

    many a man is walking around
    today with my cleat marks
    all over him

but i never do
any of that sort of thing
for the sport of it

    "I never deliberately
    cut a fellow
    except to protect myself"

*10.*

"My father had his head blown off
when I was 18 years old—
by a member of my own family.
I've never gotten over that."

so i manage the Tigers
from 1921–1926
and then i play one last season
for Philadelphia 1926–1927
and i retire from baseball

and i retire as a millionaire
not like King Kelly
who always lived in fear
he would run out of money
so he couldn't live in the high style

when i retire
i move all the way out to California
to Menlo Park
which is quite a ways away
from Georgia

but i make a grant
of $100,000
to start the COBB HOSPITAL
in honor of my parents
back there in the state of Georgia

on my deathbed
there is this sports reporter
who keeps asking me
    why did you fight so hard
    in baseball, Ty?
    Ty, why did you fight
    so hard?
    why did you fight so hard
    in baseball, Ty?

there is fire
in my eyes
as i answer:

"I did it for my father
who was an exalted man
they killed him
when he was still young
they blew his head off
the same week I became
a major leaguer

he never got to see me play
but I knew he was watching me
and I never let him down"

okay and add
this also be sure
to add this:

i was the first man
voted into the Hall of Fame

i was the first man

    i got 222 votes
    all the others got less
    than i got

    Walter Johnson got 189 votes
    Christy Mathewson got 205 votes
    Honus Wagner got 215 votes
    Babe Ruth got 215 votes

    i got 222 votes

i was the first man

## Babe & Lou

when babe hit
number 714 he was
playing for Boston
and washed up

he was a big tipper
a big eater a big
drinker and every
body loved the babe

lou was the iron
man and played
in 2130 consecutive
games and when he coughed
into the microphone
he said he was
the luckiest man alive

he batted clean up
right behind the babe
and together they
represented fear
power and (judging
from the full stands)
absenteeism

this was before the unions
before the depression before
the war and when the smoke

lifted the forties were over and
both men had died slowly
each weighing less
than a 100 lbs

## Jerome Herman's Higher Education

In the 1937 All-Star Game
Earl Averill bounced a
Snake blown drive off Dizzy Dean's toe.
Ol' Diz was never the same, and
This is why:
He already knew that
The toe bone is connected to the head bone.
What he was still too dumb to know is:
The sky has a limit.
After this discovery, it was all down hill.
He was a plowhorse gone to seed,
A crackerjack joke in a war museum.
Soon he learned that you could occupy
Two spaces
At the same time:
Your feet could be summering back in Texas
Flapping like two jackrabbit ears,
While your right arm hung over an enormous butte
On Chicago's North Side,
And your fingers trembled in the cold wind.
He went on though, a true fisherman, hugging
The shore of Lake Michigan, casting for catfish
In the Texarkana.

JOHN UPDIKE

## Hub Fans Bid Kid Adieu

Fenway Park, in Boston, is a lyric little bandbox of a ballpark. Everything is painted green and seems in curiously sharp focus, like the inside of an old-fashioned peeping-type Easter egg. It was built in 1912 and rebuilt in 1934, and offers, as do most Boston artifacts, a compromise between Man's Euclidean determinations and Nature's beguiling irregularities. Its right field is one of the deepest in the American League, while its left field is the shortest; the high left-field wall, three hundred and fifteen feet from home plate along the foul line, virtually thrusts its surface at right-handed hitters. On the afternoon of Wednesday, September 28th, 1960, as I took a seat behind third base, a uniformed groundkeeper was treading the top of this wall, picking batting-practice home runs out of the screen, like a mushroom gatherer seen in Wordsworthian perspective on the verge of a cliff. The day was overcast, chill, and uninspirational. The Boston team was the worst in twenty-seven seasons. A jangling medley of incompetent youth and aging competence, the Red Sox were finishing in seventh place only because the Kansas City Athletics had locked them out of the cellar. They were scheduled to play the Baltimore Orioles, a much nimbler blend of May and December, who had been dumped from pennant contention a week before by the insatiable Yankees. I, and 10,453 others, had shown up primarily because this was the Red Sox's last home game of the season, and therefore the last time in all eternity that their regular left fielder, known to the headlines as TED, KID, SPLINTER, THUMPER, TW, and, most cloyingly, MISTER WONDERFUL, would play in Boston. "WHAT WILL WE DO WITHOUT TED? HUB FANS ASK" ran the headline on a newspaper being read by a bulb-nosed cigar smoker a few rows away. Williams' retirement had been announced, doubted (he had been threatening retirement for years), confirmed by Tom Yawkey, the Red Sox owner, and at last widely accepted as the sad but probable truth. He was forty-two and had redeemed his abysmal season of 1959 with a—considering his advanced age—fine one. He had been giving away his gloves and bats and had grudgingly consented to a sentimental ceremony today. This was not necessarily his last game; the Red Sox were scheduled to travel to New York and wind up the season with three games there.

I arrived early. The Orioles were hitting fungoes on the field. The day before, they had spitefully smothered the Red Sox, 17–4, and neither their faces nor their drab gray visiting-team uniforms seemed very gracious. I wondered who had invited them to the party. Between our heads and the lowering clouds a frenzied organ was thundering through, with an appositeness perhaps accidental, "You *maaaaade* me love you, I didn't wanna do it, I didn't wanna do it . . ."

The affair between Boston and Ted Williams was no mere summer romance; it was a marriage composed of spats, mutual disappointments, and, towards the end, a mellowing hoard of shared memories. It fell into three stages, which may be termed Youth, Maturity, and Age; or Thesis, Antithesis, and Synthesis; or Jason, Achilles, and Nestor.

First, there was the by now legendary epoch* when the young bridegroom came out of the West and announced "All I want out of life is that when I walk down the street folks will say 'There goes the greatest hitter who ever lived.'" The dowagers of local journalism attempted to give ele-

---

* This piece was written with no research materials save an outdated record book and the Boston newspapers of the day; and Williams' early career preceded the dawning of my *Schlagballewusstein* (Baseball-consciousness). Also for reasons of perspective was my account of his beginnings skimped. Williams first attracted the notice of a major-league scout—Bill Essick of the Yankees—when he was a fifteen-year-old pitcher with the San Diego American Legion Post team. As a pitcher-outfielder with the San Diego's Herbert Hoover High School, Williams recorded averages of .586 and .403. Essick balked at signing Williams for the $1,000 his mother asked; he was signed instead, for $150 a month, by the local Pacific Coast League franchise, the newly created San Diego Padres. In his two seasons with this team, Williams hit merely .271 and .291, but his style and slugging (23 home runs the second year) caught the eye of, among others, Casey Stengel, then with the Boston Braves, and Eddie Collins, the Red Sox general manager. Collins bought him from the Padres for $25,000 in cash and $25,000 in players. Williams was then nineteen. Collins' fond confidence in boy's potential matched Williams' own. Williams reported to the Red Sox training camp in Sarasota in 1938 and, after showing more volubility than skill, was shipped down to the Minneapolis Millers, the top Sox farm team. It should be said, perhaps, that the parent club was equipped with an excellent, if mature, outfield, mostly purchased from Connie Mack's dismantled A's. Upon leaving Sarasota, Williams is supposed to have told the regular outfield of Joe Vosmik, Doc Cramer, and Ben Chapman that he would be back and would make more money than the three of them put together. At Minneapolis he hit .366, batted in 142 runs, scored 130, and hit 43 home runs. He also loafed in the field, jabbered at the fans, and smashed a water cooler with his fist. In 1939 he came north with the Red Sox. On the way, in Atlanta, he dropped a foul fly, accidentally kicked it away in trying to pick it up, picked it up, and threw it out of the park. It would be nice if, his first time up in Fenway Park, he had hit a home run. Actually, in his first Massachusetts appearance, the first inning of an exhibition game against Holy Cross at Worcester, he *did* hit a home run, a grand slam. The Red Sox season opened in Yankee Stadium. Facing Red Ruffing, Williams struck out and, the next time up, doubled for his first major-league hit. In the Fenway Park opener, against Philadelphia, he had a single in five trips. His first home run came on April 23, in that same series with the A's. Williams was then twenty, and played *right* field. In his rookie season he hit .327; in 1940, .344.

mentary deportment lessons to this child who spake as a god, and to their horror were themselves rebuked. Thus began the long exchange of back-biting, bat-flipping, booing, and spitting that has distinguished Williams' public relations.* The spitting incidents of 1957 and 1958 and the similar dockside courtesies that Williams has now and then extended to the grandstand should be judged against this background: the left-field stands at Fenway for twenty years have held a large number of customers who have bought their way in primarily for the privilege of showering abuse on Williams. Greatness necessarily attracts debunkers, but in Williams' case the hostility has been systematic and unappeasable. His basic offense against the fans has been to wish that they weren't there. Seeking a perfectionist's vacuum, he has quixotically desired to sever the game from the ground of paid spectatorship and publicity that supports it. Hence his refusal to tip his cap† to the crowd or turn the other cheek to newsmen. It has been a costly theory—it has probably cost him, among other evidences of good will, two Most Valuable Player awards, which are voted by reporters‡—but he has held to it. While his critics, oral and literary, remained beyond the reach of his discipline, the opposing pitchers

---

* See *Ted Williams*, by Ed Linn (Sport Magazine Library), Chapter 6, "Williams vs. the Press." It is Linn's suggestion that Williams walked into a circulation war among the seven Boston newspapers, who in their competitive zeal headlined incidents that the New York papers, say, would have minimized, just as they minimized the less genial side of the moody and aloof DiMaggio and smoothed Babe Ruth into a folk hero. It is also Linn's thought, and an interesting one, that Williams thrived on even adverse publicity, and needed a hostile press to elicit, contrariwise, his defiant best. The statistics (especially of the 1958 season, when he snapped a slump by spitting in all directions, and inadvertently conked an elderly female fan with a tossed bat) seem to corroborate this. Certainly Williams could have had a truce for the asking, and his industrious perpetuation of the war, down to his last day in uniform, implies its usefulness to him. The actual and intimate anatomy of the matter resides in locker rooms and hotel corridors fading from memory. When my admiring account was printed, I received a letter from a sports reporter who hated Williams with a bitter and explicit immediacy. And even Linn's hagiology permits some glimpses of Williams' locker-room manners that are not pleasant.

† But he did tip his cap, high off his head, in at least his first season, as cartoons from that period verify. He also was extravagantly cordial to taxi-drivers and stray children. See Linn, Chapter 4, "The Kid Comes to Boston": "There has never been a ballplayer —anywhere, anytime—more popular than Ted Williams in his first season in Boston." To this epoch belongs Williams' prankish use of the Fenway scoreboard lights for rifle practice, his celebrated preference for the life of a fireman, and his determined designation of himself as "The Kid."

‡ In 1947 Joe DiMaggio and in 1957 Mickey Mantle, with seasons inferior to Williams', won the MVP award because sportswriters, who vote on ballots with ten places, had vengefully placed Williams ninth, tenth, or nowhere at all. The 1941 award to DiMaggio, even though this was Williams' .406 year, is more understandable, since this was also the *annus miraculorum* when DiMaggio hit safely in 56 consecutive games.

were accessible, and he spanked them to the tune of .406 in 1941.* He slumped to .356 in 1942 and went off to war.

In 1946, Williams returned from three years as a Marine pilot to the second of his baseball avatars, that of Achilles, the hero of incomparable prowess and beauty who nevertheless was to be found sulking in his tent while the Trojans (mostly Yankees) fought through to the ships. Yawkey, a timber and mining maharajah, had surrounded his central jewel with many gems of slightly lesser water, such as Bobby Doerr, Dom DiMaggio, Rudy York, Birdie Tebbets, and Johnny Pesky. Throughout the late forties, the Red Sox were the best paper team in baseball, yet they had little three-dimensional to show for it, and if this was a tragedy, Williams was Hamlet. A succinct review of the indictment—and a fair sample of appreciative sports-page prose—appeared the very day of Williams' valedictory, in a column by Huck Finnegan in the Boston *American* (no sentimentalist, Huck):

> Williams' career, in contrast [to Babe Ruth's], has been a series of failures except for his averages. He flopped in the only World Series he ever played in (1946) when he batted only .200. He flopped in the playoff game with Cleveland in 1948. He flopped in the final game of the 1949 season with the pennant hinging on the outcome (Yanks 5, Sox 3). He flopped in 1950 when he returned to the lineup after a two-month absence and ruined the morale of a club that seemed pennant-bound under Steve O'Neill. It has always been Williams' records first, the team second, and the Sox nonwinning record is proof enough of that.

There are answers to all this, of course. The fatal weakness of the great Sox slugging teams was not-quite-good-enough pitching rather than Williams' failure to hit a home run every time he came to bat. Again, Williams' depressing effect on his teammates has never been proved. Despite ample coaching to the contrary, most insisted that they *liked* him. He has been generous with advice to any player who asked for it. In an

---

* The sweet saga of this beautiful decimal must be sung once more. Williams, after hitting above .400 all season, had cooled to .39955 with one doubleheader left to play, in Philadelphia. Joe Cronin, then managing the Red Sox, offered to bench him to safeguard his average, which was exactly .400 when rounded to the third decimal place. Williams said (I forget where I read this) that he did not want to become the .400 hitter with just his toe over the line. He played the first game and singled, homered, singled, and singled. With less to gain than to lose, he elected to play the second game and got two more hits, including a double that dented a loudspeaker horn on the top of the right-field wall, giving him six-for-eight on the day and a season's average that, in the forty years beween Rogers Hornsby's .403 (1925) and the present, stands as unique.

increasingly combative baseball atmosphere, he continued to duck bean-balls docilely. With umpires he was gracious to a fault. This courtesy it-self annoyed his critics, whom there was no pleasing. And against the ten crucial games (the seven World Series games with the St. Louis Car-dinals, the 1948 playoff with the Cleveland Indians, and the two-game series with the Yankees at the end of the 1949 season, when one victory would have given the Red Sox the pennant) that make up the Achilles' heel of Williams' record, a mass of statistics can be set showing that day in and day out he was no slouch in the clutch.† The correspondence col-umns of the Boston papers now and then suffer a sharp flurry of arithme-tic on this score; indeed, for Williams to have distributed all his hits so they did nobody else any good would constitute a feat of placement un-paralleled in the annals of selfishness.

Whatever residue of truth remains of the Finnegan charge those of us who love Williams must transmute as best we can, in our own personal crucibles. My personal memories of Williams began when I was a boy in Pennsylvania, with two last-place teams in Philadelphia to keep me com-pany. For me, "W'ms, lf" was a figment of the box scores who always seemed to be going 3-for-5. He radiated, from afar, the hard blue glow of high purpose. I remember listening over the radio to the All-Star Game of 1946, in which Williams hit two singles and two home runs, the second one off a Rip Sewell "blooper" pitch; it was like hitting a balloon out of the park. I remember watching one of his home runs from the bleachers of Shibe Park; it went over the first baseman's head and rose methodically along a straight line and was still rising when it cleared the fence. The trajectory seemed qualitatively different from anything anyone else might hit. For me, Williams is the classic ballplayer of the game on a hot August weekday, before a small crowd, when the only thing at stake is the tissue-thin difference between a thing done well and a thing done ill. Baseball is a game of the long season, of relentless and gradual averaging-out. Irrelevance—since the reference point of most individual contests is re-mote and statistical—always threatens its interest, which can be main-tained not by the occasional heroics that sportswriters feed upon but by players who always *care;* who care, that is to say, about themselves and their art. Insofar as the clutch hitter is not a sportswriter's myth, he is a vulgarity, like a writer who writes only for money. It may be that, com-pared to such managers' dreams as the manifestly classy Joe DiMaggio and the always helpful Stan Musial, Williams was an icy star. But of all team sports, baseball, with its graceful intermittences of action, its im-mense and tranquil field sparsely settled with poised men in white, its

† For example: In 1948, the Sox came from behind to tie the Indians by winning three straight; in those games Williams went two for two; two for two; and two for four. In 1949, the Sox overtook the Yankees by winning nine in a row; in that streak, Williams won four games with home runs.

dispassionate mathematics, seems to be best suited to accommodate, and be ornamented by, a loner. It is an essentially lonely game. No other player visible to my generation concentrated within himself so much of the sport's poignance, so assiduously refined his natural skills, so constantly brought to the plate that intensity of competence that crowds the throat with joy.

By the time I went to college, near Boston, the lesser stars Yawkey had assembled around Williams had faded, and his rigorous pride of craftsmanship had become itself a kind of heroism. This brittle and temperamental player developed an unexpected quality of persistence. He was always coming back—back from Korea, back from a broken collarbone, a shattered elbow, a bruised heel, back from drastic bouts of flu and ptomaine poisoning. Hardly a season went by without some enfeebling mishap, yet he always came back, and always looked like himself. The delicate mechanism of timing and power seemed sealed, shockproof, in some case deep within his frame.‡ In addition to injuries, there was a heavily publicized divorce, and the usual storms with the press, and the Williams Shift—the maneuver, custom-built by Lou Boudreau of the Cleveland Indians, whereby three infielders were concentrated on the right side of the infield.* Williams could easily have learned to punch singles through the vacancy on his left and fattened his average hugely. This was what Ty Cobb, the Einstein of average, told him to do. But the game had changed since Cobb; Williams believed that his value to the club and to the league was as a slugger, so he went on pulling the ball, trying to blast it through three men, and paid the price of perhaps fifteen points of lifetime average. Like Ruth before him, he bought the occasional home run at the cost of many directed singles—a calculated sacrifice certainly not, in the case of a hitter as average-minded as Williams, entirely selfish.

After a prime so harassed and hobbled, Williams was granted by the

---

‡ Two reasons for his durability may be adduced. A non-smoker, non-drinker, habitual walker, and year-round outdoors-man, Williams spared his body the vicissitudes of the seasonal athlete. And his hitting was in large part a mental process; the amount of cerebration he devoted to such details as pitchers' patterns, prevailing winds, and the muscular mechanics of swinging a bat would seem ridiculous, if it had not paid off. His intellecuality, as it were, perhaps explains the quickness with which he adjusted, after the war, to the changed conditions—the night games, the addition of the slider to the standard pitching repertoire, the new cry for the long ball. His reaction to the Williams Shift, then, cannot be dismissed as unconsidered.

* Invented, or perpetrated (as a joke?) by Boudreau on July 14, 1946, between games of a doubleheader. In the first game of the doubleheader, Williams had hit three homers and batted in eight runs. The shift was not used when men were on base and, had Williams bunted or hit late against it immediately, it might not have spread, in all its variations, throughout the league. The Cardinals used it in the lamented World Series of that year. Toward the end, in 1959 and 1960, rather sadly, it had faded from use, or degenerated to the mere clockwise twitching of the infield customary against pull hitters.

relenting fates a golden twilight. He became at the end of his career perhaps the best *old* hitter of the century. The dividing line falls between the 1956 and the 1957 seasons. In September of the first year, he and Mickey Mantle were contending for the batting championship. Both were hitting around .350, and there was no one else near them. The season ended with a three-game series between the Yankees and the Sox, and, living in New York then, I went up to the Stadium. Williams was slightly shy of the four hundred at-bats needed to qualify; the fear was expressed that the Yankee pitchers would walk him to protect Mantle. Instead, they pitched to him. It was wise. He looked terrible at the plate, tired and discouraged and unconvincing. He never looked very good to me in the Stadium.† The final outcome in 1956 was Mantle .353, Williams .345.

The next year, I moved from New York to New England, and it made all the difference. For in September of 1957, in the same situation, the story was reversed. Mantle finally hit .365; it was the best season of his career. But Williams, though sick and old, had run away from him. A bout of flu had laid him low in September. He emerged from his cave in the Hotel Somerset haggard but irresistible; he hit four successive pinch-hit home runs. "I feel terrible," he confessed, "but every time I take a swing at the ball it goes out of the park." He ended the season with thirty-eight home runs and an average of .388, the highest in either league since his own .406, and, coming from a decrepit man of thirty-nine, an even more supernal figure. With eight or so of the "leg hits" that a younger man would have beaten out, it would have been .400. And the next year, Williams, who in 1949 and 1953 had lost batting championships by decimal whiskers to George Kell and Mickey Vernon, sneaked behind his teammate Pete Runnels and filched his sixth title, a bargain at .328.

In 1959, it seemed all over. The dinosaur thrashed around in the .200 swamp for the first half of the season, and was even benched ("rested," Manager Mike Higgins tactfully said). Old foes like the late Bill Cunningham began to offer batting tips. Cunningham thought Williams was jiggling his elbows;‡ in truth, Williams' neck was so stiff he could hardly

† Shortly after his retirement, Williams, in *Life*, wrote gloomily of the Stadium, "There's the bigness of it. There are those high stands and all those people smoking— and, of course, the shadows . . . It takes at least one series to get accustomed to the Stadium and even then you're not sure." Yet his lifetime batting average there is .340, only four points under his median average.

‡ It was Cunningham who, when Williams first appeared in a Red Sox uniform at the 1938 spring training camp, wrote with melodious prescience: "The Sox seem to think Williams is just cocky enough and gabby enough to make a great and colorful outfielder, possibly the Babe Herman type. Me? I don't like the way he stands at the plate. He bends his front knee inward and moves his foot just before he takes a swing. That's exactly what I do just before I drive a golf ball and knowing what happens to the golf balls I drive, I don't believe this kid will ever hit half a singer midget's weight in a bathing suit."

turn his head to look at the pitcher. When he swung, it looked like a Calder mobile with one thread cut; it reminded you that since 1954 Williams' shoulders had been wired together. A solicitous pall settled over the sports pages. In the two decades since Williams had come to Boston, his status had imperceptibly shifted from that of a naughty prodigy to that of a municipal monument. As his shadow in the record books lengthened, the Red Sox teams around him declined, and the entire American League seemed to be losing life and color to the National. The inconsistency of the new super-stars—Mantle, Colavito, and Kaline—served to make Williams appear all the more singular. And off the field, his private philanthropy—in particular, his zealous chairmanship of the Jimmy Fund, a charity for children with cancer—gave him a civic presence matched only by that of Richard Cardinal Cushing. In religion, Williams appears to have been a humanist, and a selective one at that, but he and the abrasive-voiced Cardinal, when their good works intersect and they appear in the public eye together, make a handsome pair of seraphim.

Humiliated by his '59 season, Williams determined, once more, to come back. I, as a specimen Williams partisan, was both glad and fearful. All baseball fans believe in miracles; the question is, how *many* do you believe in? He looked like a ghost in spring training. Manager Jurges warned us ahead of time that if Williams didn't come through he would be benched, just like anybody else. As it turned out, it was Jurges who was benched. Williams entered the 1960 season needing eight home runs to have a lifetime total of 500; after one time at bat in Washington, he needed seven. For a stretch, he was hitting a home run every second game that he played. He passed Lou Gehrig's lifetime total, and finished with 521, thirteen behind Jimmy Foxx, who alone stands between Williams and Babe Ruth's unapproachable 714. The summer was a statistician's picnic. His two-thousandth walk came and went, his eighteen-hundredth run batted in, his sixteenth All-Star Game. At one point, he hit a home run off a pitcher, Don Lee, off whose father, Thornton Lee, he had hit a home run a generation before. The only comparable season for a forty-two-year-old man was Ty Cobb's in 1928. Cobb batted .323 and hit one homer. Williams batted .316 but hit twenty-nine homers.

In sum, though generally conceded to be the greatest hitter of his era, he did not establish himself as "the greatest hitter who ever lived." Cobb, for average, and Ruth, for power, remain supreme. Cobb, Rogers Hornsby, Joe Jackson, and Lefty O'Doul, among players since 1900, have higher lifetime averages than Williams' .344. Unlike Foxx, Gehrig, Hack Wilson, Hank Greenberg, and Ralph Kiner, Williams never came close to matching Babe Ruth's season home-run total of sixty.[*] In the list of major-league batting records, not one is held by Williams. He is second in walks drawn, third in home runs, fifth in lifetime average, sixth in runs

[*] Written before Roger Maris' fluky, phenomenal sixty-one.

batted in, eighth in runs scored and in total bases, fourteenth in doubles, and thirtieth in hits.† But if we allow him merely average seasons for the four-plus seasons he lost to two wars, and add another season for the months he lost to injuries, we get a man who in all the power totals would be second, and not a very distant second, to Ruth. And if we further allow that these years would have been not merely average but prime years, if we allow for all the months when Williams was playing in sub-par condition, if we permit his early and later years in baseball to be some sort of index of what the middle years could have been, if we give him a right-field fence that is not, like Fenway's, one of the most distant in the league, and if—the least excusable "if"—we imagine him condescending to outsmart the Williams Shift, we can defensibly assemble, like a colossus induced from the sizable fragments that do remain, a statistical figure not incommensurate with his grandiose ambition. From the statistics that are on the books, a good case can be made that in the *combination* of power and average Williams is first; nobody else ranks so high in both categories. Finally, there is the witness of the eyes; men whose memories go back to Shoeless Joe Jackson—another unlucky natural—rank him and Williams together as the best-looking hitters they have seen. It was for our last look that ten thousand of us had come.

Two girls, one of them with pert buckteeth and eyes as black as vest buttons, the other with white skin and flesh-colored hair, like an under-developed photograph of a red-head, came and sat on my right. On my other side was one of those frowning chestless young-old men who can frequently be seen, often wearing sailor hats, attending ball games alone. He did not once open his program but instead tapped it, rolled up, on his knee as he gave the game his disconsolate attention. A young lady, with freckles and a depressed, dainty nose that by an optical illusion seemed to thrust her lips forward for a kiss, sauntered down into the box seat right behind the roof of the Oriole dugout. She wore a blue coat with a Northeastern University emblem sewed to it. The girls beside me took it into their heads that this was Williams' daughter. She looked too old to me, and why would she be sitting behind the visitor's dugout? On the other hand, from the way she sat there, staring at the sky and French-inhaling, she clearly was *somebody*. Other fans came and eclipsed her from view. The crowd looked less like a weekday ballpark crowd than like the folks you might find in Yellowstone National Park, or emerging from automobiles at the top of scenic Mount Mansfield. There were a lot of competitively well-dressed couples of tourist age, and not a few babes in arms. A row of five seats in front of me was abruptly filled with a woman and four children, the youngest of them two years old, if that. Someday, presumably, he could tell his grandchildren that he saw Williams play. Along with

† Again, as of 1960. Since then, Musial and Willie Mays may have surpassed him in some statistical areas.

these tots and second-honeymooners, there were Harvard freshmen, giving off that peculiar nervous glow created when a sufficient quantity of insouciance is saturated with enough insecurity; thick-necked Army officers with brass on their shoulders and steel in their stares; pepperings of priests; perfumed bouquets of Roxbury Fabian fans; shiny salesmen from Albany and Fall River; and those gray, hoarse men—taxi drivers, slaughterers, and bartenders—who will continue to click through the turnstiles long after everyone else has deserted to television and tramporamas. Behind me, two young male voices blossomed, cracking a joke about God's five proofs that Thomas Aquinas exists—typical Boston College levity.

The batting cage was trundled away. The Orioles fluttered to the sidelines. Diagonally across the field, by the Red Sox dugout, a cluster of men in overcoats were festering like maggots. I could see a splinter of white uniform, and Williams' head, held at a self-deprecating and evasive tilt. Williams' conversational stance is that of a six-foot-three-inch man under a six-foot ceiling. He moved away to the patter of flash bulbs, and began playing catch with a young Negro outfielder named Willie Tasby. His arm, never very powerful, had grown lax with the years, and his throwing motion was a kind of muscular drawl. To catch the ball, he flicked his glove hand onto his left shoulder (he batted left but threw right, as every schoolboy ought to know) and let the ball plop into it comically. This catch session with Tasby was the only time all afternoon I saw him grin.

A tight little flock of human sparrows who, from the lambent and pampered pink of their faces, could only have been Boston politicians moved toward the plate. The loudspeakers mammothly coughed as someone huffed on the microphone. The ceremonies began. Curt Gowdy, the Red Sox radio and television announcer, who sounds like everybody's brother-in-law, delivered a brief sermon, taking the two words "pride" and "champion" as his text. It began. "Twenty-one years ago, a skinny kid from San Diego, California . . ." and ended, "I don't think we'll ever see another like him." Robert Tibolt, chairman of the board of the Greater Boston Chamber of Commerce, presented Williams with a big Paul Revere silver bowl. Harry Carlson, a member of the sports committee of the Boston Chamber, gave him a plaque, whose inscription he did not read in its entirety, out of deference to Williams' distaste for this sort of fuss. Mayor Collins, seated in a wheelchair, presented the Jimmy Fund with a thousand-dollar check.

Then the occasion himself stooped to the microphone, and his voice sounded, after the others, very Californian; it seemed to be coming, excellently amplified, from a great distance, adolescently young and as smooth as a butternut. His thanks for the gifts had not died from our ears before he glided, as if helplessly, into "In spite of all the terrible things that have been said about me by the knights of the keyboard up there . . ." He glanced up at the press rows suspended behind home plate. The crowd tittered, appalled. A frightful vision flashed upon me, of the press gallery pelting Williams with erasers, of Williams clambering up the foul screen to slug journalists, of a riot, of Mayor Collins being crushed. ". . . And they *were* terrible things," Williams insisted, with level melancholy, into the mike. "I'd like to forget them, but I can't." He paused, swallowed his memories, and went on, "I want to say that my years in Boston have been the greatest thing in my life." The crowd, like an immense sail going limp in a change of wind, sighed with relief. Taking all the parts himself, Williams then acted out a vivacious little morality drama in which an imaginary tempter came to him at the beginning of his career and said, "Ted, you can play anywhere you like." Leaping nimbly into the role of his younger self (who in biographical actuality had yearned to be a Yankee), Williams gallantly chose Boston over all the other cities, and told us that Tom Yawkey was the greatest owner in baseball and we were the greatest fans. We applauded ourselves lustily. The umpire came out and dusted the plate. The voice of doom announced over the loudspeakers that after Williams' retirement his uniform number, 9, would be permanently retired—the first time the Red Sox has so honored a player. We cheered. The national anthem was played. We cheered. The game began.

Williams was third in the batting order, so he came up in the bottom of the first inning, and Steve Barber, a young pitcher born two months before Williams began playing in the major leagues, offered him four pitches, at all of which he disdained to swing, since none of them were within the strike zone. This demonstrated simultaneously that Williams' eyes were razor-sharp and that Barber's control wasn't. Shortly, the bases were full, with Williams on second. "Oh, I hope he gets held up at third! That would be wonderful," the girl beside me moaned, and sure enough, the man at bat walked and Williams was delivered into our foreground. He struck the pose of Donatello's David, the third-base bag being Goliath's head. Fiddling with his cap, swapping small talk with the Oriole third baseman (who seemed delighted to have him drop in), swinging his arms with a sort of prancing nervousness, he looked fine—flexible, hard, and not unbecomingly substantial through the middle. The long neck, the small head, the knickers whose cuffs were worn down near his ankles—all these cliches of sports cartoon iconography were rendered in the flesh.

With each pitch, Williams danced down the baseline, waving his arms and stirring dust, ponderous but menacing, like an attacking goose. It occurred to about a dozen humorists at once to shout "Steal home! Go, go!" Williams' speed afoot was never legendary. Lou Clinton, a young Sox outfielder, hit a fairly deep fly to center field. Williams tagged up and ran home. As he slid across the plate, the ball, thrown with unusual heft by Jackie Brandt, the Oriole center fielder, hit him on the back.

"Boy, he was really loafing, wasn't he?" one of the collegiate voices behind me said.

"It's cold," the other voice explained. "He doesn't play well when it's cold. He likes heat. He's a hedonist."

The run that Williams scored was the second and last of the inning. Gus Triandos, of the Orioles, quickly evened the score by plunking a home run over the handy left-field wall. Williams, who had had this wall at his back for twenty years,‡ played the ball flawlessly. He didn't budge. He just stood still, in the center of the little patch of grass that his patient footsteps had worn brown, and limp with lack of interest, watched the ball pass overhead. It was not a very interesting game. Mike Higgins, the Red Sox manager, with nothing to lose, had restricted his major-league players to the left-field line—along with Williams, Frank Malzone, a first-rate third baseman, played the game—and had peopled the rest of the terrain with unpredictable youngsters fresh, or not so fresh, off the farms. Other than Williams' recurrent appearances at the plate, the *maladresse* of the Sox infield was the sole focus of suspense; the second baseman turned every grounder into a juggling act, while the shortstop did a breathtaking impersonation of an open window. With this sort of assistance, the Orioles wheedled their way into a 4–2 lead. They had early replaced Barber with another young pitcher, Jack Fisher. Fortunately (as it turned out), Fisher is no cutie; he is willing to burn the ball through the strike zone, and inning after inning this tactic punctured Higgins' string of test balloons.

Whenever Williams appeared at the plate—pounding the dirt from his cleats, gouging a pit in the batter's box with his left foot, wringing resin out of the bat handle with his vehement grip, switching the stick at the pitcher with an electric ferocity—it was like having a familiar Leonardo appear in a shuffle of *Saturday Evening Post* covers. This man, you realized —and here, perhaps, was the difference, greater than the difference in gifts—really desired to hit the ball. In the third inning, he hoisted a high fly to deep center. In the fifth, we thought he had it; he smacked the ball hard and high into the heart of his power zone, but the deep right field in Fenway and the heavy air and a casual east wind defeated him. The ball died. Al Pilarcik leaned his back against the big "380" painted on the right-field wall and caught it. On another day, in another park, it would have been gone. (After the game, Williams said, "I didn't think I could hit one any harder than that. The conditions weren't good.")

That afternoon grew so glowering that in the sixth inning the arc lights were turned on—always a wan sight in the daytime, like the burning headlights of a funeral procession. Aided by the gloom, Fisher was slicking through the Sox rookies, and Williams did not come to bat in the seventh. He was second up in the eighth. This was almost certainly his last time to come to the plate in Fenway Park, and instead of merely cheering, as we had at his three previous appearances, we stood, all of us, and applauded. I had never before heard pure applause in a ballpark. No

---

‡ In his second season (1940) he was switched to the left field, to protect his eyes from the right-field sun.

calling, no whistling, just an ocean of handclaps, minute after minute, burst after burst, crowding and running together in continuous succession like the pushes of surf at the edge of the sand. It was a sombre and considered tumult. There was not a boo in it. It seemed to renew itself out of a shifting set of memories as the Kid, the Marine, the veteran of feuds and failures and injuries, the friend of children, and the enduring old pro evolved down the bright tunnel of twenty-two summers toward this moment. At last, the umpire signalled for Fisher to pitch; with the other players, he had been frozen in position. Only Williams had moved during the ovation, switching his bat impatiently, ignoring everything except his cherished task. Fisher wound up, and the applause sank into a hush.

Understand that we were a crowd of rational people. We knew that a home run cannot be produced at will; the right pitch must be perfectly met and luck must ride with the ball. Three innings before, we had seen a brave effort fail. The air was soggy, the season was exhausted. Nevertheless, there will always lurk, around the corner in a pocket of our knowledge of the odds, an indefensible hope, and this was one of the times, which you now and then find in sports, when a density of expectation hangs in the air and plucks an event out of the future.

Fisher, after his unsettling wait, was low with the first pitch. He put the second one over, and Williams swung mightily and missed. The crowd grunted, seeing that classic swing, so long and smooth and quick, exposed. Fisher threw the third time, Williams swung again, and there it was. The ball climbed on a diagonal line into the vast volume of air over center field. From my angle, behind third base, the ball seemed less an object in flight than the tip of a towering, motionless construct, like the Eiffel Tower or the Tappan Zee Bridge. It was in the books while it was still in the sky. Brandt ran back to the deepest corner of the outfield grass, the ball descended beyond his reach and struck in the crotch where the bullpen met the wall, bounced chunkily, and vanished.

Like a feather caught in a vortex, Williams ran around the square of bases at the center of our beseeching screaming. He ran as he always ran out home runs—hurriedly, unsmiling, head down, as if our praise were a storm of rain to get out of. He didn't tip his cap. Though we thumped, wept, chanted "We want Ted" for minutes after he hid in the dugout, he did not come back. Our noise for some seconds passed beyond excitement into a kind of immense open anguish, a wailing, a cry to be saved. But immortality is nontransferable. The papers said that the other players, and even the umpires on the field, begged him to come out and acknowledge us in some way, but he refused. Gods do not answer letters.

Every true story has an anticlimax. The men on the field refused to disappear, as would have seemed decent, in the smoke of Williams' miracle. Fisher continued to pitch, and escaped further harm. At the end of the inning, Higgins sent Williams out to his left-field position, then instantly replaced him with Carrol Hardy, so we had a long last look at

Williams as he ran out there and then back, his uniform jogging, his eyes steadfast on the ground. It was nice, and we were grateful, but it left a funny note.

One of the scholasticists behind me said, "Let's go. We've seen everything. I don't want to spoil it." This seemed a sound aesthetic decision. Williams' last word had been so exquisitely chosen, such a perfect fusion of expectation, intention, and execution, that already it felt a little unreal in my head, and I wanted to get out before the castle collapsed. But the game, though played at by clumsy midgets under the feeble flow of the arc lights, began to tug at my attention, and I loitered in the runway until it was over. Williams' homer had, quite incidentally, made the score 4–3. In the bottom of the ninth inning, with one out, Marlin Coughtry, the second-base juggler, singled. Vic Wertz, pinch-hitting, doubled off the left-field wall, Coughtry advancing to third. Pumpsie Green walked, to load the bases. Willie Tasby hit a double-play ball to the third baseman, but in making the pivot throw Billy Klaus, an ex-Red Sox infielder, reverted to form and threw the ball past the first baseman and into the Red Sox dugout. The Sox won, 5–4. On the radio as I drove home I heard that Williams, his own man to the end, had decided not to accompany the team to New York. He had met the little death that awaits athletes. He had quit.

## Not Quite Galahad

Outside the multipurpose stadium in St. Louis, in the vaulting shadow of the Gateway Arch, a hulking statue purports to represent Stan Musial at bat. It is a triumph of ineptitude over sincerity.

St. Louis baseball writers who watched Stan Musial play baseball for almost a quarter of a century engaged a sculptor named Carl Mose to cast Old No. 6 in bronze. Then someone composed an inscription for the pedestal:

> HERE STANDS BASEBALL'S PERFECT WARRIOR;
> HERE STANDS BASEBALL'S PERFECT KNIGHT.

The shoulders are too broad. The torso is too thick. The work smacks of the massive statuary that infests the Soviet Union. It misses the lithe beauty of The Man.

"I saw the sculptor when he was working on it," Musial said. "I told him I never looked that broad. He said it had to be that broad because it was going to be against the backdrop of a big ball park. He missed the stance, but what kind of man would I have been if I'd complained. The writers were generous to put it up. The sculptor did his best. Look, there's a statue of me in St. Louis while I'm still alive."

A pregnant woman, armed with an autograph book, charged. "Write for my son Willie," she commanded. Musial nodded, said, "Where ya from?" and signed with a lean-fingered, practiced hand.

"Thank you," the pregnant woman said. "Willie is coming soon. After he gets here and learns to talk, I'm sure he'll thank you, Mr. Musial."

Inside the round stadium, the Cardinals were losing slowly in the wet Mississippi Valley heat. The final score would be Cincinnati 13, St. Louis 2. We had left after the fourth inning when baseball's perfect knight passed his threshold of anguish over the bad game being played by the home team.

To reach most old ballplayers, even millionaire old ballplayers like Hank Greenberg, you simply call their homes around dinner time. A pleased, remembered voice comes through the phone. "I had a good day playing tennis. How've you been? Who've you been seeing lately? Say, if you're ever in town, come over and we can talk about the old days."

To reach Musial, you call the office of the resort and restaurant corporation called Stan Musial & Biggie's, Inc. When I did, a secretary said crisply but politely, "I'm sorry, but Mr. Musial is on a goodwill tour of Europe. He'll be back briefly in two weeks. Then he's flying to the Montreal Olympics. We'll try to fit you in, but could I have your name again and could you tell me what this is in reference to?"

It was in reference to one thing. Stan Musial, neither a perfect warrior nor any sort of knight, is my particular baseball hero. I once heard a teammate who knew him well call him a choker. "Considering his ability, he didn't drive in enough runs," the man said. Musial heard about that remark, but would not stoop to make a response. During his 22 years with the Cardinals, Musial batted in a total of 1,951 runs. That is the fifth highest total in the history of the major leagues. According to Jackie Robinson, Musial remained passive in baseball's struggle to integrate itself. "He was like Gil Hodges," Robinson said. "A nice guy, but when it came to what I had to do, neither one hurt me and neither one helped." But four years ago Musial worked quietly for the election of George McGovern as President. He is a political activist, and on racial questions he favors the men whom Robinson almost certainly would have preferred.

Musial is a man of limited education, superior intelligence, a somewhat guarded manner, a surface conviviality and a certain aloofness, because he knows just who he is. Stan Musial, Hall-of-Famer, great batsman and, 13 years after he last cracked a double to right center field, still an American hero.

We were rambling about baseball in one of his offices in St. Louis when my wife, who can be more direct than I, interposed five questions.

"By the time you got to be 35," she said, "and your muscles began to ache, did you still enjoy playing baseball?"

Musial nodded, touched his sharp chin and said, "I always wanted to be a baseball player. That's the only thing I ever wanted to be. Now figure that I was in the exact profession I wanted and I was at the top of that profession and they were paying me 100,000 a year. Yes. I enjoyed playing baseball very much right up to the end of my career."

"About politics?" Wendy asked.

"I'm a Democrat. Tom Eagleton, the Senator, says he remembers sitting in my lap when he was a kid visiting our spring-training camp years ago."

"What do you think of Jimmy Carter?"

Musial laughed to himself. "I'd have to say he's very unusual for a candidate."

"You worked for Lyndon Johnson?"

"He asked me to run his physical fitness program and I did. I believe in physical fitness. I'm 55 years old, and I still swim two or three hours every day."

"But didn't you find Johnson vulgar?" Wendy said.

Musial looked impersonally at me, then at my wife. "No," he said, "because we only talked politics."

If I read him correctly, Musial had said in quick succession that

Wendy's first question was naive, that Carter was the prince of peanut growers and that Johnson would have sounded obscene in a roaring dugout. Just as he hit home runs without seeming to strain, Musial had implied all these things without a suggestion of rancor.

People were always mistaking his subtlety for blandness. An agent employed by both Musial and Ted Williams once said to me, "If you want to make some money selling articles, stick with Williams. The other feller's nice, but there isn't any electricity to him." Then one of the editors at *Newsweek*, where I was working, directed me to prepare a cover story on Musial. "Pick up the Cardinals out in Pittsburgh," the editor said, "and make Musial take you back to Donora. It'll work well, putting him back on the streets of the Pennsylvania factory town where he grew up."

At Forbes Field, Musial said that he was driving to Donora the next day and I was welcome to ride along with him—provided I promised not to write about the trip.

"Why not?"

"I promised someone I'd visit sick kids in the hospital. If you write that, it'll look like I'm doing it for publicity. And my mother lives above a store there. That's where she wants to live. We had her in St. Louis, but she missed her old friends, so she went back home and found a place she liked. No matter how you write that, the magazine will come out with a headline: STAN MUSIAL'S MOTHER LIVES ABOVE A STORE."

"Well, I have to come back with a story."

"We'll spend some time and maybe come up with something," Musial said.

We talked batting for three days. To break a slump, he hit to the opposite field. He remembered a day at Ebbets Field when he had gotten five hits, all with two strikes, and he remembered a year he suffered chronic appendicitis and played 149 games and hit .312. He remembered the doubleheader at Busch Stadium when he hit five home runs. He could even recall the different pitches that he hit.

"Do you guess at the plate?" I asked.

The sharp-featured face lit. "I don't guess. I know." Then Musial spun out a batting secret. He had memorized the speed at which every pitcher in the league threw the fastball, the curve, the slider. He picked up the speed of the ball in the first 30 feet of its flight, after which he knew how the ball would move as it crossed home plate.

About 80 pitchers worked in the National League then. Musial had locked the speed of about 240 different pitches into his memory. I had asked the right question, and Musial responded with a story that was picked up by a hundred newspapers.

They oversimplified, as newspapers often do. Even if you can identify a pitch 30 feet away, you are left with only a tiny fraction of a second to respond. Musial's lifetime batting average of .331 was not the product of a single secret. It was fashioned of memory, concentration, discipline, eyesight, physical conditioning and reflexes.

Going for his 3,000th hit, Musial neglected to concentrate and took his stride too early. But he kept his bat back, as all great hitters do. On sheer reflex, he slugged a double to left.

Now in his office, Musial looked much as he had 15 years before. The same surprisingly thin wrists. The same powerful back. A waistline barely thicker than it had been. The deceptive self-deprecation also persists.

"I'm semiretired," he insisted, but twice he politely broke off our interview to take business calls. Stan Musial & Biggie's, Inc., a family-held company, owns two Florida hotels and a restaurant and a hotel in St. Louis.

"Are you a millionaire like Hank Greenberg?" I asked.

"Just write that I'm not hanging for my pension. A long time ago I knew that I couldn't hit forever, and I knew that I didn't want to be a coach or manager. So Biggie Garagnani, who died young, and I started the restaurant in 1949. Biggie knew the business, and I knew that just my name wasn't enough. I put in time. I like mixing with people up to a point, and my being here was good for business. I still walk around in the place six nights a week when I'm in town. So while I was playing, I was building a permanent restaurant business, and that just led naturally into the hotels. What's my title? President of Stan Musial & Biggie's, Inc."

Unlike many self-made men from poor backgrounds, Musial is a liberal, and his liberalism seems to deepen as he ages.

"I don't think Polish jokes or Jewish jokes or black jokes are really funny," he said. "My dad came out of Poland and worked like hell all his life. What was funny about that? Pulaski came out of Poland and helped out in the American Revolution. Was that a joke? I've just come back from Poland, and I enjoyed the country, the people and seeing them work hard building high rises. Some of them me. I brought my harmonica along and played a little."

"Polish songs?"

"Yeah. Like *Red River Valley.*"

At the park, fans flooded toward his box, demanding autographs and making it difficult to study the game. Musial singled out Pete Rose for praise and said he felt embarrassed that so many major-leaguers were hitting in the .200s. "There's no excuse for that. You know why it happens? They keep trying to pull everything, even low outside sliders. You can't do that. Nobody can. If you're a major league player, you ought to have pride. Learn to stroke outside pitches to the opposite field. That's part of your job. A major league hitter is supposed to be a professional."

"Do you miss playing?" I said as Rose rapped a single up the middle.

"No," Musial said. "Nice stroke, Pete. I quit while I still enjoyed it, but I put in my time. I like to travel now, but not with a ball club. Have you ever seen Ireland? Do you know how beautiful it is?"

After the game, we drove back to Musial's restaurant, and a crowd surrounded him in the lobby. He said to each, "How are ya? Where ya from?" One 50ish man was so awed that he momentarily lost the power of speech. He waved his arms and sputtered and poked his wife and pointed. Musial clapped the man gently on the back. "How are ya? Where ya from?" Musial said to him again. The man looked as if he might weep with joy. At length he recovered sufficiently to say a single word, "Fresno."

"Does this happen all the time?" I asked.

"Isn't it something?" Musial said. "And I'm 13 years out of the business. You know what Jack Kennedy said to me once? He said they claimed he was too young to be President and I was too old to be playing ball. Well, Jack got to be President, and two years later, when I was 42 years old, I played 135 games and I hit .330."

"Ebbets Field, Stash," I said. "They should have given you the right-field wall when they wrecked the place. You owned it, anyway."

"What do you think my lifetime average was in Brooklyn?" Musial said.

"About .480."

"It only seemed that way," he said. "Actually my lifetime average there was .360."

I can't imagine Galahad, the perfect knight, as a baseball hero. He was priggish and probably undersized. That doesn't matter. Having Stanley Frank Musial is quite enough.

## To Nelson Fox

Nellie, you arrived
at Connie Mack's
wartime tryout camp
on the back of your old man's
pickup truck

You were so short
that when you stood up
you could barely see over
the side panels

But that didn't stop you
from going on to become
the greatest second baseman
in the history of the American League

Your chaw of tobacco
was as big as you were
and it was always moving
because you were always moving

Al Lopez said you "hustled
your way to stardom"
and if anybody ought to know
it's *El Senor*

As a kid, I took you for granted
the way only something necessary
can be taken for granted

I never appreciated your
talent for getting hit by pitches
as much as I should have

You did it 17 times one season
who knows how many of those bruises
became permanent?

Little man, you were so tough
that when you went into the hospital last fall
to die of cancer
you told everybody you were feeling fine

**PAUL GORRIN**

## For Micky Mantle's 500th H.R. Hit
## Off Stu Miller, Yankee Stadium,
## Mother's Day, 1967

You are my natural piety
        thick-necked, reticent
        frozen locked knees without cartilege
        legs bandaged before each game,

        Yellowhaired golden cripple hero.

My heart, yes it still leaps each time you swing

when I was eight
now that I am a man

I was at the Stadium when
Memorial Day, 1956, you hit one that
still rising
struck
the uppermost cornice

Mother's Day 1967
    You redeem us
    War befouls the spring, the land barren

    The Yahoo's—the Jew Goldberg (shonda)
    MacNamara
    the red 'possum eyed Rusk
    the dead whore Stevenson
ride the trajectory of your infield flies

But, O yellow haired, noble All American
    soft spoken
    Your home runs, your pride, your great heart

O Chairman of the Board of Swat

they bind my little days each to each.

## Mel Stottlemyre

"but what have you
  done for us lately?"

they asked him,
                the knife
hidden in one hand,
                the release
clear as a bell (school's out)
in the other
and ended his chance for
the World Series
that he could never pitch
them into
                alone
Like a mistress
                they don't want
you for your mind:

        at the end they
        send you out with
        the garbage
                only
to tell you,
                too late,
that you
                ARE
the garbage

## Hank Aaron

magically smooth across the forehead

the barest hint of anger in the eyes

at certain moments he is able to focus
on the shamefully simple pleasure
that is derived from smacking
a well pitched ball out of the park

but this is an entire history
a conjunction of events and moments
that trails us as we live our century
as unreflexively as we can

the biceps are muscles of the soul
engaged in warfare of the flesh
a spiritual angst that cannot be relieved
a senseless struggle against the light

turns flesh into gold
a mystery of the heart

from Mobile Alabama a straight line
across the continent and twenty five years
of political shit to fill our television
soul with love until we cannot sit still

he is hopelessly in love

his home runs are but the surface of his love

what a life must become if it is known
made hero of and fills the sky with hope

a ripple of the muscles beneath
the darkness of the skin

worlds exploding where the angels live

the barest hint of anger in his eyes
the hopefulness of anger in his eyes


# BERNADETTE MAYER

## Carlton Fisk Is My Ideal

He wears a beautiful necklace
next to the beautiful skin of his neck
unlike the Worthington butcher,
Bradford T. Fisk (butchers always
have a crush on me), who cannot even order veal
except in whole legs of it.
Oh the legs of a catcher!
Catchers squat in a posture
that is of course inward denying orgasm
but Carlton Fisk, I could
model a whole attitude to spring
on him. And he is a leaper!
Like Walt Frazier or, better,
like the only white leaper,
I forget his name, in the ABA's
All-star game half-time slam-dunk contest
this year. I think about Carlton Fisk
in his modest home in New Hampshire
all the time, I love the sound of his name
denying orgasm. Carlton & I
look out the window at spring's first

northeaster. He carries a big hero
across the porch of his home to me.
(He has no year-round Xmas tree
like Clifford Ray who handles the ball
like a banana.) We eat & watch the storm
batter the buds balking on the trees
& cover the green of the grass
that my sister thinks is new grass.
It's last year's grass still!
And still there is no spring training
as I write this, March 16, 1976,
the year of the blizzard that sealed our love
up in a great mound of orgasmic earth.
The pitcher's mound is the lightning mound.
Pudge will see fastballs in the wind,
his mescaline arm extends to the field.
He wears his necklace.
He catches the ball in his teeth!
Balls fall with a neat thunk
in the upholstery of the leather glove he puts on
to caress me, as told to, in the off-season.
All of a sudden he leaps from the couch,
a real ball has come thru the window
& is heading for the penguins on his sweater,
one of whom has lost his balloon
which is floating up into the sky!

## Interview with Graig Nettles

*Young:*   If I can find my . . . some general questions.

*Nettles:*   Could a got Jerry Dahms over here. (Our highschool coach)

*Young:*   I was thinking about Jerry. Jerry knows all about baseball. I could skip you.

*Nettles:*   He taught me everything I know.

*Young:*   I know.

*Nettles:*   He *was* a good coach. A damn good coach.

*Young:*   Because there's only a few things you have to know, and he played some Double A ball. He was a great catcher, but a confirmed "lunger" at the plate.

*Nettles:*   He told me a lot of things that I didnt really hear again until I got to Triple-A baseball. Guys were telling me little things that they thought I didnt know yet. I said, goddam I learned this stuff in high school.

*Young:*   Did you play third in high school, after I left?

*Nettles:*   No. I played short and 2nd.

*Young:*   What did Froebel Brigham play? Your mother and I were trying to work that out today.

*Nettles:*   When you played 2nd I played short and then my senior year I played 2nd and Froebel played short.

*Young:*   Oh you played 2nd.

*Nettles:*   And at San Diego State I played shortstop and one year at 3rd base. And then I signed as a 2nd baseman, and played 2nd base the first half of my first year.

*Young:*   You must have been a gangly big 2nd baseman, comparatively.

*Nettles:*   Not really. I was never really very big. When I signed to play pro ball I was 6 ft. 180 pounds. Good size, not big, not skinny. But then half way through my first year they said, "Well we got this guy named Carew, and he's a step ahead of you, you know, and would you like to move to 3rd base?" I said, sure. I could tell he was going to be good.

*Young:*   You seem like now to have the perfect physique for the 3rd baseman. You know, paunchy and slow.

*Nettles:*   Yeah.

*Young:*   You're not expected to run.

*Nettles:* I couldn't play 2nd or short now, no way, because I dont have the range, I dont have the speed. I have good quickness, the first 4 or 5 steps I'm good, and that's all you need at 3rd.

*Young.* If you get out of the blocks at all.

*Nettles:* If your chest holds up! What kind of notes you got there?

*Young:* I was going to ask you about the Yankees in general. Because you know, we were all rabid Yankee fans growing up, front-runners indeed. But I was wondering, when you shift uniforms, say, coming from the Twins to the Indians, and then to the Yankees, if there are things that are particularly Yankee. Like a tradition. Something that characterizes that team that *isn't* the Indians, or the Twins.

*Nettles:* One of the best things about playing for the Yankees is that when you tell somebody you play for the Yankees, all of a sudden it means something. If you say I play for the Indians, it's less clear. Stanford? Cleveland? They dont know. Especially my first year with New York, which was the last year of Yankee Stadium. Shit, there was so much tradition associated with Yankee Stadium. Babe Ruth, Lou Gehrig, Joe Dimaggio, all that kind of stuff.

*Young:* Did that feeling extend into the locker room?

*Nettles:* No.

*Young:* They've pretty much up-tempo'ed everything?

*Nettles:* They had the monuments in Yankee Stadium, and the plaques on the centerfield wall, but other than that, in the locker room there's no sign over anything that says this is where Babe had his locker or anything like that. Although I asked, because the guy who is our clubhouse man now, who does all the dirty work, the old guy, he was a clubhouse man when Babe Ruth was playing too. He's about, Christ he's 75 years old. He told me where Babe's locker was. It was something I found interesting. There's a lot of tradition involved with the Yankees. I remember the first time, because you know, Yankee tradition, Yankee tradition, all this blah-blah gets pounded into you, and the first time they had an Old-Timer's game in Yankee Stadium all the Old Timers come in and they use our lockers, so I'm at my locker and there's 2 or 3 Old Timers dressing in my locker and one of the guys was Gene Woodling. We were sitting there talking, and I can remember him saying "Fuck this uniform! That fucking uniform dont mean a thing," he says. "You're playing this game for yourself. When they dont like you anymore they trade you off like a piece of meat. Fuck that uniform." He says, "Fuck that tradition." Now there's one guy who really didnt . . . he saw everything right like it is. He didnt go for all that romantic crap.

*Young:* Yeah, the attachment to that myth.

*Nettles:* It is sort of a myth, too, really. Because you are playing the game for yourself, you're not playing it for Ruth or Gehrig.

*Young:* You're playing it for the team you're on, maybe?

*Nettles:* Oh yeah, for the team, and for yourself, at that time, but you dont say let's win one for the Babe. Rah rah Notre Dame.

*Young:* Did you get a bonus when you signed?

*Nettles:* Yeah, my bonus amounted to about, there were different things involved. I collected probably $23,000.

*Young:* Things have changed. Already the big bonuses have been cut back. Dave Moorhead (Hoover High School, San Diego, 1961) got $75,000 in 1961 with the Red Sox.

*Nettles:* There were guys getting $100,000 at that time, still, but I was not a phenom. I couldnt do everything super. I could do certain things well. I had good power for a second baseman. That's why my first year of playing they wanted to move me to centerfield. My manager came to me and said, we're gonna make a Mickey Mantle out of you. I said, now wait a minute. I didnt know if I was going to be a 20 homerun a year man in the Majors like I am. I thought, if I can hit anywhere from 10–15 homeruns, as a 2nd baseman, that's good, that's doing great, but if they move me to the outfield then Christ, I'm *expected* to hit 25–30. So I put a stop to that. I said, I'm a 2nd baseman and I want to play 2nd base. As it turned out they moved me to third base and third basemen as a rule are expected to hit some homeruns and provide some power.

*Young:* So it worked. It's like your body directed you. When it filled out to a certain . . . you went to that position.

*Nettles:* I'm still glad I told 'em No. At the time the Twins were rich in outfielders and I figured the best way for me to move up would be as an infielder with some power.

*Young:* Who was playing third then?

*Nettles:* At the time Rich Rollins was, and he was doing well, but he wasnt going to be the star that Carew ended up being. Everybody could see that Carew was going to be a star.

*Young:* And then you got traded to Cleveland and it was actually a good trade for you.

*Nettles:* Best thing that ever happened. Got a chance to play.

*Young:* Hadnt you played much prior to that? Steadily?

*Nettles:* Not really. I played. I think I got to bat 250 times the year before the trade, and that's not very regular. When you're playing everyday you get to bat somewhere between 550–600 times. When I got over to Cleveland they said you can play, they said, I hear you can play 3rd base, and I said yeah, and he said, well you're my 3rd baseman.

*Young:* Who was that?

| Nettles: | Alvin Dark. And right away I started out badly, I started out in a slump, but I was fielding real well, and he left me in the line-up, then I got hot. |
|---|---|
| Young: | You tend to be a streak hitter. In fact, I've never seen anything like it. |
| Nettles: | Oh yeah. I'm streaky as hell. |
| Young: | Even in June (1975), you were so hot last June. |
| Nettles: | Last June and July I *was* hot. That was when I was making my push toward the All-Star team. |
| Young: | But after the All-Star break, there was a real definite . . . and the Yankees completely fizzled . . . was it injuries? Like Elliot Maddox? |
| Nettles: | Yeah. That's what killed us the worse, because he's probably the best centerfielder in the league and he got hurt. |
| Young: | He was hitting .210. |
| Nettles: | And balls were falling in that he would catch easily. And that just killed us. |
| Young: | Did Bonds contribute a good year? |
| Nettles: | He contributed, sorta. But you know about him. He's the type of guy, he hits 30–40 homeruns a year but he *can't* hit in the middle of the line-up, something about his head, you know. He strikes out too much, for one thing. To have a guy drive in a lot of runs hitting in the middle of the line-up, you need somebody who can get a basehit with a man on second. If there's a guy on 2nd, Bonds is either gonna hit a HR or strike out. He's gonna strikeout a lot more than he's gonna hit a homerun. That's why he was hitting lead-off, because he got on base some. But if you needed a really clutch pressure rbi, he couldnt do it. |
| Young: | How's Mickey Rivers gonna do? |
| Nettles: | Rivers gonna do alright. He's gonna hit lead off and he's gonna get on a base a lot. |
| Young: | He's quick? |
| Nettles: | Christ he's fast. And strong too. He can drive the ball between the outfielders. He cant hit it up in the air for a long ways, but he swings down on the ball and rides it through the outfield. Shit, if he gets a ball into the gaps there in Yankee Stadium, it's an inside the park homerun. He's the fastest guy I've ever played against. |
| Young: | No kidding. |
| Nettles: | I play him 30 feet in from 3rd base, expecting him to bunt, and I *know* if he gets it down he's gonna beat it out. |
| Young: | Great! |
| Nettles: | That's how much he shakes me up. |
| Young: | How about Finley's brain child, the orange ball? A possibility? |
| Nettles: | I dont think so. I've never seen them though. |

*Young:* But tennis made that rapid jump to yellow balls, and lately I've seen blue tennis courts, and against blue those yellow balls are pure Alice in Wonderland.

*Nettles:* Yeah. But as of now I'd say no. However, all of Finley's other things everybody thought were crazy end up coming about: World Series night games, white shoes, colored uniforms, they've all come about. I'd have to play with an orange ball to find out if I liked it.

*Young:* But the thing is, baseballs are so white, they dont get lost that much. You dont have that much trouble, do you?

*Nettles:* No, not really. You know, baseball is a lot different than tennis, because tennis you're not really watching the spin on the ball. In baseball you become accustomed to seeing a white ball with red seams spinning this way or spinning that way. It'd be a little tough with an orange ball with red seams. You wouldn't be able to pick up those seams.

*Young:* They'd have to be white.

*Nettles:* You'd have to do something to offset the color, because so much of it depends on you seeing which way the ball is spinning. I never knew that in high school, we could never see the ball spin. I couldnt, you know. Now I can.

*Young:* I dont think I *ever* saw the rotation of the seams. It was rather a question of adjusting quickly to the *speed,* trying to pick up the curve as it hung.

*Nettles:* Sometimes it's easier to hit in the Minor Leagues under the bad lights than it is in the Major Leagues under the good lights, because in the Majors when the lights are so bright the ball coming in is just a white blur.

*Young:* So much light bouncing off the ball.

*Nettles:* Yeah. It's just a white *thing.* But in the Minor Leagues you can see the ball spin. It's a little darker. Sometimes those really good lights can work against the hitter.

*Young:* Have you ever chronicled your stats and figured out what you hit in day games and what you hit at night?

*Nettles:* No.

*Young:* Wouldn't that be an important thing to know?

*Nettles:* Yeah. But I wouldnt have any idea.

*Young:* If I was hitting .350 during the day, and .220 at night, I'd like to know.

*Nettles:* Yeah. I know I'm probably hung over in the day games, so I dont know if I'd like all day games or not. I do know it's a lot easier to *see* in the day games.

*Young:* I've been playing some softball, and it's a travesty, these lights. The sandlots of Berkeley. You cant see the ball, when it's hit, and I'm playing outfield. I need radar. I joined a team that already had an infield, so . . .

*Nettles:* They needed your bat, so they put you out to pasture!

*Young:* They just needed my mouth, you know, I talk all the time. But the outfield is different territory. Throwing to the right base. I've come to like it. If nothing else, I keep warm running in and out. You played some outfield?

*Nettles:* I played some for a year in 1969.

*Young:* Daytime it's great, but night-time is tricky. Frustrating.

*Nettles:* Night-time is really bad. The ball gets lost *in* the lights and on the fields you're playing on, sometimes the ball goes *above* the lights. Christ, you're in trouble.

*Young:* Do you talk about pitchers with other hitters?

*Nettles:* Yeah.

*Young:* You literally do discuss what a guy's got, what he's throwing.

*Nettles:* Sure. What he throws in what situation. One of the things I hate more than anything is to face a new pitcher. Say a kid just up from the minors, or a new guy in the league. Because I dont know what his ball does, I dont know what he's gonna do in a certain situation, whereas guys who've been around 4 or 5 or 10 years, I've faced these guys for that length of time. I know just about what they're gonna throw me when they're ahead, or when I'm ahead.

*Young:* Ted Williams said, a great pitcher, if he strikes you out with his *best* pitch on a 2–2 count, the next time he faces you and it's a 2–2 count, he's gonna throw that *best* pitch again. That's the great pitcher. The not-so-great pitcher will try to psyche you out and go to his second pitch, in that same situation. Williams was always looking for *that* guy. Because he always knew if the guy was great or not.

*Nettles:* He never thought too much of pitchers. He thinks all pitchers are stupid.

*Young:* Because he studied harder. He also said it wasnt how hard you swung either. The big thing was bat control, and always swinging at strikes.

*Nettles:* He had such a good eye. All hitting is, really, is discipline. You have to discipline yourself not to swing at pitches you cant handle. If there's a pitch low and away, dont swing at that pitch, even if it's a strike, unless you have 2 strikes on you and have to guard the plate. He was so disciplined he wouldnt do it. And then he got such a reputation that if it was down and away for a strike, he could take it and the umpire would call it a ball. The great hitters get away with that stuff. I never hardly ever saw 'em call a strike on Kaline with 2 strikes and that kinda intimidates the umpire. They wouldnt call 'em.

*Young:* Got such discipline that they've defined the strike zone religiously. So there are no arguments.

*Nettles:* Sure.

*Young:*  How about umpires coming down on you if you get a little pissy with 'em? Do they hold it on you?

*Nettles:*  Some guys will. You know, umpires are human. Some hold grudges, some dont.

*Young:*  How about Paul Runge? (San Diego High School, 1959, and son of Ed Runge, former longtime umpire in the American League) Is he in your league?

*Nettles:*  No, he's in the National League. I've talked with guys who've played in games he's umpired, and they say he's a real red ass.

*Young:*  Yeah?

*Nettles:*  They say he's a real prick.

*Young:*  You werent at San Diego High yet when Runge was King Shit, the senior catcher behind the plate. I remember riding around in his brand new blue Impala, nineteen fifty-nine.

*Nettles:*  His old man was one of the worst!

*Young:*  I thought Ed Runge was one of the Deans.

*Nettles:*  I tell you what, my first time, this is my 3rd big league at bat, I'm in there and Ed Runge's behind the plate.

*Young:*  Does he know you as a San Diego boy?

*Nettles:*  So I walk up there to pinch hit, this is 1967, go up to the plate, and the catcher calls a time out to go and talk with Joel Horlen, who's pitching. I cant think of the catcher's name now but anyway, he goes out to talk about me, because we were both in the pennant race at the time and he didn't want Joel screwing up. So as they are out there talking on the mound, Runge says, "Hey Graig, congratulations on making it to the big leagues, hope you do a good job, San Diego boy, good luck to you." So I say to myself, Alright Uncle Ed! First pitch Horlen throws a curve ball and Josephson (that's the catcher's name) goes out on one knee and catches the ball right off the ground and I take it. Runge goes "Strike one." I thought, Oh shit.

*Young:*  Really bad pitch?

*Nettles:*  Terrible, terrible. But I'd heard, Dont say anything to Runge because he likes to test rookies. So I didnt say a thing to him. So the next pitch I'm figuring he's gonna throw something outside again and I'm looking out there like that, and he throws a pitch in here (waist high). It must have been about 5 inches on the plate and Runge goes "Ball one."

*Young:*  Justice!

*Nettles:*  He made it up. He was testing me on the first pitch, made up for it on the second pitch, and from then on, the whole rest of the time that he was in the league, he gave me all kinds of breaks.

*Young:*  If you had mouthed off?

*Nettles:*  If I'd a mouthed off he'd a stuck it up my ass for the next two years. But he's like that. Maybe his son Paul is like that too. I dont know.

*Young:*  That must be the umpire's fun. To get some psychological games going. To stay awake, so to speak.

*Nettles:*  Some umps will give breaks. Others are pricks and want to stick it to you. And some are just terrible. They cant help it either way.

*Young:*  How about the famous Ron Luciano?

*Nettles:*  He's crazy.

*Young:*  I bet he's fun, though.

*Nettles:*  He's funny, but I'll tell you, I hate it when he's umpiring 3rd base because he talks to me the whole game. You know, endless chatter, and it bothers my concentration.

*Young:*  What about concentration? I know, now that I play one game a week, and I've worked all day and I'm just a sandlot asshole out there having fun, I dont know how many outs there are! At times . . .

*Nettles:*  (laughter)

*Young:*  I used to have that concentration, like I always knew.

*Nettles:*  That happens to me still. You know, Major League player, I forget. But I've been lucky.

*Young:*  Havent blown it bad?

*Nettles:*  Havent blown it real bad. Sometimes you start to go off the field and I'm lucky, our dugout's on the first base side, so I'll take a few steps and just trot over to the pitcher. I'm the last guy to get the ball to give to the pitcher, so I'll just be right there, toss it to him, and tell him some weak shit, and trot back. But I've seen guys field the ball, say the shortstop with one out, and he makes his throw to first and tears off the field, gets about half way, and comes back.

*Young:*  Yeah. It's only really brutal when there are men on base, or you *don't* make the double plays.

*Nettles:*  What's really embarrassing is if I get a quick one hopper and throw a little toss to 2nd for the force, for what *I think* is the 3rd out, and there was only one, then Christ, the 2nd baseman gets killed, because (laughing) I've given him a little lob toss.

*Young:*  Why dont you describe the slider to me, what you see it doing. We didnt see it in high school, to say the least.

*Nettles:*  Some guys throw a slider and it breaks down like that (3 or 4 feet) and they call it a slider but it isnt. A good slider should break about that far (one foot). They kinda hold it like a football, like that. It's like a cut fastball is all you're doing. And it looks like a fastball and it goes Chooof! Right at the last it just breaks.

*Young:*  Can you pick up the rotation?

| | |
|---|---|
| *Nettles:* | Yeah, sorta. The best way to gauge a slider is the speed of it. It's a little slower. The guys that throw a real hard one are impossible. If they've got a good short one and throw it hard, shit, it's on your fists. |
| *Young:* | How does Catfish Hunter get away with it? |
| *Nettles:* | Smart. |
| *Young:* | When I saw you at the Oakland game last year, the first time Hunter faced his ex-teammates, you got the hit that scored the only run you needed, and Catfish threw 88 pitches and burned down the A's. That was the most beautifully pitched game I've ever seen. The guy's in a groove, such a rhythmic flawlessness. Concentration like impeccable, like Mindless! Not a thing on his mind. And all that weight just perfectly controlled. |
| *Nettles:* | He's good. He's damn good. He's worth the money. |
| *Young:* | And he lost so many close ones last summer, 1–0, 2–1. You guys were not getting runs. |
| *Nettles:* | But he's the same. If he happened to be 20–0, or 0–15, he'd be the same. He's one of the few guys I've ever seen who can go out the night before he pitches and drink and go crazy. Pitchers, 99% of 'em, always the night before they pitch get their rest. They dont drink, oh they might have a few cocktails, but they'll get their sleep. Catfish'll stay out all night long, "playing cards," drinking, and come in the next day and pitch the best fucking game. Strange, but he's so goddam strong. |
| *Young:* | I guess he has to burn up that tension *in order* to pitch. |
| *Nettles:* | I guess so. |
| *Young:* | He never "suffers" when he doesnt win? |
| *Nettles:* | No, not really. |
| *Young:* | I mean, he never says, "Hey you fuckers, Bingo, huh!" |
| *Nettles:* | No. |
| *Young:* | He never comes in and says "Let's get some runs."? |
| *Nettles:* | Never. Never. It wouldnt . . . |
| *Young:* | Do pitchers? |
| *Nettles:* | Oh yeah, some of 'em do. "Come on, get me some runs." You know, like they're about to cry. Like they take it personal! Like we're really fucking them on purpose. We're trying like hell. You know, I mean, some pitchers you go, shit, why are they saying that? Because we dont come in and jump on their ass when they give up two homeruns in a row, or something. |
| *Young:* | So shut up. |
| *Nettles:* | So shut the fuck up. |

February 21, 1976
San Diego

## 2nd Interview with Graig Nettles

*Young:* How does it feel to be leading the team in Home Runs? New York Slugger.

*Nettles:* Strange, you know. It's a funny year for homeruns. There hasn't been a lot of homeruns this year.

*Young:* Bando gets 4 or 5, then you get 4 or 5, and then no one gets any.

*Nettles:* I was stuck on 15 for about 3 weeks, then all of a sudden in a two week period I hit seven. That's typical of me, though. I always hit in streaks.

*Young:* When you're not hitting well, does the batting coach ever offer comments, like, hey, you're way ahead of the ball?

*Nettles:* Not really. Mickey Mantle is our batting coach and he shows up about twice a year.

*Young:* Loaded on LITE beer!

*Nettles:* He shows up in the Spring, and then he shows up for a couple of Old Timers' games and that's it. Yogi Berra helps some guys. You know, they help you if you ask. I never really ask that much. I'll ask some of the other players on the team if they can see anything.

*Young:* What's Yogi's job?

*Nettles:* Yogi's job is coach. Hang around the dugout, hit ground balls. Look good in the lobby.

*Young:* I saw him out by the pool yesterday. White mafia belt, white patent leather shoes. Looked like he just walked off the showroom floor at Sears. But strong. Didnt look like he'd gained a pound.

*Nettles:* Oh he's getting kinda fat.

*Young:* Yeah. So do the gorillas in the zoo.

*Nettles:* But he takes batting practice every once in a while and he can still hit the ball hard.

*Young:* He's a little guy.

*Nettles:* Yeah, he is really little. I kid him about it. "How did you ever play before they lowered the mound? You couldn't see to throw it to second base." He's a good guy to have around. I like him.

*Young:* I saw Finley leaving the park last night. He's sporting a new white rug.

*Nettles:* He was in the lobby of the hotel the night we got in. Guys were saying "Hey Catfish, there's yr daddy, Cat, hey Cat."

*Young:* I heard that same riff yesterday. Mickey Rivers was in the coffee shop when Holtzman walked in for lunch. When Rivers sees him, he starts whispering "There's Finley, there's Finley." Holtzman starts looking around, sees Rivers, and smiles.

*Young:* You signed at last. Did you have an agent?

*Nettles:* No. I talked with Steinbrenner in Yankee Stadium once, and we didnt get anywhere. And then finally, I asked Billy Martin to talk to him for me. I said, "Billy, if you talk with Steinbrenner tomorrow, find out what his plans are for me. I'd like to know if he's going to plan on me being around here, or am I going somewhere else, or what." So Billy came and told me the next day, he said "Why dont you go up and talk with him, he's in a pretty good mood right now." I went up and we talked for 5 minutes and I signed.

*Young:* Does the signing of a 3 year contract mean you cant be traded?

*Nettles:* Not that I cant be traded, it's that I get all that money. It's called a no-cut contract, which means they cant cut the salary at all.

*Young:* Do you mind telling us what that salary is?

*Nettles:* No. When I first started talking contract over the winter the best they were going to offer was 90 for this year and a hundred for next, and I said no, I want a 3 year contract. That was a big thing to them. And so I just started making my demands out of sight. I got em up so darn high that no way they could meet em. So when they got serious about signing me they said, OK, let's try to meet in between there, which is what I wanted anyway. So I end up signing for 120 for this year, 120 for next year, and 145,000 for 1978.

*Young:* You bastard!! I dont believe it!

*Nettles:* Yeah. By them making me wait, they could have signed me for a lot less than that if they'd been serious.

*Young:* You went down to Florida in the Spring asking for 100 a year for 3 straight years.

*Nettles:* That's what the papers thought.

*Young:* Give me that again. 120, 120, 145.

*Nettles:* And in the 4th year, it says that he wont cut me the 20% if I want to play out my option. So if I have a good year in that 3rd year, and I'm still around, then they're gonna have to pay me at least 145 for that 4th year.

*Young:* Bravo.

*Nettles:* But I had them spread it out over 10 years. I took 40,000 a year for 10 years. That way I dont get killed on taxes.

*Young:* That's better for the owner, too.

*Nettles:* Better for him, better for me, better for everybody.

*PA:* That's what 1st place will do to you. He can give out the money now.

*Nettles:*   Money's never been a problem with him. I think Steinbrenner's the type of guy that wants you to say, he wants you more or less to kiss his ass and say, "I want to be a Yankee and I want to play for you & blah blah blah." I'd never said that before, and I kinda mentioned it that day, I said "We have a good team and I want to be a part of this team for the next few years." Kinda softened him up a little bit.

*Young:*   Sure.

*B:*   But for that kind of money, I'll kiss anyone's ass! (laughing)

*PA:*   When he made everyone cut his hair . . .

*Nettles:*   That was his big deal, yeah.

*Young:*   Il Duce . . .

*Nettles:*   He thinks that because back in the fifties when the Yankees were winning they had short hair, so he doesnt realize that that was the way everybody wore their hair, then. What the hell.

*Young:*   I can see Oscar Gamble having to cut his hair, but Catfish shouldn't have to cut his hair for anyone!

*Nettles:*   It was a big deal at the beginning of the year. Now the guys are letting their hair grow a little bit and he hasn't said too much. Maybe it's our big lead?

*Young:*   You've seen Mark Fidrych a couple times now. Have you hit safely against him?

*Nettles:*   Oh yeah. I got a couple hits off him the first time we faced him. It was on National TV. It was funny because he was out there talking to the ball, so just when he started to wind up for his 1st pitch, I stepped out of the batter's box, and I started talking to my bat. I said "Now dont you listen to that ball. When it comes in here you hit it right here (pointing to meat of bat), and hit it right up in that upper deck up there" and I was pointing to the upper deck.

*Young:*   Anything for TV!

*Nettles:*   And I popped up! Came back to the bench and said "God-damm, I just realized I was using a Japanese bat. Doesnt understand English."

*Young:*   Do you think of yourself as superstitious?

*Nettles:*   Not really. But I can tell you something about omens.

*Young:*   Alright.

*Nettles:*   The other day we were down in Anaheim playing and we were like in the 15th inning. And there was a guy over in the stands behind 3rd base who waved at me in about the 2nd inning of the game, and I waved back. I knew I recognized him but I couldnt think of where. It was buggin me the whole game, and then in the 15th inning all of a sudden it clicked. I knew who the guy was. He works in a place where I get my car worked on in Newport Beach. It clicked right there. And I came in and I said, "That's it, we're gonna win, we're gonna win big now. I just finally figured out who this guy was that I've been trying to figure out this whole game." We go and score 5 runs in the 15th inning and win 5–0. And it was a nothin-nothin game at the time.

August 31, 1976
Oakland
with Paul Auster

## TOM CLARK

### To Vida Blue

Vida, for a while there
no one in America
didn't know who you were
and suddenly that included yours truly

You rescued me from something
with your strikeouts
your sprint to the mound
and your blue glove

I don't know what it was exactly
that you rescued me from
but Fontella Bass
couldn't have needed a life preserver more

## To Bill Lee

Spaceman, how was your trip to Peking?
I hear you didn't have such a great time
and you're off to a terrible start
this season
with an earned run average of 12.12 per game
having given up 26 hits and 11 walks
in your first 16 innings
which is a hell of a shame
because when you're not doing well
the reporters don't like to talk to you so much
and when they don't talk to you I don't find out what you say

It could be when you're going this lousy
you don't say much anyway
I wouldn't blame you
but don't worry
the season's still young
I know you're not
I don't mean I know you're not young
I mean I know you're not worrying
because as you've said many times
for example after Tony Perez hit that painful home run off
    you in the Series
you'll still be alive tomorrow
barring a traffic accident
or cardiac arrest

You are of a philosophical cast of mind I know
even though you are a little temperamental those two traits
    can exist side by side
I mean I have seen you stomping around in the dugout
and screaming at umpires as though you wanted to kill them
but I also know you've read a lot of serious books and have
    many interesting thoughts
such as about whether intelligent life exists on other planets

and about Pyramid Power, of which you are a devotee
and about the Bermuda Triangle, which when you told him
     about it Bernie
Carbo thought you were talking about pussy, and told his
     gorilla so,
and also about ginseng, which you use before you pitch
the way Popeye uses spinach
before he saves Olive Oil by punching out Bluto, and of
     which you are thus an exponent,
and about Eastern Religions too
after many years of inquiry into which
you've concluded that techniques of wacked-out meditation
can be applied in the practical field
a baseball field say
so that for instance in your best example
a Tibetan priest could make a baseball disappear
and then materialize again down the line in the catcher's mitt

"*There*," you say, describing it,
"is my idea of a relief pitcher"

You're telling the truth, as usual
and as usual all the writers are
cackling like you were doing standup comedy

You're also telling the truth when you say that people don't
     generally realize how hard you really work
How for instance you're always one of the first guys to get out
     to the park
How you help set up the batting cage
How you shag fly balls and run a couple of miles every day
and how you actually work on catching ground balls behind
     your back
because you have this theory that because of your exaggerated
     follow-through
you have to

Remember the time you tried your theory out on the late Don
     Hoak?

It was in 1968 at Winston-Salem in the Carolina League
You were a cocky punk just out of USC
You gloved a ball one handed behind your back
That play started a game ending twin killing
and it also made Don Hoak, then your manager
want to kill you

Hoak chased you all the way to the bus screaming his head
    off
and when you got on
he stayed outside, yelling at you and pounding on the window

This is your life, Bill Lee, was not what he was saying

Don Hoak never understood you, Spaceman
It wasn't in the stars
Don's nose was just too hard, I reckon
He couldn't conceive of people like you and Hans Arp
who hurl the truth into the bourgeois face of language

People like Reggie Smith and Pudge Fisk
will never understand you either
because you tell it like you see it

You told it like you saw it that time with Ellie Rodriguez
and lost a few teeth for it
but what are a few teeth in the face of the truth?
You tell it like you see it in Spaceman Language like your
    spiritual grandfather Picabia
even when it gets you into hot water
like it did last summer when you shot off your mouth
about how you thought Busing was a pretty good idea
and about how you thought the Boston fans
Who disagreed with you were bigots with no guts

Those contentions were sensible enough I grant you
and I happen to agree with them
but then it's easy for me, I don't have to pitch in Boston
and you do and did
and it wasn't easy last summer
for although you were in the midst of a fine season
the populace was growing weary
of your smart remarks, your blooper pitches
and behind the back catches. Tibet
and Pyramid Power never did
interest Sox fans much, so that when
on May 20 you shut out the A's
with a quasi-spectacular one-hitter
no one seemed to notice,
the response was merely polite,
no one seemed to understand how well
you were pitching, how no lefthander
to put on a Red Sox suit

since Mel Parnell
or even just possibly
the legendary Robert Moses "Lefty" Grove
had pitched quite as effectively
and consistently
as you were doing;
it was as though everybody was just waiting for you
to fuck up.
And you kept on
not fucking up.
On July 27 your unique sinker was never better
than in a 1–0 masterpiece over Catfish Hunter,
the breathtaking parabola of your blooper ball
never more tantalizing or bizarrely elongated.
But still you were not approved of
as you would have been had you not been
funny in the head. You began to speak
curiously after victories.
On August 9 you beat the A's again
and afterwards said they looked
"emotionally mediocre, like
Gates Brown sleeping on a rug."
What did you mean by that?
On August 24 you beat the White Sox 6–1
in a downpour at Fenway. It was one
of your greatest days. At one point you fielded
a ground ball behind your back by sticking
your glove up over your left shoulder,
spearing the ball, and from a sitting position
starting a double play that ended up with
you lying flat on your back in front of the mound.
Still, when it was over, you sensed the contempt
of the writers and fans. They loved you
but they did not love you. "When I'm through,"
you said, "I'll end up face down in the Charles
River." Spaceman, why did you say that?

That was your seventeenth victory
the third year in a row you'd won 17 games
and this time it looked like
you had a good shot at 20 or
better. Little did you know you'd go
through the playoffs, the Series, the winter
and the first two months of a new season
still looking for that next victory. Or
*did* you know, and is

that what you meant about the Charles River?
You had arm trouble, sure. Then Johnson
kept you out of the playoffs even though
you'd beat the A's twice and called them
emotionally mediocre earlier. In the Series
you pitched well in the second game
but Drago lost it in the ninth. After
the infamous Fisk/Armbrister non-obstruction dispute
in Game Three you said that if you'd
got to ump Larry Barnett you'd have "Van
Goghed" him. You meant you'd have chewed
his ear off? Johnson scheduled you
to start Game Six. "It's not often a
mediocre pitcher gets to start in the
sixth game of a World Series," you said.
(You turned out to be right.) When someone
in the gang of writers asked you if this
was the biggest game you'd ever been asked
to pitch, you said, Nope, this is nothing
compared to the 1968 College World Series.
"That was real baseball," you said. "We
weren't playing for the money. We got
Mickey Mouse watches that ran backwards."
And then when someone else asked what you'd
do if you won and forced the Series into
a seventh game, you said you'd declare an
automatic 48 hours of darkness so Tiant
could get another day's rest. "That's what Zeus
did when he raped Europa," you said.
"He asked the sun god, Apollo, to stay
away for a few days."
                    The next
three days, it rained. Apollo, perhaps
hearing your words on a Tibetan wavelength,
split, and not only did Zeus favor you
by washing out the sixth game, which was set
back from Saturday to Tuesday—he ordained
Tiant to pitch it. And you were pissed
off with Zeus and with Darrell Johnson. You sulked.
But when Carbo's pinch homer tied it
in the 8th, I saw you climb up on the rim
of the dugout and wave out toward the left field
wall, where Carbo's ball had gone,
urging your teammates on. Four innings
later, Pudge Fisk's homer over the same wall
won it for Boston, and you danced in the

dugout with the other Sox,
happy as in Frank Lima's perfect phrase
a bunch of fags in Boystown.
                              That left
the seventh game up to you. You pitched
your ass off, serious for once, and took
a 3–0 lead into the 6th, but then Pete Rose
busted up a double play by banging into Burleson
and up came Tony Perez. I know you hate
me to mention what happened next but it's
a part of the story, Spaceman. You tried to
float your blooper pitch past The Dog
for the second time in one night. That was
once too often, like Tony said later.
You thought you could do it;
you were gambling; that's why
they call you Spaceman. They call
Perez The Dog because he persists. "I saw
him all the way," he said later; "I was
ready for it." Boom! The ball
disappeared into the screen. Two runs. An
inning later you came out with a blister
and a one run lead that was gone by
the time you hit the showers. So much for
Tom Yawkey's World Series Dream. You
sat in the locker room with your head down
amidst your sad teammates later. "I just
went out there and did my job," you said,
in your disappointment using the cliché for once.
"I went out there and threw the shit out
of the ball." The blooper ball you threw
Perez? "Hell, I live by that pitch
and I'll die for it," you said half-
tragically. This time nobody laughed.

And then you left for China.

## Clemente
## (1934–72)

won't forget
his nervous
habit of
rearing his
head back
on his neck
like a
proud horse

# 10

# Following a Team

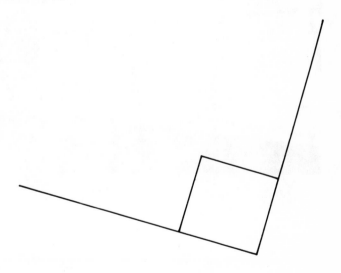

**TOM CLARK**

---

## Interesting Losers

*for Bill Veeck*

Although I had felt many emotions
The meaning of the word "pity" remained
A mystery to me until 1951
When at the age of ten
I discovered the St. Louis Browns

Then
For three short years
A more pitiable spectacle could not have been disclosed

At first base the Brownies had Hank Arft—no kidding—
At second who but the unmemorable Bobby Young
At short the scrawny yet not untalented Billy Hunter
At third a variety of persons including the unsung Fred Marsh
And the washed up Vern Stephens
Who hit the highest popups
In the entire universe

In left field grazed the confused but impassive Dick Kokos
Whose visage lay inert in my mind until one minute ago
When I remembered that baseball card from around 1950
Which showed
A beautiful aerial view of Dick Kokos swinging
Or rather
The conclusion of his swing
Which seemed to involve Dick in a strange state of contortion
Whereby his bat having achieved a 360° arc
Came around and hit him in the back of the head

Meanwhile in center field there was the baby faced Polish hopeful
Johnny Groth
And in right the handsome rapist Jim Rivera who perfected the kamikaze
    slide

Not to mention the deep thighed Don Lenhardt
The insouciant George Schmees
or the pretentious Jim Pisoni

Ah and the Brownies had some great pitchers
They had the wee Ned Garver who somehow won 129 games
The ageless Satchel Paige who was meant for something better
The fiery Virgil Trucks
The bitter Lou Kretlow
The ravaged Gene Bearden
The pissed off Tommy Byrne
The useless Bob Cain
And the deteriorating Ray Coleman
And behind the plate
And the greatest of them all
Was scrappy Clint Courtney
Who couldn't play worth shit
But was so tough
He once swallowed an old jockstrap full of rusty nails
For a promotional stunt
Between losses of a double header

That's what's called a St. Louis Browns Taco nice going Clint!

## Son of Interesting Losers

Eddie Gaedel came from Chicago

In 1951 he was 26 years old and stood 3 feet 7 inches tall

Bill Veeck signed Eddie Gaedel to a St. Louis Browns contract on
   Saturday night July 18, 1951, the night before a big doubleheader in
   Sportsmans Park against the Detroit Tigers, a Sunday doubleheader
   celebrating the Golden Anniversary of the American League

Veeck's promise of a holiday promotion brought out better than eighteen
   thousand people

Nobody was disappointed or surprised when the Browns lost the first game to the Tigers

Between games, members of the ground crew wheeled a huge birthday cake out onto the field, the cake had 50 candles, one for each American League season

The midget Eddie Gaedel stood at his full height inside the birthday cake, wearing his white St. Louis Browns home uniform, with the number "⅛" on the back in brown

Eddie was nervous it was dark inside the cake

When they got to home plate the bearers put the cake down and knocked on the side to let Eddie Gaedel know it was time to come out

He came out

The crowd cheered

Bill Veeck, the one-legged war vet, wearing his famous open-neck sports shirt, grinned from the press box

The second game started

While the Tigers batted in the first inning, Browns manager Zack Taylor helped Eddie Gaedel tie his shoelaces in the dugout

Eddie's hands were shaking

The Tigers finished batting and came off the field

Carrying a tiny kid's bat, Eddie climbed out of the dugout and approached the plate

He informed umpire Ed Hurley that he would be a pinch-hitter for the Browns' lead-off man, Frank Saucier

Hurley stood apart from his mind for a moment and took a second look

Gunfighter-fashion, his strike hand shot back to his pants pocket where it got a good grip on the rule book

Zack Taylor loped out of the dugout to show Hurley Eddie Gaedel's official contract with the St. Louis Browns

The mists of time cleared from the umpire's eyes

Eddie Gaedel stepped into the batters box

Bob Cain, the Detroit pitcher, wound up and fired

The ball exploded into the catcher's mitt a foot above Eddie's head for
ball one

The next two pitches blasted in high and wide of Eddie's tiny strike zone

Bob Cain swore softly and spat into the grass in front of the mound

"Shit," he thought, and then he threw the softest pitch he could throw:
Eddie never saw it: he had his eyes squeezed shut

"Ball Four," said Hurley

Eddie Gaedel trotted off to first base

Immediately Zack Taylor replaced him with a pinch runner

The next day the American League banished midgets from its playing
fields for all time

League President Will Harridge ordered that Eddie Gaedel's statistics be
erased from the record books for all time, and it was done

Bill Veeck paid Eddie Gaedel a hundred bucks

The Browns went on losing, Zack Taylor's hair kept falling out, Bill Veeck
split, the Browns went off to Baltimore and became winners, and Eddie
Gaedel got bookings on the after dinner circuit

Over meat and potato leavings he told the fathers of high school letter
winners about his day in the big leagues

Years passed

In the late 50's Bill Veeck got back into baseball with the Chicago White
Sox

One day he called Eddie Gaedel and asked him to drop by with a couple
of his pals

Veeck dressed the four midgets up in plastic outfits to look like Men from Mars

Then he hired a helicopter and had it circle over the infield at Comiskey Park

Eddie Gaedel and his fellow Martians came down the sky ladder and landed at second base, where they captured two White Sox infielders at raygun-point

It was like a St. Louis Browns Reunion!

JOHN E. MAXFIELD

## Hard Core Support

My mother-in-law is a Senator's fan.
Even now—the team long moved,
The first to Minnesota
The second, Texas.
She'd root for anyone in Washington.

I watched her, years ago
During a particularly long drought.
Once again an early lead blown
The pitcher wild,
Seemed planted in the mound.
She stomped across and stretched to reach the mantel
Switched off her small transistor:
"I can't stand listening to another
Mismanaged baseball game!"

But every little while she'd stop—
Click it on, confirm and click it off
Then stalk away, red hair flying—
A bristling banty hen whose chicks
Persisted in their foolish straying.

ELSTON HOWARD
Sr. and Jr.

# JOEL OPPENHEIMER

## My Father

my father was born in 1893. he was a new york giants fan. my son nathaniel was born in 1966. he is a new york mets fan. i was born in 1930 and i was a dodger fan and am a mets fan, and i hate the yankees. i have more self-confidence now, and have learned the virtues of passion, whether for or against.

my father, having switched to the mets with a desperation similar to mine, had problems devoting full energy to them because he had known the giants. but he was interested in rooting for and watching the national league, and they were the only national leaguers around, so they became his team. but i had twenty-five years of training with the dodgers, which meant i was able to take the mets to my bosom completely, from opening day in '62 on. his death came in August of '69, and so he never saw the pennant race, he never saw the series, and he never saw his grandson in a mets uniform. he did see my play on occasional visits to summer camp, where he watched as i hit texas leaguers from the three, four, or five slot and dropped a great many fly balls out in right field. maturity brought me the wisdom to move to the pitcher's mound, where the other guys are expected to do the fielding.

in any event, it occurs to me now that between the three, we've seen and will keep seeing the history of baseball, and that's a comforting thought. it lends a continuity to life which allows you to believe that the past really happened in a time when you ain't quite sure of it. john mcgraw was my father's motto, and i can't see he suffered by it. i, on the other hand, have always found something to bitch about with managers, although it took until just recently to get me mad at durocher.

well, what is this game? i'd like to think it is peculiarly "american," but i can't see any reason to do that aside from the empirical one that it grew up here and has few relatives anywhere else. it's a game in which time and space are warped into totally artificial limits, and i suppose that's part of it: games, after all, have always seemed to me to involve a suspension of reality so we can mess with a specific number of variables inside a rigid framework, thus getting away, for a little bit, from that hassle called life.

well, by golly, it sure happens—sometimes so much that nothing happens. the dream is of a game that goes on and on, the last out never being made —or a batter fouling, fouling, fouling, so that no ball is ever fair and again the game goes on. thus time and space so carefully denoted are forever destroyed, or at least put on the shelf. i'm talking about the sag of spirit when you realize in the top of the ninth that you're five runs ahead and that unless the other team scores five the game will be over and you won't get to bat again. it happens to me whether i am playing or watching. *i want the game to go on.* that's an unrealistic view of the universe. every other game i can think of tells you when it's going to end either by an actual clock or by a defined goal in points. in tennis they've even gotten dissatisfied with that kind of end, so they have the tiebreaker. terrific. if you want a game to end quickly why start it in the first place? but baseball does more than take you out of time and space, because it allows for a set of records and statistics that mean you don't even have to watch the game to enjoy it. now that *is* wacky and american, i guess. i mean there are guys who wouldn't go to a ball game if you paid them, yet they are fans in the truest sense. al koblin and wes joice own a bar where i hang out and they won't let you turn a ball game on the house television, although i swear i've seen bowling matches on, on slow days there, and yet neither of them can keep out of a trivia war, or a favorite-all-time-team discussion, or a day-by-day prognosis of the season. in horseracing if you bet without at least thinking you know something about the horse you're a fool, but baseball is constructed to let everybody be a specialist. dave markson is my age, grew up in albany watching kiner clout homeruns up there, and can give you every batting average in both leagues from 1935 to 1945. he hasn't seen a game since 1947, but he's my consultant for "his" ten years. vic ziegel specializes in the outré, so that when i wanted to know why jimmy wilson caught an entire world series for the cincinnati reds while they had ernie lombardi he gave me a complete dossier in ten minutes: lombardi sprained his ankle; they reactivated wilson who was then past forty, and he went on to be the hero of the series, with, among other things, the only stolen base. you can't do this with any other game, but then who would want to?

# A. BARTLETT GIAMATTI

## The Green Fields of the Mind

It breaks your heart. It is designed to break your heart. The game begins in the spring, when everything else begins again, and it blossoms in the summer, filling the afternoons and evenings, and then as soon as the chill rains come, it stops and leaves you to face the fall alone. You count on it, rely on it to buffer the passage of time, to keep the memory of sunshine and high skies alive, and then just when the days are all twilight, when you need it most, it stops. Today, October 2, a Sunday of rain and broken branches and leaf-clogged drains and slick streets, it stopped, and summer was gone.

Somehow, the summer seemed to slip by faster this time. Maybe it wasn't this summer, but all the summers that, in this my fortieth summer, slipped by so fast. There comes a time when every summer will have something of autumn about it. Whatever the reason, it seemed to me that I was investing more and more in baseball, making the game do more of the work that keeps time fat and slow and lazy. I was counting on the game's deep patterns, three strikes, three outs, three times three innings, and its deepest impulse, to go out and back, to leave and to return home, to set the order of the day and to organize the daylight. I wrote a few things this last summer, this summer that did not last, nothing grand but some things, and yet that work was just camouflage. The real activity was done with the radio—not the all-seeing, all-falsifying television—and was the playing of the game in the only place it will last, the enclosed, green field of the mind. There, in that warm, bright place, what the old poet called Mutability does not so quickly come.

But out here on Sunday, October 2, where it rains all day, Dame Mutability never loses. She was in the crowd at Fenway yesterday, a grey day full of bluster and contradiction, when the Red Sox came up in the last of the ninth trailing Baltimore 8–5, while the Yankees, rain-delayed against Detroit, only needing to win one or have Boston lose one to win it all, sat in New York washing down cold cuts with beer and watching the Boston game. Boston had won two, the Yankees had lost two, and suddenly it seemed as if the whole season might go to the last day, or beyond, except here was Boston losing 8–5, while New York sat in its family room and put its feet up. Lynn, both ankles hurting now as they had in July, hits a single down the right field line. The crowd stirs. It is on its feet. Hobson, third baseman, former Bear Bryant quarterback, strong, quiet, over 100 RBIs, goes for three breaking balls and is out. The goddess smiles and encourages her agent, a canny journeyman named Nelson Briles.

Now comes a pinch hitter, Bernie Carbo, one-time Rookie of the Year, erratic, quick, a shade too handsome, so laid back he is always, in his soul, stretched out in the tall grass, one arm under his head, watching the clouds and laughing; now he looks over some low stuff unworthy of him and then, uncoiling, sends one out, straight on a rising line, over the center field wall, no cheap Fenway shot, but all of it, the physics as elegant as the arc the ball describes.

New England is on its feet, roaring. The summer will not pass. Roaring, they recall the evening, late and cold, in 1975, the sixth game of the World Series, perhaps the greatest baseball game played in the last 50 years, when Carbo, loose and easy, had uncoiled to tie the game that Fisk would win. It is 8–7, one out, and school will never start, rain will never come, sun will warm the back of your neck forever. Now Bailey, picked up from the National League recently, big arms, heavy gut, experienced, new to the league and the club; he fouls off two and then, checking, tentative, a big man off balance, he pops a soft liner to the first baseman. It is suddenly darker and later, and the announcer doing the game coast to coast, a New Yorker who works for a New York television station, sounds relieved. His little world, well-lit, hot-combed, split-second-timed, had no capacity to absorb this much gritty, grainy, contrary reality.

Cox swings a bat, stretches his long arms, bends his back, the rookie from Pawtucket, who broke in two weeks earlier with a record six straight hits, the kid drafted ahead of Fred Lynn, rangy, smooth, cool. The count runs two and two, Briles is cagey, nothing too good, and Cox swings, the ball beginning toward the mound and then, in a jaunty, wayward dance, skipping past Briles, feinting to the right, skimming the last of the grass, finding the dirt, moving now like some small, purposeful marine creature negotiating the green deep, easily avoiding the jagged rock of second base, traveling steady and straight now out into the dark, silent recesses of center field.

The aisles are jammed, the place is on its feet, the wrappers, the programs, the Coke cups and peanut shells, the detritus of an afternoon; the anxieties, the things that have to be done tomorrow, the regrets about yesterday, the accumulation of a summer: all forgotten, while hope, the anchor, bites and takes hold where a moment before it seemed we would be swept out with the tide. Rice is up, Rice whom Aaron had said was the only one he'd seen with the ability to break his records, Rice the best clutch hitter on the club, with the best slugging percentage in the league, Rice, so quick and strong he once checked his swing halfway through and snapped the bat in two, Rice the Hammer of God sent to scourge the Yankees, the sound was overwhelming, fathers pounded their sons on the back, cars pulled off the road, households froze, New England exulted in its blessedness, and roared its thanks for all good things, for Rice and for a summer stretching halfway through October. Briles threw, Rice swung, and it was over. One pitch, a fly to center, and it stopped. Summer died in New England and like rain sliding off a roof, the crowd slipped out of Fenway, quickly, with only a steady murmur of concern for the drive ahead remaining of the roar. Mutability had turned the seasons and translated hope to memory once again. And once again, she had used baseball, our best invention to stay change, to bring change on. That is why it breaks my heart, that game—not because in New York they could win because Boston lost; in that, there is a rough justice, and a reminder to the Yankees of how slight and fragile are the circumstances that exalt one group of human beings over another. It breaks my heart because it was meant to, because it was meant to foster in me again the illusion that there was something abiding, some pattern and some impulse that could come together to make a reality that would resist the corrosion; and because after it had fostered again that most hungered-for illusion, the game was meant to stop, and betray precisely what it promised.

Of course, there are those who learn after the first few times. They grow out of sports. And there are others who were born with the wisdom to know that nothing lasts. These are the truly tough among us, the ones who can live without illusion, or without even the hope of illusion. I am not that grown-up or up-to-date. I am a simpler creature, tied to more primitive patterns and cycles. I need to think something lasts forever, and it might as well be that state of being that is a game; it might as well be that, in a green field, in the sun.

(1977)

## CHARLES BARASCH

### World Series

Why, when Carlton Fisk
hit the home run,
did the man in section 22,
down the third base line,
raise his hands for joy,
forgetting his fat wife
at home with the teenage daughter,
and driving home
why did he remember his wedding night,
and even the first night
parked by the river,
which is why he married her
in the first place?

# 11

# At the Ballpark

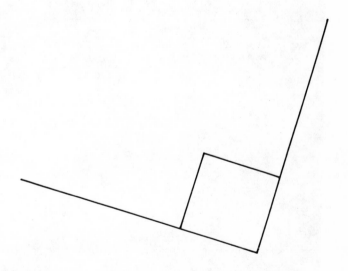

## Leo 1675

### *from Two Penny Lane,* a Novel

Von Joshua led off for the Giants hitting .326 on a cool cloudy Saturday afternoon out at Shea.

Asa and I were sitting in the third deck along with a whole slew of kids and a good sprinkling of cigar smoking beer drinking World War One & Two vets and other assorted pensioners and creature people applauding as Joshua flied out to Unser.

After the catch he threw it in to Phillips at short and after the ball was tossed around, then it went back to Seaver as Derrel Thomas stepped in, bounced a hard shot to Phillips who went to Torre at first (6–3), and after they again threw the ball around it went to Seaver as Willie Montanez dug in hitting .295. The first pitch was a ball, the second a strike, the third a strike and so was the fourth and me and Asa and the fans cheered as the Mets ran in.

They're lovely, Asa smiled. In their sparkling white uniforms.

I nodded, marking down the totals on my scorecard. K for Montanez, as I said white at home, gray on the road. An American Airlines jet made an arc not all that high over left field, like a lazy mechanical fly, and headed east to—Suez, its roaring breezy racket trailing after. Del Unser got the bat he wanted and walked out to the plate. Dave Rader threw the last of Montefusco's warmup pitches to second base and the Giant infield peppered it around, tossed it to their pitcher and the bottom of the first inning began as Unser, hitting .288, hit a drive toward the left field corner.

Which I thought Gary Matthews in a flicker the way he leaned forward ward, and then saw it, made a little misjudge, but then he began to run back as Unser was around first and digging hard to second, Matthews, with his back to the infield yet watching the ball over his shoulder and his left (glove) hand outstretched, in two deer-like leaps, and in the middle of the last leap, glove extended, his right arm outstretched laterally but on a downward angle and his whole body diving up and out to the extreme of its reach as he snagged it, round, small, white, against the sienna and black of his glove as his body came down hard in a forward pitch, lunging forward, right hand out to cushion the impact when he slammed against the wall as Unser rounded second, and slowed while Matthews managed to brake without hitting the wall and Unser jogged across the infield into the dugout. Matthews threw the ball in to Chris Speier, say it like spire, who even without throwing pebbles still reminds me of Marty Marion, more than anyone, in fact, and I made the mark on my scorecard (7), and there was one out. The Met fans showed their curious courtesy—it was the first inning—and cheered the catch, as Millan, say it me-yahn, with his respectable .294 second baseman's average, slashed a drive down the right field line which Montanez intercepted with a fine backhanded catch, and in a little trot stepped on first. I marked down 3, there were two down, Millan ran back into the dugout and I thought that the first two hits had been pretty hard, but Kranepool came in to strike out and straighten out my thinking. The fans made unhappy noises because Kranepool is a favorite, as he should be. He's hit in the desperate clutches only the Mets create, those weird late-in-the-game trickster situations that call for the level force of Kranepool, and on the hit which extricates his team, the Met fans spin off into Met-extasy, and prove somebody's point whoever it is, for every warp there's a whap, and besides Kranepool is the only original Met left, what's that, Joel? Thirteen years?

I did the totals and Asa remarked it was looking more like rain than ever. I raised my eyes and saw that the sky was in too many different levels, and said no, it won't rain (it didn't), and she said how do you know and I said I used to play outfield I know what rainclouds look like.

But, she said, pushing a finger into my left shoulder: that was over twenty-five years ago!

Don't bug me, I said.

Aw, she pouted, gee Lucky.

Some things you don't forget, I explained, and besides I did a lot of farm work, in my day.

What a bore.

I don't talk much at ballgames, I said.

We should come more often, she said, and Gary Matthews stepped in. Seaver rubbed the ball around and looked at Matthews, and then, in about fourteen pitches struck out the side: Matthews .283, Speier .280, and Thomasson .219, as it might be remembered that the high batting averages of yesteryear that glamorized the game have vaporized in the modern baseball that's all pitching. On my scorecard, in the vertical column of the top half of the second inning it was all Ks and I wrote at the bottom, in the little box divided by a diagonal line, an ideogram not unlike the sign which stands for percent, as Asa yawned, lit a filter, scratched the back of my neck and slumped back in the seat humming he's a reeeeeel nowhere man and I laughed looking out over the field. No hits, no runs, and maybe Seaver's gotta no-hitter (wrong. Wuzza 5-hitter).

The big curly red-headed batter Montreal had loved stood outside the batter's box watching the Giant infield snap the ball around, and then he stepped in with, as is his style, his pants high on the leg and his hard plastic batter's cap clamped down over his curls with the bill so low he has to tip back his head to see, or at least it looks like that, and for some reason I think of Christopher Robin, and an old fashioned biglittleboy image of a major leaguer like the tiger in the coloring book and the tiger in the zoo, on Leo 1675 when Rusty Staub stepped in. Very cool. Casual a man as you could see, except when he makes those running catches and doesn't dive for it like Mays and the others, but in the flash before he gets it, he sits down and with his feet out makes the catch in his lap while he slides along the grass as the kids go wild.

What's he like? Asa asked, I've heard of him.

While the fans cheered Staub leading off the Met second, I said, remembering the Pete Rose incident, that Staub was a fine ballplayer, and evidently responsible, and I yet see him out there in left with Berra, facing the furious crowd, making the gesture of no more throwing things at Rose. Pete Rose is as popular at Shea as Ted Williams was at Fenway in the Forties.

Staub is, I said, a bachelor, popular with the ladies, and a great cook. They called him *Le Gran D'orange* in Montreal.

The delight of the fans, whose bounding hopper Speier turned into an easy out 6–3, as in telling Asa about him, Staub, I suddenly remembered a fifteen year old girl I once knew who would have called him cute: he the cleanup hitter, the cool red-headed Christopher Robin tiger, he whose first definition German name means powder, dust as on the wings of butterflies, made the righthanded turn at first and loped back into the dugout as casual as if he was out in the hallway and went back to get the cigarettes he forgot.

Staub out, 6–3. Joe Torre walked, Garrett struck out and Jerry Grote slapped a liner to first which Montanez fielded (unassisted, 3), and the Mets were down 0/0 on my scoreboard as a big United jet glided across the first base side of the sky and banked down over left out of sight.

I like the white little ball rolling around, Asa said as I was writing. "Me too," I said. She slipped her arm through mine and we sat back close together looking out beyond the big black cliff of the scoreboard to the parking lot and Queens County beyond, in soft Saturday smog, in New York. Staub means a lot of things.

I smiled to myself all this fuss over that little white ball: *must* be psychic, I thought.

She nodded. Chasing the world, I thought. The Bird.

Yes, I continued to think. I thought eagerly. We looked at each other warmly as Seaver looked in to Grote for the sign. Rader was on first with a single which goes to show what love will do, you miss things, and then Steve Ontiveros (.272) walked, which put men on first and second with nobody down and Seaver's no-hitter gone. Montefusco, the Giant's pitcher (10–6 ERA 3.23), came to bat. Seaver struck him out. The leadoff hitter,

Von Joshua again, who had flied out to Unser in the first, came up and hit a hard shot about two feet to the right of second base, and as the ball was clearly destined for the alley up right center, and Rader was on his way in to and then around second, and Ontiveros was coming into second, Millan, in a headlong, but not utterly headlong, dive with his glove out blocked the ball, and in his forward momentum did a sort of three-quarter somersault in a cloud of dust scrabbling around to get it he got it and flipped over somehow so when the dust cleared and Ontiveros was almost to second, Millan lay on his back in the dirt about fifteen feet to the right of but behind the base with the ball in his hand and his head up, he had a calm and patient expression on his face as he watched Phillips, the Met shortstop, flash to second, and just before Phillips got there, Millan lobbed the ball to the bag. And the ball looped in no hurry as Phillips crossed the bag in a roar as Ontiveros was in the middle of his slide and the force out was made, there were two down and, most importantly, the run didn't score nor were the bases loaded, and as Millan got to his feet and dusted himself off the threat was no longer so great. Asa tapped me on the shoulder, her eyes wide and bright from the remarkable play, she pointed, and there was the beer vendor! So as Thomas stepped in I saw the union man at the keyboard of the linotype machine typing away what the sportswriter had written and the editor had polished up, tomorrow's sub-head under the Met victory calling Millan's play the play of the game, which it was and which they printed, right there in tomorrow's paper, without the sound of the crowd, the cloud of dust, Millan's head-up calm and patient expression, and the sense of the sight of the touch in the vision surrounding that little white ball floating through the air to second base as Phillips snatched it and the force was made. No sense of the collective heightened empathetic impact—never. No sense of the beautiful girls who are at every game—no sense of Asa in her cutoffs, of her gorgeous legs, her sneakers without socks, and the brief crisp white tanktop, those spare garments over her long and elegant figure, tan from the beaches and the sun, no sense of her long glowing coal black hair, combed straight back from her forehead, so her whole face shone—no sense of any *body*, not even of those on the field, whose bodies are what the game consciously is intuitively, as I descended—carefully—the steps to the beer vendor and Derrel Thomas took a strike. I made the happy purchase and returned up to Asa, sat down beside her and as one of the World War One soldiers in the section to our right lit a cigar, watching me over the flame, he smiled, and as Asa took the beer she saw him and smiled and so did I she was so madly lovely. Strike one. We both sipped beer.

Jesus that's good, she said, and with a Hey Lucky and a little nudge— how about some vodka!

Well, I am. Lucky scores again! reaching into my raincoat pocket and took out the small glass jar that had previously, once, contained herring in sour cream, but which this Saturday held (80 proof) vodka, and after I, after I myself sipped it was delicious as she sipped and Thomas smacked a grounder to Millan who flipped to Phillips for the force and the Mets were out of the inning. I marked down, at the bottom, 1/0, also marking in the H (hit) column at the far right, 1 (for Rader), he'd gotten the single, as Asa sipped again and swallowed and cried out as the old vet watched her, as he puffed on his cigar, the jealous old lech, and Asa said holy *shit,* It ain't beer, I said, and she handed the jar to me and I sipped and capped it, returned it to my raincoat pocket and sipping beer I watched the Giants toss the ball around in the pre-third inning warmup.

I looked into the great space before me.

And as baseball is 99% consciousness and concentration the one percent of sensation happens in a step by step process that to those who don't know happens all of a sudden, but to those who know, one thing creates the next thing, and in all that space where fractions count and something happens, guys who have played a lot of ball get to in a certain way know when something's gonna happen before it does, and in the bottom of the third as Phillips stepped in I had that old feeling again, and I smiled.

Phillips took a strike.

My vision crystallized, and on the next pitch my body felt like a tuning fork as Phillips swung and me and Asa rose to our feet as the ball flew on one great straight line over the second baseman's head up the right center alley, and Phillips raced in to first and around on his way to second as the two Giant outfielders Thomasson (right) and Joshua (center), converged to it in a roar and the glory of a cloud of dust Phillips slid hard into second with the throw too late and we had a man on second, nobody out, and Seaver who is a helluva hitting pitcher at bat and everybody from here to Rangoon knowing he was gonna bunt, which he did, and lemmie tell ya Ontiveros at third had to *hustle* on his throw to first to get Seaver, which he did, he got him on a perfect bunt, and there was one out, with.

Phillips was on third.

All the fans sat down, and got that hard-eyed look fans get when they *know* they're gonna get a run. Unser was up and the kids began to pipe.

The Mets are a trickster team and fans are tricksters too, and when Unser slammed the double into left center and Phillips scored it was a trickster hit in a refreshing new definition of the word team-ster—smacked with authority, and after Asa and I had finished clapping and cheering and had sat down again, we had a little more of that (Russian) water followed by a slug of beer as I made the appropriate signs on my scorecard and Felix Millan came to bat, and after a lull and a little hum, he sent a thunderbolt to Montanez at first who caught it and stepped on first for the out, and then Kranepool came up and much to the distress of the fans, flied out to center and Unser got stranded at second. But.

We'd had two hits and we gotta run! It was us ONE, them nix.

As the Giants came to bat.

Top of the fourth.

I looked at Asa who was looking at my scorecard and asking me what the numbers meant, and while I explained, I thought about her, objectively, as well as the other way.

She was lovely in a disturbing way. Her skin was rich, resilient, and tawny. She had long dark hair and very dark emotional eyes above a little button of a nose, round cheeks and her constant and helpless full-lipped pout, which with her lean and graceful figure, and style of (marching) walking (head high), generally sent guys on the streets into fits. She was nineteen.

She had, and it was true, a heart of gold. And following the metaphor in metals, she was as tough, or as defensively hard as iron. The gold was given, but she had become iron the hard way, forged out of a miserable childhood in a rotten city across the gray river.

I had a sort of haggard look, gazing at her: call me Mary Shelley. Call me Dr. Frankenstein. Call me Lucky.

I'm hungry, she said.

So am I, I said, but the lines at the refreshment stand are each a mile long and in each line ten thousand kids drive countermen and women crazy because the kids forget.

You should write an essay, she interrupted.

Maybe I will, I said.

Maybe I mean it, she said.

Maybe I will, I repeated.

I bet you won't.

We'll see, I said, watching Seaver warming up.

She lay her head on my shoulder and slipped her arm through mine, and yawned, saying she thought she was getting drunk. Then she took her arm away, raised her head, sat back, folded her hands in her lap and scowled. I watched her.

She looked at me and her eyebrows went into an upside down v as her eyes got imploring, and she said I really *am* hungry, Lucky, couldn't you get us a couple of hotdogs and some more beer?

Montanez stepped in and Seaver looked for the sign as I said oh well Goddamn and handed her the scorecard and pencil. Told her to write down what happened, and walked down the steps finishing my beer and watching Montanez's hit drift lazily over Phillips' head into left where Kranepool caught it as the crowd applauded and cheered. A big United jet glided up on a rising curve from left field, and headed east. I turned, and flashed a seven sign up to Asa, saw her write it down, and continued on my way.

Down the walkway under the stands to the long lines at the refreshment stand. I tossed the plastic cup in a trashcan and took my place at the rear of what looked like the shortest line, and set myself to be patient. There were about sixteen kids, and in the line to my left I saw another adult, standing just ahead of me. He was wearing a pork pie hat and a plaid sportscoat. He was over forty, around five eight, plump and husky, and sweat ran down the side of his face. He sighed, and sensing me watching him he turned, and our eyes met. We smiled, and we each shook our head at being back in line again and the hopelessness of it all ho hum *fuck*. As a matter of fact he looked like a cop. White. Pockmarked in the hollows of his cheeks. White shirt open at the collar, and actually he looked—he looked like the Continental Op! Was this *The Shea Caper?* May be! as around us kids chirped, laughed, and cried out as they messed around clutching their Met pennants with their blue Met ballcaps askew, and like Rusty Staub, so low on their foreheads they had to raise their heads to see before them, which was kind of amusing, but not to the people behind the counter at the refreshment stand who served them, who were just about to explode from frustrating rituals that'd driven even Jesus to wits end.

Watcha want! barked the counterman.

Little voice, eyes wide, peering up: a hotdog.

The counterman took the dog off the rotating grid, put it in a bun and gave it to the boy who said Two.

The counterman took a deep breath. His eyes bugged out of his head, and his face got red as he prepared by rote the other hotdog thinking ahead—the kids were too small to reach up to the mustard and ketchup dispensers, so the counterman took a good grip on reality and went through his sequence which began with which did they want mustard or ketchup, thus oh gee whiz, gosh, golly, decisions, decisions, a grimy index finger between parted lips ummmm mustard mustard ketchup ketchup ketchup mustard with questions written in his eyes while the gang behind him carried on and the adults in the line ground their teeth and stared at the floor, remembering.

Ketchup! cried the boy.

The counterman, cursing architects that designed refreshment stand counters so high, slopped ketchup on the two hotdogs and handed them back to the boy, each dog in shallow paper containers with a napkin for each, and after the boy paid the counterman he, the counterman, with an incredible, yet sort of doomed expression, like a bee in a blizzard, and his face criss-crossed with broken capillaries, glanced at the next kid, who was in a batch—who was a batch—began to relate, while yet the first little boy looked up, and with the two hotdogs in his hand, he remembered Mommy had said ice cream.

I laughed, and saw the agency detective grinning.

The counterman turned the color of raspberry sherbert, leaned partly over the counter and asked what kind d'ya want, in a tone of Huckleberry Hound gone mad, and the boy bit his lip and looked up at that big face and didn't say anything as his little face under that big major league Rusty Staub ballcap went pink and then red and then pale white as he gathered courage, and then, in an awfully small voice asked what kind did the counterman have?

Vanilla/chocolate vanilla/strawberry growled the counterman in an evil voice, and the boy lowered his head and sighed, looked at the hot-dogs in his hands and thought, hard, in fact, the bill of his ballcap all but obscuring his face, and he thought and thought, and thought and thought and thought and then looked up to the counterman who was turning a darker color, heading toward plum, and the boy parted his lips, and with his eyes wide and honest injun, said, but almost in a whisper,

I don't know!

The counterman's face was heading toward a funny green and I thought he was going to flip, VANILLACHOKLIT cried the boy, which he got, along with a plastic spoon. The counterman took the boy's money, made change and gave it to the boy and the boy left and that's the way it went until it finally came my turn. I made my order which I quickly re-ceived, and as he rang up the sale I put mustard on the four hotdogs, and put them in along with two cold beers in the box, and when the counter-man gave me my change I took the singles and gave him the silver as a tip, for which he thanked me, and as our eyes met we both smiled.

You gotta be patient, I said.

It's a lousy job, he said, and I agreed. It was, as he sipped from a paper cup, something kin but amber to my little water in my herring & sour cream jar, tossing me a wink over the rim, and we grinned. I moved out of the shrill swirl of waiting kids, and headed toward the ramp and as I emerged into the vista of the stadium Staub stepped into the batter's box. I finally made my way up the steps to Asa, and as I sat down I saw the distant figure of the agency detective settle himself in his seat on the far end of the next section, and take a bite from his hotdog and a long pull of beer. He was alone.

"Hot dog!" Asa laughed. She took 'em and bit one hungrily, and chewed and drank beer thirstily. As she told me what had happened I made the marks on my scorecard.

Matthews had grounded out third to first, Garrett had made a fine play, Speier had walked and somehow, which neither of us could figure out, there had been two out when Thomasson flied out to left to end the in-ning. So the bottom of the fourth and the Mets were up. I ate a hotdog and drank beer. Asa put her arm around my neck, kissed my cheek, told me this was wonderful, more fun than she'd ever dreamed. She'd never been to a major league game. I took her hand in mine and kissed her fingers, looked in her eyes and said a word or two. She agreed, and we breathed hotdogs, mustard, beer, vodka and cigarette tar on each other as we laughed, and Staub took a strike and, as is his habit, looked back to the umpire. Strike confirmed. Staub resumed his forward bending stance, bat straight up. Asa finished her second dog, sipped beer, sat back, lit up a cigarette and watched him with a neat little smile.

It was I guess because of the cool cloudiness that the big crowd stayed away, but I was glad because we could stretch our feet across the seats before us, as the two rows of seats were empty. Thought of Penny Lane. I hummed some. Staub hit a liner foul down the first baseline and one of the vets to our right yelled Hit one like that *fair,* and when, on the next pitch which Staub hit down the *third* baseline foul, the vet yelled the same thing, and on the next pitch, which was a ball, which the red-headed power as on the wings of butterflies took, he, on the next pitch, fouled it onto the screen behind home and the old guy on our right shouted The other way! pointing to centerfield, and half out of his seat, cigarbutt between fingers around a beer.

Staub hit the next pitch into center for a single.

I bet that vet felt like Babe Ruth.

Staub stood on first base casually taking off his batting glove like he was waiting for a streetcar in a small town in Ohio, and then took his lead. But Torre struck out. Garrett walked and Staub jogged down to second as Grote came up, dug in, and in an effort to hit into right field behind the runners, unusually good Met thinking, he sent a smart hopper to Thomas at second who tossed to Speier crossing second who on the pivot threw a straight line to Montanez at first for the double play and the Mets were down. One hit no runs, and I filled everything in on my scorecard. So far, going into the top of the fifth, Seaver had pitched a one hit shutout, walking only one and striking out five.

I have a hunch this is going to be Seaver's all the way, I said to Asa, also thinking it might be his best year yet. She said she wished she knew more about it, although she admitted she had played softball and was, in fact, a good player, but still, she further admitted, she wished she had kept up with *base*ball and I said I wished I had too. A Pan Am 747 drifted over the ballpark, heading east to exotic places with a trailing rushing roaring wind behind, and Dave Rader, who had gotten the only hit off Seaver so far, came to bat as the Mets finished throwing the ball around. Garrett threw it to Seaver and Seaver rubbed it around and watched Rader dig in, and I think it was on a two and one count that Rader hit a hard grass-cutter to Phillips who grabbed it, and in a motion like conductors make to the trumpets in the approach to the end of the fourth movement, Phillips laced it to first for the out. 6–3, one down and a ripple of applause swept over the crowd. The infield fired the ball around and again Garrett tossed it to Seaver who rubbed it hard and looked in to Grote for the sign, as Ontiveros, the Giant third baseman, waited for the pitch which he subsequently drilled into left for a single BUT then bingo suddenly another terrific play.

The Giant pitcher, Montefusco, hit a high hopper to the mound which Seaver went up for and got, turned and threw to Phillips as Phillips swept across second base and in a slashing motion threw to Millan at first for the doubleplay bam, like that, except it had been slightly different, because Met second baseman Millan covered first because Met first baseman Torre had gone in toward home on the chance of a bunt, and it was really nifty to see 'em move so professionally and that Millan was so absolutely there for Phillips' throw. Millan made a gesture of excellence to Phillips who acknowledged it with a nod and they ran off the field together. I wondered if Millan was getting Phillips ready to take control of the infield, as Harrelson (out on injuries), seemed to have lost, and that cannot be.

One hit, no runs: 1/0. Seaver had again figured in the vital sense.

It was the bottom of the fifth, and, in the mystery of order, as in the secret surprise in the unfolding of normal expectations, suddenly, marvelously, Phillips was up.

You could almost see it—we all felt it. A certain restless happy apprehension, a certain sparkle, something almost invisible, but not quite, like a shimmer in the air, a subtle tingle in the sensibilities which felt great, and I leaned forward intently. Asa was absorbed in it too, and was reading my scorecard, murmuring to herself. I said,

How about a little water?

She laughed and nodded, eagerly, so we had a nip and a chaser of beer, good, I lit up a smoke and waited for what I was certain would happen, yet not knowing how it would, and I rubbed my hands. She made a merry little laugh as Phillips took a strike.

The clouds had seemed to lift a bit, and I was certain it wasn't going to rain. Another one of those inbetween days. The crowd, not being able to stand the suspense, began to clap and a scattering of kids across the park began to chant Let's go Mets, in their piping voices, and Phillips took a ball, and in my own pleased apprehension I put my beer, scorecard and pencil on the empty seat before me.

Why are you doing that? Asa asked.

Just in case, I grinned, and the fans clapped louder and in more volume as he took ball two, but it died down and the ballpark got quiet when he took a strike, and in the tingling and silent suspense in the crowd the place was so quiet you could hear a glove drop, but on the next pitch—on a two and two count—on what looked like an outside fast ball Phillips met it perfectly: a fraction too late and right on the button sending a long *hard* hummer over the second baseman's head into and up the alley in right center and as he dug around first the ballpark was on its feet, me and Asa too, as Joshua and Thomasson converged on it, Joshua getting the jump, but the hand of Fate gave the Giants a raw deal, for as Joshua, the Giant center fielder, got there and was correctly prepared to hold Phillips to a long single, the ball hit a pebble in the grass, or a tiny ridge made from someone's spikes, and took a bad hop and went behind Joshua, and Phillips raced toward second. Thomasson overran the ball, and Joshua ran hard toward the wall, chasing the bounding ball, which he got as Phillips rounded second, and went toward third with everything he had as Joshua made the long throw to second which Thomas took, pivoted, and threw a strike to Ontiveros at third *just about* when Phillips slid in—but not quite, because Phillips came in under the glove and before the tag and when Ontiveros made the tag the umpire, in the drama some of them love, quickly stooped and threw his arms out wide: hands down and Phillips was in safe with a triple—a buckeye triple, but still a triple—and the cheers and the applause rocked the stadium.

*We* had a guy on third. Nobody out.

Seaver came to bat and everybody remained standing as on the end of the diving board happily, while Seaver took a couple of pitches and we all gradually sat back down again, and on what looked like a low curve strike that hung a little on the outside corner Seaver swung down, and hit the ball hard, on the nose, sending it bouncing between first and second into right field for a single and Phillips scored and everybody in tumult, the ballpark on its feet again all of us crazy and hollering and all and me and Asa with our arms around each other, oh those sluggin' pitchers! the score was two to *nuthin'!* as the batboy ran out and Seaver put on the blue jacket, and stood on first base as people clapped and cheered and the batboy ran back into the dugout.

Seaver took a couple of steps off the bag as the Giant pitcher went into his motion, and Unser, at bat, waited.

But he flied to center. Joshua got it handsomely and threw it in to Speier. One down.

We were in our seats again and I said: Phillips has two hits, a double and a chancey triple, he's scored twice and both those runs are because of Seaver. Not bad!

She nodded, and I warmed at the sight of her profile, and her intense gaze on Millan as he crossed himself as he walked to the plate. Then he stepped in and took his stance. Choking the bat, like he does, way up, the Braves were fools to let him go, but they did and there he was, and he whacked a liner about two inches off the ground on the chalk line—all the way down into the right field corner, and went in to and tore around first, lost his cap, and then went into second at the last moment slowing for a stand up double as the ballpark tilted in a solid cheer and Seaver ran and ran and ran and ran as we cheered and cheered and he slid safely into third—well WELL!

Thus Kranepool walked and Staub came up with the bases loaded. The kids were piping, shrilling, shouting and yelling and cheering and carrying on somethin' terrific. Staub took a couple & then—he hit the ball into left center, just a shade toward center, but in left field, and not very deep as Seaver tagged up and the tension was wonderful! The ball wasn't in any hurry, it hung around in the air, but after a while it dropped into Joshua's waiting glove and Seaver took off as fast as he could toward home, and as he came in positioning his body for the slide, Torre, the next batter, held his hands up like Hands Up! and Seaver stayed on his feet and crossed home plate on a run, the throw was cut off, there were two out and the runners held. Score, three zip.

Seaver ducked down into the dugout and his teammates surrounded him as Torre stepped in.

Oh, Asa said, Seaver's *beautiful.*

Want a beer? I asked, there's the beer man—

She shook her head and I walked down and got one, came back, sat down drinking, Torre took strike two, and as I marked everything down on my scorecard, he struck out, so at the bottom of the fifth it was total five hits and three runs for us and two hits and *nuthin'* for them.

Seaver lasted the sixth and the seventh and big jets flew east to Kiplingland, but in the top of the eighth after Rader flied out, Ontiveros walked, and Adams, pinch hitting for Giant pitcher Montefusco, singled and McMillan came out and we saw Seaver nod, and as he walked off the field he got a standing ovation, as pitcher Jerry Koosman came in. Berra wouldna done that.

But it was a good move, as Seaver was exhausted. On one of the last pitches he threw, we saw him pushing, trying too hard—the hitting and all that running he'd done did it.

Asa laughed seeing that bizarre auto in the form of a baseball with a Met's cap on top putter in, Koosman got out, went to the mound and began his few warmups, and I wondered. I'd seen enough of Koosman to know how good he is, but—well, in the (this) clutch, I wasn't sure.

But he got 'em. On a force at second and a snappy 6–4–3 Phillips to Millan to Torre doubleplay to end the inning. And after Speier pulled off a dazzling doubleplay of his own, which wiped out the Mets in their eighth, the Giants came to bat in the top of the ninth. Montanez singled, Koosman took a hard *mean* grounder from Matthews, whirled, and because Phillips, on the righthanded hitter, was playing for the ball to come on that side, Millan covered second and was the pivot man for a terrific doubleplay.

Two down, and all the crowd—everybody—kids, vets, vendors, cops, poets and other types including me and Asa—watched Koosman strike out Speier to end the game, as in a universal cheer *hooray*.

We sat down, and leaned back, and then, as everybody rose and began to leave the ballpark, I notated the K, made the totals, lit up a smoke and then lit Asa's smoke, and we shared the last of the beer and watched the cops line up along the first and third baselines, as the field attendants rolled out the big tarp cylinder, and began covering the infield, and, like memories of me, pieces of stray paper blew across the deserted outfield. Days gone by.

Then we stood up too, stretched, and walked down the steps to begin the long journey home. That long walk to the subway, and the long subway ride, the transfer, and then—at Grand Central we decided to take a cab, which we did, and Asa, who said she wanted to go home and clean up her place, it was a mess, she said, & we crossed the city. She got out on the corner of the street where she lived—not, however, before I'd gotten a warm hug and a kiss that is yet on my lips. Just as her words are still in my ear: *Thanks Lucky, it's been wonderful.*

I watched her elegant figure walk briskly away as the machine I was in moved off on a tangent, and so I went my way too, suddenly deciding right then and there that the next day's papers would, in their usual dry style, report the same dull shit about Seaver's beautiful 17th win. More news in the same old language written by the same old hack reporters who work for the same old editors who work under the fist of the same old publishers, so! as I had my scorecard, and all the people, the ballpark, and the whole feel of the whole game in my mind, why not write it the way it really *ought* to be written? Something I'd wanted to do anyway, just about all my life. I'd suffered that dull old daily baseball reportage frustration in daily newspapers since I was a boy, and even then, when I was fifteen & I'd gotten my first typewriter, a black Royal portable, second-hand, I'd wanted to write about DiMaggio, & Musial, & Mize, Jack Robinson and Ned Garver and Williams in *my* way—

Thus this story.

I didn't go to the ballgame with Asa. I went by myself. But that's what the reporters called reality, which I, being real, will know in another, different story which one day I'll write—but anyway I don't much bother with what they call real. Being forty-five years old, alone at a major-league ballgame with my memories. That's real, okay. But I do something else—I do what I do, and what I do is what I call my art, my mythology, my self.

And there, as Kipling wrote, in the last sentence of a story called *The Man Who Would Be King*, the matter rests.

## GEORGE KIMBALL

## Opening Day at Fenway

Years ago—only a few years ago, actually, but still years before the miracle year of 1967 and years before it became chic to root for the Red Sox—the centerfield bleachers at Fenway were traditionally the habitat of the most diehard of Sox afficianados. If the bleacherites weren't the most knowledgeable fans, they were close to it, and they were certainly the most faithful. I suspect I was exposed to more genuine baseball lore, more understandings of the subtleties and strategems of the game, and perhaps most importantly, more sheer love for the sport by sitting exclusively in the bleachers from boyhood through my early twenties than I've encountered in any reserved seat press box since.

This, of course, was back in the days when the Red Sox were drawing so poorly that they had to schedule night games around the Hatch Shell concerts in the summer and when a gate of 20,000 on Opening Day was considered spectacular. But from April through September the coterie in center field retained a fidelity unmatched anywhere else in the American League. And while the businessmen who bought season tickets might sit next to someone in an adjacent box all season long and never exchange six words, there were people out there who'd been friends for twenty-five years yet never seen each other outside Fenway Park.

There were the beaten old men who looked like they'd just panhandled the 50 cent admission price, the retired gentlemen with their transistor radios and the truck drivers who took their shirts off on hot summer days. There were two old ladies from Dorchester, both named Mary, who attended the afternoon games as faithfully as they attended Mass. They left home early in the morning, bringing their Official Big League Scorebook along to Church, and after lunch in Kenmore Square, showed up at the park before batting practice started. They never went to night games, but the Boys from Chelsea did.

The Boys from Chelsea—three of them, Felix, Vinny, and Joe, all cab drivers, I believe, invariably turned up at night, and two or three of their friends often made it—were inveterate gamblers. They came to games weighted down with 50 cent rolls of pennies, and would wager with each other and anyone else on every conceivable facet of the game, from whether the next batter would get a hit (3 to 1 for Mantle or Williams; 6 to 1 for most pitchers) to an error on the next play (usually about 25 to 1, but you could always haggle) to the possibility of Casey Stengel being ejected during the course of the game. (If you got a bet down at the prevailing 7½ to 1 odds on Jackie Jensen hitting into a double play at every available opportunity, you usually made out over the course of a season.)

And there was Fat Howie. Fat Howie was on speaking terms with every centerfielder in the league. He'd sit right next to the rope (the section in straightaway center, directly in the batter's line of vision, *always* used to be roped off; since the space is needed now, the seats are painted green and customers are allowed to sit there, provided they wear dark clothing) and carry on a running dialogue. Howie would lean over the wall between innings and yell out to Bob Allison: *"Hey, Bob, what's happening in Cleveland?"* (The scoreboard on the left field wall can't be seen from the bleachers in center.) And Allison would check the score and holler back: *"4 to 2 Indians, Howie."* Howie was always there, day or night. I don't know what he did for a living; maybe he took his summers off.

And, of course, there was the gang I hung out with in college. We'd usually catch about 20 or 30 games a year, always going in a group of four or five and always with a case of beer. Back then there was no hassle about bringing your own beer into the bleachers; everyone did it, and probably would still be able to except for one particularly raucous occasion in the spring of 1964 when the bleachers were invaded by a few hundred Friday night beer drinkers posing as baseball fans.

Along about the sixth inning they were very drunk and very angry. The Red Sox were being humiliated by the lowly Kansas City Athletics (commonly referred to at the time as the "Kansas City Faggots," since they wore bright gold suits with green trim, long before mod uniforms became fashionable), and someone heaved an empty beer can in the direction of Jose Tartabull, the A's centerfielder. An umpire ran out to retrieve it, and was greeted by a fusillade of beer cans. This brought the park police out on the field, and the shelling exploded for real. One cop was cold-cocked by a beer can—a full one—and the barrage continued for about ten minutes, abating not because the park announcer warned that the umpires were threatening to forfeit the game, but only because the assholes ran out of ammunition. After that they started checking you out for beer when you came through the gate, and—at 55 cents a cup—the price of drinking went up considerably in center field.

Besides me, there were 34,516 other paying customers there last week. I hadn't been to an opener at Fenway for seven years, though I caught a couple at Shea Stadium and K.C. Municipal. I looked around for Howie and the two Mary's, but I didn't see them. I suspect they'd be pretty uncomfortable out there these days anyway; the bleachers last Tuesday were packed with a crowd that would've been indistinguishable from the occupants of the cheap seats at the Fillmore East: freaks sporting Mao buttons, long-haired college kids, high school hippies, and even teeny-boppers, with bells, beads, and blemishes.

Initially, anyway, that was relieving. For several years now I've found myself trembling whenever the National Anthem is played at sporting events, not out of patriotic sentiment but of fear that some flag-crazed lunatic sitting in back of me will be overcome by his emotions and seize the opportunity to bludgeon me from behind with his souvenir Louisville Slugger. Since the first ball on Opening Day was thrown out by a Vietnam veteran, a former POW, the new crowd did thus provide at least a reassuring measure of collective security during the pre-game ceremonies, helping to compensate for the nostalgic loss of old ambience.

On the very first play of the game, Yastrzemski made an incredible diving, sliding catch by the left field line off Horace Clarke's bat, rolled over and held the glove aloft. Now in the old days Jimmy Doyle from East Boston would've been yelling *"Atta boy, Carl Baby"* in his booming fog-horn voice, a voice so loud that even in the middle of 35,000 fans Yaz would've heard him. But the ovation from the bleachers was only polite applause by comparison. *"That was a pretty nice catch,"* commented one of the kids behind me.

Ray Culp retired the Yankees 1-2-3 in the first, but despite two hits the Sox' half of the first was scarcely more auspicious. Luis Aparicio led off with a smash over third base, which Jerry Kenney backhanded with a superb stab observed by everyone in Fenway Park except Aparicio and first base coach Don Lenhardt, who waved Luis around toward second— directly into a rundown. Reggie Smith followed with another single but, after Yaz flied out, Reggie, the team's top base thief, was thrown out trying to steal second.

The Yankees went down in order in each of the next two innings. As the Sox trotted off the field after the third, one of the kids behind me turned to his companion and breathlessly uttered: *"He's pitching a no-hitter!"*

Now, according to every sacred tradition of the game's etiquette, this is something which is *never* mentioned aloud—particularly after only three innings have been played. I was on the verge of turning around and instructing him on the point when his friend smugly added: "He's pitching a *perfect game.*"

Fat Howie would have thrown them both over the wall.

I sat seething as the Red Sox went down 1-2-3 again, and then decided that it was time to make a beer run. "My turn," I said, and after entrusting my scorecard to the guy sitting next to me, began making my way down the aisle. I paused at the top of the runway just in time to see Thurman Munson chop a slow-roller to the third-base side of the mound.

A pitcher fleeter afoot would have handled it with ease; Sox pitching coach Harvey Haddix, about 50 now, could *still* have eaten it alive. Culp himself could probably have made the play three times out of four, but as he lumbered off the mound he not only overran the ball but momentarily blocked out Petrocelli racing in from third. Rico barehanded the ball and whipped it to first in one motion, but too late to catch Munson. An infield single; the Yankees had their first hit, and I knew exactly where the blame lay. *"Smart-ass punks!"* I shook my fist at them as I descended the stairs.

I returned with the beer to find Reggie Smith on second with a double and Yastrzemski coming to bat. Taking my scorecard back, I matter-of-factly threw out *"Here comes the first run of the season!"*, which would've immediately been covered at 7 to 2 by Felix or Vinny. There was no response to the challenge here, though, and naturally Yaz responded with a run-scoring double.

Between innings the guy who'd been keeping my scorecard wanted to know what the funny little illegibly-scrawled notes in the margin were all about. I briefly considered a number of spectacular fabrications, but finally admitted that I wrote for the *Phoenix* and planned to do a story of some sort about Opening Day.

"Oh *yeah?*" He eyed me strangely. "If you're a sportswriter why the fuck are you sittin' *here*," he gestured toward the press box. "Instead of up there?" The fact of the matter was that the Red Sox had declined to provide the paper with press tickets, but for some reason I mumbled that I liked it better in the bleachers. At one time that would've been true; today it made me twice a liar.

The middle innings were largely uneventful, except for Duane Josephson knocking Kenney squarely on his ass while breaking up a double play, and the fact that somebody nearby produced a hash pipe. Since the hash was still being circulated when the time came, the people next to me remained sitting through the seventh inning stretch, yet another tradition shot to hell. We did come up with another run in the seventh anyway. Following two singles, a sacrifice, and an intentional walk to pinchhitter Joe Lahoud, Culp hit a sure double-play ball to short, but John Kennedy, running for Lahoud, bowled over Clarke at second, knocking the ball away and allowing the run to score.

New York led off the eighth with their second and third hits. After an error and two putouts, the bases were loaded, two out, when Clarke stroked a base hit to right apparently certain to score two runs, but Josephson perfectly blocked the plate long enough to get Smith's throw to home and somehow the tying run was out at the plate. *"Perfect throw,"* approved one of the morons behind me. It was *not* a perfect throw; it bounced three times and Scott almost cut it off and the runner had it beaten by at least ten feet had Josephson not had his body in the way.

The Sox scored their third run the way they are supposed to be scored: Yaz singled, went to third on a single by Rico, and came home on Scott's sacrifice fly. Unspectacular, but it is the sort of thing that games are won by. Just as I'd called Josephson a "mediocre catcher" in print that morning—he came through with three hits and that key play at the plate that afternoon—I also picked the Sox to finish second behind Baltimore. One game does not a season make, but I'm looking forward to having reason to revise both assessments. I'm also looking for a new place to sit.

April 1971

**TOM CLARK**

## What Happened

## During Outfield Practice

Jay Johnstone
walked under the bleachers
with a blocky woman
hugging and talking
(was it his mother?
we may never know!)

Billy C.
did some shoulder stands

Deep knee bends
were performed
by Bill North
as the sky grew dark

The lights went on

## September in the Bleachers

In the bathroom the bad dudes
are putting money on Ali & Kenny Norton
up & down the row of stalls
little coveys of guys with tiny radios
calling out the blow by blow:
Round two to Muhammad! Whoo!

I listen to all this while I'm pissing
& the national anthem's playing outside
then make it back up thru the hot dog line
to catch the first inning, grinning,
my heart tells me Vida will shut out Kansas City tonight

He goes right ahead & does it before my eyes

## Great Catch

With one away
in the seventh
and Terry Crowley on base
Pina threw
a side arm curve
to Earl Williams
who golfed it
high 'n deep
to left

Joe Rudi
pedaled back
to the warning path
sidewise, watching
the towering drive
as it peaked
and began to fall

with one hand propped
against the wall he
crouched, and leaped
and hung
            motionless
in a bath of light
his glove
a foot above the top
                speared it!

—and then he fell back down
into the sound


STEPHEN CORMANY


## Culture vs. Nature


Every so often in Yankee Stadium
Mantle or Murcer had to contend with the monuments.
A long drive would get sandwiched between
The Sultan of Swat
The Iron Horse and
The Yankee Clipper.
Mickey, if he had been given to such gab
May have called the protuberances
The Stonehenge Pinball Machine.
On the other hand,
Take the case of Cleveland's Municipal Stadium:
No monuments there
Nay, in fact before 1946
No fence.
In a game against Philadelphia
In the early thirties
Rangy Earl Averill
Chasing a towering drive off the bat of
Al Simmons
Was bowled over by a polar bear.

## The Boudreau Shift

On one side
It was like a church school picnic
All the ringers had attended
On the other . . .
The hot corner of Pluto

## Gumbo

In August or June of '65 or '3
Off Paul Foytack of Los Angeles
In a game already hopelessly won
Paradise was given a cursory
Revisitation.
Held, Francona, and Ramos
Who normally could not whistle a tune on a Jew's harp
Cashed their angels in altogether
And popped three rockets off a sinking ship.
Next Brown,
                plainest of shortstops
                bat lighter than a candlewick
Timed a hung curve just so:
                hitting the salami
                missing the Swiss cheese—
Off it went:
                a wind blown
                   bone loan
                   heaven sent
                   Oriental style
                   Chimpanze kite

After the fourth firecracker had popped
The Fan-O-Gram unearthed this news:

            "So happens they have tied a
            record for coincidence."

Kirkland stepped up.
Hadn't had a hit in two weeks
Grave already dug
Was hunting with his penknife for his
.200
Fan told him he could piss it farther than
He could.
Foytack, mopping the L.A. sewer system
Hardly even bothered with a windup.
Kind of a fast
                    heave-ho
                                catch-as-catch-can
                                            slider.

Kirkland saw Gumbo
Rifled it for a single.

## "Will You Sign
## My Brand-New Baseball,
## Louie?"

the best thing in my head
of baseball and Kansas City
is the Royals playing the
Red Sox and the drunk trying
to get Louie Aparicio
to sign his brand-new baseball:
every time Louie comes loping in
from shortstop at the end
of the half inning there he is
the drunk elbowing his way
from high up in the grandstand
down into the box seats and all
those turned-around wrinkled
foreheads and goddammits and
uplifted cups of Hamms and
Dr. Pepper with amazing
timing to catch his man
exactly at the screen except
that Louie every time
fields with his eyes that
white routine ball coming
out of the crowd and drops
his look and speeds up just
a little then disappears
into the dugout safe as the
fans cheer and cheer and
cheer for both of their heroes

## Riverfront

Fine drops of rain
run down like young streams from
plastic summer parkas
down the arms of curved chairs
falling from the hair of
three men in row 38B
in row C
an elegant young face intense
carved mahogany, small rivulets
carelessly sliding from aquiline nose
upon a knee
make random patterns
merge with cement water then
continue through the human sea
past soggy red-hots Hudepohl and
staggering shells from peanuts delved
now forgotten in one
unanimous need for sun.

billows of tarp begin to wave
rolling tossing toward home plate
slowly moving to the low buzz-sung
stanza of hawkers, families, fans
a man wearing a blue hat
is on the mound
reds near the dug-out
swing various wooden bats
rhythmic oars skimming water from air
beating the haze clear
at last
high up near the flying flags
sings an accented bird-like voice
"vaya, Perez, vaya"
far below a small voice echoes
"let's go Bench"
sun drenches the stands.

## Night Game

*Only bores are bored,*—wrote William Saroyan—
And I was a bore, and so I went to the ball game;
But there was a pest who insisted on going with me.
I thought I could shake him if I bought one ticket,
But he must have come in on a pass. I couldn't see him,
But I knew he was there, back of third, in the row behind me,
His knees in my back, and his breath coming over my shoulder,
The loud-mouthed fool, the sickly nervous ego,
Repeating his silly questions, like a child
Or a girl at the first game ever. *Shut up,* I told him,
*For Christ's sweet sake, shut up, and watch the ball game*
He didn't want to, but finally subsided,
And my attention found an outward focus,
Visible, pure, objective, inning by inning,
A well-played game, with no particular features,—
Feldman pitched well, and Ott hit a couple of homers.

And after the ninth, with the crowd in the bleachers thinning,
And the lights in the grandstand dimming out behind us,
And a full moon hung before us, over the clubhouse,
I drifted out with the crowd across the diamond,
Over the infield brown and the smooth green outfield,
So wonderful underfoot, so right, so perfect,
That each of us was a player for a moment,
The men my age, and the soldiers and the sailors,
Their girls, and the running kids, and the plodding old men,
Taking it easy, the same unhurried tempo,
In the mellow light and air, in the mild cool weather,
Moving together, moving out together,
*Oh, this is good,* I felt, to be part of this movement,
This mood, this music, part of the human race,
Alike and different, after the game is over,
Streaming away to the exit, and underground.

# 12

# Layers of Sound

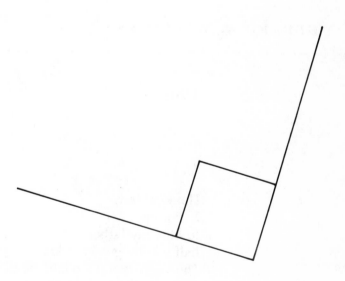

## RICHARD COUTANT

### layers of sound: Fisch Farm

from all sides beyond, songs
of invisible birds;
behind my head, through screen,
the kettle boils.
further within, faintly,
the Red Sox trail, 3–2,
while through moist air, miles away,
a truck shifts down, climbing.


## GERARD A. MULLIGAN

### Home

*I*

Home at last,
I step up
to him, my father,
half a halting way to kiss
(one generation too late, or early—
my son will kiss his father,
as my father his);
we clasp, instead,
our hands.

## II

And in the kitchen,
where my younger father and I
in the tiplight of a Lucky Strike,
heard Williams hit homers in the dark
(to let her sleep),
I know The Kid is gone,
and Piersall,
and Buddin
(whom I, constant bobbler
of vicious grounders
at the long shortstop of my time,
sort of liked),
and I am home.

## III

And later I leave,
on another long road trip,
on, as it happens,
a Saturday afternoon
(Bosox vs Chisox),
listening to the game up the Turnpike,
losing it around New Haven

## 7th Game  :  **1960 Series**

*for Joel*

Nice day,
sweet October afternoon
Men walk the sun-shot avenues,
                                  Second, Third, eyes
                                  intent elsewhere
ears communing with transistors in shirt pockets
                    Bars are full, quiet,
discussion during commercials
                        only
Pirates lead New York 4–1, top of the 6th, 2
Yankees on base, 1 man out

What a nice day for all this—!
Handsome women, even
dreamy jailbait, walk
                        nearly neglected  :
men's eyes are blank
their thoughts are all in Pittsburgh

Last half of the 9th, the score tied 9-all
Mazeroski leads off for the Pirates
the 2nd pitch he simply, sweetly

                    C R A C K !

belts it clean over the left-field wall
Blocks of afternoon
acres of afternoon
Pennsylvania Turnpikes of afternoon        One
              diamond stretches out in the sun
                          the 3rd base line
                          and what men come down
                          it

                    The final score, 10–9

Yanquis, come home

## George Brett/October 14, 1976

ABC thought it was what we wanted to see
the side of the coin
that didn't turn up
as last night that white voyeuristic eye
came to lick sweat

in your Kansas City clubhouse
plunged into the finality
of all that lost sweetness
it hurt

You hurt

You said, There's nothing to say, really,
when you lose, the team loses,
when you win, it's the team that wins

A hopeless Warner Wolf at last
got sensitive
to the numb gloom of the Almost
as his every useless question
outraged the manhood
of a nation

George Brett, the tears
in your eyes

## The End of the Right Season

my brother-in-law is a very good fan but he knows little about magic and nothing at all about naps. which figures, since he is studying to be a doctor, and they don't consider either to be a part of real life.

i discovered this lack in him on monday, may 29, which was, according to the government and the travel agencies, memorial day. the national league having also accepted it as such we had an afternoon game scheduled with st. louis. in addition, the schools had accepted this abomination, too, which meant that nathaniel was home and raising hell all day, so that when philip and judy called and said they were coming over, i figured it meant good company for me while watching the game and good company for helen while not.

philip and i watched, with a somewhat quiet nathaniel, since his uncle was here and that was company and the score went to 6–3 their favor and we all sort of gave up. not really of course, but there was no sense in sitting and hurting, so philip went into the kitchen with helen and judy, and nathaniel decided to paint in his room, and i was free for my midgame nap. i tilted the set a little toward the couch, carefully adjusted the sound so i could hear it but not so it was intrusive, assured nathaniel, who had popped back out of his room, that nothing new had happened, and stretched out on the couch. it worked. improbably shortly after i closed my eyes boswell hit his first homer of the season with two men on and the score was tied. philip walked in, checked the score, and walked back to the kitchen. i heard him tell helen that i was asleep and had missed it. two minutes later they replayed the homerun, but he thought it was another one and started screaming about me missing the two of them and did helen think he ought to wake me? without opening my eyes and as clearly and loudly as i could i announced that it was a replay and why the fuck did he think i had lain down anyhow if not to get the score tied?

agee was on, staub was up. i went back to the business of napping and winning the game. i heard philip and nathaniel come in, quietly, as philip warned nathaniel not to bother me. staub reached, mays reached, and agee scored on a wild pitch. we had koosman warm for the last of the ninth so i felt secure finally and settled myself. and promptly fell into a deep, beautifully comforting sleep. i was awakened by a great silence and a deep malaise. the idiot had turned the set off after the last out! any napper knows this is critical. the full nap, with the set droning quietly, is one of god's great gifts to mankind. but how can you convince a third-year medical student of anything relating to body or soul? the consequence was a horrible late afternoon and evening that was only saved by helen producing a fantastic chocolate mousse pie.

when the nap had been broken i had turned on the tail-end of the yankee game to see if swoboda was playing (he had started over the weekend and gone four for eight—and I like to think that that had happened because he had cancelled out on dinner with us, and he had cancelled out because he was bugged about not playing—but that's an entirely different kind of magic). it took only one minute to remind me again why i am not a yankee fan. bill white was talking about some guy's average and said that some of the players figure if they get fifteen hits every fifty times at bat they ought to hit .300. i had to wonder what he thought the rest of the guys figure, and i even had a kind thought for bob murphy.

on tuesday night matlack shut out philadelphia. what will we do if he is double figures by the all-star break? he could have sixteen wins by then—or more if tom terrific lets the other guys go on a four-day schedule. not that i want tom terrific to sit down. but it would be interesting to see if there's any way two guys, say, could pitch every fourth day, tom every fifth, and two more bounce in and out to make up the difference. i'll work it out—and it's possible that that's how it worked with the preacher and with whitey ford.

in any event matlack really looks okay, capra is spotty but shows signs, and koosman has looked good the last two times in relief. yogi is quoted as saying one more good go and he starts, and finally, while i still refuse to believe in mcandrew, he may do it to me yet. he looked terrific the last time out against st. louis, and he wasn't that bad at all in the montreal game.

in fact, for the end of may, things look very rosy. we shall see what we shall see, of course, but it is a fact that the world at large—i.e., all those who do not understand my fascination with the game, with the team, and with the season—think of the mets as twenty-four guys limping or being hauled along behind tom terrific and it would be nice to have that impression corrected. just as it's nice to see agee, harrelson, and grote doing something as well as staub, mays and fregosi. and when cleon starts hitting it's going to be nicer. as it is, i haven't had the heart to tell nathaniel that cleon is slumping.

the one thing we americans can't seem to accept is finesse, and we're always looking for the leader, the strong man, the guy on the white horse, even though those are the guys we (at least the white european segment of the population) left home to get away from.

for example, nixon's astonishing rise in popularity as attested by the ubiquitous polls right after the mining speech. it was direct action, a lot of steam on the ball, blow it right past them, baby.

on friday night, on the other hand, phil niekro got booed at shea stadium on his way to a three-hit win for atlanta, and it wasn't a met defeat they were upset about, it was niekros knuckleball, a pitch which has always seemed vaguely unamerican to fans. and on saturday tom terrific just couldn't stop bitching about ralph garr's three-for-three, which in tom's inimitable term "didn't make ninety feet between them."

this was new york, where, like they say, excellence is appreciated—and it usually is, too, except when it smacks somehow of conniving instead of strength, brains instead of brawn.

the boos came mainly whenever niekro threw his floater, a big nothing rising high and dropping around the plate, and they were the biggest the one time it dipped over for a perfect strike. they call this kind of pitching shit. even the name notes the utter contempt in which it's held. i've thrown a floater, and a lot of other junk pitches, but it's true that the floater bugs even the umpire. nobody notices that hardly anyone ever hits it. i know, i know, that once rip sewell tried to throw one past ted williams in an all-star game, and williams blasted it, but williams was the greatest, and nobody else much that season hit it big that i recall. sewell won 143 games and lost 97 for a pittsburgh team that finished as high as second only once in his ten years, and the rest of the time was fourth or worse, so he can't have been that bad a pitcher. he called the ball an "ephus," which is enough to remember him for.

you see, it's like a betrayal, that a pitcher should throw a pitch that by its very nothingness is hard to hit. a rex barney heaving a bullet past you is a hero, even if he hardly ever throws a strike, because that's strength, man, and power. now don't get me wrong, because i get suckered by that mystique too, and indeed, one early spring day in the fifties went out to the ball park in asheville, north carolina, to see what was to be barney's last appearance in a dodger uniform, although we didn't know it then. the brooks were playing their asheville farm on the way up to brooklyn, and they'd announced that barney would pitch in rotation until he pitched himself on or off the club. it was beautiful. he threw his smoke and threw his smoke and then he threw his smoke ten feet over the catcher's head, and then he gave up a triple and a double and then he put his glove down on the mound and pulled himself and walked to the bench and out of the game.

the point is that the junk pitcher exists by brains alone, fooling you by where the ball is, or might be, or ought to be, and by changing speeds from slower to slowest, and making the ball dip and break or not until you're crazy. you've also got to supply all the power—you can't just meet the ball and watch it sail. this is, of course, what causes all the hostility, since everyone is the same: if they get beat they want to get beat by a haymaker, not nibbled to death, or fall stumbling over their own feet.

kiner was really upset, having been a slugger, and went on and on about knuckleballers until i expected to hear that he had lobbied vinegar bend mizell into having federal legislation introduced banning them. he was so shook that he erred about washington's famous staff in the forties which at one point had four (wolff, niggeling, leonard, and heffner), not three knuckleballer starters—you could look it up. it may in fact be that staff that started me on my deviant way, since my american-leaguer team in those days was the senators.

but the simple fact is that all the rules of the game call for is that the pitcher throw the ball in such a way that it pass through the strike zone and is hard to hit, and it don't nowhere in all the fine print say anything about that ball having to be a high hard one or a fast-breaking curve.

the same basic truth holds for garr's three hits, since his job is to get on base safely, and the fact that he beat out two bunts and an infield grounder, and that, in fact, he did the same thing consistently all last season, ought to be to his credit, as much at least as kiner hitting homeruns year after year. but we really can't accept this kind of thinking, and we underrated clemente next to mays or aaron because he hit a lot fewer homeruns—and indeed, in san francisco the fans like willie himself less than cepeda and mccovey for exactly the same reason. we like goliath, the big lug, is the simple fact; deep in our souls we really despise david, we think he was cheating somehow.

in the same fashion the landy-bannister race i mentioned earlier found everybody really admiring landy and somehow sneering a little at bannister, who after all, didn't even finish properly. he had given so much to win he fell down after finishing, whereas landy had the grace and style to run his extra lap out.

i'm sure there's something pertinent here in regard to the candidates and the issues and the new theories of populism in all this, but i haven't got the slightest idea what it might be. maybe, in the end, it all comes back to trust. maybe we just don't trust, can't believe in, the man who is so transparent we see what he's throwing, what he's doing, and yet we still can't hit it, or the hitter who dumps one that should be handled, it looks like, but it can't be; maybe we can only buy the pitch that can't be seen, the hit that can't be touched.

it would certainly be a simple universe that way, and yet, and yet. when we were playing those sunday games ten years ago emilio cruz spent a whole summer screaming at me and my shit, but in one hundred at-bats he got ninety-eight pops to second, a grounder to short, and a scratch single through the hole, so who won that one, and who's better, if you're counting?

it's also significant to me that the three met hits were all gotten by john milner, who's really too young and inexperienced to know that niekro's unamerican. he just went up and tried to hit the pitches.

there'd be no key to the city presented if hoyt wilhelm signed with the mets, but i'd love to see him out there, an old man with a knuckleball and a lot of wins and a lot of saves and a low era and also, a large set of pitching brains. if he lost, it'd be goddamned banjo hitter beat him, scratching for a hit, screwing around on the bases, sliding home under the tag. mr. kiner, mr. seaver, mr. amurrican, that also happens to be baseball. and, fortunately for all of us, it's life too.

# 13

# Baseball Math and Abstract Games

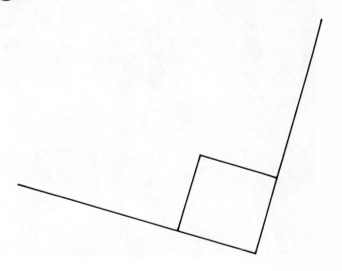

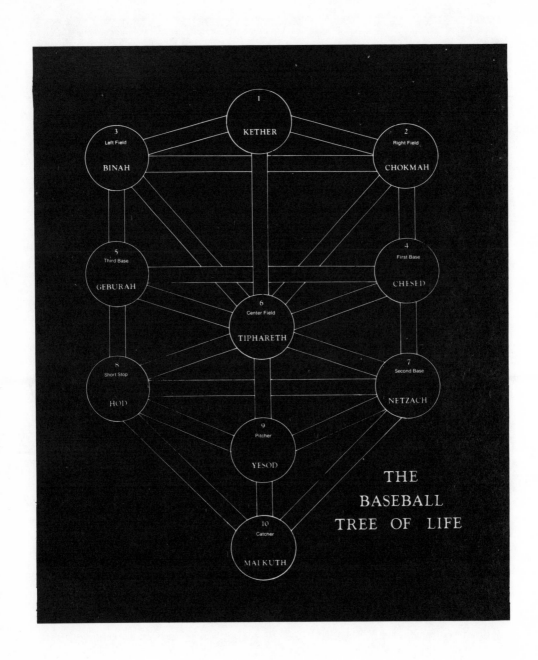

# ROGER ANGELL

## Box Scores

Today the *Times* reported the arrival of the first pitchers and catchers at the spring training camps, and the morning was abruptly brightened, as if by the delivery of a seed catalogue. The view from my city window still yields only frozen tundras of trash, but now spring is guaranteed and one of my favorite urban flowers, the baseball box score, will burgeon and flourish through the warm, languid, information-packed weeks and months just ahead. I can remember a spring, not too many years ago, when a prolonged New York newspaper strike threatened to extend itself into the baseball season, and my obsessively fannish mind tried to contemplate the desert prospect of a summer without daily box scores. The thought was impossible; it was like trying to think about infinity. Had I been deprived of those tiny lists of sporting personae and accompanying columns of runs batted in, strikeouts, double plays, assists, earned runs, and the like, all served up in neat three-inch packages from Pittsburgh, Milwaukee, Baltimore, Houston, and points east and west, only the most aggressive kind of blind faith would have convinced me that the season had begun at all or that its distant, invisible events had any more reality than the silent collision of molecules. This year, thank heaven, no such crisis of belief impends; summer will be admitted to our breakfast table as usual, and in the space of half a cup of coffee I will be able to discover, say, that Ferguson Jenkins went eight innings in Montreal and won his fourth game of the season while giving up five hits, that Al Kaline was horse-collared by Fritz Peterson at the Stadium, that Tony Oliva hit a double and a single off Mickey Lolich in Detroit, that Juan Marichal was bombed by the Reds in the top of the sixth at Candlestick Park, and that similar disasters and triumphs befell a couple of dozen-odd of the other ballplayers—favorites and knaves—whose fortunes I follow from April to October.

The box score, being modestly arcane, is a matter of intense indifference, if not irritation, to the non-fan. To the baseball-bitten, it is not only informative, pictorial, and gossipy but lovely in aesthetic structure. It represents happenstance and physical flight exactly translated into figures and history. Its totals—batters' credit vs. pitchers' debit—balance as exactly as those in an accountant's ledger. And a box score is more than a capsule archive. It is a precisely etched miniature of the sport itself, for baseball, in spite of its grassy spaciousness and apparent unpredictability, is the most intensely and satisfyingly mathematical of all our outdoor sports. Every player in every game is subjected to a cold and ceaseless accounting; no ball is thrown and no base is gained without an instant responding judgment—ball or strike, hit or error, yea or nay—and an ensuing statistic. This encompassing neatness permits the baseball fan, aided by experience and memory, to extract from a box score the same joy, the same hallucinatory reality, that prickles the scalp of a musician when he glances at a page of his score of *Don Giovanni* and actually hears bassos and sopranos, woodwinds and violins.

The small magic of the box score is cognominal as well as mathematical. Down the years, the rosters of the big-league teams have echoed and twangled with evocative, hilarious, ominous, impossible, and exactly appropriate names. The daily, breathing reality of the ballplayers' names in box scores accounts in part, it seems to me, for the rarity of convincing baseball fiction. No novelist has yet been able to concoct a baseball hero with as tonic a name as Willie Mays or Duke Snider or Vida Blue. No contemporary novelist would dare a supporting cast of characters with Dickensian names like those that have stuck with me ever since I deciphered my first box scores and began peopling the lively landscape of baseball in my mind—Ossee Schreckengost, Smead Jolley, Slim Sallee, Elon Hogsett, Urban Shocker, Burleigh Grimes, Hazen Shirley Cuyler, Heinie Manush, Cletus Elwood Poffenberger, Virgil Trucks, Enos Slaughter, Luscious Easter, and Eli Grba. And not even a latter-day O. Henry would risk a conte like the true, electrifying history of a pitcher named Pete Jablonowski, who disappeared from the Yankees in 1933 after several seasons of inept relief work with various clubs. Presumably disheartened by seeing the losing pitcher listed as "J'bl'n's'i" in the box scores of his day, he changed his name to Pete Appleton in the semi-privacy of the minors, and came back to win fourteen games for the Senators in 1936 and to continue in the majors for another decade.

## Baseball & Classicism

Every day I peruse the box scores for hours
Sometimes I wonder why I do it
Since I am not going to take a test on it
And no one is going to give me money

The pleasure's something like that of codes
Of deciphering an ancient alphabet say
So as brightly to picturize Eurydice
In the Elysian Fields on her perfect day

The day she went 5 for 5 against Vic Raschi

## Pool Table Baseball

Divide the pool balls into two teams.
Assign a batting order. Choose one ball as pitcher.
Put the cue ball and eight ball out of play.

The player representing the fielding team stands at one end of the table, batter at other. Pitcher rolls the ball down the table toward the batter. Batter must throw his ball out to meet the pitcher's ball and attempt to strike it so that it rolls, after contact, into one of the four pockets in front of him, i.e., the two side pockets, and the two pockets at the pitcher's end. Side pocket to batter's right is a single. Side pocket to batter's left is a double. Corner pocket to the batter's right on the pitcher's end is a triple. Corner pocket to the batter's left at the pitcher's end, home run. A single advances each base runner one base, double two bases, etc.

If the batter fails to cause the pitched ball to go into one of the four "fair" pockets, but hits a cushion in fair territory instead, it is an out. If the batted ball hits a cushion in foul territory, i.e., on the batter's side of the side pockets, it is a foul ball. If the pitched ball is not "swung" at by the batter and it lands between the two center diamonds, it is a strike. If it lands outside these diamonds it is a ball.

A sacrifice "bunt" is achieved if the batter hits a pitched ball in such a manner that it stops rolling, in fair territory (pitcher-wards of the imaginary line connecting the two side pockets), before either striking a cushion or falling into a pocket.

Pitched balls should not be "fast" for safety's sake. Fast pitched balls may tend to jump the table when struck. The pitcher's art is to accomplish subtle curves, change-up screwballs, and sliders by experimenting with finger english.

The eight ball and cue ball are put out of play because of their inordinate power.

Generally we found the five ball and three ball to be excellent batsmen, and the thirteen to be an exquisite craftsman on the mound.

**JAMES BOGAN**

## "You're Too Far in the Future"

Playing shortshop for a local town league team made up of ex-convicts, public relations men, chemical engineers, students, poets, and welfare recipients—KENMARK SPORTING GOODS emblazoned on orange shirts—if you remember to bring it. Anyway in the bottom of the 7th we are ahead 13–7 and before 3 men have batted they have loaded the bases and scored 3 runs—or so it seems. Then another run leaving men on second and third. A hard ground ball is hit into the box which much to my surprise I get to and pick up. Quickly I tag the man standing on second and then the base. Time enough to watch the runner make it to first. Everybody by this time including myself "saw" and then—and this is the story—for all to hear came the voice of an eight year old who was sitting on the opposition bench—"You're too far in the future, Shortstop!"

## Prose 43

The minotaur was on second base. The
lower part wanted to steal but the rest
seemed to hesitate. The reliever was
still wet from the sea; he was trying
to hold it together with a string
stretched from his right foot sixty
feet and six inches to the plate. His
receiver waited there on one knee with
his left arm extended and the gloved
hand raised. But his eyes kept shifting
from the string to the runner on second,
half bull and half man, and back again.
After a while he asked for time out and
headed toward the mound.

## A Note on Poetics, 1974

Let us suppose a baseball team with Kurt Schwitters at third,
Louis ("Hit-em-where-they-ain't") Zukofsky at short, Peter
Kropotkin at second, and Anon at first. Art ("Frenchy")
Rimbaud is in left, Willie the Lion Smith in center, and
Gertrude Stein in right. On the mound Werner Heisenberg, whose
notorious indeterminacy pitch has made him the club's un-
challenged "stopper." Alternating behind the plate are John
Cage and Master Canterel, and the manager is Ludwig ("the Barber")
Wittgenstein, whose rep around the circuit as a staunch
disciplinarian is largely undeserved.

Then let us suppose that there's no field, no ball, and no
other team. What would the final score be?

## Lineups

San Francisco ss
Munich cf
Paris lf
Rome c
Madrid 3b
London rf
Athens 1b
Istanbul 2b
New York p

Orange ss
Blue lf
Green 3b
Purple cf
Red 1b
Tan c
Brown rf
Pink 2b
Yellow p

Legs ss
Hips rf
Breasts 1b
Genitals lf
Buttocks c
Stomach cf
Feet 2b
Arms 3b
Head p

*A Day at the Races* rf
*The Maltese Falcon* lf
*Rules of the Game* 3b
*Children of Paradise* cf

*On the Waterfront* 1b
*The Lady Vanishes* ss
*The Baker's Wife* 2b
*Odd Man Out* c
*Masculine Feminine* p

Patio 2b
Bathroom ss
Dining Room cf
Living Room 1b
Bedroom 3b
Foyer lf
Hall rf
Garage c
Kitchen p

Pope ss
Keats 2b
Shakespeare cf
Milton 1b
Spenser rf
Chaucer 3b
Jonson lf
Yeats c
Donne p

Carrots (raw) 2b
Beans rf
Tomatoes lf
Potatoes c
Eggplant 1b
Brussels Sprouts ss
Spinach cf
Squash 3b
Lettuce p

*The Trial* 2b
*Remembrance of Things Past* lf
*Middlemarch* cf
*War and Peace* 1b
*The Brothers Karamazov* 3b
*Ulysses* ss
*Moby Dick* rf
*The Magic Mountain* c
*The Wings of the Dove* p

Polio rf
Syphilis (Gonorrhea) lf
Heart Disease ss
Cancer cf
Hepatitis 1b
Cirrhosis 3b
Measles c
Common Cold 2b
Influenza p

Vivaldi 3b
Chopin 2b
Mozart cf
Beethoven c
Wagner 1b
Brahms lf
Debussy ss
Handel rf
Bach p

### *All Star Team*

| | |
|---|---|
| P- | Dizzy Deneb |
| C- | Yogi Betelgeuse |
| 1st- | Stan "the Moon" Mizar |
| 2d- | Red Rigel |
| 3d- | Casey Canopus |
| SS- | Chico Spica |
| OF- | Duke Sirius |
| OF- | Babe Vega |
| OF- | Hank Aldebaran |
| | |
| MVP- | (Most Variable Pulsar) |
| | Sonny Sol |

# NINE BIG LEAGUE POETS by Mikhail Horowitz

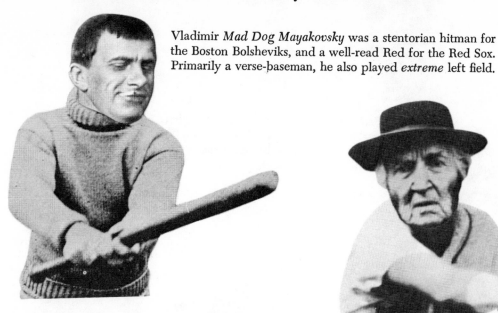

Vladimir *Mad Dog Mayakovsky* was a stentorian hitman for the Boston Bolsheviks, and a well-read Red for the Red Sox. Primarily a verse-baseman, he also played *extreme* left field.

Robert *Goat Boy Graves* played for the Majorca Magi. Each year at the Spring Training Equinox, he was entrusted with the burning of ritual incense to the White Goddess of the White Sox.

Jonathan *Jo Jo Swift* was a misanthropic shortstop for the Brobdingnag Giants whose "Modest Proposal"—that bankrupt owners eat their bonus babies—so enraged the Commissioner's Office that he was drummed out of the league and reduced to vending peanuts in Lilliput.

*Sad Sam Beckett* spent most of his career in the stadium parking lot, waiting for Lefty Godot. The terse, hermetic hurler is also remembered for dishing up Joe Krapp's Last Tape Measure Homer.

Banned from appearing in most of the respectable ballparks of his day, Charles *Babe Baudelaire* was nevertheless a mainstay of the Oshkosh Opiumeaters notorious "Merdeerer's Row." Most Valuable Madman three times, he died after attempting to smoke one of the Minotaur's turds in the bullpen.

Allen *Gus Ginsberg* saw the best bats of his generation destroyed by spitballs . . . Most Visionary Player in 1956, Gus is the only active chanter to have ever slammed an Om run onto the Bardo Plane.

Ishmael *Alto Reed* was a stickman with
almost magical abilities who played for
the Los Angeles Loas in the late '60's
and early '70's . . . a "fringe player,"
he was finally barred from active
competition after one-too-many
accusations of "doctoring" his bat,
putting a "spell" on the opposing pitcher,
and turning the umpires into toads.

*David Herbert Lawrence* was poetry's 1st DH.

*T. S. Sweeney* (also known as *Apeneck
Eliot* to the more vociferous boo-birds of
Wasteland Park) played his college ball
with the Princeton Prufrocks and later
joined the Indianapolis Imagists of
the *Ty Pound* era. For a long time,
Sweeney and Pound were the game's
most polyphrenogenitive one-two punch.
Apeneck eventually wound up with the
Hoboken Hollow Men, and ended his
playing days "not with a bang, but a balk."

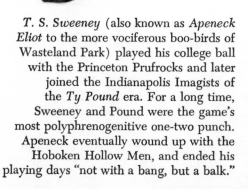

## Howl for Casey

I saw the best bats of my generation destroy'd by spitballs,
    curving elliptically plateward, dragging themselves thru
    the Little Leagues at dawn, looking for an angry hit;
Ruthian sluggers staggering on stadium roofs illuminated,
    rounding incredible bags & coming home;
Who singl'd, & doubl'd, & tripl'd, & homer'd hosanna! into
    the grandstand down the ramp & ending up ecstatic & holy
    w/peanuts & Ballantine Beer in the zen bleachers;
Who slump'd, & watch'd their Louisville timbers go limp, &
    boo'd their fate under celestial arclights, as the rabid
    fans in madness also boo'd;
Who emerging from dugouts dugouts dugouts into the navel's
    ondeck circle were dished up umbilical curveballs by
    embryonic portsiders;
Who loned it along Ohio baselines, looking for visionary
    Cleveland Indians who WERE visionary Cleveland Indians;
Who toed the old rubber w/Gaylord Perry, foot queens fondling
    the southpaw's quivering mound;
Who balled the whole ballpark at the Astrodome, first to open
    & then to catch their flies;
Who poured prick into Ford Frick, six inches too short for the
    shortstop, the league's Most Voluptuous Player, Nookie-
    of-the-Year, relieved by the Lord when their love was
    knocked out of the box;
Who ruled in right field by divine right, fungo Bodhisattvas
    reciting the Diamond Sutra;
Who pitched for Paradise, & Paradise Lost, & were banished down
    down down to the hot stove circuitry of Burning Bush Leagues;
Who stole third base to support their habit, snorting the astro-
    turf w/some dark Benway in Fenway Park;
Who peered trembling into the wet Tibetan facemask of Yogi
    Berrananda, coming thru those catchers in the rye;
Who molested bonus babies, a hot flash in the pan, whizzing
    into the eager mitts of Whiz Kids;
Who mastered Tai Chi w/the invincible Ty Cobb, but could not
    nail sweet Jesus at the plate;
Who slugged Om runs, & utilized their flaccid tools of ignorance
    to open up the keystone, no hits no runs no Eros, only to
    find the jissom of Pee Wee Reese;
Who got hot pants for Billy Cox at the hot corner, & were
    buggered by grumbling umps whilst waiting for Lefty;

Who split hairs w/the old Barber in Kiner's Korner, insatiable
backstops w/foul balls, lumbering on Buddhist shinguards
for the Lost Bunt;
Who chained themselves to the endless scoreboard for 23
innings this actually happened & vanished high on opiated
crackerjacks into oblivious bullpens;
And CASEY, secret hero of this poem, the cupid of Mudville,
sailing mashnotes on paperplanes to nubile batboys,
abandoned to boobirds & pulling his pud in the batter's
box, weeping & thinking, You can't strike out w/out
having Visions;
Ah Casey, while YOU are a bum, I am a bum, & now you're truly
gloveless, alone & broken in the poor old winter Polo
Grounds of God, a prime candidate for the Hall of Shame,
& even the groundskeeper hands you a raincheck;
Down to the Diamond! He saw the All Stars! Angels in the
outfield! Bearded twirlers on Biblical mounds! Seraphic
hotdog vendors in heavenly aisles! He played the game!
Scarf'd pennants! Sniff'd Red Sox! Blew down the Pirates!
Yam-yanker for the Yankees! Cincinnati Wetlegs! Double-
maidenheaders! Base on balls & Frenchkiss'd Leo the Lip!
-the dirt in his cleats an edible joy, good to nibble a thousand
innings.

## JACK KEROUAC

## *from* Desolation Angels

To while away the time I play my solitaire card baseball game Lionel and I invented in 1942 when he visited Lowell and the pipes froze for Christmas—the game is between the Pittsburgh Plymouths (my oldest team, and now barely on top of the 2nd division) and the New York Chevvies rising from the cellar ignominously since they were world champions last year—I shuffle my deck, write out the lineups, and lay out the teams— For hundreds of miles around, black night, the lamps of Desolation are lit, to a childish sport, but the Void is a child too—and here's how the game goes:—what happens:—how it's won, and by whom:—

The opposing pitchers are, for the Chevvies, Joe McCann, old vet of 20 years in my leagues since first at 13 age I'd belt iron rollerbearings with a nail in the appleblossoms of the Sarah backyard, Ah sad—Joe McCann, with a record of 1–2, (this is the 14th game of the season for both clubs), and an earned run average of 4.86, the Chevvies naturally heavily favored and especially as McCann is a star pitcher and Gavin a secondrater in my official effectiveness rulings—and the Chevvies are hot anyway, comin up, and took the opener of this series 11–5 . . .

The Chevvies jump right out ahead in their half of the first inning as Frank Kelly, the manager belts a long single into center bringing home Stan Orsowski from second where he'd gone on a bingle and walk to Duffy—yag, yag, you can hear those Chevvies (in my mind) talking it up and whistling and clapping the game on— The poor greenclad Plymouths come on for their half of the opening inning, it's just like real life, a real baseball, I cant tell the difference between this and that howling wind and hundreds of miles of Arctic Rock without—

But Tommy Turner with his great speed converts a triple into an inside-the-park homerun and anyway Sim Kelly has no arm out there and it's Tommy's sixth homerun, he is the "magnificent one" all right—and his 15th run batted in and he's only been playin six games because he was injured, a regular Mickey Mantle—

Followed immediately back to back by a line drive homerun over the rightfield fence from the black bat of old Pie Tibbs and the Plyms jump out ahead 2–1 . . . wow . . .

(the fans go wild in the mountain, I hear the rumble of celestial racing cars in the glacial crevasses)

—Then Lew Badgurst singles to right and Joe McCann is really getting belted (and him with his fancy earned run average) (pah, goes to show)—

In fact McCann is almost batted out of the box as he further gives up a walk to Tod Gavin but Ole Reliable Henry Pray ends up the inning grounding out to Frank Kelly at third—it will be a slugfest.

Then suddenly the two pitchers become locked in an unexpected brilliant pitching duel, racking up goose egg after goose egg, neither one of them giving up a hit except one single (Ned Gavin the pitcher got it) in the second inning, right on brilliantly up the uttermost eighth when Zagg Parker of the Chevs finally breaks the ice with a single to right which (he too for great super runner speed) unopposed stretches into a double (the throw is made but he makes it, sliding)—and a new tone comes in the game you'd think but no!—Ned Gavin makes Clyde Castleman fly out to center then calmly strikes out Stan the Man Orsowski and stalks off the mound chewing his tobacco unperturbed, the very void— Still, a 2–1 ballgame favor of his team—

McCann yields a single to big bad Lew Badgurst (with big arms southpawing that bat) in *his* half of the eighth, and there's a base stolen on him by pinch runner Allen Wayne, but no danger as he gets Tod Gavin on a grounder—

Going into the final inning, still the same score, the same situation.

All Ned Gavin has to do is hold the Chevvies for 3 long outs. The fans gulp and tense. He has to face Byrd Duffy (batting .346 up to the game), Frank Kelly, and pinch hitter Tex Davidson—

He hitches up his belt, sighs, and faces the chubby Duffy—and winds up— Low, one ball.

Outside, ball two.

Long fly to center field but right in the hands of Tommy Turner.

*Only two to go.*

"Come on Neddy!" yells manager Cy Locke from the 3rd base box, Cy Locke who was the greatest shortstop of all time in his time in my appleblossom time when Pa was young and laughed in the summernight kitchen with beer and Shammy and pinochle—

Frank Kelly up, dangerous, menacing, the manager, hungry for money and pennants, a whiplash, a firebrand—

Neddy winds up: delivers: inside.

Ball one.

Delivers.

Kelly belts it to right, off the flagpole, Tod Gavin chases, it's a standup double, the tying run is on second, the crowd is wild. Whistles, whistles, whistles—

Speedboy Selman Piva is sent out to run for Kelly.

Tex Davidson is a big veteran chaw-chawin old outfielder of the old wars, he drinks at night, he doesnt care— He strikes out with a big wheeling whackaround of the empty bat.

Ned Gavin has thrun him 3 curves. Frank Kelly curses in the dugout, Piva, the tying run, is still on second. *One more to go!*

The batter: Sam Dane, Chevvy catcher, old veteran chawidrinkbuddy in fact of Tex Davidson's, only difference is Sam bats lefty—same height, lean, old, dont care—

Ned pitches a call strike across the letters—

And there it comes:—a booming homerun over the centerfield barrier, Piva comes home, Sam comes loping around chewing his tobacco, still doesnt care, at the plate he is mobbed by the Kellies and the crazies—

Bottom of the 9th, all Joe McCann has to do is hold the Plymouth— Pray gets on an error, Gucwa singles, they hold at second and first, and up steps little Neddy Gavin and doubles home the tying run and sends the winning run to third, pitcher eat pitcher—Leo Sawyer pops up, it looks like McCann'll hold out, but Tommy Turner simply slaps a sacrifice grounder and in comes the winning run, Jack Gucwa who'd singled so unobtrusively, and the Plymouths rush out and carry Ned Gavin to the showers atop their shoulders.

Tell me Lionel and I didnt invent a good game!


Finally I buy a St. Louis *Sporting News* to catch up on the baseball news, and a *Time* Magazine, to catch up on world news and read all about Eisenhower waving from trains, and a bottle of Italian Swiss Colony port wine, expensive one of the best—I thought— With that I go cutting back down the drag and there's a burlesque house, "I'll go to the burlesque tonight!" I giggle (remembering the Old Howard in Boston) (and recently I'd read how Phil Silvers had put on an oldtime burlesque act in some burlesque somewhere and what a delicate art it was) — Yes— and is—

For after an hour and a half in my room sipping that wine (sitting with stockinged feet on the bed, pillow back), reading about Mickey Mantle and the Three-I League and the Southern Association and the West Texas League and the latest trades and stars and kids upcoming and even reading the Little League news to see the names of the 10-year-old prodigy pitchers and glancing at *Time* Magazine (not so interesting after all when you're full of juice and the street's outside), I go out, carefully pouring wine in my polybdinum canteen (used earlier for trail thirsts, with red bandana around my head), stick it in my pocket of jacket, and down into night—

# VICTORIA M. RATHBUN

## Death by Disappearance

Willie Waltz divided his time between pinball &
baseball on TV. Although stubborn scenes of tenderness
persisted in his life, like really great kittens waiting
to be let out, their voices didn't travel far in such
an overcrowded atmosphere. Events! Plot! Mitchell Page
throws up on his own shoes right before Vida Blue's
first pitch. Ty Cobb's second cousin, the pinball champ
of the financial district, shows him how to rake it in.
Willie's indigent punk nephew steals a car & winds up
in jail, & the wife goes back to visit her folks in Corpus
Christi. At this point, Willie takes a good look at his
life. It's all springs & pings, bright lights, the buzz
of the crowd, the grey of cathrode ray, the green of
astro-turf. It's beautiful. Down the alley, he gets a
whiff of burnt sugar—cotton candy? Further on, he
can smell cold beer & a million hamburgers. Lines of
neon beckon like three or four warm winters, like the
fingers of an elegant hand. Spirituality & Marilyn
Monroe, those perfect twins, turn to look at him from
the counter as he enters the Studio Diner. He's an AP
wirephoto of Joe DiMaggio, he's a paragraph in tomorrow's
paper, he's a well-turned phrase, he's a comma.

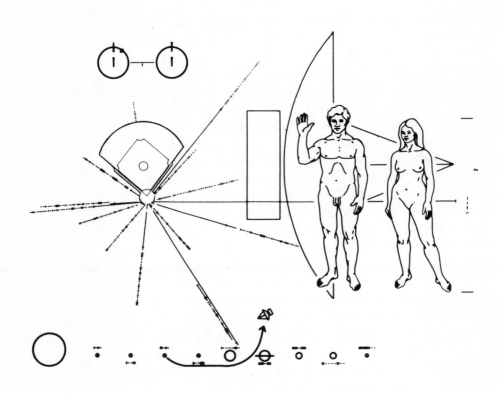

# 14

# Visions and Voodoo

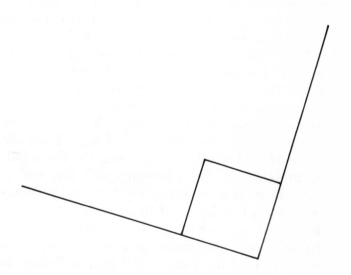

## RICHARD GROSSINGER

## Baseball Voodoo

On October 17, 1971, Steve Blass won the seventh game of the World Series. He pitched an aesthetic, almost flawless game. Five days earlier he stopped an Oriole team that had gone through nine Pirate pitchers in two days in Baltimore, on sixteen runs and twenty-four hits. Before the largest crowd in Pittsburgh history, he struck out eight and gave up only one run. In 1972 he won nineteen games, eleven more than he lost; he had an earned run average of 2.48. In 1973 he couldn't get anybody out, for the Pirates and not for any of the minor league teams to which they sent him.

Steve Blass was basically an ordinary pitcher. He didn't have great speed or overpowering stuff, but through the years he became one of the Pirates' most reliable pitchers until, by the 1971 Series, he was the ace of the staff. They found themselves entrusting their "must" games to him, although they couldn't say, in so many words, why he was effective. And when it was *the* game for the Pirates, number seven, or the whole season on the hundred-and-seventy third, it was clear that Blass would pitch and would be as effective as any pitcher in the game.

Surely the Pirates must have used him with an intuitive trepidation, but baseball has always been played on an open field with real bats and real balls. The final score emerges from a chaos of irretrievable experiments not the radar clocking of a Nolan Ryan or Herb Washington. It's like creation. We can't say how it would have been better if God had been able to throw harder than the speed of light. Each first inning is how beautiful it would be, back at the beginning, the Earth just at the warm edge of the Pleistocene, the lakes reviving with fins and gills from ancient frozen eggs. Only as many teams as there were players, the balls seized whole from rivers that had held them in their teeth for millennia, the bats from hazel and oak, whose crashing down brought rainwater. These original ballfields now lie under seas and cities, or sit as mummified relics, forerunners of the Pima and Papago ballcourts in the Old World deserts. Man has only ancestors back then. And only then. So Steve Blass can pitch without fear he might be anyone else or that the hand-axes scattered on the margin of a Rhodesian lake might have been left there without a scorekeeper. The caribou dice are thrown, and we too, we alone, are the final score.

There have been pitchers with incredible stuff who have never been able to win in the Major Leagues, while many ordinary pitchers have been effective, through savvy, rhythm, experience, luck, the scouts grade them with numbers as if they were quantities but often they have no idea. Steve Blass' lack of outstanding stuff is provocative only after the demise. The coaches begin working on how to get him to recover it; they look over films of Steve Blass before and Steve Blass after. —Recover what?— He looks exactly the same pitching to the Orioles in 1971 as getting nobody out in the International League in 1972. Only then do they start saying—there's nothing surprising about this; the only real question is, how did he do it in the first place?— (—With mirrors—is the joke line, not really a joke at all).

Pitchers have torn muscles, broken bones, been operated on, had ligaments grafted; they have altered everything about their delivery and rhythm that made them a pitcher in the first place. They have come back from rotary cuff surgery, from not being able to lift their arms for a year and a half, and they have won ball-games. Occasionally, like Jim Palmer and Luis Tiant, they have pitched the best baseball of their lives after the actual physical equipment was seemingly taken away. It is almost as though the outer throwing form is an illusion. If you learn how to do it in terms of a strong healthy body, the skill remains, the ability to put it over, long after the body ceases to back it. An inner image of the entire pitching sequence is regenerative, like a reptile limb.

Baseball men said they could recall no other case in which the ability left a player that quickly. It made no sense to them; it made no sense to the Pirates either, and, against their better judgement, they kept giving him fresh chances. But it was like playing the man off the street; he could go through the motions convincingly enough from having played as a kid and from having watched enough games, but there was no way he could get real hitters out. And in the end they stop asking questions and say simply: —He lost it. They're sorry. They return to present business. True, some clubs call in hypnotists, TM trainers, Silva Mind Control operators, How-To-Succeed-in-Business positive-thinking Christians, but these are novelties, and such instructors do not replace the coaches, do not revise the game plan, they do not go far enough. Sometimes a single player will come upon an amazing streak after a session with one of these trainers; he may even lead the league in hitting or become a star for years. But then he is accepted as a reality of his own acts rather than the product of an initiation. If the ceremony is debunked, the fall from grace is equally unavailable. You just fall and fall. Performance and result determine the gestalt, and inner cause is thought about only in very literary sports pages, like those of *The New Yorker* and *Psychology Today*.

After the game Steve Blass had a childlike amazement: what have I done! As close to horror as delight. He kept talking about how, because he remembered it now in a kind of numbness, how, as a kid, he had had this daydream about pitching the seventh game of a World Series, pitching it and winning it. —Steve Blass winds and fires. Strike three! It's all over. The Yankees win. Steve Blass winds and fires. Curve ball. Batter swings above it. Strike three! . . . . . winds and comes in sidearm, picks up the outside corner, strike . . . . . gets him with a hard slider . . . . . winds and, he pops it up . . . . . fires . . . . . low outside . . . . . but I guess he swings, and strikes out anyway . . . . . he swings over the slider, ground ball to short . . . . . Strike three! He threw it right by him. It's all over.—

Not that he was the only kid in America pitching in his head, but he recalled it, he wanted to recall it, in perfect clarity, even after the reality. The seventh game in 1971 did not dim or overwhelm all the seventh games of his mind.

There are different theories as to what happened to him. A long article in *The New Yorker* by Roger Angell summarizes the problems and possibilities. Perhaps the death of his team-mate, Roberto Clemente, in a plane crash affected him morbidly; maybe he lost something in his rhythm, then lost his confidence, and couldn't recover; was he an inflexible pitcher?; did he lost interest in winning?

It is clear that Steve Blass made a pact with the devil—if not the devil, then some other angel—to be able to pitch in the Major Leagues, someday to win the seventh game of a World Series. He kept going for a year after the pact had expired, on sheer mantra perhaps, he was sailing, he put in another good season. The Pirates won the division; they almost won the pennant. In fact, Blass had the deciding game of the play-offs with Cincinnati in his grasp when the agents came to claim their due. —Get him out of there—, said his guardian. —It's time for him to try something else—. The big hook. Then the relief pitchers lost it for him, the winning run scoring on a wild pitch thrown by Bob Moose. A wild pitch? At a time like that? But Moose only *threw* the ball; he was just an innocent by-stander.

"I looked into Bob's eyes after the game," his wife said, "and I saw right away it wouldn't change him." Not so for Steve Blass. He never came back. Whether it was the wild pitch thrown by another man, the plane crash in another land, the end of the daydream, the action behind the scenes, little matters, for these are metaphors, and they converge in the ambiguity, the overall ambiguity of our time.

We may forget it in our daze, but what happens in a game is as much a consequence of ritual performance as it is directly-applied physical will. American Indian tribes knew this when they included sporting competitions in rain dances and harvest ceremonies. The players shared an occasion with shamans and priests. The ball they kicked up and down a field that was also a sand-painting was filled with seeds that were also corn-stalks and trees, the same seeds the chanting and dancing raised to the power of rain. Where the sacred feathered runners of the corn ceremony (the sunbirds) become the rushing opponents of lacrosse, there is no clear break; no clear break of intelligence—no departure from a landscape of huts and dry grass; patchwork planting, wild flowers, and soft counter-positional circles drawn in the dust. And the rain swept over the abandoned field, past the equinox, in the same harmonics, the same wave—different site—that drove the seed-packed hide between two goal posts, gold posts, two tridents, polarities, North and Red, South and Blue—each "yard-" marker, as they cross it, an actual transcendence, from one space and mind to another.

They continued to recognize this even after colonization, and they outlawed from their baseball games witch-doctors chanting for the other side. There was nothing whimsical or hysterical about it; the rule read: too many men on the field, nothing less blatant.

"Twice in the previous week I had been cautioned to 'watch out for their (the Braves) magic.' I did not have to wait long. After the game had been tied up at one—one for four innings and the tension was increasing, the skies suddenly darkened, lightning flashed and thunder rolled, but no rain fell. A huge pre-storm wind swept across the valley and lifted clouds of sand many feet into the air. The field was obliterated and players crouched down to avoid being blinded by the stinging dirt."

But there was no way out of the game, no way it could be called, either in sandstorm or tornado. The mortals who had raised these forces now had to see them through.

We think we do not have witch-doctors, but we recognize the mysterious home-team advantage. If it is not telepathic, it is at least in that ballpark. Coaches and managers speak of a player's incredible desire to win, they recognize clutch performers, ones who are able to hit home runs when everyone on the other team, including the pitcher, is poised against the possibility. They are Bobby Thomson, Hal Smith, Frank Robinson, Jerry Lynch, Chuck Essegian, Cliff Johnson; they are the same person. A player catching a winning touchdown in the last seconds of a game says the ball miraculously stuck to his elbow; he didn't even see it. The coach acknowledges grittiness, as if the power were masculine and macho, despite the older association of Athena and Hera with supernatural feats of war. They prefer physical mechanics, so grotesque as to be pornographic, to any supplication, any yielding, any grace. If victory is to be a winged woman, they don't want it. No one claims he gave the ball an extra telekinetic push, or that the strike-out that won the game occurred when the pitcher curved the ball after it left his hand. This is too dangerous a possibility, too provocative and profound in its implications, not only for sports, but for the society that honors them as physical events.

In 1973 Dave Augustine, a rookie just up from the minors, hit a "home run" at Shea Stadium that "won" the pennant for the Pirates. But the ball did not leave the field; its flight broke just above the grandstand and it dropped onto the railing, then bounced, not in the direction momentum should have taken it (into the stands for a home run anyway), but back into the glove of Cleon Jones, who threw out the lead run at home plate. Two nights later Steve Blass made one last try (against Tom Seaver and a stadium full of screaming fans), but he was clearly a dead man pitching out of turn. The Mets won the 1973 pennant. Now the fortunes of the New York teams directly reflect the financial and moral crisis in the city, not as an irony but a fact. The 400 plus points the Jets gave up was the leakage of corrupt money. The teachers in Queens may root for the Knicks to come back, but their plush pension fund makes it impossible, makes it certain the league will not permit them to sign George McGinnis, nor will the Federal Government come quickly to the aid of the Rangers, even as they are humiliated by the Russians. That the Yankees failed to win the pennant with Bobby Bonds and Catfish Hunter is proof that money alone cannot buy them out of the cosmic slump. Exactly because the spreading hardcore porn depicts only mechanics and gymnastics, it is not sexual or sensual at all. The Yankees won all too many pennants on and off Broadway for them ever to be able to fall in love again. But one hot summer in Detroit a rush of ghetto violence finally brought the Tigers the pennant and the Series the following year. It was always a floating Chinese zodiac. And we are totally ignorant when we smile, condescendingly, at The Year of the Dragon or The Year of the Bear. They are so much bigger than we are it's like they come down from a higher league.

There is a continuous psychic vying going on in games, the lesser sunspots and ice ages that occur within the astrology of the greater ones. They are good for a run of herring or ancient man to move North to the caves of Tibet or one hot summer. They are good for that even if they are not the major rhythms of the star. They are so subtle they change nothing at any discrete moment or in a flash of revelation, but they continue to work, and if one team's fans hire a witch doctor for the World Series, the management of the other team is going to do exactly the same, straight from Africa, like an imported soccer-style kicker. They can claim it's for publicity and entertainment, but then they don't know that themselves. As they avoid stepping on the first-base line and jump to attention when the star Puerto Rican player tells them to get those bats uncrossed. In a laboratory in Moscow one can see the dish lifted from the table, no strings attached. In the midst of a football game, there is so much energy and collision, one could accept any outcome, any cause, as Franco Harris grabs the errant pass off a pinball machine and runs for the winning touchdown, as George Blanda writes a sentimental script of game-winning passes and kicks, and O. J. Simpson, using a combination of t'ai chi and psi, throws off blockers and dashes through openings. Julius Erving is as much a creature of mental brilliance and mind-play as physical skill.

Or is there a difference? Not for an animal in the jungle. Not for a lion compelling a gazelle to come to him, a zebra compelling a lion not to notice.

"The game should have been halted until the sand cleared but the Braves insisted on continuing to play. So play went on sporadically between sharp bursts of wind, swirling sandstorms and the crashing of thunder. And still no rain fell. Sun Chief describes how if, instead of rain, at the end of a Katsina dance only a strong wind blew spreading sand, then this showed that those who sent for the Katsinas had bad hearts and had done evil. This feeling was present at the Cochiti game. Thunder, lightning and storm clouds which bring only the dead dust and no life-giving rain are the worst of portents. One Redskin going out to bat fell on his knees, crossed himself and muttered a prayer."

But baseball in America is not an Indian ritual; it is not a daydream or fantasy. It is big business. Winning the World Series has immediate financial implications. Whereas once these were downplayed beside the romance, now athletes discuss cash with pride and misty eyes and rarely talking about winning in any other context. It would betray the physicality. the maleness of the whole thing. It would make them less heroic. They cannot see how their inflation dollar-bill dance looks to a ninety-year old Pueblo chief.

When the baseball season ends, like when the bank closes, business begins again when it re-opens, in the morning or next spring. If you make a million dollars one day, the rising sun tells you you have to go out and do it again. And this has nothing to with Steve Blass' daydream.

The only symptom his team-mates report is that he remained pleasantly indifferent through the whole crisis; he was not intransigent in any stubborn sense; he simply did not fight his condition. It looked to them as though he regarded it objectively, as something happening to someone else. From the vantage of a bus in the Florida State League, the seventh game of the World Series is a fantasy all over again, with this one difference: it has come true somewhere; he can find it written into the records under his name. The young players look ahead into the future as imaginarily as he looks back into the past. There is no time warp between them.

—Groovy—, says Baba Ram Dass. —You want to be god of the Winds? Okay. Howl away for fifteen thousand years. You done with that one? What next? You want to win the seventh game of the World Series? Fantastic. Coming right up. One for each of you. Seventh game of the World Series. You don't have to worry. As long as you desire it, it will be here. Nature won't rest until all that karma is fulfilled. No hurry. We've got eternity—.

The last football player on Earth will still be saying: "I want to be compensated, and the last I heard they was doing it in money." Long after New

York City has washed the last dollar bills into the sewer in the spray from the street-washer manned by no one riding out his option and all that's left are the same Indian games that were here before it began.

When it's a new season, nobody cares who won the previous year. For a pitcher with marvellous physical ability, the pitching and the winning can be painless. In all sports there are effortless opaque stars, Jimmy Connors, Joe Namath; they succeed by habit and without interest; they lose without tension. But for Steve Blass the wonder of a beautiful fantasy had become the ordinariness of daily baseball and the American formula for success. To go on pitching was impossible. Back through the Charleston Charlies, the Thetford Mines, in the Florida State League, he began to understand, in retrospect, what he had done. He began to make that one game real and give it some value and dignity beyond simply having to come back and do it again, fiscal year after fiscal year. It was the only way out he had. The alternative would be to become a professional hero, until there is nothing, nothing at all out there in the sun.

No one knows it, but it is the summer softball leagues in Madison, Wisconsin, and Enosburg Falls, Vermont, and Berkeley, California, and Oklahoma City, where the real games are played. All those who dropped out earlier and still love the game, unpaid, on bumpy fields, but each field different, the pastures and mountains or moraine and gravel lots beyond, as only a place could be, in the angle of sun to leftfield and the run-off to the rivers, the odd banks and home run ponds and ground rule double pines. This is what they mean when they adore the big wall in Fenway, the ivy in Chicago. This is the October series broken down into a hundred thousand atomistic possibilities, one for each Indian clan, for each daisy dandelion field or gravel lot. Barry Gifford, ex-University of Missouri star, hitting over .500 in obscurity in San Francisco; he could be Bobby Murcer but Bobby Murcer could not be him. Geoff Young, from San Diego, making all the plays for The Best Minds of Our Generation softball team; his buddy Graig Nettles made it, and gets to sit around hotel lobbies and drink beer; he didn't. The catcher singing riffs the whole game. ANDY'S PIZZA on the shirt of the pitcher; batter says, "Make this one with mushrooms and cheese."

When the sportswriter finds Steve Blass, he is coach of his son's Little League team. The players keep asking him why he's not with the Pittsburgh Pirates today. Back at his home, he and the writer play a game, going through the Cincinnati Reds' line-up, the writer calling the out the player and Blass saying how he would pitch him, pitch by pitch as the writer invents the results. He pitches to Pete Rose, Joe Morgan, Johnny Bench, Tony Perez, mixing up his stuff, getting them out. In his head! He is hitting the corners, jamming the batters, putting them off-balance with off-speed stuff. He is starting to give away his secret. He did it once, for real, so he wouldn't have to keep coming back and doing it again in some repetitive irrevelant way. To fail totally, so strong is his guilt for being an imposter, so unexamined is his life.

As the sportswriter sends up the batters, he continues to pitch to them. He is back suddenly in the 1971 Series. —That's how it was then—, he cries out, as if he were remembering Bridey Murphy herself. —I could see each thing ahead of time—.

Now the sportswriter has Perez take a fastball up and in, "and then Blass threw him an intentional ball—a very bad slider inside. Perez had shortened up on the bat a little, but he took the pitch. He then fouled off a fastball, and Blass threw him another good fastball, high and inside, and Perez struck out, swinging, to end the inning."

The sportswriter comments that it was a "pretty good inning," and they both laugh.

" 'Yes, you know the *exact* sequence has happened to Perez many times,' Blass said. 'He shortens up and then chases the pitch up here.'

"He was animated. 'You know, I can almost *see* that fastball to Perez, and I can see his bat going through it, swinging through the pitch and missing. That's a good feeling. That's one of the concepts of Dr. Harrison's program, you know—visualization. When I was pitching well, I was doing that very thing. You get so locked in, you see yourself doing things before they happen. That's what people mean when they say you're in the groove. That's what happened in that World Series game, when I kept throwing that big slop curveball to Boog Powell, and it really ruined him. I must have thrown it three out of four pitches to him, and I just *knew* it was going to be there. There's no doubt about it—no information needed. The crowd is there, this is the World Series, and all of a sudden you're locked into something. It's like being plugged into a computer. It's "Gimme the ball, *boom!* Click, click, click . . . *shoom!*" It's that good feeling. You're just flowing easy.' "

And you see Luis Tiant twirling them in. You see them all.

[After this piece was written, I ran across the following quote from Bill Lee, who started the seventh game of the 1975 World Series for the Red Sox and strangely blew an apparent win with a soft giveaway pitch to Tony Perez:

"Now those guys can sit naked in the snow at 18,000 feet and they have such powers of mental discipline that if they put their mind to it, hell, they can generate enough heat to melt snow for twenty feet around. Now you put that Tibetan priest on the mound, naked or not, with a baseball in his palm, and he'll take that power of concentration and make the ball disappear and then materialize down the line in the catcher's mitt. *There's* my idea of a relief pitcher."

I mean the image is there, and it's going to persist until we get in under it, or, more likely, it gets in under us.]

NOTES:

This is a piece of myth-fiction constructed almost entirely from the information in two pieces: primarily "Down the Drain" by Roger Angell [*The New Yorker,* June 23,

1975], and, secondarily, "Pueblo Baseball: A New Use for Old Witchcraft" by J. R. Fox [most recently, *Io*/16, Winter, 1973]. The two descriptions of the Pueblo baseball game come from Fox, who borrows some of his material from *Sun Chief*, the Hopi autobiography collaborated on by Sun Chief himself and the sociologist Leo W. Simmons [Yale University Press, 1942]. *All* the Blass material comes from Angell's sensitive and inspired research. In the closing interview with Blass, Angell, of course, is the sportswriter feeding him the imaginary game.

This tale borrows its form and genre from the mode, fairly common in anthropology, of revising and reconstructing the fieldwork of a previous century according to current theory. In that spirit, it is a sort of spoof on the anthropological version of "truth," which is little more than a passing academic fashion at any given time. In such accounts, the work of the modern ethnologist blurs with original source in such a way that they are indistinguishable at points, so much does the current writer appear, in his own mind, the person who actually conducted the interviews and collected the data. His revision justifies a reliving of the whole field experience, and his own account absorbs the earlier one as one version of a myth absorbs another. The author has remained faithful to the style of that genre. However, he does not wish, in reality, to disguise the contribution of Roger Angell to this piece. *He* did the full ethnography on Steve Blass, and the story is entirely his work. This version merely reconsiders his account in terms of other anthropological documents.

## The Athlete

Teamwork, dedication, and a winning attitude—these are the three graces which descend on all the members of the league leading Hibernian Hall Class "B" Softball Team.

Pagan Baseball, Cu Chulainn as the "Ump," and John Baxter, formerly of the I.R.A., champion of the Native Games, connects . . . the ball sailing over the Protestant left fielder's head where it is seized by a flight of Ravens who carry it halfway back to Erainn. O Lug, the game is over; the Irish have defeated Rowaton.

There are still ages when the old magics prevail. Some have the myths, others the rituals: put them together, the Coach is saying, and you change the imagination of the World.

He learns his Irish both at home and down at the Hibernian Hall. Old Men sitting in the corner, nursing their drafts, dream aloud of the glorious days of the Sinn Fein—the Sinn Fein, MacNeill's brilliant Gaelic League, and Connolly's green socialism—an agrarianism via Marx tailored to fit the old, abused yet still pregnant Irish soil. At no time in the last four hundred years is Ireland quite as profound as on the eve of her own revolution.

We must play Greenwich for the regional championship—Greenwich, the wealthiest Yankee community in all of this region—Greenwich will now host a gathering for the sons & daughters of the Clan na Gael.

Standing on second base, the wet winds of Long Island Sound blowing in across his face, he looks down past Johnny Long's strong right arm, and watches Oliver Cromwell come to the plate.

A low lying cloud floats in from the Sound, and three old women— Brigit, Maude Gonne, and Grace O'Malley—step out of the silver air and take their place, like the witches in Macbeth, on the green aside his brother who is holding the line down at third base.

The score is 3 to 2, Irish.

The Greenwich team has two aboard, one out, and it is the bottom of the fatal seventh.

Strike two.

Johnny Long has put Cromwell in the hole.
Now the Witches begin to mumble.
Blessed be the Holy Name of Ireland.
Blessed be the Sacred Heart of Breed.
"I am the Hag of Beare, and dream
of the rich cloth I no longer wear . . ."
Cromwell hits a scorcher down the third base line.

His brother, perfectly positioned, pounces on the ball, the moves of a cat, and he feels it hit his own glove as he pivots over second, and throws Cromwell out at first by more than a yard and a half.

The stands erupt, the tenant farmers cheer, and the witches turn into beautiful Irish women who rush onto the field to greet him.

We had to win this one, he tells the Davis brothers. I felt it was in the air.

## Understanding Alvarado

Castro thought it was no accident that Achilles "Archie" Alvarado held the world record for being hit in the head by a pitched ball.

"Because he was a hero even then," Fidel said, "because he stood like a hero with his neck proudly over the plate."

When people asked Mrs. Alvarado what she thought of her husband's career, she said, "Chisox OK, the rest of the league stinks. Archie, he liked to play everyday, bench him and his knees ached, his fingers swelled, his tongue forgot English. He would say, 'Estelle, let's split, let's scram, *vámonos a* Cuba. What we owe to Chisox?'

"I'd calm him down. 'Arch,' I'd say, 'Arch, Chisox have been plenty good to us. Paid five gees more than Tribe, first-class hotels, white roomies on the road, good press.'

"'Estelle,' he would say, 'I can't take it no more. They got me down to clubbing in the pinch and only against southpaws. They cut Chico Carasquel and Sammy Esposito and Jungle Jim Rivera. What we owe to Chisox?'

"When it got like that, I would say, 'Talk to Zloto,' and Zloto would say, 'Man, you Latinos sure are hotheads. I once got nine hits in a row for the Birds, was Rookie of the Year for the Bosox. I have the largest hands in either league and what do you think I do? I sit on the bench and spit-shine my street shoes. Look there, you can see your greasy black mug in 'em.' Zloto always knew how to handle Alvarado."

Zloto came to Havana, showed Fidel his hands, talked about the '50s.

Fidel said, "They took our good men and put them in Yankee uniforms, in Bosox, Chisox, Dodgers, Birds. They took our manhood, Zloto. They took our Achilles and called him 'Archie.' Hector Gonzalez they called 'Ramrod,' Jesús Ortiz they made a 'Jayo.' They treated Cuban manhood like a bowl of chicos and ricos. Yes, we have no bananas but we got vine-ripened Latinos who play good ball all year, stick their heads over the plate and wait for the Revolution. Fidel Castro gave it to them. It was three and two on me in Camagüey around November 1960. There were less than two dozen of us. Batista had all roads blocked and there was hardly enough ammunition left to kill some rabbits. He could have starved us out but he got greedy, he wanted the quick inning. When I saw that he was coming in with his best stuff with his dark one out over the middle, I said to Che and to Francisco Muniz, 'Habana for Christmas,' and I lined his fascist pitch up his capitalist ass."

"I'm not impressed," Zloto said. "When I heard about the Bay of Pigs I said to myself, 'Let's wipe those oinks right off the face of the earth.' You took Cuba, our best farm property, and went Commie with it. You took our best arms, Castro, our speed- and our curve-ball artists. You dried up our Cuban diamonds."

"Zloto, Zloto," Fidel said. "Look at this picture of your buddy, 'Archie' Alvarado. Don't you like him better as 'Achilles'? Look at his uniform, look at his AK 47 rifle."

"I liked him better when he was number twenty-three and used a thirty-six-inch Hillerich and Bradsby Louisville Slugger to pound out line drives in Comiskey Park."

"There's no more Comiskey Park," Fidel said. "No more Grace, no more Chuck Comiskey to come down after a tough extra-inning loss and buy a drink for the whole clubhouse. No more free Bulova watches. The Chisox are run by an insurance company now. You punch a time clock before batting practice and they charge for overtime in the whirlpool bath."

"That's goddamn pinko propaganda," Zloto said.

"You've been outta the game, big Victor," Fidel said. "You've been sitting too long out in Arizona being a dental assistant. You haven't been on the old diamonds, now astro-turfed, closed to the sun and air-conditioned. You have not seen the bleachers go to two-fifty. While you've been in Arizona the world changed, Zloto. Look at our Achilles, four fractured skulls, thirteen years in the big time. Played all over the outfield, played first and played third. A lifetime mark of two ninety-nine and RBIs in the thousands. He never got an Achilles day from Chisox, Bosox, Tribe, or Birds. When he came home Fidel made him a day, made him a Reservist colonel. I did this because Achilles Alvarado is not chickenshit. You, Zloto, know this better than anyone.

"Achilles said to me the first time we met, 'Fidel, the big time is over for Archie Alvarado, but send me to the cane fields, give me a machete and I'll prove that Alvarado has enough arm left to do something for Cuba.' A hero, this Achilles 'Archie' Alvarado, but they sent him back to us a broken-down, used-up pinch hitter with no eye, no arm, and no speed.

"'Achilles, Archie,' I said, 'the Revolution was not made for Chisox, Bosox, Bengals, and Birds. We didn't take Habana for chicos and ricos. Cuba Libre doesn't give a flying fuck for RBIs. The clutch hit is every minute here, baby brother. Cuba loves you for your Cuban heart. I'll make you a colonel, a starter in the only game that counts. Your batting average will be counted in lives saved, in people educated, fed, and protected from capitalist exploitation.'"

"Cut the shit, Fidel," Zloto said. "I'm here because Archie will be eligible for his pension in September. He'll pull in a thousand a month for the rest of his days. That'll buy a lot of bananas down here, won't it?

"You may think that you understand Alvarado, Fidel, but I knew the man for eight years, roomed with him on the Chisox and the Bosox. I've seen him high, seen him in slumps you wouldn't believe. I've seen him in the dugout after being picked off first in a crucial situation. You wouldn't know what that's like, Castro. I'm talking about a man who has just met a fast ball and stroked it over the infield. He has made the wide turn at first and watched the resin of his footprint settle around the bag. He has thrown off the batting helmet and pulled the soft, long-billed cap from his hip pocket. The coach has slapped his ass and twenty, thirty, maybe forty thousand Chisox fans start stomping their feet while the organ plays 'Charge,' and then he is picked off in a flash, caught scratching his crotch a foot from the bag. And it's all over. You hear eighty thousand feet stomping. The first baseman snickers behind his glove; even the ump smiles. I've seen Alvarado at times like that cry like a baby. He'd throw a towel over his head and say, 'Zloto, I'm a no-good dummy. Good hit and no head. We coulda won it all here in the top of the ninth. The Yankee pitcher is good for shit. My dumb-ass move ruined the Chisox chances.' He would sit in front of his locker taking it real hard until the GM or even Chuck Comiskey himself would come down and say, 'Archie, it's just one game that you blew with a dumb move. We're still in it, still in the thick of the race. You'll help these Sox plenty during the rest of the year. Now take your shower and get your ass over to a Mexican restaurant.' The Alvarado that I knew, Castro, that Alvarado could come back the next afternoon, sometimes the next inning, and change the complexion of a game."

Fidel laughed and lit a cigar. "Zloto, you've been away too long. The Archie you knew, this man went out of style with saddle shoes and hula-hoops. Since the days you're talking about when Alvarado cried over a pick-off play, since then Che and Muniz are dead and two Kennedys assassinated. There have been wars in the Far East and Middle East and in Bangladesh. There have been campus shootings, a revolution of the Red Guard, an ouster of Khrushchev, a fascist massacre in Indonesia, two revolutions in Uruguay, fourteen additions to the U.N. There has been détente and Watergate and a Washington-Peking understanding and where have you been, Zloto? You've been in Tucson, Arizona, reading the newspaper on Sunday and cleaning teeth. Even dental techniques have changed. Look at your flourides and your gum brushing method."

"All right, boys," Mrs. Alvarado said, "enough is enough. What are we going to prove anyway by reminiscing about the good old days? Zloto means well. He came here as a friend. Twelve grand a year for life is not small potatoes to Archie and me. In the Windy City or in Beantown we could live in a nice integrated neighborhood on that kind of money and pick up a little extra by giving autographs at Chevy dealerships. Fidel, you know that Archie always wanted to stay in the game. In one interview he told Bill Fuller of the *Sun-Times* that he wanted to manage the Chisox someday. They didn't want any black Cuban managers in the

American League, not then. But, like you say, Fidel, a lot of water has gone under the bridge since those last days when Archie was catching slivers for the Bosox, Chisox, and Birds. These days, there might even be some kind of front-office job to round off that pension. Who knows, it might be more than he made twenty years ago when he led the league in RBIs."

Castro said, "Estelle, apart from all ideological arguments, you are just dreaming. Achilles was never a U.S. citizen. After a dozen years as one of Castro's colonels, do you really think Uncle Sam is going to say, 'C'mon up here, Archie, take a front-office job and rake in the cash'? Do you really think America works that way, Estelle? I know Zloto thinks that, but you've been down here all this time, don't you understand capitalist exploitation by now?"

Estelle said, "Fidel, I'm not saying that we are going to give up the ideals of the Revolution and I'm not deluded by the easy capitalist life. I am thinking about only getting what's coming to us. Alvarado put in the time, he should get the pension."

"That's the whole reason I took a week off to come down here," Zloto said. "The commissioner called me up—he heard we were buddies—and said, 'Zloto, you might be in a position to do your old friend Alvarado some good, that is if you're willing to travel.' The commissioner absolutely guaranteed that Archie would get his pension if he came back up and established residence. The commissioner of baseball is not about to start mailing monthly checks through the Swiss embassy, and I don't blame him. The commissioner is not even saying you have to stay permanently in the U.S. He is just saying, 'Come up, get an apartment, make a few guest appearances, an interview or two, and then do whatever the hell you want."

Fidel said, "Yes, go up to America and tell them how mean Fidel is, how bad the sugar crop was, and how poor and hungry we Cubans are. Tell them what they want to hear and they'll pension you off. The Achilles I know would swallow poison before he'd kowtow to the memory of John Foster Dulles that way. They sent an Archie back home, but Cuba Libre reminded him he was really an Achilles."

"Fidel, let's not get sentimental," Mrs. Alvarado said. "Let's talk turkey. We want the twelve grand a year, right?"

"Right, but only because it is the fruit of Achilles' own labor."

"OK, in order to get the money we have to go back."

"I could take it up in the United Nations, I could put the pressure on. Kissinger is very shaky in Latin America. He knows we all know that he doesn't give a fuck about any country except Venezuela. I could do it through Waldheim, and nobody would have to know. Then we could threaten to go public if they hold out on what's coming to him."

Zloto said, "America doesn't hold out on anybody, Castro. Ask Joe Stalin's daughter, if you don't believe me. You guys are batting your heads against the wall by hating us. There's nothing to hate. We want a square deal for everyone. In this case, too. As for Kissinger, he might carry some weight with the Arabs, but the commissioner of baseball cannot be pressured. That damned fool Alvarado should have become a citizen while he was playing in the States. I didn't know he wasn't a citizen. It was just crazy not to become one. Every other Latin does."

"But our Achilles, he was always different," Castro said. "He always knew that the Chisox, Bosox, Birds, and Braves didn't own the real thing. The real Achilles Alvarado was in Camagüey with me, in Bolivia with Che, with Mao on the Long March."

"The real Achilles was just too lazy to do things right," Mrs. Alvarado said. "He didn't want to fill out complicated papers, so he stayed an alien. As long as he had a job, it didn't matter."

"Zloto," Fidel said, "you one-time Rookie of the Year, now a fat, tooth-cleaning capitalist, you want to settle this the way Achilles would settle this? I mean why should we bring in Kissinger and Waldheim and everyone else? I say if a man believes in the Revolution, what's a pension to him? You think I couldn't have been a Wall Street lawyer? And what about our Doctor Che? You don't think he would have made a big pension in the AMA? I say our Achilles has recovered his Cuban manhood. He won't want to go back. Estelle does not speak for him."

"Fidel is right," she said, "I do not speak for Archie Alvarado, I only write his English for him."

"If Estelle wants to go back and be exploited, let her go. Do you want those television announcers calling you Mrs. Archie again as if you had stepped from the squares of a comic strip? does the wife of a colonel in the Cuban Army sound like a comic-strip girl to you, Zloto?"

"Fidel," Estelle said, "don't forget the issue is not so large. Only a trip to the Windy City or Beantown, maybe less than two weeks in all."

"You are forgetting," Fidel said, "what happened to Kid Gavilan when he went back to see an eye surgeon in New York. They put his picture in *Sepia* and in the *National Enquirer,* the news services showed him with his bulging eye being hugged by a smooth-faced Sugar Ray Robinson. They wanted it to seem like this: here are two retired Negro fighters. One is a tap dancer in Las Vegas, the other has for ten years been working in the cane fields of Castro's Cuba. Look at how healthy the American Negro is. His teeth are white as ever, his step lithe in Stetson shoes, while our Kid Gavilan, once of the bolo punch that decked all welterweights, our Kid stumbles through the clinics of New York in worker's boots and his eye bulges from the excesses of the Revolution. They degraded the Kid and the Revolution and they sent him home with a red, white, and blue eye patch. That's how they treated Kid Gavilan, and they'll do the same to Achilles Alvarado."

"Well, goddamn," Zloto said, "I've had enough talk. I want to see Alvarado; whether he wants to do it is up to him."

"That," Castro said, "is typical bourgeois thinking. You would alienate the man from his fellows, let him think that his decision is personal and lonely, that it represents only the whims of an Alvarado and does not speak for the larger aspirations of all Cubans, and all exploited peoples. The wants of an Alvarado are the wants of the people. He is not a Richard Nixon to hide out in Camp David surrounded by bodyguards while generals all over the world are ready to press the buttons of annihilation."

"No more bullshit, I want to see Alvarado."

Estelle said, "He is in Oriente Province on maneuvers with the army. He will be gone for . . . for how long, Fidel?"

"Achilles Alvarado's unit is scheduled for six months in Oriente. I could bring him back to see you, Zloto, but we don't operate that way. A man's duty to his country comes before all else."

"Then I'm going up to see him and deliver the commissioner's letter. I don't trust anybody else around here to do it for me."

"We'll all go," Fidel said. "In Cuba Libre, no man goes it alone."


## II

### On Maneuvers in Oriente Province

The Ninth Infantry Unit of the Cuban Army is on spring maneuvers. Oriente is lush and hilly. There are villages every few miles in which happy farmers drink dark beer brewed with local hops. The Ninth Army bivouacs all over the province and assembles each morning at six A.M. to the sound of the bugle. The soldiers eat a leisurely breakfast and plan the next day's march. By two P.M., they are set up somewhere and ready for an afternoon of recreation. Colonel Alvarado is the only member of the Ninth Infantry with major-league experience, but there are a few older men who have played professional baseball in the minor leagues. Because there is no adequate protective equipment, army regulations prohibit hardball, but the Ninth Infantry plays fast pitch softball, which is almost as grueling.

When Fidel, Zloto, and Estelle drive up to the Ninth Army's makeshift diamond, it is the seventh inning of a four–four game between the Reds and Whites. A former pitcher from Iowa City in the Three I League is on the mound for the Reds. Colonel Alvarado, without faceguard or chest protector, is the umpire behind the plate. His head, as in the old days, seems extremely vulnerable as it bobs behind the waving bat just inches from the arc of a powerful swing. He counts on luck and fast reflexes to save him from foul tips that could crush his adam's apple.

When the jeep pulls up, Reds and Whites come to immediate attention, then raise their caps in an "Olè" for Fidel.

"These are liberated men, Zloto. The army does not own their lives. When their duties are completed they can do as they wish. We have no bedchecks, no passes, nobody is AWOL. If a man has a reason to leave, he tells his officer and leaves. With us, it is an honor to be a soldier."

When Zloto spots Alvarado behind the plate, he runs toward him and hugs his old friend. He rubs Alvarado's woolly black head with his oversize hands. Estelle is next to embrace her husband, a short businesslike kiss, and then Fidel embraces the umpire as enthusiastically as Zloto did. An army photographer catches the look of the umpire surprised by embraces from an old friend, a wife, and a Prime Minister in the seventh inning of a close game.

"Men of the Revolution." Fidel has advanced to the pitcher's mound, the highest ground. The congregated Reds and Whites gather around the makeshift infield. "Men of the Revolution, we are gathered here to test the resolve of your umpire, Colonel Alvarado. The Revolution is tested in many ways. This time it is the usual thing, the capitalist lure of money. Yet it is no simple issue. It is money that rightfully belongs to Colonel Alvarado, but they would degrade him by forcing him to claim it. To come there, so that the capitalist press can say, 'Look what the Revolution has done to one of the stars of the fifties. Look at his stooped, arthritic back, his gnarled hands, from years in the cane fields.' They never cared about his inadequate English when they used him, but now they will laugh at his accent and his paltry vocabulary. When they ask him about Cuba, he will stumble and they will deride us all with the smiles of their golden teeth.

"The commissioner of baseball has sent us this behemoth, the Polish-American veteran of eleven campaigns in the American League, Victor Zloto, who some of you may remember as Rookie of the Year in 1945. This Zloto is not an evil man, he is only a capitalist tool. They use his friendship for the colonel as a bait. Zloto speaks for free enterprise. He has two cars, a boat, and his own home. His province is represented by their hero of the right, Barry Goldwater, who wanted to bomb Hanoi to pieces. Zloto wants the colonel to come back, to go through the necessary charade to claim his rightful pension and then return to us if he wishes. Mrs. Alvarado shares this view. I say no Cuban man should become a pawn for even one hour."

"What does the colonel say?" someone yells from the infield. "Does the colonel want to go back?"

The umpire is standing behind Castro. He is holding his wife's hand while Zloto's long arm encircles both of them. Castro turns to his colonel. "What do you say, Achilles Alvarado?"

Zloto says, "It's twelve grand a year, Archie, and all you have to do is show up just once. If you want to stay, you can. I know you don't like being a two-bit umpire and colonel down here. I know you don't give a shit about revolutions and things like that."

Castro says, "The colonel is thinking about his long career with the Chisox, Bosox, Tribe, and Birds. He is thinking about his four fractured skulls.

He justifiably wants that pension. And I, his Prime Minister and his friend, I want him to have that pension, too. Believe me, soldiers, I want this long-suffering victim of exploitation to recover a small part of what they owe to him and to all victims of racism and oppression."

Colonel Alvarado grips tightly his wife's small hand. He looks down and kicks up clouds of dust with his army boots. He is silent. Zloto says, "It's not fair to do this, Castro. You damn well know it. You get him up here in front of the army and make a speech so it will look like he's a traitor if he puts in his pension claim. You staged all this because you are afraid that in a fair choice, Archie would listen to reason just like Estelle did. You can bet that I'm going to tell the commissioner how you put Archie on the spot out here. I'm going to tell him that Archie is a softball umpire. This is worse than Joe Louis being a wrestling referee."

"Think fast, Yankee," one of the ballplayers yells as he lobs a softball at Zloto's perspiring face. The big first baseman's hand closes over the ball as if it were a large mushroom. He tosses it to Castro. "I wish we could play it out, Fidel, just you and I, like a world series or a one-on-one basketball game. I wish all political stuff could work out like baseball with everybody where they belong at the end of the season and only one champion of the world."

"Of course, you would like that, Zloto, so long as you Yankee capitalists were the champions."

"The best team would win. If you have the material and the management, you win; it's that simple."

"Not as simple as you are, Zloto. But why should we stand here and argue political philosophy? We are interrupting a game, no? You have accused Fidel of not giving Alvarado a fair opportunity. I will do this with you, Zloto, if Achilles agrees, I will do this. Fidel will pitch to you. If you get a clean hit, you can take Alvarado back on the first plane. If not, Alvarado stays. It will be more than fair. This gives you a great advantage. A former big-leaguer against an out-of-shape Prime Minister. My best pitch should be cake for you. You can go back and tell the commissioner that you got a hit off Castro. Barry Goldwater will kiss your fingertips for that."

Zloto smiles. "You're on, Castro, if it's okay with Archie and Estelle." Colonel Alvarado still eyes the soft dirt; he shrugs his shoulders. Castro says, "Do you think this is a just experience for you, Achilles Alvarado? This is like a medieval tournament, with you as the prize. This smacks of capitalism. But this once, Fidel will do it if you agree that your fate shall be so decided."

"What's all this about fate and justice," Estelle says. She takes the ball from Castro. "Archie had eleven brothers and sisters and hardly a good meal until he came up to the Chisox. He cracked his wrist in an all-star game and that cost him maybe four or five years in the big leagues because the bones didn't heal right. It's a mean, impersonal world with everything always up for grabs. Alvarado knows it, and he accepts it. He is a religious man." She throws the ball to her Prime Minister. "Get it over with."

The teams take their places, with Castro replacing the Three I League pitcher. Zloto removes his jacket, shirt, and necktie. He is six five and weighs over 250. His chest hairs are gray, but he swings three bats smoothly in a windmill motion as he loosens his muscles. Castro warms up with the catcher. The Prime Minister has a surprisingly good motion, more sidearm than underhand. The ball comes in and sinks to a right-handed batter like Zloto. Colonel Alvarado takes his place behind home plate, which is a large army canteen.

"Achilles Alvarado," says Castro, "you wish to be the umpire in this contest?"

"Why not?" Zloto says. "It's his pension, let him call the balls and strikes. If it's a walk or an error, we'll take it over. Otherwise, a hit I win, an out you win."

"Play ball!" the umpire says. Castro winds up twice, and his first pitch is so far outside that the catcher diving across the plate cannot even lay his glove on the ball. Fidel stamps his foot.

"Ball one," says the umpire.

The infield is alive with chatter: "The old dark one, Fidel," they are yelling. "Relax, pitcher, this ox is an easy out, he can't see your stuff, there's eight of us behind you, Fidel, let him hit."

Zloto grins at the Prime Minister. "Put it down the middle, Mr. Pink, I dare you."

Fidel winds and delivers. Zloto's big hands swing the bat so fast that the catcher doesn't have a chance to blink. He has connected and the ball soars a hundred feet over the head of the left fielder who watches with astonishment the descending arc of the power-driven ball.

"Foul ball," says the umpire, eyeing the stretched clothesline which ended far short of where Zloto's fly ball dropped.

The power hitter grins again. "When I straighten one out, Castro, I'm gonna hit it clear out of Cuba. I never played in a little country before."

Castro removes his green army cap and runs his stubby fingers through his hair. He turns his back to the batter and looks toward his outfield. With a tired motion he orders his center fielder to move toward left center, then he signals all three outfielders to move deeper. Estelle Alvarado stands in foul territory down the first-base line, almost in the spot of her complimentary box seat at the Chisox home games.

Zloto is measuring the outside corner of the canteen with a calm, deliberate swing. He does not take his eyes off the pitcher. Castro winds and delivers another wild one, high and inside. Zloto leans away but the ball nicks his bat and dribbles into foul territory, where Estelle picks it up and throws it back to Castro.

"One ball, two strikes," says the umpire.

"Lucky again, Castro," the batter calls out, "but it only takes one, that's all I need from you."

The Prime Minister and the aging Rookie of the Year eye one another across the sixty feet from mound to plate. Castro rubs the imagined gloss from the ball and pulls at his army socks. With the tip of a thin Cuban softball bat, Zloto knocks the dirt from the soles of his Florsheim shoes. The infielders have grown silent. Castro looks again at his outfield and behind it at the green and gentle hills of Oriente Province. He winds and delivers a low fast ball.

"Strike three," says the umpire. Zloto keeps his bat cocked. Estelle Alvarado rushes to her husband. She is crying hysterically. Fidel runs in at top speed to embrace both Alvarados at home plate. Zloto drops the bat, "It was a fair call, Archie," he says to the umpire. "I got caught looking."

"Like Uncle Sam," Castro says, as the soldiers stream in yelling, "Fidel, Fidel, the strikeout artist." Castro waves his arms for silence.

"Not Fidel, men, but Achilles Alvarado, a hero of the Cuban people. A light for the Third World."

"Third World for Alvarado. Third strike for Zloto," an infielder shouts, as the Ninth Army raises Fidel, Achilles, and Estelle to their shoulders in a joyful march down the first-base line. The Prime Minister, the umpire, and the lady gleam in the sun like captured weapons.

Zloto has put on his shirt and tie. He looks now like a businessman, tired after a long day at a convention. Fidel is jubilant among his men. The umpire tips his cap to the army and calms his wife still tearful atop the bobbing shoulders of the Cuban Ninth.

"Alvarado," Estelle says, "you honest ump, you Latin patriot, you veteran of many a clutch situation. Are you happy, you fractured skull?"

"Actually," Alvarado whispers in her ear, "the pitch was a little inside. But what the hell, it's only a game."

# ROB BREZSNY

## Qabalistic Sex*Magick
## for Shortstops and Second Basemen
## (*excerpts*)

As a child I was a boy but I thought I was a girl too. I thought I was the two of us, growing up together, taking turns creating each other. The night was my dream of her and the day was her dream of me. We used the same baby, shared the eros of a single zygote, split apart so that one was miasma and the other prophecy, one mammal and the other archetype, one beast and the other angel.

I suffered as the boy in the body. Day was shadow, my time apart from her. At night I celebrated dissolution, ritually offering sacrifice to our reunion. Before falling to sleep I gave her my orgasms, the day's accumulated psychic energy—blankets pulled over my face and kleenex stuffed in my ears to shut out all sensations from the outside world, a ring of stuffed animals encircling the bed and sealing the sanctified space.

My guardian and guide into dreams was a big totem-body borrowed from the chief of the stuffed animals, Tony the (Detroit) Tiger. Dressed in his baseball uniform, Tony lay always on my pillow directly to the left of my head. He gave way to the map of a gargantuan tiger-crocodile through which I entered my double dream-body.

In some of my more self-conscious day-dreams I resurrected my favorite map-veils from the land of sleep and built them into a buffer-body between my vulnerable flesh and the external world. I was gradually able to sneak my dream-girl into this body, so that in time we were inseparable. She came to inhabit roughly the same space as the body of flesh but jutted out a little beyond the skin. She felt like a halo, holding me in suspension and making me permanently dizzy.

I felt her but never really *saw* her during the day. She never gave me a face and figure to visualize. And at night she was too maniacal and hydra-headed ever to remain very long in one name and shape.

So I contacted and communed with her by evoking the sensation of MAP-ness. Two maps in particular came to serve as my entrance to her world, by day or by night.

The first map is the more ancient. In later years it has been radically transmuted. The second map was originally formulated to be more versatile and universal than the first map, a means to a more thorough exploration of the world of my dream-girl. But ironically, when it finally came into full use, I lost her entirely.

MAP #2

A totem of the Tiger-Crocodile Body: a porously-woven gem engraved with the complete geo-anatomical image of the Baseball Diamond.

The MAP began always as an abstract insinuation. It had to be re-invoked each time it was used.

The Call was made:

A geometric ghost of Earth-light irradiated the Eye-Gland, discharging a shivering, rarified hissing. Coiling and uncoiling like a Breather, the vibration formed a vaporous sarcoma. Dry, husky veins materialized within, diagramming the skeletal magnetic fields of disembodied WORDS.

The WORDS coagulated, began to bleed Barbarous Names, and the diagram collapsed into a sea of chthonic lights, an infernal bath roiling with the black glowing chromosomes of exfoliated homunculi.

A yeasty Vampire-King steamed forth from the multitudes and breathed an instant condensation:

The mature MAP, a docile and adamantine Diamond Germ, a brilliant Star Granulated Kernel glutted with iridescent cartoons of sacrosanct baseball games.

It was then infinitely elastic and could assume any size, according to the desired destination.

It bubbled to the size of solar system and enacted baseball myths with the planets as heroes.

It blanketed the Earth and depicted the crystal lattice-work of the sacred planetary anatomy.

It contracted to cellular size and portrayed baseball-idylls among the nuclear chromatins.

On June 23, 1956 I discovered the sacred world of the ancestors at a game between the Tigers and the Boston Red Sox. Until then I had practiced my magics with greedy secrecy. I had not guessed that others before me had shared the Silence and had even evolved ceremonies to enter it at will.

My father had decided to take me to my first major league game on the occasion of my sixth birthday. We arrived at Briggs Stadium at twilight.

We entered the outer shell of the stadium and made our way towards our seats in the reserved section behind third base. When I first glimpsed the field my uncensored impulse was that I was looking at a "dream-window," a compact, rarified area that I had often watched intrude into my dreams and suck into itself all the seemingly-flimsier material around it.

In fact, I was looking at the field through a concrete doorway opening onto the grandstand. As we stepped across the threshold I was stricken with the overpowering sense of HOLY. A dome of gauzy vibration surrounded the field and bound it in a deeper, denser dimension. Inside, the pristine emerald green of the field emanated an ethereal violet haze. The players themselves were dressed in purest white. I could see shimmering shrouds of light around their bodies. They warmed up for the game with an utter self-possession that I had never before witnessed. They were standing in sacred space.

It was years later, after I had begun to investigate the occult, that I realized the baseball field is a near-perfect analogy of the Tree of Life, the conventional meditation glyph of the Qabalah . . . . .

I regard it as no coincidence that the arrangement of positions of the baseball field corresponds so closely to the alignment of the sephiroth on the Tree of Life. I now perform, with the air of the Tree of Life, some of the same imaginative exercises which I once practised using the baseball field map. But I have not completely abandoned the original map, merely incorporated it into a very personalized version of the Tree of Life.

I probably would have become violently insane had I not received my first (disguised) initiation into the Qabalistic-Baseball System of Meditation around this time. It was my salvation. With it I began to be able to control and channel the incredible sexual exchanges for which I had become the focus.

It happened during the spring of fourth grade. I was acknowledged to be the best baseball player around, so I was called upon to manage the baseball team representing our class in a tournament against the other classes. For this special tournament, school rules required that at least three girls be included in each starting line-up. The other boys in the class thought this a stupid, emasculating rule. But I saw it as a sexual opportunity, a thrilling new element to be used in my alchemical dramas . . . . .

There was no hierarchy of baseball talent among the fourth grade girls of Sudman School, Allen Park, Michigan in 1960, so I could without guilt choose my three favorites, the three sexiest girls in the class, Gail Musa, Patti McQueen and Nancy Lebenta. I immediately began to include them intimately in my orgiastic pre-sleep rituals. My dream-girl began exclusively to portray herself with their faces. As the experiments proceeded, though, Gail Musa's dark, sultry, Venusian face prevailed, dominating my fantasies and giving my dream-girl a definite and specific form she had not previously had. . . .

The erotic *Qabalistic* experiments began when I installed Gail within the nerve nexus of SECOND BASE in my baseball field map and abandoned my phantom dream-lover. It is the story of my initiation into the mysteries of NETZACH, the Qabalistic equivalent of SECOND BASE.

As central ganglion of SECOND BASE, Gail became Queen of NETZACH and received all the attendant powers, privileges, and responsibilities. She organized my training for initiation around an investigation of the terrain between SHORTSTOP and SECOND BASE.

This area I later recognized to be Twenty-Seventh Path on the Tree of Life: Connecting NETZACH and HOD (the eighth sephirah, or SHORTSTOP) and ruled by the sixteenth card of the traditional Tarot deck, the Tower, card of the planet Mars. Within the environs of this path she aided me in learning how to regulate and control the unbalanced debilitating forces that were deposited in me through the Totem and Radio: the Toy Witch dimension of the baseball field map.

At the core of our work was the rite of *congressus subtilis,* or sexual union with a non-material entity. Even though Gail was at home in her own bed and I in mine, I was able to fertilize her astral body with my astral seed and conceive with her a brood of elemental children. And so together we broke down the haunting love-death of the elementals into names and forms and birthed them in our own image. Where before they had bedeviled me to the verge of criminal insanity, they now became my willing servants. With them at my command I was then formally initiated into the mysteries of NETZACH by Gail, the Queen of that sephirah.

I have been prepared for the use of Qabalistic magick since my youth. The baseball field map served as the surrogate system, building in my aura a vivid image of the archetype of the Tree of Life. In fact, baseball provided a more effective program for the work than a formal course in the Qabalah.

If astral structures are to become potent talismans, they must be nourished with the stuff of personal emotional associations. The abstruse theorems contained in the Qabalistic texts would not have roused my imagination to crystalize a miniature Tree of Life in my aura.

And would my mother have allowed the revolutionary teachings of the Qabalah to reach me had they been offered in the weird occult tongues of the Angels and Archangels? Would she have invited trance-intoxicated wizards into her house to teach her son to meditate upon the example of Aleister Crowley? Of course not. To be indoctrinated by the Great American Game was the perfect subterfuge:

BASEBALL IS THE MODEL FOR THE
GUERRILLA MEDITATION TECHNIQUES
OF MODERN AMERICAN QABALISTIC
MAGICK.

The following is a description of a dream-artifact. It appeared on February 29, 1972, four hours before I boarded a plane in London to depart for New York after a six-months' stay in Europe.

I was one of the extra-terrestrial guides of the planet Earth, a Martian member of the Great White Brotherhood of the Solar System come to protect and preserve the realm of the Old Gods, the beings which *homo sapiens* had displaced and banished to the secret places of the planet.

I could not actively intercede and nullify the oppressive politics of the ruling species, and so I erected a Gargantuan Bubble—a dazzling musical globe—where I took representative members of the Old Gods, like a latter-day Noah. I kept them inside in a kind of suspended animation: Until the day when the human civilization would disappear.

The elves and the dwarves, the nymphs and the fauns and the satyrs, the sylphs and undines, the griffins, the sphinxes, the centaurs, the titans, the muses . . .

From each I extracted and memorized the essential genetic information.

Eons passed. I waited for a sign.

When the Magic Baseball Game began I knew it was time for the Old Gods to be released and returned to Earth.

The little statues and idols in which they had been trapped for so long shivered and squealed. Slowly and inexorably they took their places over the vast baseball diamond spread across the inside of the great Bubble.

I strode to the pitcher's mound and checked my fielders. My beloved griffins, patina-encrusted, fidgeted near Third Base. The Great God Pan squatted behind Home Plate. A small host of sphinxes hovered over my head. At Second Base was my sultry Venusian Hetaira, Gail Musa. And at Shortstop, a winged, mercurial salamander with the face of my singer-hero David Bowie.

We began our lethal incantation, led by the strident voices of the griffins:

> Lithosphere on Fire
> Lucifer's Desire
> Lithosphere on Fire
> Lucifer's Desire . . .

And from an infinitesimal prick at the very Crown of the Bubble appeared a race of Reptile Men adorned with cartilaginous diamond crests and riding black winged horses.

I grasped the magic baseball in my right hand and raised it high over my head.

All together we bellowed the materialization of Fire. I threw the ball straight up.

As it fell it broke into a multitude of miniscule Earths. Our Reptile Men and their steeds rushed to envelope them, then with a burst of Black Fire extinguished every one.

The Old Gods blinked out, reassembled outside the Bubble, and went forth once again to populate the planet.

At the time of the dream I had not yet discovered that BASE-BALL=QABALAH. But three years later when Mercury appeared to me again in the shape of David Bowie, this time mixed with Philadelphia Phillies Shortstop Larry Bowa, I finally guessed.

There were two dream-visitations in June of 1975. In each, Bowie-Bowa led me underground, as Mercury often does, through a labyrinth of shadowy rooms and halls. This was the catacombs of his immense domed vehicle, which was a kind of flying saucer with the guts of a baseball stadium. It was an appropriate home for the image-flesh that he had borrowed.

In the visitation of June 2, 1975, he led me into a dark and dank room, empty except for a television. There I watched a show exhibiting the "latest styles in Tarot-card images," which were modeled by a series of undulating boxes that resembled the 1957 baseball cards. The "modern" images were predominately weird, shimmering portraits of the players of the 1957 Detroit Tigers, my all-time favorite team—including Al Kaline, Charlie Maxwell, Frank Lary, Jim Bunning, and Harvey Kuenn.

The outlines of the faces and the shapes of the features remained relatively fixed but the color of the skin pulsed rhythmically with iridescent greens and protoplasmic purples, and tiny phosphorescent explosions flickered from all the orifices. Clusters of eggs and worm-like jewels writhed around the boundaries of the faces, sometimes penetrated the skin and disappeared.

I thought the cards looked like little televisions themselves, and for a moment—imagining "television within a television"—I felt the familiar maddening sensation of "map of a map of a map of a . . ."

I re-experienced all the thrills I felt when I first discovered baseball cards, relived the satisfaction of studying the records and vital statistics, memorizing the faces, sorting the cards according to various systems of classification (by teams, by position, by age, by how much I liked them), and inventing card games using only my favorite cards.

Accompanying these feelings was a rush of a different kind of familiarity, emotions that also felt like memories but more compacted. I found no way to describe this to myself later except to say that the portraits on the cards reminded me of the noble faces used to illustrate the virtues in old physiognomy textbooks. The crude blank look of modern profane man was conspicuously absent.

Yet they were the same faces I had preserved so vividly in my inner eye for more than fifteen years. Centerfielder Bill Tuttle still had that hazy, evasive Cancerian look (born under the sign of the Crab). Frank Lary had the fixed, bulldog jaw; though the pupils of his eyes were so contracted that he appeared to be in a trance. Duke Maas had the characteristic cleft in his chin. Reno Bertoia was the passionate, temperamental adolescent Italian. Al Kaline looked like my father as I imagined my father looked when I was born.

At the bottom of Harvey Kuenn's card was a signature—"Huysmans." It made sense if Huysmans was the creator of these cards, I thought, since he painted medieval scenes. I was confusing and combining the decadent French author of *Against the Grain* with the modern scholar who wrote *The Waning of the Middle Ages*.

Charlie "Paw Paw" Maxwell flowed across the screen three times, the only card to appear more than once. The third time he showed I transfixed him on the screen with an act of dream-will. I wanted to examine him in detail and report back to my brother Tom. Maxwell and Tom are both left-handers and when I was young they together embodied my archetype of left-handedness. Moreover, Maxwell was Tom's favorite player, the Young-Father image equivalent to my Al Kaline.

To my surprise Maxwell's position was listed as Second Base. I had never heard of a left-hander playing Second. But then I remembered that Tom had been an All-Star Second Baseman in Little League.

I expected to find Maxwell's batting record on the back of the card. Instead there was an intricate network of red hieroglyphics splayed across a black background. A cartoon from outside the card migrated into the midst of the hieroglyphics and announced that they were the voice-print of the Star Sirius coding instructions for work on the Twenty-Eighth Path. (Between NETZACH and YESOD, the seventh and ninth sephiroth; a reference to the "pathworkings" of the Qabalah.)

I guessed during the dream that the Charlie Maxwell card was the "modern" version of the seventeenth card of the traditional Tarot, The Star. In checking an occult reference book the next day I found that The Star card is in fact the traditional symbol for the Twenty-Eighth Path.

In the next dream-visitation, on the summer solstice of 1975, Mercury escorted me to the heart of the mysteries of Sirius. This time I did not simply observe the cards. I became a co-creator. I intruded into a previously-undifferentiated region of the baseball field map-plasm and designed for it an articulate configuration of sound: a poem-talisman enclosed within the body of my own Tarot card. It gave me access to that part of the map that links the map as a whole to its prototype.

The dream began in the underworld. Bowie-Bowa took me by the hand and led me through smoky glass doors into a lightless crypt reeking of ammonia. I ran my free hand along the wall and felt a fine, damp fur. After a few cautious steps we came upon a row of gnarled sarcophagi which emitted a faint glow. They reminded me of bioluminescent worms. At the foot of the last one, a withered old black woman lay, squirming and stroking herself. She squealed out jumbled clusters of syllables as if speaking in tongues. But in listening closely, I clearly distinguished the words of the English language. In fact she was merely mimicking the standard rap of the Christian fundamentalist preachers. The fit was genuine. But it seemed more like a chemical disturbance or epileptic seizure than a divine communion.

"Through the city of black buzzing." That phrase carried us through a kind of black porous diaper composed of swarming insects. We alit on a broad phosphorescent baseball field in a perfectly flat, horizonless land oppressed by a very low black sky. The sole source of light was the ground.

A game was in progress. We watched from the vicinity of the first base coaching box. It was the last game of the season and it didn't matter much who won. The old veteran Al Kaline was being given as many times at bat as possible since this was his last game before retiring. He was batting in both the lead-off and clean-up positions. The scoreboard gave a summary of his record thus far in the game:

|  | AB | R | H | RBI |
|---|---|---|---|---|
| Choline | 5 | 4 | 1 | 3 |

or was it Chaline? Definitely "Ch" in place of "K". I thought of acetylcholine, the chemical involved in the transmission of nerve impulses.

Then the game was over and another had begun. There was an exogamous feel to this one, the sense of a match-up between two teams that rarely played each other, that were not in the same league—like my favorite teams Detroit and Philadelphia playing in spring training or the World Series.

I was playing Shortstop for Detroit. Though I am right-handed, I was wearing a left-handed glove. Kaline, the player-manager, was in centerfield.

Near the pitcher's mound I found a little glass head or eye, an egg-shaped marble which bore a photographic likeness of my face. As I walked towards Second Base to show it to my girlfriend, a milk-white salamander ran across my path. At first it was almost two-dimensional, no more than a thin, veined membrane. But when I gave chase and tried to catch it, it puffed up into a transparent balloon-like sac and squirted away.

I noticed that I no longer had the marble. It was now suspended like an eye at the center of the salamander-sac. I followed it as it floated towards Third Base. There, standing on the Third Base bag, was Al Kaline. He stopped me and handed me a huge, three-dimensional baseball card in the shape of a cereal box. It was similar to the cards I'd seen on television on June 2.

The name of the player on the card was BERQ QALQAS. He played for the TIBETAN GUERRILLAS. I took "guerrilla" to be a pun on "gorilla" implying that the guerrilla is a more sophisticated and glamorous beast to have as one's totem than the gorilla.

Qalqas looked much like the Reptile Men from the dream of the Old Gods. The cartilaginous diamond crest was set in a skull shaped like an elongated hoof. Face and body were as sleek as a polished gem and black except for the crest. There were no facial features except for slits around the eye area. There was a double set of scaly wings. He was seated, or perhaps attached to, a squat, black winged horse.

On the back-side of the box-card was a diagram representing a pitcher pitching to a catcher. An arrow at the end of a dotted line connected a circle, image of the pitcher's mound, with a similar circle behind an up-side-down pentagram symbolizing home plate. The diagram and its caption:

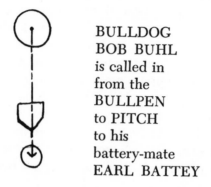

BULLDOG
BOB BUHL
is called in
from the
BULLPEN
to PITCH
to his
battery-mate
EARL BATTEY

Kaline hinted that this card could be used to perform an act of talismanic magick. And that I should "think sexy thoughts and let the astral plane spore (me) for a change." In fact, he suddenly became very funny.

Earl Battey, he said, was like "a scarab crawling from a shitty meditation."

And since "Bob Buhl 'swings both ways,' Graves (Robert Graves, author of *The White Goddess*) wrote him into the script as the poet in the labyrinth." (Ariadne's web or Arianrhod's castle?)

And "Battey is the Salt of the Battery." (sounded like "assault and battery")

And "The Black dog
The black bull
As black as the pitch
In Hecate's Eye"

In second phase of my introduction to MAGICK, Mercury confirmed that the Tree of Life was the prototype of the Baseball field map and that together they would lead me back to MAGIC. He taught me a diabolical lesson: that I should seek the holy in the midst of the most mundane, the spiritual in the midst of the most biological, the universal in the midst of the most personal. He appeared in the dual image of Larry Bowa and David Bowie to demonstrate that I had long known him intimately but never recognized him.

Since I was a child I have believed in Shortstop as the peculiar emotional location of androgynous information. When I play Shortstop, I love to feel myself in my body—sleek, lithe, smooth, graceful, vibrating from the inside in a kind of perpetual sexual excitement. I feel like my body is as feminine as a man's body is permitted to be, yet I don't feel like a woman. I feel anomalous, super-charged, outside the game altogether and yet the focus of the action. I am aggressively confident of my defensive skill. I feel potent in my ability to field, handle, and manipulate the raw force of the batted ball. All the other players are less balanced than I, more completely consumed in one extreme or the other. They look to me as a catalyst and mediator, as the central point of equilibrium around which opposing forces circulate.

Larry Bowa is my prototypical Shortstop—a consistent defensive star since 1970 for my favorite team of later years, the Philadelphia Phillies. Small and light in comparison to his teammates (5'11", 155 pounds), he lacks brute power but is proficient in the subtler offensive skills. In the field he is impeccably accurate, agile, fleet-footed, rangy, graceful.

For years I have played with the imagination of David Bowie as androgynous extra-terrestrial messenger from the stellar gods, using rock and roll as his medium. At first I elaborated the outlines of the story he had suggested with his album *Ziggy Stardust and the Spiders from Mars*. But with the appearance of *Diamond Dogs* I began to weave his myth into my own.

In the winter of 1973 I received what I regard as a direct transmission from the Dog-Star Sirius concerning the Star's envoy to Earth, Dionysius, the "Lame God of Light." The entire thirty thousand word message was delivered over a period of three weeks, during which time I remained almost continually in trance. I was not a mature medium—the result was a dense, tangled, unreadable story that I typed up and called "The Revolt of the Lame and the Last Sacred Acts." It became a potent, if weirdly-formulated, talisman which steadily attracted new information concerning the link between Sirius and the Earth. In time I began to identify myself as an extra-terrestrial visitor from Sirius fleshing out the inexpressible Word of Dionysius.

In *Diamond Dogs* I detected the insinuations of the same mysteries revealed in "The Revolt of the Lame . . ." Bowie at once joined my conspiracy of Sirians. I began to attribute to him the same androgynous, homunculian, transvestitic, tricksterian, agathodaimonic, and mercurian qualities which I have imagined myself to possess as extra-terrestrial messenger and which I have vividly sensed while playing Shortstop. I even imagined we were in secret contact via dreams, planning and coordinating future transmissions.

Mercury revealed that he was not different from Larry Bowa and David Bowie. His body had been formed in me from the stuff of my baseball and extra-terrestrial fantasies. I did not, until June of 1975, ever think of calling him by the name "Mercury," nor did I consciously invoke his aid.

Nevertheless he had served as mediator between alchemical husband and alchemical wife, heaven and earth, god and human, celestial father and chthonic mother. I was able to use his peculiar state of consciousness simply by arousing the personal memories and associations which share his nature.

1) From DAATH, the silent sephira, Vision of The Conference of the First Swirlings, Assiatic Division of the Great Magic Baseball Body:

| LEAGUE OF SEVERITY | LEAGUE OF MILDNESS |
|---|---|
| Tibetan Guerrillas | Neptune Egg-Demons |
| Orgone Blue Spankings | Holy Ghost Parasites |
| Chichen Itza Syllabaries | Dionysian Trance- |
| Zen Trans-Biogrammarians | Migrations |
| Black Solar Heat | Samhain Maenads |
| Rememberers | Yezidi Witch-Tricksters |
| Ectoplasma Gland- | Anti-Christ Clowns |
| Mesmerizers | Lunatic Cartoons |
| Quasi-Stellar Punks | |

LEAGUE OF MERCY

Venus Whoremoans
Enochian Dream-Works
Red Bush Succubi
Sphinx Orgasms
Autismeros Ruptured
   Gametes
Akasha Homunculi
Lesbian Clones

2) From the Twenty-Second Path, between Tiphareth and Geburah, Vision of the Line-Up for the Play-Off Game between the Tibetan Guerrillas and the Neptune Egg-Demons:

| TIBETAN GUERRILLAS | NEPTUNE EGG-DEMONS |
|---|---|
| 1. Female Acid of Windows, RF | 1. Microwave Beehive Star, 3B |
| 2. Prakriti Bricoleur, SS | 2. Bombastic Amino, RF |
| 3. Berq Qalqas, CF | 3. Babylon-with-Full-Hands, 2B |
| 4. Reptile Rodeo Man, LF | 4. Wild Rashy Lila, C |
| 5. Nostradamus Impetigo, C | 5. Haploid Pulsar, LF |
| 6. Chesed Guevara, 3B | 6. Nemesis Pimpdragon, SS |
| 7. Aqua Bilge de ma Grotesque, 2B | 7. Chloroplaste Philosophe, 1B |
| 8. Anaerobe Blistercuffs, 1B | 8. Humus Azoth, CF |
| 9. Violet Cloaca-Protein, P | 9. Ark-Brute Witch-Whorl, P |

Below are excerpts from a very simple sample meditation of modern Qabalistic sex-magick. It is reprinted from the pamphlet "Qabalistic Sex-Magick for Shortstops and Second Basemen":

Imagine the diamond to be located on the Martian equator, longitude 32° West . . . Imagine yourself the naked cynocephalic Shortstop running to your left and behind Second Base for a pop-up.

Just as you are about to snare the ball in the web of your glove (which is on your left hand), imagine ramming your erect phallus into the upturned vulva of the Second Baseman, a red-haired woman crouching on all fours. Her number is 7. Her uniform is the gauzy green gown of a priestess of Isis but is pulled back from her haunches to expose her genitals . . .

POSTSCRIPT

Note: Brezsny and Geoff Young met at a party on October 28, 1978, and argued the merits of their respective "heroes." Brezsny said that Larry Bowa had improved his hitting a hundred points since getting his mantra from TM. Young howled a few times in disrespect of that possibility. Then he said that Bucky Dent put that black paint under his eyes because he knew it was going to be bright, and he simply went out and did his job, a good tough southern kid. Russell, on the other hand, blew it entirely. Brezsny agreed in part, but suggested that Dent had vamped (as in vampire) Russell, and that he was in the service of Hecate. He offered Young a mantra; Young refused, so he chanted Bowa's mantra. Then he added that Bowa was taking flying lessons and was going to become the first invisible shortstop. "Can you imagine what that will do to the game?" he asked. Young was totally outraged. He said: "I want my shortstop like Bucky Dent, with his spikes in the good hard ground; you know, like on this plane, none of this mantra bullshit."

## VICTORIA M. RATHBUN

## Three and Two

Your friends call you up with a great idea.
"How about if we pick you up, then go to the
liquor store because you're the only one who looks
old enough to buy booze, then we go pick up the girls?"
You go buy a gallon of Ten High & start to pick up
the girls. After three girls it becomes apparent that
there's no girl for you. You grab one of your friends.
"What happened?" "Well, see, she called up at the last
minute & said she couldn't go because her dog chewed
up her last pair of shoes. Do you want to just go
home?" "Shit no," you say, and wind up in a burger
joint. As you fall asleep ogling the factory girls,
you dream about being the hottest nineteen-year-old
pitcher in the world. Everyone is totally amazed by
your fast ball. When you wake up, you've just been
passed up for the majors because your curve & slider
were unreliable & you walk four consecutive guys.
The manager is shaking you. "You just didn't know
how to mix 'em up," he says.

## *The Nether World Series*

It's high noon in Hell
You're stationed at 2nd base
for the Dead Sox
at Styx River Stadium

The infield's a bottomless pit

You're playing naked,
& every man on the opposite team's

Ty Cobb

# RICHARD GROSSINGER

## Three Repeating Baseball Dreams

I come by a huge train. I know it is a train because I was waiting at the station, but, now that I am riding on it, it seems more like a party spread indefinitely in all directions. The people are going to a ball game uptown. We leave the train, and it is clear that it is the middle of winter. There is snow on the houses, and the stadium is covered with ice. The ramp leading off the train goes directly into the stadium, which turns out to be an indoor arena so large that it simply seems to be summer everywhere. There are baseball fields on every tier, but also lakes and brooks, and a beach leading to the ocean. I try to look down onto the field that is central to my interest, but it lies at the bottom of a deep canyon, and I can see it only as a faint etching in the dirt. It is in my mind's eye (within the dream) that I now see the players in brilliant white uniforms. I see their game from the center, as in a flock of birds, with players moving in all directions, carrying out, collectively, the movements of a whole game, or maybe a whole season, or maybe even all the games ever played. On each tier of the stadium they are going on, hundreds of them, thousands of them, but they are compacted into instants, so the scores appear to go up on computer board (like a changing train schedule) faster than I can keep track of them. Only a second ago it was April, and there was so much promise. Now the season is almost over, and the teams are locked into position. After a while I become frustrated at there being no one game to watch, and I try to leave, but I find myself in an endless series of adjoining underground train platforms, with fans leaving the games covering them so densely that it is a constant crowd.

I am headed toward the World Series, walking in view of the stadium. It is two teams I don't care about, the most invincible in each league. As I begin to enter the crowd, I overhear that one of the teams is unable to play (the reason is unclear, but quite official). The team I was rooting for has been asked to replace them. I can't understand why. Not only did they not finish second, but they finished fifth or sixth, well below the team they are replacing. Now I seem to recall (or understand) the reason why none of the teams above them can play. I approach the stadium with a new sense of excitement as I imagine the players I followed challenging this great opponent, but I am also slightly guilty and feel that I am getting away with something. I want to be excited, but an inner awareness warns me not to be taken in by this change.

I look at the schedule and find that the team I am following is playing a team in the other league (it might be San Diego against the Minnesota Twins, or the New York Mets against the Boston Red Sox). I turn on the game and it is terribly mysterious, like the first games I heard when I was a kid. The whole possibility is unknown. Now I look back over the results of the season and realize that each team has been playing each team in the other league three times, half of them at home and half of them on the road. I review what has happened over the season and I gain a new appreciation of relative relationships. Some relatively unsuccessful team like the Chicago Cubs or the Montreal Expos has beaten the Yankees all three times. The pitching match-ups today are strange, and there is no sense that the game could be on TV. It can be gotten only on an old red radio.

NOTES:
The first dream might be called "The Cumulative Baseball Game." It seems to be using baseball as a metaphor for life—the swiftness and simultaneity of it all as one's age increases. The fact is that whole seasons do, finally, telescope into single images and fragments that cannot be assigned to any season with surety. The same thing happens to those years of our life. We cannot tell second grade from third or fourth grade, and it is unclear what happened in 1952 or 1953. Somewhere inside us the events are discrete and linear, but our experience of our own life is more of an accumulation, a thing that grows and coalesces. In dreams we certainly have access to other moments in our life, which shows that they are still alive *in the present* in our memories. The Cumulative Ballgame is like an encyclopedia of baseball, personal rather than public —just those images that impressed themselves on us and the over-all collective result of the games we watched and the seasons we followed—a much denser and more fulfilling event than any single championship game in any sport because we experience it from within.

Baseball is clearly a cue to memory. We locate years by remembering who won the pennant and then remembering what we were doing at that time. I recently checked out of the library for my nine-year-old son a history of the first eight years of the Mets, and, from reading it, I experienced such rushes of memory, not so much about baseball as about how my life was then, that I was totally disoriented after an hour, and even confused about what house I was living in. The sheer names of players brought back things I had totally forgotten, proving how much is in the fan's association with a player's name. It is locked into the whole set of feelings it occurs alongside. Different names from the fifties each recall slightly different aspects of our own lives then. The Ashburn of ourselves is somewhat different than our Scarborough or Suder. We have a Klippstein and a Temple, a Grim and a Zernial. As we see the names again we realize it is true, that these things not only existed but continue to exist in us.

When the Mets and Colt 45's (now the Astros) were formed, I played a whole season on a spinner game, using the expansion draft rosters plus otherwise acquired players, with the result that people like John De Merit or Bob Botz, who played very little or not at all for the actual Mets, have as strong images for me as some who played the whole season. The 1962 Mets might not have been a good ball team, but the sheer complexity of movement on them (Cook, Daviault, Chiti, Moford, etc.) gave voice to a whole range of feelings about mythological origins. In a sense, it gave very subtle new names, archetypal perhaps, for primary particles, or trickster figures.

The second dream seems to foreshadow divisional play (in which the best team doesn't always appear in the World Series) even as the first dream foreshadows the domed stadium and the last dream foreshadows interleague play. All three dreams began, though, in slightly other forms in my childhood.

The World Series dream points out the arbitrariness of rooting for any one team. Just as one's own team could replace the winning team by some disaster (implied in the dream), so can one's own team be substituted in the imagination during the World Series for a team actually playing. In fact, both teams, all teams, are made up of arbitrarily assigned human beings. Trades and, now, free agencies prove that they are interchangeable. Admittedly Rusty Staub of the Tigers is a different entity than Rusty Staub of the Expos or Astros or Mets, but imagination bridges the gap and makes interesting things of it, just as in the dream it is able to substitute one team for another.

The interleague dream shows how we measure relative values between systems that have never been tested in fact. That is the beauty of the World Series, and the relative depradation of it that interleague play would bring. We not only do not know who will win, but we do not know how our images of the different leagues, in their separate realities, will change as a result of the series of games. Similar things happen of course in wars between nations, migrations of whole peoples, and political and economic crises. The events have not yet occurred, so, no matter what image we have of what could happen, we are left with awaiting the outcome to know what everything that came before meant. The relations of the United States with the different countries of Africa or China are like World Series beween different leagues.

# 15

# When Will You Grow Up?

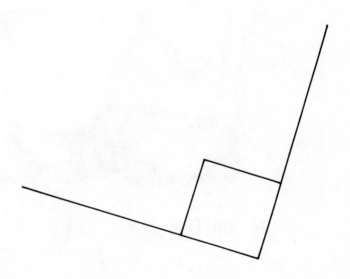

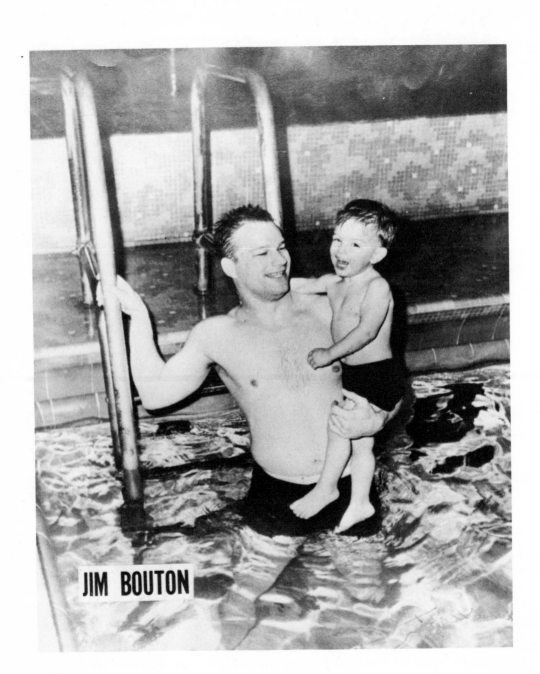

JIM BOUTON

# KEVIN KERRANE

## Screwball

In Huntington, West Virginia, where I went through the motions of grow-ing up, we sometimes called it "stickball"—but its only resemblance to big-city street stickball was the bat, usually a broomstick, and anyway as we got bigger we preferred an old-style softball bat, long and very thin. Among the other alias of screwball were "wall ball," "pitching in," and "one-on-one." The game is, in fact, the best one-on-one version of baseball I've ever found, though it can still be interesting with two on a side.

A rough strike zone is chalked on a wall. The batter stands in and pro-tects it, while the pitcher fires from about fifty feet away—or whatever feels right to the players: the difference of a few feet in pitching distance can alter all the other balances in a game. It's best to use a tennis ball, one with most of the fuzz gone but still with plenty of rabbit. A smooth wall makes a nice catcher, bouncing most balls right back to the pitcher. There are no bases, and all runners are imaginary. If a batter hits a fair ball, its value depends on how far it carries on the fly—past the elm tree for a double, say, and into the street for a triple, across the street for a homer. Cleanly fielded grounders are outs, as automatic as caught flies, provided the pitcher snares them in front of an agreed-upon line.

So screwball is essentially a pitching-hitting game, the only running coming on tough fielding plays. From fifty feet a decent pitcher can bring a tennis ball at what seems to be 80-plus mph, or break off sharp curves and sliders, remembering and imagining as he works. Playing the game at thirty-seven I can occasionally psych myself into feeling that I have bet-ter natural stuff right now than I did half this life ago. Some well-mean-ing people say screwball must be bad for your arm. But a tennis ball's probably too light to do real damage to muscle tissue, even if you throw at top speed. I usually have a good post-game soreness that's all gone within three or four days, in time for another start. —And what, these days, would I be "saving" this arm for anyway? To be more nimble in reaching for the bills in my mailbox?

Hitting offers rich imaginative possibilities too. Standing in against balls that dart like hummingbirds, balls that you can hear as they whoosh past, can simulate batting against the best baseball pitcher you ever faced. And you can train yourself to hang in: getting conked by a tennis ball might sting for a second, but it doesn't produce much fear—and in most versions of the game it doesn't even count as a hit batsman; it's just a "ball." The most unrealistic element is that you can often smack an extra-base hit just by meeting the ball squarely, even if you don't take a full swing. Screwball rewards, and develops, punch hitters with honed reflexes; it also encourages interesting experiments in switch-hitting.

If I used these hand-eye skills to play more tennis, fewer people would think me crazy, or ask with their eyes: "When will you grow up?" But I can't make the break, and I'm grateful to tennis mainly for providing me with game balls for screwball. One way that screwball most resembles tennis is the difficulty of finding the right opponent, one who brings out a sharp but bonded competitive edge in you, who remains earnestly honest about line calls (strike-or-ball when pitching, fair-or-foul when batting), and who isn't a bore to return to reality with after a game. My all-time all-opponent team is Jack Carpenter. Memorable moment: in a crucial situation he works me to a full count, then takes a six foot four power stance and smiles out: "It's down to you and me, turkey." . . .

In West Virginia, North Carolina, New York, and Delaware I've experimented with these rule variations:

* After two strikes, a foul tip into the box is a strikeout.

* When the batter takes a pitch, the box is only a *guide* to the strike zone. Two honest players can usually agree if a breaking pitch that drops into the box was high or inside when it passed the batter.

* With a man on first, a one-hopper back to the pitcher is a double play. No fair letting pop-ups bounce.

* Any fair ball that rolls dead is a hit. (This is especially important when the playing surface is grass instead of playground asphalt.)

Still another wrinkle, learned from my big brother a quarter century ago, is the use of imaginary lineups. The opponents "represent" two major-league teams, perhaps in a final playoff or Series game, and each at-bat is announced as the appropriate player in the order. You bat left-handed for left-handed batters, right for righties; and, though it's allowable to juggle a team's usual lineup, at least three of your nine starters must bat "other-handed," opposite the side you normally hit from.

Baseball is a kids' game played by adults; screwball, as I play it now, is that squared. Adolescent, replete with butch clichés, an ego substitute for pitching semi-pro (which was itself a substitute)—sure, sure, but I pity anyone who simply equates fantasy with regression: in some measure we need it to live, and it's one link to imagination, the play-impulse finally freeing us from mere ego as we improvise roles and create box scores. Richard Grossinger is right: the game, in all its guises, flowers upward toward transcendent possibility and, as body-knowledge, goes down the brain-stem, down the spine, a thick taproot to our hidden selves.

. . . Jack Carpenter stands in as Ted Simmons. Did he say "turkey"? I reach back, Sudden Sam McDowell reaches back, and we strike his ass out on a rising fast ball that sails in on the hands and thwocks into the box as if to rattle the bricks. "Gobble, gobble."

**PHILIP ROTH**

---

## from *Portnoy's Complaint*

So I ran all right, out of the hospital and up to the playground and right out to center field, the position I play for a softball team that wears silky blue-and-gold jackets with the name of the club scrawled in big white felt letters from one shoulder to the other: S E A B E E S, A.C. Thank God for the Seabees A.C.! Thank God for center field! Doctor, you can't imagine how truly glorious it is out there, so alone in all that space . . . Do you know baseball at all? Because center field is like some observation post, a kind of control tower, where you are able to see everything and everyone, to understand what's happening the instant it happens, not only by the sound of the struck bat, but by the spark of movement that goes through the infielders in the first second that the ball comes flying at them; and once it gets beyond them, "It's mine," you call, "it's mine," and then after it you go. For in center field, if you can get to it, it *is* yours. Oh, how unlike my home it is to be in center field, where no one will appropriate unto himself anything that I say is *mine!*

Unfortunately, I was too anxious a hitter to make the high school team —I swung and missed at bad pitches so often during the tryouts for the freshman squad that eventually the ironical coach took me aside and said, "Sonny, are you sure you don't wear glasses?" and then sent me on my way. But did I have form! did I have style! And in my playground softball league, where the ball came in just a little slower and a little bigger, I am the star I dreamed I might become for the whole school. Of course, still in my ardent desire to excel I too frequently swing and miss, but when I connect, it goes great distances, Doctor, it flies over fences and is called a home run. Oh, and there is really nothing in life, nothing at all, that quite compares with that pleasure of rounding second base at a nice slow clip, because there's just no hurry any more, because that ball you've hit has just gone sailing out of sight . . . And I could field, too, and the farther I had to run, the better. "I got it! I got it! I got it!" and tear in toward second, to trap in the webbing of my glove—and barely an inch off the ground—a ball driven hard and low and right down the middle, a base hit, someone thought . . . Or back I go, "*I* got it, *I* got it—" back easily and gracefully toward that wire fence, moving practically in slow motion, and then that delicious DiMaggio sensation of grabbing it like something heaven-sent over one shoulder . . . Or running! turning! leaping! like little Al Gionfriddo—a baseball player, Doctor, who once did a very great thing . . . Or just standing nice and calm—nothing trembling, everything serene—standing there in the sunshine (as though in the middle of an empty field, or passing the time on the street corner), standing without a care in the world in the sunshine, like my king of kings, the Lord my God, The Duke Himself (Snider, Doctor, the name may come up again), standing there as loose and as easy, as happy as I will ever be, just waiting by myself under a high fly ball (*a towering fly ball*, I hear Red Barber say, as he watches from behind his microphone—hit out toward Portnoy; *Alex under it, under it*), just waiting there for the ball to fall into the glove I raise to it, and yup, there it is, *plock*, the third out of the inning (*and Alex gathers it in for out number three, and, folks, here's old C.D. for P. Lorillard and Company*), and then in one motion, while old Connie brings us a message from Old Golds, I start in toward the bench, holding the ball now with the five fingers of my bare left hand, and when I get to the infield—having come down hard with one foot on the bag at second base—I shoot it gently, with just a flick of the wrist, at the opposing team's shortstop as he comes trotting out onto the field, and still without breaking stride, go loping in all the way, shoulders shifting, head hanging, a touch pigeon-toed, my knees coming slowly up and down in an altogether brilliant imitation of The Duke. Oh, the unruffled nonchalance of that game! There's not a movement that I don't know still down in the tissue of my muscles and the joints between my bones. How to bend over to pick up my glove and how to toss it away, how to test the weight of the bat, how to hold it and carry it and swing it around in the on-deck circle, how to raise that bat above my head and flex and loosen my shoulders and my neck before stepping in and planting my two feet exactly where my two feet belong in the batter's box—and how, when I take a called strike (which I have a tendency to do, it balances off nicely swinging at bad pitches), to step out and express, if only through a slight poking with the bat at the ground, just the right amount of exasperation with the powers that be . . . yes, every little detail so thoroughly studied and mastered, that it is simply beyond the realm of possibility for any situation to arise in which I do not know how to move, or where to move, or what to say or leave unsaid . . . And it's true, is it not?—incredible, but apparently true—there are people who feel in life the ease, the self-assurance, the simple and essential affiliation with what is going on, that I used to feel as the center fielder for the Seabees? Because it wasn't, you see, that one was the best center fielder imaginable, only that one knew exactly, and down to the smallest particular, how a center fielder should conduct himself. And there are people like that walking the streets of the U.S. of A.? I ask you, why can't I be one! Why can't I exist now as I existed for the Seabees out there in center field! Oh, to be a center fielder, a center fielder—and nothing more!

# 16

# Season's End

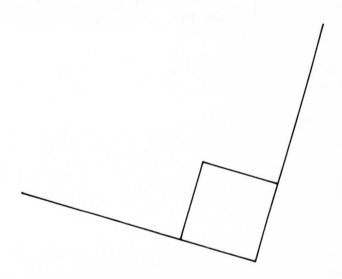

# DANIEL CURLEY

## After the Game Is Over

It is night and the ball park is deserted.
I am running in the dark, telling
each base with my feet like beads,
touching all I missed in the afternoon.
God, my dear, what a mess I made of it.
O for four, and the one time I reached,
thrown out stealing and it wasn't even close.
I made two errors and threw once to the wrong base,
and once the scorer gave a hit out of pure mercy.
Oh, I am going back, breaking my neck in the dark
and touching the bases after the game is over,
touching Susan and Norma and Betty Jo,
throwing out Marjorie at the plate,
and going five for five off everyone
their staff can throw against me.
None of it will appear in the box score,
and the averages will go on down and down,
and next year my contract will not be renewed.
I'll be out in the sticks and then out of the game—
sitting at home, drinking beer, and watching heroes on T.V.

## Baseball Psalm
## *from* The Slag of Creation

After a summer of no baseball at all, the poets from South Londonderry come, rouse me, and I am standing in the outfield with Mørk while Shepherd Ogden, in his West Virginia sweatshirt, name and number on it, hits them out, high and tiny into the sky. I start to do usual baseball warm-ups, but I find myself in a combination of them and t'ai chi, then only t'ai chi. The game comes alive, and I feel speed and breath. I am an animal running. I throw the forever daylight of my biology back. Is this what baseball was? all the time? simply the body? and dancing free and wild? across intermontane flatlands mixed of rocks and mantle beneath the garden and centerfield weeds?

There is no chi involved. But the chi, with its Asian and medicinal lineage, its surety of a life current in a body of veins and arteries, is a clue to the sequence of motions, *baseball isn't neutral either,* not while I'm alive, while I'm scooping, flung beyond myself, glove to the webbing, tumbling as I snag it, the missile of disintegrating time.

This is Vermont and October, and I have never played before. I have never known how big the Indian games were, for the real plains, their bumpiness and scars, and not just the calm village green, how farflung the spaces, the chase of sewn and bound objects, the flow and slink of deer and beaver and weasel, stopped from the pellet center of animal selves. I collide with the ball for the moment it is solid/I am whole, running it out of impossibly blue sky, the few clouds, the sun intense but fallen, the leaves red and ochre, the cold breath of those who have lived into the eleventh month of their thirtieth year. I love the field of play and its realness, its grassness and that it is prairie; I love the ball as a pinpoint, a connection, a sting. There is rhythm and orb and breath and deep awe of sky, whether daylight here of its inner phenomenal splay or night-blazed with our whole history, strung out in eternity, true faces of those who would be our gods. And though the ball is not a planet, and a meteorite only in a lark, it is a sky object for the way it loses itself in the blue and then comes down on the parabola I can measure without a second's thought, that precise occluded moment at which we come together, because I learned to do it, the t'ai chi class a recent memory, the sparrow's tail of what we can yet become.

I want the scar-tissue to open, the fear and desire to mesh, where autumn is more brilliant than left-field, *and* the only spectator, fire in my blood, the imaginary applause of iron, running in my ears, as at twilight Mars sings and a hundred stars appear sultry, subtly, the billion that do not, like the suffusion in liquid/life once was, coacervate warm on the dilute robes of the missing dakini. All these things have to do with baseball, stars and cells and deer and Indians and rough sewn objects to stand for the whole of creation, their worldness, their cosmological completion; don't ask me why; I don't think of it while I'm playing. They make their way into my baseball piece always, by stealth and association; it's a wonder they don't take it over, and leave me frozen and silent, a player on some remote field where the game has either ceased or not yet been invented, because everywhere else I am a historian, a gimp astronomer—there alone am I the magician and the prince.

Mørk says: "When you catch the ball it's like you're catching the whole world," and so opens for me a kind of wonder I have suspected all along, that is greater than my knowledge, and I have fled because it made me a forever child. I lie bare and arms open, before the powers of sky. Did I think I was playing some kind of jock adult game, when I was dancing openly, writing baseball liturgy and myth?

Now it's gone. And I am proud to stand with Shep and his brother Lash, talking shop on the big stone by our house, kicking the autumn leaves. Let the trees like giant men enter into their discourse with the stars. We will stay small, and shy, and imperfect, for we are approximations anyway, and if we are babes, these are our rightful toys.

## A Difference

Something fallen out of the air, some
thing that was breathing there before
stopped: or say it is a difference

felt quickly on turning from one's work
to the window, and seeing there the same
trees the same color, the sky still without clouds,

changed only in reference to the trees
which also seem to have turned away.
The world still external but less distinct

at its center. For a few
seconds. Fall. The centerfielder drifts under
the last fly ball of the summer, and puts it away.

## HOWARD SENZEL

## Baseball and the Cold War (*excerpts*)

At Hebrew school, we used to play a game called Chinese baseball. This consisted of throwing a tennis ball against the back wall behind the Holy Ark. It would rebound into a cinder-topped parking lot of fielders. There were specific delineations for singles, doubles, and triples. Over the cliff was a home run, but there were those who were robbed by death-defying, climbing-down-the-cliff catches.

All base-running and scoring took place only within the minds of the players, but the image was absolutely complete. The reality of the situation was no more than throwing a tennis ball, but this time in company, and that made the experience as total as any big-league game. Despite the limitations, we all had our baseball personalities. The bunter, just trying to get on base, would use position and angle rather than strength, and try to get the ball to fall just over a jutting shed roof. The power hitters would take a long run and shoot for the cliff. All the tactics, strategy, and drama of real baseball, we had off that back wall.

Even as a young child, I knew, from my cousins, about Monopoly, Parcheesi, Clue, and The Great Game of Sorry, but my board game was All-Star Baseball. It was a simple affair. The board consisted of some glossy printing and two mounted spinners. The players consisted of round disks marked off in numbered sections. The numbers stood for various kinds of hits and outs. The game consisted of placing the disks over the spinners and awaiting fate's control of the spin.

It was a simple game, but still, the players were personalized. Each year, new disks were issued, based on last season's all-star team. Duke Snider had the largest angle of possibility for a home run, although my uncle's old set from the thirties was sometimes brought out by my cousin, and that had Babe Ruth, with a home run angle even larger than Snider's. It was my understanding that the game was scientifically designed so that if you played an entire season of games, each cardboard disk would reproduce the exact performance of that player in that season. Even though I knew baseball wasn't like that, I trusted the statistics to intensify the metaphor. And besides, if you could have Duke Snider, Willie Mays, and Hank Aaron on the same team, you didn't like to ask too many questions.

I played with my cousins and always kept score. Since the action existed only as an abstraction, keeping score was all that the game actually was. I kept the score sheets in the bottom of my night table, until the drawer was so full it cracked. Then I threw them all out and began again. The summer we moved to the suburbs, where I didn't know anyone, I played a ninety-nine-game season of all-star games between the National and American League teams of the previous year. At the end of the season, I computed every imaginable statistic for every player. It was not quite science. Four hundred hitters were quite common, and the average number of runs per game was nearly twenty, more than double the number of runs produced in real baseball. As I look back and see the amount of energy and concentration that went into the cardboard disks and spinners, I am amazed by the way this game was able to pull me into total transcendence. At school, I was never very good at arithmetic. But I did all of the computation for all the various averages, and I was accurate. Arithmetic was a discipline, and something I was not good at, but baseball statistics were simply the logical extension of the need to know. They had to be done correctly, and besides, they were never a chore if you knew that at the end of the arithmetic you would have an up-to-the-minute batting average.

When I was about twelve, David Friedman, my old KPAA captain and my friend, sent away for a very expensive, fancy, mail-order game called APBA. What the initials stood for is something I never inquired about and never found out. I spent many days of my life playing that game, but, really, it came too late. I had moved to the suburbs and begun to dream driving automobiles and chasing after fast women before APBA ever had a chance to get its hooks into my imagination. Had the game come into my life when my dynasty of internal baseball was ascending, rather than collapsing, who knows how different my life might have been.

The game was very complicated, with many throws of different-size dice. There were different categories of pitchers, and the meaning of the roll of the dice varied accordingly. The batters were thrown with double-digit dice, allowing for the possibility of nearly every number between 11 and 66. A card for each batter translated the roll of the dice into that batter's performance, scientifically calculated on the basis of last year's actual performance. It was all very scientific and as manager you could duplicate the strategy decisions of real baseball. Yet the transformation from board game to mental baseball was never made for me by APBA as it was by All-Star Baseball. The trouble with the game was that it made you feel that you were always on the verge of mastering it, when it was clear that the game required at least a lifetime of devotion just to be comfortable with its mechanics. I kept waiting for the time when I would be able to jump up after throwing the dice and yell, "Eleven, home run, we win, yippie!" But that was a point I never reached. I seemed forever stuck at a primitive stage. The roll of the dice was always followed by "Eleven . . .

Let's see, right-handed pitcher, Class C . . . No plus or minus, right? . . . Okay . . . Let's see, Roy Campanella . . . eleven . . . I think it was a home run, just let me check and make sure I looked in the right column."

What strikes me all these years later is not that APBA failed to consume me, but the extent to which it was given its chance. During that winter, my friend and I did manage to get through the entire National League season. That represents about six hundred games. And with the countless readings of all the cumbersome charts and tables, our commitment represents, by the standards of ordinary behavior, an overwhelming devotion to APBA baseball. Partly, this had to do with the scale of the game's price tag and our respectful desire to get our money's worth. But much more than this was the fact that we were not baseball novices. We knew the world of internal baseball, and we knew all kinds of other forms of transportation to get there. APBA was complicated, but nothing was more complex than real baseball, and so, with our difficulty, we came to believe that we were approaching a more complex, more exciting, and, therefore, a higher form of internal baseball.

And now I could remember Teddy Gold. In 1970, a young radical named Theodore Gold, who had been a leader of SDS at Columbia University, joined the Weathermen and went underground. A short time later, he was killed in the townhouse explosion in New York's Greenwich Village. He died attempting to execute the highly dangerous and extremely risky political act of calling for a civil war in order to see if the citizens will take you as seriously as the authorities. He died trying to make the bombs that would announce the revolution to a population that had to finish making their car payments before they could contemplate anything so drastic. But Ted Gold died for an ideal. And however remote his dream might seem to other people in other times, his seriousness cannot be doubted. He risked, and sacrificed, his life for what he believed.

And what he believed in was the truth of his own alienation. That this society and its institutions and human relationships were so bankrupt, corrupt, disordered, and awful that it would be worth risking his life in order to set in motion the forces that would change them. The first step was to destroy the illusions and the myths that hold up the institutions, and then perhaps even the odd bit of federal real estate or corporate headquarters.

And because he was known to be thoughtful, and intelligent, and serious, and because he gave his life, we also know that Ted Gold thought about these things. And thought about these things to a point where he was driven to become a bomber.

And in the end, Ted Gold was the Weatherman, the bomber, part of the fringe dismissed as lunatic by regular America. A very marginal member of society, indeed. Of all the kinds of people that this society produces, none had less stake in things as they are than Ted Gold. None was less committed to the preservation of traditions and institutions. None more desperate for change, and none more eager for total change. Ted Gold was not just willing to participate; he was willing to give his life.

And at the same time, Ted Gold was a fanatic follower of the New York and, later, the San Francisco Giants. He read the box scores every morning. And he was quoted as saying that he would have to wait until Willie Mays retired before he could become a true communist.

Now, the radical understanding of the function of professional baseball is: circus. Its effect was to divert the people from their natural inclination to think about their lot, and to keep them from getting restless. It was an opiate. It gave people room in which to tolerate intolerable circumstances. For a good radical, it was a joy of childhood, but definitely not worthy of serious consideration for anyone seriously political.

And baseball was also hero worship, and the star system, and the worst kind of indulgence in the American cult of the rugged, unique, superior individualist. A good communist was not interested in baseball. And so Ted Gold, who was committed enough to sacrifice his life for the cause, could not think of himself as a good communist. He was not prepared to give up baseball.

And now, in the middle of the World Series, near the very last moments of the baseball season, I finally understand Ted Gold's position.

Alienation is emotional, but radicalization is an intellectual process. Proposition, conclusion, and then anger. The process of becoming a radical is not only creating but channeling anger. And as the propositions and anger increase, they begin to form a pattern. It changes the way that the world is perceived. It changes the way that you live and the things that you want from life. The illusion is that the process is one of genuine rebirth, causing a new and different human being to emerge from the same consciousness. But the evidence is to the contrary.

The evidence is that there are depths beyond which an intellectual process cannot go. The evidence is that there are aspects of your own identity so strongly established that they cannot be penetrated by conviction, not to mention thought. There are things about our own identity that we cannot alter by decision. And baseball is one of those things.

The baseball fan does not decide, and in fact cannot decide, about baseball if it has seeped into the deepest sense of self. Because if baseball is there, that is who you are.

It is not that I realized I was declaring myself for baseball, but just that I got so totally and un-self-consciously into the baseball that I forgot all about the work. And it is not that I abandoned my job, but that the excitement of the baseball caused such disarray in my mind and my notes that categories dissolved. And I could feel every bone in my body vibrating to the beat of the detente. And then, "From across the water came Cuban Pete, He was doin' the boogie to the rhumba beat," came from my record player, and Hank Snow's voice synchronized all the other patterns. It's the rhumba boogie done the Rhumba-Cubanal style. It's Luis Tiant pitching. It's Fidel Castro being respected instead of patronized, imperialism revenged. It's a reminder of the passions that baseball produces, and a mutual forgiveness between my childhood and myself. And, of course, it is regulation baseball.

The baseball was superb, which should have been enough. And it was more than enough, but the evidence for my personally observed system had begun to go awry. The Tiant family had started to go to Hollywood. In the last game of the Series, they entered into a comfort with their celebrity. They were now mugging for the camera in ways that suggested they might have had a few lessons during the rain.

And their son, Luis, now aiming for immortality and even higher tax brackets, began to mix the metaphors in my mind. Luis Tiant, as he pitched, began the recounting of the storming of the Moncada Barracks, the young revolution's bleakest hour and most severe defeat. The stage had been set for the triumphal march into Havana. Instead, Tiant fell apart and was chased out in the seventh inning.

The ceremonial first pitch of the seventh game was thrown out by Joey Tramontana, a crippled boy representing the Jimmy Fund. The announcer told us that the Jimmy Fund was an old Boston Braves charity for crippled children that was taken over by the Red Sox when the Braves left for Milwaukee. A communal health problem in a culture which has destroyed community, I thought. But what did that make of the politics of the ceremonial first pitch, and wasn't it ever so slightly perverse to be looking there?

The national anthem was sung by the Winged Victory Chorus of the U. S. Third Army Airborne Division. They wore green sequined tuxedos and destroyed Boston's image as a city of conservatories. They were also a mistaken context for organized baseball. Baseball has prospered and streamlined its image for the corporate era. What were they doing, singing in sequined tuxedos?

But the World Series ended, and with it the impossible threads that I had felt obliged to pursue. And besides, I had relearned the joys of baseball and the subtleties of Cuban detente it might contain. There have been some hard knocks. Luis Tiant will be remembered as a King, but the very nature of the Series did not allow for the kind of solo heroism that political consideration desired. National television exposure, as well as diplomatic recognition, would have to wait. Detente, in a pretty successful trial balloon, was nevertheless set back a few cosmic places in the grand order of things. But Luis Tiant planted a metaphor in the consciousness of the American television public that was certain to bear fruit, one day. Just not today.

The media, as fickle as any superficial fan who pays attention to the World Series and nothing else, shifted their focus to the winning Cuban. A newspaper report of the last game highlights Tony Perez. The story wanders off the game and tells how, fifteen years ago, a teen-age ball-player named Perez got discouraged and decided to return home to Cuba.

"Cuba had just fallen into the hands of Fidel Castro, and he had suddenly banned Cubans who played in America from going back, once they came home."

One sentence later, Perez was saying nice things about baseball, and in return, he was certified a World Series hero. Anyone who has studied the case will remember the president of the United States imposing an embargo, but no matter. My professional expert opinion on the matter is that the baseball expert at the State Department's Cuba Desk had staked not only some political judgment, but probably a lot of money, on Luis Tiant and the Boston Red Sox. And though Tiant came through beautifully, all the money behind Boston was lost. Hostility followed regret, and revenge was taken in the only area available. Tony Perez's heroism would be used to throw one last baseball insult at Fidel Castro. It was a small-minded exercise in bitter face-saving. Too insignificant a matter to alter the movement of baseball detente. Too futile a gesture, even, to mollify a bureaucrat's gambling losses.

The World Series was finally won by Cincinnati, the tie-breaking run being scored on a bloop single by Joe Morgan, with two out in the ninth inning of the seventh game. Which was typical. This was the most even match there ever was, and it produced the most exciting baseball anyone has ever seen. As World Series go, this was a jewel, and a classic, and, some said, the greatest ever.

For me, this World Series was baseball's final seduction. I found many things in the course of the baseball season. But the World Series' final note rang in the deepest part of myself that I found, and that was baseball.

As I look back to the images of amazing baseball, there are too many instances too memorable to be contained in any one event. I think of Luis Tiant, bending and twisting and studying centerfield in the middle of his windup; base-running with his face as much as his legs; playing both cat and mouse to Joe Morgan's famous lead off first base. And by contrast, in between Tiant's appearances, Reggie Cleveland throwing sixteen straight pitches to first base to hold Morgan, all of them, eventually, in vain.

And that glorious sixth game. Tiant's shellacking, Dwight Evans' catch, Bernie Carbo's second pinch-hit home run, and Carlton Fisk's game-winning hit, a home run worthy of announcing a candidacy upon. And too many more feats simply to catalogue. They were all part of the dramatic pattern, and therefore more spectacular than their story will ever sound. I have never seen a more interesting sequence of heroic activities organize themselves into a baseball game. Not to mention my new respect for the subtleties of Cuban detente.

And so, amidst tears and laughter, and songs of praise of motor oil, antifreeze, and beer, the cameras cut directly from the world champions' locker room to the Johnny Carson show, and the summer ended. Pete Rose, still covered in World Series sweat, had just finished saying, "I wish opening day was tomorrow." I did too.

And though this is certainly not the time or place to ask, there is a part of me that has been in turmoil all this time, and which still asks me, Why this baseball? Why not Greek tragedies and symphonies? Why not economics, history, and philosophy? And if it must be so esoteric, why not something closer to a master plot? Why get stuck in a metaphor that does not even hope to ring universal?

And now, finally, I can answer that question, because this baseball is now a part of me that I can see. And I can see that it runs deeper than other culture. Not traditional philosophy, and not traditional history, because in my identity, baseball runs deeper. Baseball is so deeply rooted that it is not subject to will. Baseball is the strongest, least vulnerable, and most confident piece of myself that I am in touch with. And so I am able to see all I see, and do all I do, through the metaphor of baseball. And no other framework could do this for me, because no other framework could ever allow me the same kind of access to myself.

And so it is by baseball that I am able to examine and express myself. And now this no longer seems odd or embarrassing to me. This is who I am.